Bridge Leadership

Connecting Educational Leadership and Social Justice to Improve Schools

A volume in
Educational Leadership for Social Justice

Series Editor:
Jeffrey S. Brooks, *University of Missouri-Columbia*
Denise E. Armstrong, *Brock University*
Ira Bogotch, *Florida Atlantic University*
Sandra Harris, *Lamar University*
Whitney H. Sherman, *Virginia Commonwealth University*
George Theoharis, *Syracuse University*

Educational Leadership for Social Justice

Jeffrey S. Brooks, Denise E. Armstrong, Ira Bogotch, Sandra Harris,
Whitney H. Sherman, and George Theoharis, Series Editors

*Bridge Leadership: Connecting Educational Leadership
and Social Justice to Improve Schools* (2009)
edited by Autumn K. Tooms and Christa Boske

*Leadership for Social Justice:
Promoting Equity and Excellence Through Inquiry and
Reflective Practive* (2008)
edited by Anthony H. Normore

Bridge Leadership

Connecting Educational Leadership and Social Justice to Improve Schools

edited by

Autumn K. Tooms and Christa Boske
Kent State University

Information Age Publishing, Inc.
Charlotte, North Carolina • www.infoagepub.com

Library of Congress Cataloging-in-Publication Data

Bridge leadership : connecting educational leadership and social justice to improve schools / edited by Autumn K. Tooms and Christa Boske.
   p. cm. — (Educational leadership for social justice)
   Includes bibliographical references.
   ISBN 978-1-60752-349-9 (pbk.) — ISBN 978-1-60752-350-5 (hardcover) — ISBN 978-1-60752-351-2 (e-book)
   1. Educational leadership. 2. School management and organization. 3. Social justice. I. Tooms, Autumn K., 1965- II. Boske, Christa.
   LB2806.B733 2009
   371.2   dc22
                                                                    2009043799

Copyright © 2010 IAP–Information Age Publishing, Inc.

All rights reserved. No part of this publication may be reproduced, stored in a retrieval system, or transmitted in any form or by any electronic or mechanical means, or by photocopying, microfilming, recording or otherwise without written permission from the publisher.

Printed in the United States of America

DEDICATION

Autumn would like to dedicate this book to her firstborn academic son, Dr. Charles A. Smialek. His actions as a scholar, principal, and devoted husband and father, remind her regularly that hope always looms around the corner on the road not taken.

Christa would like to dedicate this book to her 6-year-old daughter Angely, who protested on her school bus, identifying herself as a "civil justice person who will carry the sign like the people in *Hairspray*."

ADVACE PRAISE FOR BRIDGE LEADERSHIP

"*Bridge Leadership* is a powerful and fascinating new volume that explores the intersections of social justice and educational leadership. What distinguishes it from other social justice work is that it is much more personal than most such texts. Many of the book's authors share poignant excerpts of their life stories and connect them to the theoretical constructs, historical events, and political struggles of social justice.

The foregrounding of these personal stories and the bridges they create with social justice gives the volume a raw power not found in other social justice works. I could not put the volume down!"

—*Ulrich C. Reitzug,*
University of North Carolina, Greensboro

"*Bridge Leadership: Connecting Educational Leadership and Social Justice to Improve Schools*" provides a provocative look at the linkage between practicing social justice and improving schools in a global context. The contributors address the role and interplay of feminism, activism, homophobia, social justice discourse, complexity, cultural relevancy and the increased awareness of the global context and how these social pieces affect leadership preparation for improving schools. Furthermore, this set of narratives portray the internal and external struggles experienced by those committed to school improvement.

—*Alan R. Shoho,*
University of Texas, San Antonio

CONTENTS

Foreword
  Margaret Grogan ix
Series Editor Preface
  Jeffrey S. Brooks xv
Introduction: Social Justice and Doing "Being Ordinary"
  Christa Boske and Autumn K. Tooms xvii

SECTION I
LOOKING INWARD

1. Surviving While Dismantling One's Professional Culture:
   The Honor/Struggle for the Feminist Academic
   Catherine Marshall 3

Scenic Overlook: Chapters 1 and 2 27

2. A Time to Grow: Workplace Mobbing and the
   Making of a Tempered Radical
   Christa Boske 29

Scenic Overlook: Chapters 2 and 3 57

3. What's a Nice Dyke Like You Embracing This
   Postmodern Crap?
   Catherine A. Lugg 59

Scenic Overlook: Chapters 3 and 4 95

4. "Fire in the Belly": Igniting a Social Justice Discourse in
   Learning Environments of Leadership Preparation
   Gaetane Jean-Marie 97

THE LEADERSHIP BRIDGE

5. Leading Justly in a Complex World
   Carolyn M. Shields *125*

SECTION II
LOOKING OUTWARD

6. The Miseducation of a Professor of Educational Administration: Learning and Unlearning Culturally (Ir)relevant Leadership
   Jeffrey S. Brooks *153*

Scenic Overlook: Chapters 5 and 6 .... *171*

7. Individual Transformation for Global Impact: Increasing Global Citizenship Through Study Abroad
   Colleen L. Larson and Teboho Moja *173*

Scenic Overlook: Chapters 6 and 7 .... *207*

8. Unlocking the Door to International Collaboration: The Power of Interpersonal Relationships and Learning Communities
   Bruce Barnett and Gary O'Mahony *209*

Scenic Overlook: Chapters 7 and 8 .... *255*

9. Personal Reflections on an Organizational Transformation: UCEA's Re-Emerging Role in a World of Interdependent Nations
   Stephen Jacobson *257*

SECTION III
THE REFLECTING POOL

10. Looking Back on the Road not Taken
    Autumn K. Tooms and Christa Boske *281*

11. Epilogue
    Ira Bogotch and Dilys Schoorman *293*

About the Authors *307*

FOREWORD

Margaret Grogan

In 2001, I approached the editor of the *Journal of School Leadership* (JSL), Rick Reitzug, to suggest that the journal publish a special issue on social justice. Rick was enthusiastic about it. He gave me the go ahead to put out a call to see if any submissions came in. Both he and I were surprised at the overwhelming response. I don't remember exactly how many manuscripts I received, but I do remember that we got so many good ones that after reviews and revisions there were enough for two special issues in JSL! In the introduction to these issues, I said that I was prompted to put out the call because the term social justice had just begun to find its way into the literature and general discourse of educational leadership. I wasn't sure that I knew what it meant and I really wanted to see what others meant when they wrote about it. Well, that seems like another era now. Not only is the term used frequently in the literature today, but several educational leadership books and articles have also been written with social justice in the titles. Scholars in the field of educational leadership and other fields of education are writing about work that pertains to bringing about change in the schools and in society writ large that addresses widespread injustice. You will find references to this body of work in the chapters that follow. These chapters build on the earlier contributions to enrich and broaden the conversation. The narratives and essays in *Bridge Leadership: Connecting Educational Leadership and Social Justice to Improve Schools* refer to social justice with an ease of familiarity that suggests the term has a firm place in our lexicon. Generally speaking, the authors in this book are talking about human rights, the debilitating effects of poverty, racism and sexism, homophobia, equity, equality of opportunity, the value of diverse opinions and of cultures, and the increased consciousness of the relations of power.

I am very glad about this development. In my own academic life, I have survived a time when to use any of those terms above was to invite suspicion. Moreover, the ideas associated with the terms were often interpreted as a personal attack on White males and/or anyone with conservative views. I can see where the discomfort came from. Most of the terms above, and by association the term social justice, came from Marxism, critical theory, postmodernism, poststructuralism, radical feminism, and queer theory to name a few sources. One common thread in all those theories is challenge to the status quo, which is upheld by the dominant groups. And, newer theories such as postcolonial theory, LatCrit, and Critical Race Theory have opened up the discussion about power relations even further. However, at the time, this sense of *personal* threat, made it hard to get much of a hearing for ideas that interrogated the fundamental power structures in schools, although, as a White, middle class, heterosexual academic, I was sheltered from any real pushback. I think that's why it was okay for me to suggest doing a special issue on social justice—possibly because I was not seen as having too much of an axe to grind. I was writing about women's issues, but by the early 2000s, many believed that the days of discriminating against women had ended—the suffragettes and episodes of bra burning relegated to the history books. Indeed, the backlash was in full swing and we were hearing from (middle-class) women employed as lawyers that they wanted to go back to being moms. This is the same year 2000 when women led only about 10% of school districts across the country despite the large majority of women in education and in education doctoral programs.

So I am pleased that it is more than acceptable to advocate for social justice today. The School of Educational Studies at Claremont Graduate University (CGU) where I am currently professor and dean is committed to social justice and accountability. When I interviewed for the position, it was made very clear to me that a commitment to social justice without accountability suggested merely understanding that there was widespread injustice. The additional commitment to being accountable for bringing about justice was necessary for change to occur. The faculty at CGU stressed that recognizing inequities was not enough. Michael Dantley and Linda Tillman (2006) describe the same sentiment as "the hard work required to move notions of social justice from rhetoric to effective action"

(p. 26). Other colleges of education also use the term. The College of Education at Portland State University declares that one of their priorities is to "Promote diversity and social justice"[1] and one of the Pennsylvania State University College of Education's goals is to "Enhance the commitment of faculty, staff, and students to the centrality of diversity, social justice, and democratic citizenship."[2] Duquesne University's College of Education states "We will demonstrate our commitment to service and social justice through community outreach activities."[3] In addition, the University Council for Educational Administration (UCEA) identifies "Diversity, equity, and social justice in all educational organizations"[4] as one of their values.

As I reflect on the past 8 years since the special issues were published, I am encouraged by the fact that schools of education and departments of educational leadership have embraced social justice as a value and made commitments to action. Although there are sometimes heated debates about what *exactly* social justice means, using the term allows us to conduct the discussion. Like many ideas, until there were phrases coined that gave a name to a phenomenon, it could not be discussed. Take "global warming" for instance, a highly contested term, but, under its umbrella, necessary research has been conducted and prolonged debate has been sparked. Finally, now, in 2009, years after the concerns were voiced, some widespread global attention is being paid to world climates and the human contributions to serious, negative changes that have occurred. Whether the problems stem from the warming or the cooling of temperatures, or from some other interrelated set of factors, reducing the emission of greenhouse gases is generally understood to be critical to human survival. Will the debates end? Not at all. "Climate change" has begun to displace "global warming" and offers an even wider set of concepts for our consideration. This is an inevitable and uncontrollable process of language and concept development.

Another example closer to home is the "achievement gap." I remember doing a study in Virginia in the early 2000s trying to understand how school superintendents were dealing with the disparities in test scores of different groups of students. It was just after Virginia introduced the Standards of Learning (SOL) tests, but before No Child Left Behind (NCLB) gave us the term achievement gap. Whitney Sherman and I found that one or two larger districts already disaggregated their SOL and other test score data and were comfortable initiating a community-wide discussion about how to address their blatant failure to serve all students. But these were the exceptions. Most districts in our study refused to disaggregate their data and absolutely refused to discuss publicly the disparities they knew existed. All this changed when NCLB gave districts no choice in the matter. Test scores were not only disaggregated but the results were made public, and schools and districts held accountable for their continuing failure to address the disparities.

Like global warming, achievement gap is also a contested term. It suffers because standardized-test score baggage is associated with it, and because it focuses the discussion too narrowly on academics instead of on the whole student. However, think of the deafening silence before the term was coined. Every educator knew that countless students were leaving schools unable to read and write. Those that bought into the notion of the bell curve were even comfortable about it. We can certainly argue the merits of how the act has been implemented and of the unintended consequences of it, but we must acknowledge that the naming of the gap has allowed us to be outraged about our failures and to put resources into disrupting racist, sexist, homophobic, and other discriminatory practices that account for these failures.

At the same time, we must be wary of the way such phrases can be used to legitimate the status quo. Much bad pedagogy has been utilized in the name of addressing the achievement gap. Curricula have been watered down, recall has replaced learning, and the arts have been removed from the schedule in many districts. The school day has been harnessed to the engine of NCLB that threatens to drive all creativity and imagination from the classroom. So the process of creating terms and naming phenomena must be continuously interrogated. Chris Weedon (1997) argues that "language is the place where actual and possible forms of social organization and their social and political consequences are defined and contested" (p. 21). We have seen how groups like *Leaders for Social Justice* (LSJ) emerged under the guidance of Catherine Marshall. After several years of existing in *ad hoc* spaces created in organizations such as UCEA and the American Educational Research Association (AERA), LSJ is now a legitimate Special Interest Group (SIG) at AERA. As a founding member, I heard many lively conversations about the relative advantages and disadvantages of remaining "off the grid" as opposed to becoming part of an established organization. I'm happy to note that the group is thriving in its new home. Jeff Brooks plays a pivotal role in the SIG by maintaining the listserv and communicating many opportunities for LSJ members to engage in activities that further social justice conversations. For instance, just the other day we learned about the First International Conference of the Society for the Study of Gloria Anzaldua: El Mundo Zurdo being held in San Antonio, Texas cosponsored by the Women's Studies Institute and the University of Texas-San Antonio. And we heard of a new publication: *Research Is Ceremony: Indigenous Research Methods* by Shawn Wilson. This listserv helps to shape the discourse about social justice leadership. Together with the conversations at the annual meetings, the sessions sponsored by the SIG, and the growing list of publications with social justice in the title, the meaning of the term is evolving.

A recent addition to the entities organized around the concept of social justice leadership is the new UCEA *Center for Educational Leadership and Social Justice* at Duquesne University under the leadership of Jim Henderson. Center activities and research agendas are still under discussion, but the very fact of its existence reinforces the acceptance of the term and provides future opportunities for assignment of meaning to the term. Having participated in the inaugural convening of leadership practitioners, scholars and students to discuss the mission and goals of the center, I am glad to report little agreement on how social justice should be defined. I am pleased because disagreement keeps meaning from being too narrowly ascribed. And more than anything else at this stage, I would not like to see social justice become associated with a limited set of beliefs for the reason noted above. Business as usual could be celebrated in the name of social justice. We must ask always "justice for whom"? I am reminded of Jean-François Lyotard's warning to us. "Consensus has become an outmoded and suspect value. But justice as a value is neither outmoded nor suspect. We must thus arrive at an idea and practice of justice that is not linked to that of consensus" (Lyotard, 1979/1993, p. 66).

Debate and dissensus are vital to sustain this work—as is the emphasis on the *practices* of justice. The term social justice may evolve into something else. It doesn't matter. We may abandon it as too ambiguous in favor of more precise terms such as equity, equality, human rights, anti-racism etc. But none of these is uncontested either. Weedon (1997) believes that "To subscribe to the provisional nature of meaning is not to imply that it does not have real effects" (p. 82). Social justice provides us with space to identify where injustices lie and to arrive at ways to address them. What matters is the quality of research we conduct in the name of bringing about social justice, the discerning theory we use to interrogate the status-quo, and the level of commitment we make to action. This effort includes being watchful and paying attention to how the discourse can be appropriated for other uses. Our work is in focusing leadership preparation and development on disruptive practices and policies that turn our educational system on its head. Over the next eight or ten years, as our use of the term social justice matures and stimulates new questions to research and new avenues of inquiry, I hope to see more impatience with the lack of fundamental change. Whatever happened to the passion that ignited the phrase "We won't take this any more?" I'd like to see some of that fire burn in the work of social justice going forward. Thanks to Christa, Autumn, and all the authors included here, this book provides an excellent impetus for it.

NOTES

1. http://www.pdx.edu/education/graduate-school-education-priorities
2. http://www.ed.psu.edu/educ/about-the-college/vision-and-mission
3. http://www.education.duq.edu/aboutus/missngoal.html
4. http://www.ucea.org/values-vision-goals/

REFERENCES

Dantley, M., & Tillman, L. (2006). Social justice and moral transformative leadership. In C. Marshall & M. Oliva (Eds.), *Leadership for social justice* (pp. 16-29). Boston: Pearson Education.

Lyotard, J. F. (1993). *The postmodern condition: A report on knowledge* (G. Bennington & B. Massumi, Trans.). Minneapolis: University of Minnesota Press. (Original work published 1979.)

Weedon, C. (1997). *Feminist practice and poststructuralist theory* (2nd ed). Cambridge, MA: Blackwell.

SERIES EDITOR'S PREFACE

Jeffrey S. Brooks

I am pleased to serve as series editor for this book series, *Educational Leadership for Social Justice*, with Information Age Publishing. The idea for this series grew out of the work of a committed group of leadership for scholars associated with the American Educational Research Association's (AERA) Leadership for Social Justice Special Interest Group. This group has actually existed for many years before being officially affiliated with AERA, and has benefitted greatly from the ongoing leadership, support, and counsel of Dr. Catherine Marshall (University of North Carolina-Chapel Hill). It is also important to acknowledge the contributions of the AERA SIG's first President, Dr. Ernestine Enomoto (University of Hawaii at Manoa), whose wisdom, stewardship, and guidance have helped ease a transition into AERA's more formal organizational structures that were at times difficult to reconcile with a group that largely identified itself as a group of nontraditional scholars and continues to push toward innovation rather than settle for the status quo. I am particularly indebted to my colleagues on the SIG's publications committee: Dr. Denise Armstrong, Brock University; Dr. Ira Bogotch, Florida Atlantic University; Dr. Sandra Harris, Lamar University; Dr. Whitney Sherman, Virginia Commonwealth University; Dr. George Theoharis, Syracuse University. This committee has been a joy to work with and I look forward to future collaborations as

Bridge Leadership: Connecting Educational Leadership and Social Justice to Improve Schools
pp. xv–xvi
Copyright © 2010 by Information Age Publishing
All rights of reproduction in any form reserved.

we seek to provide publication opportunities for scholarship in the area of leadership for social justice.

The present volume *Bridge Leadership: Connecting Educational Leadership and Social Justice to Improve Schools*, edited by Autumn Tooms and Christa Boske, Kent State University, is the second book in the IAP *Social Justice Leadership Series*. Tooms and Boske have set out to reconstruct the history of social justice in educational leadership through the methods of personal reflective narratives. It is out of the new international experiences as well as local and national struggles that each of these authors have confronted institutional "ordinariness" with a renewed sense of moral purpose. We hope that you enjoy this book and find it to be a significant contribution to advancing both education and social justice in the world today.

INTRODUCTION

Social Justice and Doing "Being Ordinary"

Christa Boske and Autumn K. Tooms

Lucy Varney is a 23-year-old, fresh-faced communications major at Kent State University. She is also one hell of a waitress at a café that Autumn likes to refer to as her "satellite office." When Lucy sees Christa and Autumn walk in the door of the Wild Goats café for lunch, she immediately draws up a Diet Coke with lemon because Autumn cannot function without one. And she remembers to ask Christa about her adorable daughter's latest adventures in kindergarten.

While the secretaries at Kent State think Autumn begins her day around 10 in the morning, Lucy knows that Autumn begins work in the booth by the coffee grinder at 7 in the morning with a stack of things to read or write, a Diet Coke with lemon, and an egg white and spinach omelet.

What Lucy did not know until the day that we wrote this chapter, is that she is a wonderful teacher and editor. Because in between the omelets and furious scribbles on napkins and legal pads, Lucy will ask "what are you writing this time?" And there lies the opportunity to explain the complex stuff that we think about; the most recent project being this book. Autumn started to answer Lucy's question by reading her the title, which was a brilliant representation of the serious intellectual nature of this volume. When Lucy raised one eyebrow during midread, we understood it was time to rethink the title, and throw out the notion that pedantic equals homage to our heroes—the authors in this volume.

After a few weeks of omelets and emails, we realized the best way to respect the brave and significant work of our colleagues and authors, was to articulate that their efforts were really based on bridge building. More specifically, they were based on bridge leadership. The concept of bridge building in conjunction with school leadership has been alluded to or used by various authors (Culbertson, 1995; Firestone & Reihl, 2005; Merchant & Shoho, 2006). We like the phrase bridge leadership and define it as a kind of epistemology in which the leader understands that the core of her or his work is rooted in traversing spaces between people. These spaces cut across a gamut of parameters that include equity, opportunity, and productivity. Furthermore, the spaces are not bound by time or geography. For instance, instead of thinking about the phrase "groundbreaking work" why not consider "bridge building work." In truth, that is what many of the authors here such as Catherine A. Lugg have done. They have not only broken ground by engaging in different ways of thinking, they have also built a bridge for others to cross into spaces of equity. The same can be said of Jeffrey Brooks and Carolyn Shields who take us around the world to different spaces and the ramifications of our own ignorance.

We argue that bridge leadership is about deconstructing ones ego in order to make the complex easily understood. Such is the lesson of our good teacher, Lucy Varney. She is a brilliant, hard working, independent young woman, who showed with one raise of an eyebrow that being pedantic does not always mean begin intellectual or reverent. And so we thank Lucy for encouraging us to rework the title without saying a word. We believe that bridge leadership, as we are defining it, is at the heart of this book. Frankly, we argue that it is also the core of who we are as academics and as leaders. Bridge leadership is about the commitment to give voice to those who have no voice, and translating the complex into the easily understood. We argue that ultimately, this is the heart of being scholars/leaders. While this chapter opened with the lessons of Lucy Varney, we "begin again" (and humbly recognize this phrase is lifted from our dear friend Ira Bogotch) with an explanation of why this is an important book. In an effort to be true to our epistemology of bridge leadership, we unpacked its framework in a way that we hope is easily digestible. Enjoy. If you like, Lucy will be happy to bring you a Diet Coke with lemon.

Introduction xix

WE BEGIN AGAIN …

In 1949, Margaret Wise Brown wrote *The Important Book*, which encouraged children to wonder about "ordinary" things, like the sun, moon, wind, rain, or rainbows. The children's book had no plot, setting, conflict, heroes, or heroines. Some argued it was a feckless effort by the author to consider the world in both small and large ways. How could such a book be of any help to children; much less the teachers charged with their education?

In spite of Wise Brown's unorthodox structure and organization, *The Important Book* went on to become one of the greatest selling books of all time. If you visit Amazon.com right now (some 60 years after the first printing of *The Important Book*) you can order a new edition of this classic work. Why? Because teachers in every decade since 1949 have realized the value of working with a book that overtly invites the reader to think for themselves in the midst of learning the concrete and abstract simultaneously. A specific example of Wise Brown's prowess is found in a passage on the sixth page in what appears to be an ordinary passage:

> The important thing about rain is
> that it is wet.
> It falls out of the sky,
> and it sounds like rain,
> and makes things shiny,
> and it does not taste like anything,
> and is the color of air.
> But the important thing about rain
> is that it is wet.

A few pages later, the reader finds an ordinary picture of clouds and a blue sky with this passage:

> The important thing
> about the sky is that it is always
> there. It is true that it is blue
> and high, and full of clouds,
> and made of air.
> But the important thing about
> the sky is that it is always there.

Are you still dumbfounded as to why Wise Brown's book has stood the test of time for over 60 years? Are you wondering why on earth this scholarly chapter begins with a discussion of a children's book? We argue that the answer to both of these questions is written on the inside flap of the first edition of *The Important Book* (Wise Brown, 1949):

> The important thing about *The Important Book* is that you let your child tell you what is important about the sun and the moon and the wind and the rain and a bug and a bee and a chair and a table and a pencil and a bear and a rainbow and a cat (if he or she wants to). For the important thing about *The Important Book* is that the book goes on long after it is closed.

There is nothing ordinary about a book that can entice us to decide what is and is not important. Indeed, the greatest thing about any important book is that it teaches and inspires the soul of a reader long after it is closed. The book you are holding in your hands does not have a plot. But it is rife with conflict. And there are heroes and heroines who have grappled with it in all sorts of settings. The inspirations and lessons come not only from chapter authors telling their story, but from the chronicles of the educators, leaders, and policymakers who are wrestling with what social justice means in terms of the ordinary, everyday activities of schools and societies around the world. Like *The Important Book* (Wise Brown, 1949) this work is not simple, but it attempts to convey important messages simply, and without pretense.

We know this is an important book because of the very important and brave people who have graciously contributed chapters. Many of the chapters presented here are the first tellings of seminal work done in our field to break barriers, as in the case of Cath erine Marshall, whose first chapter starts such discussions with a resounding bang. There are accounts of lifetimes focused on building intracultural bridges as offered near the end of the book by Bruce Barnett and Gary O'Mahoney. We are particularly pleased that Margaret Grogan has agreed to tell the story of what it was like to facilitate the first formal discussion in the field of educational administration about what social justice *is*. We know this is an important book because personal narratives within it capture moments and contributions unlike any other kind of methodology used in our field.

We visualized the organization of this book through the metaphor of hiking in the hilly woods that surround our offices at Kent State University. In between the foreword and the epilogue, our book is organized into three sections, or paths of discourse, connected by a bridge. Autumn and I linked each chapter with a one half page "scenic overlook" that is a quick summation of how each author's discussion is related to its neighbor. In conjunction with the foreword, the first path, *Looking Inward*, deconstructs a history of social justice discussions and work in the field of educational administration.

Catherine A. Lugg and Gateane Jean Marie follow Marshall's opening insights with powerful stories of personal transformation and a resulting commitment to leadership. (And while Christa is too humble to put this in writing, Autumn is happy to tell you that Christa Boske's story of transcendence and mobbing in academe is profoundly courageous).

Looking Inward winds itself to the bridge that Carolyn Muriel Shields titled *Leading Justly in a Complex World*. She explains how social justice, leadership, and capitalism are inextricably linked whether we like it or not through her narrative of work Thailand. She aptly argues that economic conditions around the world hold leaders, schools, and thus learning, hostage. The conclusions of Shields' arguments bring you squarely to a new path: The second section we titled, *Looking Outward*. This section addresses the processes used in understanding our world and our role in it. Jeffrey Brooks opens the discussions by considering the yeasty problems of whose social justice counts in our global society along with the uncomfortable questions associated with the desire to serve wrapped in personal privilege and intellectual colonialism. Colleen Larson and Teboho Moja demonstrate the transformation process and understanding glocality through the eyes of their students involved in a study abroad experience. After the warmly recounted stories of colleagial bridge building in leadership preparation provided by Barnett and O'Mahoney, Dr. Stephen Jacobsen defends why thinking glocally is absolutely part of being a school leader. He also explains how international collaborations are not new to the field of educational administration.

The last section in our book is titled *The Reflecting Pool* and is a space intended for you to think through what you have read. there are two chapters, one written by Autumn and myself dedicated to considering the themes revealed in this book. Lastly, Ira Bogotch and Dyllis Schoorman provide an epilogue that fervently challenges us to think about the "so what" of all of this. They consider the future of our profession and ask us to unpack what it means to be a leader in this era of inescapable glocality.

HOW TO READ THIS BOOK

Both Autumn and I sought to address an international audience of scholars and practitioners in educational leadership with this work. Because we are (to some degree) both post modernists, we have organized this book so that one does not have to read it in any one particular order. Because we also are pragmatists and both former school principals, we have also organized this book so it can be also be read front to back in the exact order of the chapters. We invite you to walk this path with us as you wish. Also, you will see that at the end of each chapter we have listed things to think about if you are a school leader or one who prepares school leaders. Our hope is that you will read this book with pen or pencil in hand because we feel that the landscape of a books is best appreciated with scribbles in the margins.

Doing "Being Ordinary"

Some argue that the phrase social justice has lost its potency because it has become a trite rallying call in which those who use it are essentialized as nonscholars with an agenda or as the scholars who are the "ists" (as in *feminists, queer theorists, critical race theorists,* and yes, *postmodernists*). This book is considers the spectrum of social justice and how leadership in many ways is predicated on social justice work. Autumn's best friend muttered over breakfast one day that he was not comfortable as to when and where to use the term without repercussions. He struggled to decide if he even had the right to use "social justice" at all as his specialization is not in critical theory. And yet, Autumn's friend has a vita which reflects a lifetime of social justice work across the arenas of diversity, ethics, and service to the field. Like most iconic words, social justice has become politicized to the point where no one is quite sure what it really means and how it will be interpreted when it is used. What we do know is that for many, the passion to improve the lives of others is a core value of both leadership development and social justice. Why then should it be hard to see the intersections of both?

The issues that galvanized our passion for leadership as it is linked to social justice intensified for both of us over the last several decades because of personal and professional experiences. These significant experiences included Autumn's desegregation work as a principal and building a leadership preparation program at The College of The Bahamas while improving the one at Kent State University. Christa worked in predominantly impoverished inner-city schools and experienced the gift of parenthood. Such adventures and challenges energized our commitment to consider school's role in communities around the globe. We disagree with each other about what social justice means, how it is interpreted in scholarship, and how it can affect the preparation of school leaders. We realized this is not a unique phenomenon once we read Dr. Grogan's foreword. Unfortunately, we are still arguing as a profession about what social justice *is* just as we are arguing about what leadership *is*.

We are compelled to chronicle the historic social justice moments in our field because it is directly aligned with the mandatory call for glocality (which refers to the ability to think globally and act locally) as an administrative skill set (See Wellman, 2002 for a greater discussion of the term). Glocality for school leaders is an act of consciousness, recognizing the interconnectedness of both self and place. For twenty-first century school

Introduction xxiii

leaders, engaging in minimal external perspectives is not enough to lead and respond to the call for social justice. Like it or not, we live in a world that is becoming more interconnected across culture, time, and space. Edward Relph (1976), an academic geographer, notes understanding the influence of place, is essential to understanding human experience, because place provides meaning for people's lives and permeates everyday life. We argue that it is the astute school leader who recognizes the importance of place as it relates to the human experience and development of compassion and responsibility in students.

Furthermore, the problem with some calls for social justice is that the issues at hand are distracted by the pedantic arguments of woe, as if Barbara Cartland, John Dewey, and Jonathan Kozol together wrapped up the plea for change in schools with magenta charmuse. We want to capture your attention dear reader; more importantly we want to keep it. Thus, we sheepishly defer to Margaret Wise Brown below when we explain the central themes of this book:

> The important thing about this leadership book is
> it chronicles social justice *work* and *demands more*.
>
> It teaches *glocality*
> values personal narrative,
> and asks "Whose social justice *counts*"?
>
> But the important thing about this leadership book is
> It chronicles social justice *work* and *demands more*.

So there you have it; an ordinary stanza about some not so ordinary concepts. We also use this homage to Margaret Wise Brown to demonstrate how we routinely mistake important, everyday work, as ordinary. In order to understand how and why we do that, consider the insights of an ethnomethodologist named Harvey Sacks.

Dr. Harvey Sacks, a faculty member at the University of California at Berkley, tragically died at the age of 40 in a car crash. He is credited with founding the discipline of conversational analysis. His original lectures focused on understanding how people "do" particular actions, which often make their actions unnoticeable. The 1970 Harvey Sacks lecture on "Doing Being ordinary" provides us with an understanding of the significance of doing every day work. Sacks developed his notion of "ordinary" as daily life and business as usual (Sacks, 1985, p. 215). Being ordinary suggests people who go about their everyday business are invisible to themselves. For people identified as nonordinary or "not one of us," normative social demands are heightened (Bogdan & Taylor, 1994, p. 14). We intentionally or unintentionally group our efforts into those that translate into professional capital and the other stuff of an *ordinary day*.

Sacks (1985) noted we tend to organize, understand, and relate our lived experiences to each other in terms of events that are storyable. That is to say they are exciting or epic. The rest of our existence we tend to quantify as *ordinary*. Inevitably we are socialized to describe the contributions we make that carry the greatest cultural capital. The rest of our efforts we deem as part of the everydayness of our ordinary lives. We have ordinary days at the office and ordinary lives at home that are interrupted with epic events such as publication, professional recognition, marriage, divorce, or even the death of a cherished colleague. To support this argument, we ask to consider this exchange that most likely happens regularly in your life:

"Hi! What happened at work today?"

"Nothing much, it was an ordinary day".

In truth, if you are a professor, your day might have included chairing two separate doctoral dissertation defenses, mediating a fight between your colleague and your department chair, receiving notice that your manuscript had been accepted by a prominent journal, mentoring a colleague who feels frustrated with the politics she is facing, and considering the ethics of inviting a speaker to class that is a renowned sexist.

For many, nothing is ordinary about any of the above. And all of those "ordinary" actions are rooted in a moral compass set firmly toward doing what is fair and equitable. Thus, the work of social justice can be considered in some ways as "doing" being ordinary. Furthermore, the work of social justice is about doing things with consistency- hence why such actions become ordinary for some. In relation to this phenomenon, Sacks (1985) argued:

> It seems plain enough that people monitor the scenes they're in for their storyable characteristics. And the awesome, overwhelming fact is that they come away with no storyable characteristics, where presumably any of us with any wit could make of this a rather large array of things to say. But that would take a kind of effort that could make one feel uncomfortable. (p. 218)

Western civilization, which is ensconced in a Puritan ethic demands that we spend most of our time manifesting legitimate experiences centered on work, piety, and humility. The everyday experiences of an ordinary person, which may include anything other than the above are deemed in our social consciousness as illegitimate and therefore unworthy of mention in discourse (Butler, 1997; Gee, 1996; Goffman, 1959; Sacks,1985). To better understand how this happens we utilize a poststructural perspective on language, discourse, and talk.

Scholarly considerations of discourse and its impact on reality typically fall within the umbrella of post-structuralism, a philosophical and intellectual stance that originated in France in the 1960s. One of the goals of post structuralism is to deconstruct traditional views about reality and truth (Cherryholmes, 1988). Poststructuralists Michele Foucault (1975, 1980) and Jacques Derrida (1982) both examined discursive practices and their relationship to reality or truth. At the heart of poststructuralism is a concern with the deconstruction of the power relationships that permeate the texts and discourse practices of society. *Discourse* refers to the different ways in which we individually or collectively integrate language with other communicative elements when creating and interpreting a message. But what is the difference between *talk* and *discourse*?

We define talk as a social action in which those participating in a discussion coconstruct a meaning in interaction in everyday activity (Duranti, 1997). Discourse however, is "a set of norms, preferences, and expectations relating linguistic structures to contexts which speakers and listeners draw on to modify, produce, and interpret language" (Ochs, 1988, p.8). The concept of discourse can be further deconstructed into more specific terms and understandings. James Paul Gee (1996) drew on Foucault (1975, 1980) to specify understandings of discourse into something he called "Big D discourse" ("D/discourse") and "Little d discourse" ("d/discourse").

D/discourse refers to the many ways of acting and being in the world: It is a set of communicative constellations and talk patterns consisting of language working in concert with one, many, or all the following: Feelings, bodies, non-linguistic symbols, objects, clothes, interaction, action, technologies, geography, time, tools, symbols, verbal and non verbal expressions, and people (Gee,1996). D/discourse contours social practices by creating particular kinds of subjectivity in which human beings are managed and given certain forms which are viewed as self evident, rational, normal, or irrational and abnormal (Alvesson & Karreman, 2000; Derrida, 1982; Foucault,1980; Gramsci,1971).

The concept of d/discourse is centered on the pragmatics of language in use. It refers to the language bits and grammatical resources that make up interactions. It however is not talk, because talk depends on a message being created between the speaker and the receiver in discourse. Thus, a Post modern approach to interaction and language demonstrates that there are complex layers to social interaction and everyday choices in our life. The opportunities within everyday social interaction are where we can find some of the most important aspects of leadership.

To understand the power of D/discourse, leadership, social justice and doing "being ordinary" consider this:

Kent State University has a 20 year history of working with The College of The Bahamas in various program building capacities. The Bahamas only achieved independence in 1972 and still struggles with a post colonial hangover that is embedded in racism, an economy dependent on tourism and an informal caste system in Bahamian society. The true Bahamas is rarely seen by tourists. Efforts to build the first program school administrative training program began in 2002. Before then, the method of selection of school masters was typically based on gender (always preference given to males) and age (the teacher with the longest tenure was promoted). Kent States work in conjunction with the College of The Bahamas had made a noticeable impact with the Bahamian Ministry of Education, particularly as it related to schools in family islands. Family islands are small places that may or may not have electricity, running water, and public libraries with more than 50 books. Two years after the conclusion of the first cohort of masters degree students graduated from the College of the Bahamas, talks began again between Kent State University officials and Bahamain administrators from the Ministry of Education and The College of the Bahamas. Autumn was present at one such discussion which took place over a dinner in Kent, Ohio. Two of the White males from Kent State spent most of the dinner talking about the wonderful tourist experiences they had while in the country. They were not astute enough to understand that the D/Discourse in the Bahamas is that "racist, classist, White folks only see golf and scuba diving in our country and fail to understand the true Bahamain culture." Thus, the Kent State officials unknowningly insulted their dinner companions. The only saving grace for Kent State was that the third White male from Kent State realized what was happening and gently turned the conversation to discussions of family (a high Bahamian value) and of experiences he treasured that usually only Bahamians enjoy such as fresh conch salad eaten at shack called George's located in Potter's Cay. The subtle point made by the third official from Kent State was that yes, Kent State does recognize and honor the depth and complexity of Bahamian culture. Ironically when Autumn asked her colleague (the cultural offender) what he thought of the dinner, he replied, "Oh just another ordinary get to know you dinner." When she asked her colleague who shared his adventure at George's what he thought about dinner, he replied," Well that was wild ... I think we ended up showing we care—but for a moment I was really sweating it. Just another ordinary day at Kent State!"

There is nothing ordinary about how we understand discourse, (both D/d), social justice, leadership, and doing being ordinary. Leadership is often found in the mundane moments of reading a conversation and understanding how we are interpreted as individuals and the culture we represent. After you read Catherine Marshall's chapter on her daily life as a professor, ask yourself if you remember doing anything like she did in an ordinary day. Or read Jeffrey Brooks chapter to see if his ordinary day is like yours. We were inspired by the scholarly works of our peers, as well as their passion for promoting humanity in schools and raising the difficult questions of whose version of humanity counts? We hope this book will push you beyond the edges of "business as usual" and into the unknown territories of your ordinary day. Together, we will discover spaces for hope, healing, activism, and renewal. Expect to find moments of joy, sadness, guilt, discovery, and pain. We intended for the authors' stories to shed light on what it means to struggle with leading for social justice and to imagine possibilities. It is time for "doing being ordinary" to be understood as anything but ordinary. Just as the insights recorded here point to way toward understanding school leadership, leadership preparation, and yes, social justice.

SUGGESTED QUESTIONS FOR REFLECTION

For school leaders:

1. How do you identify your everyday work?
2. What does "doing being ordinary" mean to school leaders in the twenty-first century?
3. Do you think there is a relationship between "doing being ordinary" and the underperformance of children of color? Why or why not? Support your claims.
4. To what extent do you engage in authentic conversation about "doing being ordinary" about issues of human oppression?
5. What are your hopes in reading this book? What are your expectations? What are your concerns? Share and discuss your reactions with a partner, through a narrative, and/or as a large group.

For those preparing school leaders:

1. What do you consider *important* in preparing school leaders?
2. How does your insight compare with the authors' insights expressed in this introductory chapter?
3. What does "doing being ordinary" mean to you as a scholar preparing school leaders for the realities of the twenty-first century?
4. To what extent do you and your colleagues engage in authentic discussions about "doing being ordinary" and human oppression?
5. How do you understand social justice? How do you promote humanity in yoru courses?
6. What are your hopes in reading this book?

REFERENCES

Alvesson, M., & Karreman, D.(2000). Varieties of discourse: On the study of organizations through discourse analysis. *Human Relations, 53*(9), 1125-1149.
Bogdan, R., & Taylor, S. (1994). *The social meaning of mental retardation: Two life stories.* New York, NY: Teachers College Press.
Butler, J. (1997). *Excitable Speech: A politics of the performative.* New York, NY: Routledge.
Cherryholmes, C. (1988). *Power and criticism: Poststructural investigations in education.* New York, NY: Teachers College Press.
Culbertson, J. (1995). *Building bridges: UCEA's first two decades.* University Park, PA: University Council for Educational Administration.
Derrida, J. (1982). *Of grammatology.* Baltimore: The Johns Hopkins University Press.
Duranti, A. (1997). *Linguistic anthropology.* Cambridge, Egnland: Cambridge University Press.
Firestone, W. A., & Riehl, C. (Eds.). (2005). *A new agenda: Directions for research on educational leadership.* New York, NY: Teachers College Press.
Foucault, M. (1975). *Discipline and punish: The birth of a prison.* New York, NY: Vintage Books.
Foucault, M. (1980). *Power/knowledge: Selected interviews and other writings, 1972-1977.* New York, NY: Pantheon Books.
Gee, J. P. (1996). *Social linguistics and literacies.* New York, NY: Routledge.
Goffman, E. (1959). *The presentation of self in everyday life.* Garden City, NY: Anchor/Doubleday.
Gramsci, A. (1971) *Selections from the prison notebooks.* London: Lawrence and Wishart.
Merchant, E., & Shoho, A. (2006). Bridge people: Civic and educational leaders for social justice. In C. Marshall & M. Olivas (Eds.), *Leadership for social justice: Making revolutions in education* (pp. 123-125). New York, NY: Allyn & Bacon.
Ochs, E. (1988). *Culture and language development: Language acquisition and language socialization in a Samoan village.* Cambridge, England: Cambridge University Press.
Relph, E. (1976). *Place and placelessness.* London: Academic Press.
Sacks, H. (1985). On doing being ordinary. In J. Maxwell Atkinson & J. Heritage (Eds.), *Structures of social action: Studies in conversation analysis* (pp. 123-125). New York, NY: Cambridge University Press.
Wellman, B. (2002). Little Boxes, glocalization, and networked individualism. In M. Tanabe, P. van den Besselaar, & T. Ishida (Eds.), *Digital cities* (pp. 33-38). Berlin, Germany: Spinger-Verlag.

SECTION I

LOOKING INWARD

CHAPTER 1

SURVIVING WHILE DISMANTLING ONE'S PROFESSIONAL CULTURE

The Honor/Struggle for the Feminist Academic

Catherine Marshall

How does one evolve and find ways to buttress and interweave activism with an academic life? This chapter describes the clash of educational institutions and my personal realities, to my eventually finding and creating bodies of knowledge, collaborators and validation. Experiencing firsthand the underside of sexual politics of education and the professoriate, in order to live with my realities and survive, I had to challenge the dominant discourse. A bit of initial illustration: First, as pregnant teenager in the 1960s, I was kicked out of 11th grade. Later, as a teacher engaged in the women's movement, I was frustrated with educators' lack of attention to gender equity; as a graduate student I squirmed within the gendered hierarchy of educational administration. Then, as a junior faculty member, and the only woman in an educational leadership department, I faced the sickening realization that I was seen not as a serious scholar but as a sex object when I was sexually harassed by my dean.

Breakthroughs and support came, though, from interdisciplinary literatures, from international collaborations, and from persisting in scholarship that pushes the margins of educational administration and politics to include feminist scholarship and the perspectives of women and girls into educational policy discussions.

SEARCHING FOR THEORY

As a public school teacher in the 1970s, I hid, as if they were dirty secrets, my work on Women's Political Caucus legislative pushing for child care and abortion. I had to defend my inclusion of women's history in the eighth grade curriculum. I did not know what to do with anger when jock men were promoted to administrative posts but not women. Women's liberation consciousness-raising, some emerging women's studies and of course Friedan's *The Feminine Mystique* (1963) penetrated my awareness though. My need for advanced study came from frustration and anger with inequities and a desire to find ways to understand them. Title IX passed in 1972; then one of those incongruities occurred. According to the law, girls were supposed to be able to have full participation in sports but in reality they never did. I went to the American Civil Liberties Union to find support for an incredibly athletic eighth grade girl who should have been on the baseball team. No: we were "waiting for regulations." That took years and I learned the difficult lesson that laws don't make things happen. My awareness of those gender inequities catapulted me into the women's movement. I worked on getting women elected to office. I learned the limits of tokenism. Through many such experiences I learned about inequities but I couldn't find my way out of the organizational and political messes around me. I needed conceptual frameworks and looked to doctoral studies for theoretical understanding.

PUSHING BOUNDARIES IN GRADUATE SCHOOL: CONCEPTUALIZING GENDER

Initially I wanted to go to graduate school to study gender inequities in the curriculum. Then I bumped into Larry Iannacone who said, "No, it's not just about sexism in curriculum, it's about politics: That's where the power is to make change." He was so right! So I took courses like organizational theory, politics, philosophy of research, and so on. Even those traditional courses were incredibly eye opening. It was in graduate school that I began to get theories and concepts that helped me sort through anger and incongruities. Concepts like Kanter's "opportunity structure" (1977) helped me see how structures sent messages saying, "You stay back girl." I learned about the relationships between policy, politics and values. So I understood Title IX is still not being enforced decades later because dominant actors do not value its intents.

Still, picture grad school in the 1970s: no female authors of literatures or professors of educational administration! When I told one professor that I wanted to do my final project on women in school administration, imagine my confusion when one professor told me that it was not a significant topic. *Now* I know that defining a significant question has to do with the "politics of knowledge" and who gets to determine what counts as knowledge.

I see *now* that I was being put through survival testing when so many papers had red penned notes all over them. The papers were about conceptualizing research and methodology and were related to my topic on women and school administration. The message I kept getting was: you need to show that you can be objective and systematic when you conduct research. That way you will be able to use the data to defend your point rather than relying just on your passion. At the time such criticism was painful. In retrospect, I realize that those critiques helped prepare me to challenge oppressive norms and to recognize the challenges in current debates about validity in our research, and about emotion, caring, and spirituality in our field. Being tested then prepared me for my venturing and seeking ways to combine my work as "objective scholar" with my social justice and feminist advocacy.

I was angry at a system that was oppressive and because of that I was seen as somebody with a chip on her shoulder over "this women's stuff." I could either back off or I could pass the tests and prove myself. You should have seen me, in 1976-77, having shed my ladylike "teacher clothes," walking into professor's offices wearing a T-shirt proclaiming, "A Woman's Place is in the House … and in the Senate." One professor said to me, "Well, women just don't want administrative positions." I saw a different reality in my doctoral classes where more than half of the students were women. I thought: I'm not the one who is wrong here. I started to develop a coping mechanism: instead of anger, I would laugh at the absurdities. While I didn't have the feminist theory at the time, my women's movement activism helped me see realities of patriarchy supporting pompous, arrogant and wrong men, who still kept their power. I knew I needed their approval to make my way in the world. Laughing at the absurdities was my exercise of agency, giving me internal strength and power to deal with oppressive and marginalizing situations. Laughter kept me from being a victim. I couldn't laugh in people's faces but I could in private and survive and thrive.

A big breakthrough came when I persisted with the question of women in educational administration. I found Flora Ida Ortiz who was doing research on women and minorities in school administration. She became a mentor who, over the years would talk about gender and sexuality issues, about sex discrimination, about things that women have to do that men don't have to do. She understood these issues not only from the position of being a woman, but she is also tiny, and the first Hispanic female professor in educational administration in the United States. She is someone who has always had to learn to assess power situations in order to survive. She also was the one who introduced me to the concept of the marginal man. It is the idea that, although you may get a job, you may never feel included, thus always remaining marginalized. I used that concept in my dissertation to conceptualize how women leaving teaching to enter administration were left dangling. We women in educational administration have been treated like a "marginal man." *Now* we have the words of Patricia Hill Collins, naming as the "outsider-within" (Collins, 1998).

Amazingly, too, my doctoral program was very supportive of qualitative inequity for such questions that had little specific language, that borrow conceptual frameworks in literature in other fields, to describe the inequities that women faced in educational administration.

Still, in 1980 I backed off such challenges to my field, for career survival. I had been advised that I had better show I had other qualifications. So with the help of a University of California at Los Angeles and Sacramento postdoctoral fellowship I was able to develop expertise as a politics and policy scholar, which meant I had a second specialization, along with my third area, qualitative methodology, which was very rare at the time. Thus, I was three people packaged into one. Only now, decades later, I find delightful ways to integrate those three people. I actually published in all three areas but not in mainstream educational administration journals. I was getting published in anthropology, sociology, and qualitative journals and my article on stigma first appeared in Australia (Marshall, 1985, 2000). In that piece, I compared women's experiences in educational administration to Goffman's (1986) stigmatized individual. At the time many journals in educational administration were not willing to publish articles on gender issues. Years after its publication, while studying Australian government documents on gender, I was delighted to see it cited. But U.S. governments and education administration programs, to this day, are still shoving aside the dilemmas of women in educational administration.

SEARCHING FOR TENURE IN THE SNAKE PITS OF ACADEMY

In my first academic job was at the University of Pennsylvania, I was the only full-time female faculty member in the department of educational administration. I actually wore suits with little bow ties! Sexual politics were challenging at Penn and there were no protections. As a junior faculty member I was put in charge of chairing doctoral dissertations and writing new curriculum, which didn't leave a lot of time for publishing. My mentor Larry Iannacone would say stop, you have to publish to survive. He couldn't understand why I couldn't say no. Flora Ida Ortiz really helped me understand that there was a double standard for women. A graphic illustration of the powerlessness I felt was an incident that occurred in my first year in academia. I was new, untenured and overwhelmed with responsibilities so I went to my dean for help. He said he was really busy but could meet with me on a Saturday. So I went to meet with him on a Saturday and to make a horrible story short, my dean sexually harassed me. I'd gone for career support, to be taken seriously as a budding scholar, and he propositioned me!

I got out of the situation but I was emotionally paralyzed by it. I knew I would never be able to have a conversation with the man. I knew something about him that would make him want to discredit me. I would never be able to have support from him, and he was my dean!

By the time I left that snake pit there were three sexual harassment lawsuits pending against the dean. He came out of it unscathed and went on to an endowed professorship in another institution. The timing, 1980-1985, is significant because that was about the time that Anita Hill was having similar experiences with Clarence Thomas, before the term sexual harassment entered the public discourse. Hill raised the consciousness of women nationally and helped women see that patriarchy supported sexual harassment and even highly qualified strong woman, exercising agency and refusing victimhood, found little support in the legal system, the Senate, the media, and the popular culture.

So I jumped when I was offered an associate professor position with tenure at Vanderbilt. They selected me as the scholar who could design the curriculum for their doctoral students who would do case studies. My expertise in comparative state politics also helped me get that job. I had worked on a comparative state project with Douglas Mitchell and Frederick Wirt, *Culture and Education Policy in the American States* (Marshall, Mitchell & Wirt, 1989). I had credibility from two other areas of expertise even though it was risky to do gender work. I definitely did not get the job because I did wonderful gender research. A senior politics of education scholar advising me, prepromotion, "You're going to ruin yourself Catherine, with all that feminist stuff, and you started out so great, doing research on state education politics!" Even now, in 2009, getting students and courses and funding for pursuing marginalizing feminist agendas is a lonely nonsupported task.

INTELLECTUAL INSIGHTS FROM FEMINIST SCHOLARS POTLUCKS AND REVOLUTIONS

Tenure allowed me to say "no" occasionally, when male colleagues expected me to advise their students when they were off earning consulting fees. By that time, I knew enough to collaborate with other women for camaraderie and for pushing women's issues. Here's one vignette: I invited all the female professors to come to a potluck at my house. It was a Friday night, food, wine and a bit of rabble-rousing talk in my living room. During the gathering, the phone rang. It was my dean saying, "Hi Catherine. I just thought I'd call to see what you are meeting about." I knew, at least by that time, I could laugh and tell him that, in my home we can talk about whatever we want to. Nevertheless, when he called me into his office on Monday he repeated the request. There were just two other women in educational administration, Ann Austin who was being taken advantage of, teaching a number of courses and paid poorly, and Yvonna Lincoln. Both are highly regarded scholars in higher education. Then Yvonna came up for promotion and was denied, with questioning that her husband had done most of her writing! Time to get out of that snakepit. Collaboration with other women is a support but is not enough.

GAINING STRENGTHS FROM FEMINIST LITERATURES

In the 1970s and 1980s American Educational Research Association (AERA) Division A and the Politics of Education Association were bastions of White male chumminess that I entered only through sponsorship. I searched outside leadership literature for gender insights. For example, from Constantina Safilios-Rothchild I first heard the term "homosocial," which so beautifully evokes the power of male bonding in educational administration. And the AERA Special Interest Group (SIG) on Women provided space, and feminist literatures were expanding.

The prevalent liberal feminism had gained strength from the precedents of the civil rights movement and emphasized American political rhetoric about the rights of individuals to self-expression and opportunity. Thus, it yielded token policies. We accepted this underfunded and unenforced nod to feminism. We (I) believed that going to the master's house to ask through rational argument for our needs would work.

Gradually, stimulated by experiences and literatures, I sought deeper and wider feminisms. Sometime in the 1990s, Michelle Foster laughed at my moaning about male dominance in our school of education. She said "you White women are just too nice and quiet. My mamma told me, when I was very little, 'look at you with your nappy head—you're never going to get what you need being NICE and pretty and sweet'" and Michelle was SO right. Our feminist theory (and our mothers' guidance and our liberal middle class feminisms) had not given us the tools and strategies we needed. The puzzles over endarkened epistemologies (Dillard, 2003; Foster, 1993) continue, as do the dilemmas over how to combine scholarly career decorum with being interventionist and successfully activist feminists. Another blindness was illustrated when, as I was palling around with Fazal Rizvi (an Australian scholar). I pushed him away when he wanted to come to the AERA SIG on Women. Wrongly, I assumed feminism was only for women.

Many of feminisms' realizations had not permeated my (and others') knowledge: the feminist insights about race, sexuality, about how politics of knowledge legitimize men's work, about male bonding and profeminist men. I needed theorizing of how tokenism left institutional sexism firmly ensconced. I needed feminisms that moved us beyond the Western cultural emphasis on rational-legal and individual rights-orientation that left me and Anita Hill dangling. I needed to see how those cultural orientations had, through our history, been embedded in court precedents that protected a private sphere where husbands ruled families. They were embedded in workplaces and professional cultures that "protected" women from the tough (and better paid) jobs in management, leadership, and plumbing and also penalized women for their propensities to have periods, children, collaborative facilitative work styles, and caring relationships. I did not know enough of history and cultural values to critique these forces. However, my experiences with clashes of sexuality education systems, and the snake pit realities, described above, drove my search for feminist critique that encompassed women's values, activism, and collaboration and that laid bare patriarchal politics, tokenism, and andro-centric scholarship.

EDUCATION'S FOOT-DRAGGING INCLUSION OF FEMINISM

These stories above are illustrative of *my* confusions and realizations of the need for feminist scholarship that embraces power and politics, that takes us beyond essentializing middle class, ethnocentric, U.S.-centric—to feminisms that can both frame realities we live <u>and</u> identify powerful tools to challenge and reframe and to build alternatives to the master's house.

These realizations stimulated me to read evolving feminist literatures, search for support for activism, and then to develop feminist critical policy analysis, with its methods and stances that challenge political systems and institutional life.

Reading scholars in the 1980s like Gilligan (1982), Belenky, McVicker Clinchy, Goldberger, and Mattuck Tarule (1986), Noddings (1984), Jane Roland Martin (1994) helped delineate what is missed when women's voices, values, and women's ways are excluded. These literatures offered alternative arrangements, ethics, values, curricular, and pedagogical approaches that come from insights into women's ways, with potential for major reframing of educational purposes and structures. The fields of study most invested in purposes and structures are administration and policy but feminist literatures penetrated only a few enlightened, mostly curriculum and instruction and teacher education scholars' work. The potential insights for bringing to schooling the caring, hope and joy, and the potential of collaborative, collective workplaces for students and educators, (theorized in Noddings, hooks [1994], and others) was not broached as essential to rethinking schooling. They were even belittled and undermined, with attacks on methodology and with being cast to the sidelines as irrelevant and impractical (e.g. Noddings and Martin). This happened, in spite of the obvious overarching support from Sandra Hardings' (1991) demand that women's excluded voices, insights, and needs be incorporated to eliminate the andocentric biases in theory and research. Formal acceptance of my feminist approach to educational administration didn't really occur until the 90s. In "Imagining New Leadership" (Marshall, 1995) I was able to point to the fallacies in leadership theory that ignored the absence of women and minorities. But my article on "caring" (Marshall, Patterson, & Rogers, 1996) symbolizes a major change in the field. I was doing collaborative research on career assistant principals. In the data we found that individuals who serve as an assistant principal for years, talk about the ways they devoted themselves to kids. I kept looking for ways to conceptualize the data. I finally made a connection to Nel Noddings' work on the ethic of care (1984), which provided a way of conceptualizing their experiences. Calling it "Caring as Career" and submitting it to EAQ, brought us comments like, "This is strange, what leadership theories are you using, and do they fit?" The piece was nontraditional in that it used feminist theory to conceptualize educational administration. It went through at least three revisions before EAQ finally accepted it. When I look back, that may have been the point that EAQ, a prestigious but stodgy journal, started to open up to nontraditional approaches.[1]

Another breakthrough came from feminisms that rejected the view of women as one collective category, recognizing shifting and evolving identities, critiquing the idea of seeing women as "not men," as well as recognizing that women differ in identities affected by class, race, geography, politics, and so on. Breakthroughs came from Collins' *Black Feminist Thought* (1990) exposing Eurocentrism too. Many studies, then flowed from situating and focusing on the lives of women educators as they survived, and attempted to change the institutionalized sexism—from Weiler's (1988) to Chase's *Ambiguous Empowerment* (1995). A bit of historical analysis helped, too. Cynthia Dillard's (1995, 2003) and Michelle Foster's *Othermothers: Exploring the Educational Philosophy of Black Women Teachers* (1993) begin with a valuing of African American women educators and demonstrate alternative understandings of schooling and leadership that comes from such an expansion. Tyack and Hansot's (1982) *Managers of Virtue*, Blount's (1998) *Destined to Rule*, and McFadden and Smith's (2004) uncovered the cultural embeddeness of compulsory heterosexuality and masculinity in educational administration.

My election in 1990 as the first female president of the Politics of Education Association (PEA) was also critically important. When I first started going to meetings it was dominated by White males. I know I gained legitimacy in that circle through my traditional politics work. The power I gained from that position allowed me to bridge non traditional pieces such as editing a PEA yearbook entitled *The Politics of Race and Gender* (Marshall, 1993). Then there was also another piece I wrote with Gary Anderson for the 1995 *Politics of Education Yearbook* (Marshall & Anderson, 1995) that was important. It showed how the politics of education could benefit from feminist theory and cultural studies perspectives. Mainstream scholars did not really understand what we were saying. That point was abundantly clear in the AERA presentation on the yearbook. We had talked about how gender and culture were huge areas of silence. The audience was demonstrating that exact point by remaining silent on the topic! Neither the discussants, nor the audience, commented on our work. Ben Levin stood up and pointed out the irony in that moment. Again, silence. I could see that these ideas were going to continue to be ignored unless I persisted in drawing attention to them.

THE ESSENTIAL POWER AND POLITICS CRITIQUE

To move beyond a depressing, marginalized, powerless situation, a critique is essential. One eurcka moment was provided by connecting feminisms with power and knowledge-politics. Harding's (1991) exposition of androcentric biases in research methodologies and the research and theories built upon such biased science. Ferguson, too, made the connection of feminist theories with the knowledge/power dynamic. As Ferguson said, "What is lacking here is an explicit recognition of the political context within which the male and female voices develop" (Ferguson, 1984, p. 168). Without that critique, those voices, values and ways would (1) leave women doing all the caring work but with no pay or valuing for it and no alteration in the power structures, (2) allow those controlling bureaucracies and political arenas to do the value-assessments, (3) leave women's concerns in the private sphere, and (4) relegate women's issues into managed, vulnerable, noninstitutionalized units like universities' women's studies, and un- and underfunded and token concessions like the Women's Educational Equity Act. Thus, theorizing and acting needed a critique of white male power embedded in policies, politics, laws, courts, professions, and agencies, women's caring, relationship-valuing, voice.

One mainstay of the critique builds upon postmodernist and constructivist recognition that realities and identities are socially constructed. From that realization, we see the power of institutional and professional practices that label and channel, legitimize and delegitimize. *Now* we can reframe problems: for example, the problem is reframed from the pregnant girl's sexual behavior—to what are schools doing to help girls' empowered identities. With this, one can reframe the issue of few women in leadership by dismantling the white male norms embedded in the very definitions of leadership, as seen in the work of Grogan (2003), AhNee-Benham (2003), Brunner (2000), Marshall (1995), and Dillard (2003).

Still, I needed theories that moved past the marginalized-as-victim conceptualization. Realization and insights from cultural studies, and working with Gary Anderson, led to seeing "complex forms of cultural and political resistance, accommodation, and compliance rooted in the informed intentionality of social actors" (Marshall & Anderson, 1995, p. 174). So, cultural analyses of school subcultures then reveal micropolitics of identity negotiation, resistance, and agency. Thus, students' rebellion, acting out, and considering dropping out, or getting pregnant may be viewed as their exercising agency and/creating their own selves. As they negotiate the cultural and political webs of meanings, students, and educators can be seen as political agents for their own destinies. Bingo: I had found a way to bring my three selves together as a strong advocate, centered from an identity forged by surviving, and ready to lead from that center! Theory, scholarship, and my own experience and goals could finally converge.

DIVERSE, INTERNATIONAL, AND INTERDISCIPLINARY INTERCHANGES PROVIDED CHALLENGES AND SUPPORTS

Through the years, comments and events inspired my search for literatures:

Sandra Acker, over coffee in Toronto, said, "Why are you trying so hard to see that more girls love science-why do you buy into the way markets and men value what men do (e.g. science), and the devaluing of, for example, child nurturance, caring, relationship, collaboration?" Since then I, and others, "get" the possibilities of using insights from maternal feminisms to embed caring, relationship, collaboration, and valuing of nurturance into education systems. But, with a few exceptions—like a few schools with child care for pregnant teens and making subcommunities in schools to increase a sense of belonging, these feminist insights have not altered school structures.

In a continuing search, I discovered the international network of women scholars in educational administration and political science—women like Miriam David, Jill Blackmore, Nelly Stromquist, Sandra Taylor, Jane Gaskell, Jane Kenway, and many others (e.g. Arnot & Weiner, 1987; Stronquist, 1997; Weiler, 1988). They were scholars in *my* field writing about gender and politics! Even though I was an associate professor, I felt like I was a graduate student again when Madeline Arnot advised, said "You will be at a standstill until you get all the literature that connects feminism and politics. You *must* read these Australian, New Zealand, South African, and British scholars who connect feminism and politics." I had to search for them in international presses and pay in foreign currencies but I devoured these books. If I had had that type of intellectual stimulation in graduate school, my gender scholarship would have had a chance to develop earlier. Still, I was not alone anymore. That was really the beginning of me conceptualizing *Feminist Critical Policy Analysis* (Marshall, 1997a, 1997b) where I could connect politics, feminism, gender studies, and leadership. These types of connections had been missing in my graduate education, in literature in the United States, and in my own teaching.

Breakthroughs focusing on the power of the state came from legal theory, with Catherine MacKinnon's *Toward a Feminist Theory of the State* (1989) and *Only Words* (1993) and from political science, with Ferguson's *Feminist Case Against Bureaucracy* (1984), Fraser's *Unruly Practices* (1989) and Elshtain's (1979, 1982) critique of mainstream political science. Elshtain points to the huge expansion of areas for analysis once one highlights the political arenas and activities more commonly developed by women. Fraser (1994) points to the multiple hidden public spheres and the existence of "counterpublics" composed of subordinated social groups which "invent and circulate counternarratives ... oppositional interpretations of their identities, interest, and needs" (p. 84). Thus women's counternarratives have invented terms for marital rape, the triple shift, power-with leadership, and so on. Breakthroughs, too, came when feminist education scholars moved to macro arenas to study the effects of the economic and political systems, as did Weiler (1993), in her demand for a move beyond critical theory, Weis (1988, 1993), in her demonstrations of limited economic opportunities shaping high school male and female identities, and others. But this connection was greatly aided by international insights, of such authors as such as Yates (1993), Arnot and Weiner (1987), Blackmore (1998), David, Weiner, and Arnot (1997), and others.

FEMINIST CRITICAL POLICY ANALYSIS

I became whole, and an integration of research methodologist, gender scholar, and policy scholar when I published *Feminist Critical Policy Analysis* in 1997. I knew, finally, to take on policy arenas by moving beyond assumptions about a collective women's identity or women's problems to focus on "the public problems of a pervasively gender-structured society" (Disch, 1991, p. 501). This move pointed to the particular policies and political leadership (formal and informal) that create, choose and enforce patterns that have the effect of disenfranchising or denying women opportunity. By doing so, feminist scholars create powerful strategies for upsetting political assumptions and arrangements and reframing alternatives. We are also forging a strong connection between feminist critiques and theories of democracy, and thus, a feminist critique of democracy.

This is much better than the feminisms that point out our victim status and that leave us in the margins of women's studies. Feminist critical policy analysis starts with the assumptions that bias, power, and values drive the identification, labeling, and legitimation of a problem and the methods seen as useful for studying and solving it. Too, feminist analysis realizes that the appropriateness and policy-relevance of any recommendations will be judged in accordance with dominant interests. All other problems, methodologies, and solutions will be cast to the side.

I used Fraser's (1994) views of the public sphere as a "masculinist ideological notions that functioned to legitimate an emergent form of class rule" (p. 79). Fraser continues, noting those who decide the agenda in the public sphere arrange "the hegemonic mode of domination" (Fraser, 1994, p. 117). As I worked developing feminist critical policy analysis, I also developed a discussion of methodologies for policy analysis that can incorporate feminist critiques (e.g., narrative and interpretive). I proposed bringing to the forefront facets of women's experience with the demand that policies be reconstructed to address and redress. I proposed investigating and laying bare the cultural embeddendness of policies. I proposed research agendas focusing on ways that policies and programs and regulatory procedures incorporate these realities of power and control such as a focus on:

- The barrier between public and private, erected ostensibly to protect the freedom of all [is] supportive of the oppression of many (Stivers, 1991, p. 63). Policies obfuscate gender politics in the private sphere: men keep the power to control, hurt, and take advantage of women through family structures, sex, violence, and even the rituals of romance and the burdens of mothering;
- capitalism and patriarchy intertwine in policies disadvantaging women, as when domestic and caring work are un- or underpaid;
- the state, and men's control of identity- and myth-making, including assigning women roles in keeping male aggressiveness in check (Stivers, 1991);
- symbolic gender policies which are accompanied with token implementation and backlash;
- institutional structures are created for political purposes, often to women's disadvantage;
- how "gender and its regulation is not an afterthought in state policy. Rather it is a constitutive part of it" (Apple, 1994, p. 356);
- how talk is power; male management of knowledge and language is a site of political struggle;
- how "men are uncomfortable with the thought that their advantages were not necessarily earned but rather bestowed by institutions and professions structured to support them" (Marshall, 1997, p. 25).

Feminist critical policy analysis makes people uncomfortable. Still, it has been defended and demonstrated in Bensimone and Marshall, (2003). Others have taken up the agendas and approaches: See for example, example of Andre-Becheley's (2005) analysis of mothers choosing schools for their children. She used feminist critical policy analysis to uncover the oppressive dimensions of policies, to reframe policy questions, as well as to seek activist and social justice alternatives. See also, Weis' (1997) dismantling of the major national reports of crisis in education; Stromquist's (1997) identification of the token nature of U.S. policies for educational gender equity; Brunner's (2000) reframing of women's leadership, validating a power-with, rather than a power-over style; and Laible's (1997) account of a school board that just can't quite understand why a sexual harassment policy is needed. See also, Shaw's (2004) analysis of U S welfare policy, incorporating the lived realities of poor women, showing how seemingly gender-blind policy, combined with demonization of single mothers ideolog, results in policy that cuts off women's education and job opportunities.

Much fruitful work lies ahead using feminist critical policy analysis. Beyond identifying the discourse in political and institutional arenas where power is embedded, next steps include: (1) researching the resistances, since resistance to subjugating practices and subjugated knowledges are what Ferguson calls " the crafting and recrafting of particular insights into unfolding and ever-shifting unities of explanation and action" (1984, p. 157) and (2) proposing alternative assumptions and power arrangements. As Ferguson stated, "a specifically feminist discourse can suggest reformulation of some of the most central terms of political life: reason, power, community, freedom" (p. 155). Once one lays bare and sheds the androcentrism of leadership theory, one discovers exciting patterns through the exploration of women's leadership, as Brunner (2000) and Benham (2003) show. Once one acknowledges that women's policing is a valid, legitimate area for studying politics, as Andre-Bechely (2005) showed and as Elshtain (1982) demonstrated in the coalitions of mothers of the disappeared in South America, then feminism has expanded the study of political arenas multiplies exponentially, far beyond elite male-normed legislatures.

Searching for illustrations, I conducted research on teacher unions' gender activism (Marshall, 2002). I found savvy feminist educators maneuvering micro and macro politically. The American Federation of Teachers' (AFT) mission to protect teachers' rights expanded to include students' rights to gender equitable instruction, pregnancy leaves and "pregnancy-related disabilities." A state level teacher union leader in New England recounted how her union worked on better pay and status for paraprofessionals. She said, "women came alive working on substantive issues ... then learned how to accumulate power, how to make coalitions, how to win." But it was a struggle, she said, to get women teachers to challenge male domination of leadership and use "the huge power block they never had exercised.... Before my election I was viewed as 'too nice' to be president.... A guy who had fought me tooth and nails said, 'You're a real bitch.' And I said 'Thank you very much.' They were astounded that I could run a meeting." She recalled using her ethnic community connections and her connections with elementary teachers, parents and legislators as constituency-building, as well as how to use dramatic gestures when lobbying. I found similar power-savvy Australian femocrats in my research on gender equity policy in Australia (Marshall, 2000). These are examples of the kind of discoveries in politics, expaned.

This power-savvy grass-roots politicking was attuned to sexuality and beyond the white middle classes. However, in the United States, both teacher unions are federations, needing to please their locals. The conservative backlash rhetoric about feminists upsetting traditional families, government intrusion into private affairs, and any association between gender equity and the controversies over birth control, sexuality, sex education, and abortion created a fearful retreat. A Washington bureaucrat recalled firings of gender equity personnel, and "people feared strong views ... we changed the name of the research program from sex inequities to 'classroom interaction studies.'" They avoided gay/lesbian issues. Gender-related positions in state bureaucracies were shifted into more ambiguous titles like "creating healthy school environments" and focusing on "quality" education and test scores. Some maintained their feminist work by honing in on the policy interest in school violence, bullying, and harassment. Some mourned, working with little or no budgets and little hope that their positions would be filled when they retired. This research on feminists functioning in political shifts illustrates the range of issues—from culture, class, and race differences among women, confronting male backlash, grass roots collaboration, disunity and non-consensus around sexuality and abortion issues—to femocrats coping without support in the environment of governmental enmity to feminism.

Conversations and literature-sharing *have* improved, with the internet and travel. There is no funding for conferences of international feminist scholars in education, for networks and symposia. Feminist scholars in education have little interaction with those in political science, public policy, women's studies, sociology of occupations, never mind with those who make public policy. But publications now exist, albeit at the fringes of educational administration and policy.

MOVING TOWARD ADVOCACY AND COLLABORATION

To move beyond marginalization and "woe-is-me-hood," and to share the wealth of discoveries about politically savvy feminism, I sought collaboration with other equity-oriented scholars. In my field, what counted as knowledge affecting literature, preparation programs, and licensure still did not encompass gender. The creation of Leadership for Social Justice (LSJ) was a powerful breakthrough. By convening a group of scholars who wrote about equity and social justice, I found a way to multiply our efforts and to recognize and take advantage of intersectionality. LSJ members use advocacy, research, and curricular work to collaborate in the struggles against inequitable policies and practices.

LSJ has even enticed more mainstream scholars to take an interest in these ideas, providing the place for possibility for shared research and activism. Even the lone critical scholar in a department, as I often was, has an international community of scholars. Now many mission statements and job descriptions in educational administration include social justice goals.

The invisibility and marginalization of social justice in educational administration was one of the reasons I wrote *Reframing Educational Politics for Social Justice* (Marshall & Gerstl-Pepin, 2005). I wanted to use courses on politics (required usually) to show how political arrangements subtly marginalize ideas considered feminine, as an arena dominated by invisible male norms. Now educational administration is starting to develop language to name issues of marginalization. Scholars like Catherine Lugg, Larry Parker, Jim Scheurich, Michael Dantley, and Gerardo Lopez are opening the field to new ideas. Editorial boards are shifting. I loved getting the Willystine Goodsell Award in 2002 for contributions to research, scholarship, and activism for women and girls in education. So, think now of how amazing it was that I received the 2008 Roald Campbell Award for contributions to the field of educational administration. And to think I was going to ruin my career with all that stuff on gender!

WHERE ARE WE NOW?

This chapter illustrates that the "personal is political." Having Nancy Pelosi in the Senate and Title IX on paper is only token progress. Why so? Consider the selective reality of students in a gender class, choosing to believe that there is gender equity while at the same time giving personal examples of unequal treatment. Titus found that some preservice teachers "deny, dismiss, or discount women's oppression, distance themselves from feminism, or express dismay or despair in the absence of any definitive solutions to the inequalities they acknowledge" (Titus, 2000, p. 22). There is much work to be done, still.

BACKLASH AND HISTORICAL SELECTIVITY

Backlash against the women's movement is interwoven with the ways right wing Christians are challenging multiculturalism and attempting to reassert church based, Christian values through legislation and political influence (Cooper, 1997; Cudd, 2002). Willett (2002) asserts that women's liberation movement of the 1960s did not take into account the power of cultural desire for children, for the protections mythically afforded women by patriarchal institutions, and for family life. In gender equity debates, then, opponents as well as those on the fence could easily press the antifamily, antifemininity, antimarriage, and antichildren buttons. Women and young girls exploring the offerings of the women's movement, while lured by promises of equal pay and personal freedoms, were fearful of the (media-inflamed) specter of identities that seemed to limit their chances for a nice husband and children, and for being seen as "normal" and proper.

Still, the interweaving discourses of critical, critical race, queer, and feminist theory and research can empower educators. When a 23-year-old teacher, or a forties principal is exploring and negotiating her sense of self she is doing so in the school- and society-generated contexts of her neighborhood, her skin, her sexuality, her gender, as well as the expectations of her profession and her regional culture. She could benefit from theory on the intersectionality of race, class, gender, and sexuality as they allow exploration of their career, and identities. But I doubt these empowering discourses are part and parcel of the professional pre- and in-service or the teacher lounge talk of educators. Too bad. Because while these critical discourses are upsetting, they also could help educators feel comfortable with their instincts toward expanded identities, liberatory practices, and social movement participation. This would help me feel that our feminist scholarship has been worthwhile.

Now, in 2009, these literatures and insights may be used in cultural studies, women's studies, and, in education, in social foundations programs. But feminist readings appear next-to-never as powerful curricula in programs that prepare teachers and administrators. When these readings were published they did not even reach, never mind startle or overturn, the canon of educational leadership and policy. Many U.S. scholars in administration and policy may know of one or two such works at best. Those who seek (as I do) to position this scholarship at the center of administration and policy are still struggling.

The standards and accountability movement controls the curriculum in administration: administrator and teacher licensure must address diversity and federal law No Child Left Behind must address inequities in achievement but none of these policy thrusts mention gender or sexuality. NCATE shies away from any provisions that might force schools of education and educator licensing to address gender and sexuality. Funding for research or programming on gender, from governments, foundations, or programming is undermined by current rhetoric about "best practices," "what about the boys," and "protect the traditional family." These are rhetorical code phrases meaning: feminist agendas need not apply. Further, the legitimized fund-able research methods now must be "scientific" with randomized controlled experiments, thus marginalizing the methodological advances from feminist scholarship (Marshall & Young, 2006). One's opportunity to use feminism and social science to "talk back … in a spirited critique" (Devault, 1999, p. 27) is severely constrained. Thus, feminist insights are viewed as frills that might distract from the main business of training educators. They are viewed as distractions taking scholars from the main business of getting grants and consolidating pedagogy for online delivery. Within my own educational leadership program, I cannot convince my colleagues of the importance of providing a course on gender. They say it is embedded in other courses, that Title IX has solved any problems, and that we must focus on the skills required by licensing boards.

FINAL REFLECTIONS: FADE AWAY OR CAUSE A RUCKUS?

After recounting both the snake pits and the delights of a feminist scholar, I end with these as essential recommendation:

- To examine the wide context wherein the personal, the political, and the economic (e.g., third shift, women's work) as topics incorporated in research and theory;
- To see gender as a social construction, devised within unequal gender/power relations;
- To avoid essentializing and to interrupt common misrepresentations of women;
- To deconstruct and alter simplistic "add women and stir" ventures;
- To take credit for feminist methodological insights, such as, for collaboration with research participants, for embracing subjectivity, and for combining research with action for empowerment (Marshall & Young, 2006).

I do have a hopeful watch-and-see story: I, along with Lois Andre-Bechely, agreed to write a chapter for the *Handbook of Research in Education Politics*, to be called "Feminism and Education Politics: No Longer for Women Only" (Marshall & Andre-Bechely, 2008). Will the scholars in education politics read it? Will the authors of other chapters incorporate feminist insights and gender questions in their chapters on unions, on federalism, on micropolitics, interest groups, the Christian Right, school reform, school boards, urban schools, school finance, privatization? Will they be doing so by the time I retire or die? I ask this with my exhausted-from-the-struggle, why-not-just-retire voice.

However, I have another voice, a feminist, fun-and-rebellion voice. Reflecting on the meager gains from behaving like a well-socialized and proper professor, and using a cold cost-benefit feminist critical policy analysis framework, I wish to generate strategies to get for feminist scholars the benefits deserved for our decades of intellectual struggle. Using collaborative strategic feminist politics (see Mawhinney, 1997 and Henry, 1990), I think we should cause a ruckus by:

- *Creating narratives and documentation* of past experiences where male colleagues were given leadership positions then accumulated wealth, lucrative consulting contracts, and robust retirement accounts even when they barely showed up for classes and delivered less service, student advising, publications than women professors, and were excused for peccadilloes like sexual harassment (and we should name names);
- *Hiring experts for a campaign:* assemble feminist public health experts, lawyers and economists to assess the estimated loss of benefits, money, and health from the struggle to survive as feminist scholars; and align with women's caucuses in our various professional organizations and in unions; and
- *Making "outrageous" demands,* for example, for 2-year paid leaves, for example, for full funding of 20 years' worth of future conferences that solidify efforts to bring educators to us, that consolidate our work and identify ways to bring educators up to speed on feminist insights, and for example, for large outlays of reparation money from institutions that have used but inadequately rewarded woman's work, and for other ideas of rewarding and celebrating the work of feminist scholars.

We might as well cause a ruckus

"For the master's house will never be dismantled with the master's tools."

—Lorde

NOTES

1. I credit Rick Reitzug for supporting the numerous revisions I made to help connect traditional ed ad analysis with what the data were showing.

REFERENCES

AhNee-Benham, M. K. P. (2003). In our mother's voice: A native woman's knowing of leadership. In M. D. Young & L. Skrla (Eds.), *Reconsidering—Feminist research in educational leadership* (pp. 223-245) Albany: State University of New York Press.

Andre-Bechely, L. (2005). *Could it be otherwise? Parents and the inequities of public school choice.* New York, NY: Routledge.

Apple, M. (1994) Texts and contexts: The state and gender in educational policy, *Curriculum Inquiry, 24(3),* 349-59.

Arnot, M., & Weiner, G. (1987). *Gender and the politics of schooling*. London: Unwin Hyman.
Arnot, M. D., & Weiner, G. (1999). *Closing the gender gap: Postwar education and social change*. Cambridge, England: Polity Press
Belenky, M. F., McVicker Clinchy, B., Goldberger, N. R., & Mattuck Tarule, J. (1986). *Women's ways of knowing: The development of self, voice, and mind*. New York, NY: Basic Books.
Bensimon, E. M., & Marshall, C. (2003, May/June). Like it or not—Feminist critical policy analysis matters [Reply]. *The Journal of Higher Education, 74,* 337-349.
Blackmore, J. (1998). *Troubling women: Feminism, leadership and educational change*. London: Open University Press.
Blount, J. (1998). *Destined to rule the schools: Women and the superintendency, 1873-1995* Albany: State University of New York Press.
Brunner, C. C. (2000). *Principles of power: Women superintendents and the riddle of the heart*. Albany: State University of New York Press.
Chase, S. (1995). *Ambiguous empowerment: The work narratives of women school superintendents*. Amherst: University of Massachusetts Press.
Collins, P. H. (1990). *Black feminist thought – Knowledge, consciousness, and the politics of empowerment*. New York, NY: Routledge.
Collins, P. H. (1998). *Fighting words: Black women and the search for justice*. Minneapolis: University of Minnesota Press.
Cooper, D. (1997). At the expense of Christianity: Backlash discourse and moral panic. In L. Roman & L. Fry (Eds.), *Dangerous territories: Struggles for difference and equality in education* (pp. 43-62). New York, NY: Routledge
Cudd, A. (2002). Analyzing backlash to progressive social movements. In A. Superson & A. Cudd (Eds.), *Theorizing Blacklash: Philosophical reflections on the resistance to feminism* (pp. 3-16) New York, NY: Rowman & Littlefield.
David, M., Weiner, G., & Arnot, M. (1997). Strategic feminist research on gender equality and schooling in Britain in the 1990s. In C. Marshall (Ed.), *Feminist critical policy analysis I: A perspective from primary and secondary schooling* (pp. 91-105). London: Falmer Press.
Devault, M. (1999) *Liberating method: Feminism and social research*. Philadelphia, PA: Temple University Press.
Dillard, C.B. (1995). Leading with her life: An African American feminist (re)interpretation of leadership for an urban high school principal. *Educational Administration Quarterly, 31*(4), 539-563.
Dillard, C. B. (2003). The substance of things hoped for, the evidence of things not seen: Examining an endarkened feminist epistemology in educational research and leadership. In M. D. Young & L. Skrla (Vol. Eds.), *Reconsidering feminist research in educational leadership* (pp. 131-159). Albany: State University of New York Press.
Disch, L. (1991, September). Toward a feminist conception of politics. *PS: Political Science and Politics, 24,* 501-504.
Elshtain, J. B. (1979). Methodological sophistication and conceptual confusion—A critique of mainstream political science. In J. A. Sherman & E. T. Beck

(Eds.), *The prism of sex* (pp. 229-252). Madison: The University of Wisconsin Press.
Elshtain, J. B. (1982). Feminist discourse and its discontents: Language, power and meaning. In N. Keohane, M. Z. Rosaldo, & B. C. Gelpi (Eds.), *Feminist theory: A critique of ideology*. Chicago: University of Chicago Press.
Ferguson, K. (1984). *The feminist case against bureaucracy*. Philadelphia, PA: Temple University Press.
Foster, M. (1993). Othermothers: Exploring the educational philosophy of black American women teachers. In M. Arnot & K. Weiler (Eds.), *Feminism and social justice in education: International perspectives* (pp. 101-123). Bristol, PA: The Falmer Press.
Fraser, N. (1989). *Unruly practices: Power, discourse and gender in contemporary social theory*. Minneapolis: University of Minnesota Press.
Fraser, N. (1994). Rethinking the public sphere: A contribution to the critique of actually existing democracy. In Calhoun, *Habermas and the public sphere* (pp. 109-142). Cambridge, MA: MIT Press.
Friedan, B. (1963). The feminine mystique. New York, NY: W.W. Norton.
Gilligan, C. (1982). *In a different voice: Psychological theory and women's development*. Cambridge, MA: Harvard University Press.
Goffman, E. (1986). Stigma: Notes on the management of a spoiled identity. New York, NY: Simon & Schuster.
Grogan, M. (2003). Laying the groundwork for a reconception of the superintendency from feminist postmodern perspectives. In M. D. Young & L. Skrla (Vol. Eds.), *Reconsidering feminist research in educational leadership* (pp. 9-34). Albany: State University of New York Press.
Harding, S. (1991). *Whose science? Whose knowledge? Thinking from women's lives*. Ithaca, NY: Cornell University Press.
Henry, M. (1990) Voices of academic women on feminine gender scripts. *British Journal of Sociology, 11*(2), 121-135.
Hooks, b. (1994) *Teaching to transgress: Education as the practice of freedom*. New York, NY: Routledge.
Kanter, R. M. (1977). *Men and women of the corporation*. New York, NY: Basic Books.
Laible, J. (1997). Feminist analysis of sexual harassment policy: A critique of the ideal of community. In C. Marshall (Ed.), *Feminist critical policy analysis I: A perspective from primary and secondary schooling* (pp. 201-215). London: Falmer Press.
MacKinnon, C. (1993). *Only words*. Cambridge, MA: Harvard University Press.
MacKinnon, C. A. (1989). *Toward a feminist theory of the state*. Cambridge, MA: Harvard University Press.
Martin, J. R. (1994). *Changing the educational landscape: Philosophy, women, and curriculum*. New York, NY: Routledge.
Marshall, C. (1985, August). From culturally defined to self-defined: Career stages of women administrators. *The Journal of Educational Thought, 19*(2), 134-147
Marshall, C. (1995, August). Imagining leadership. *Educational Administration Quarterly, 31*(3), 484-492.
Marshall, C. (Ed.). (1997a). *Feminist critical policy analysis I: A perspective from primary and secondary schooling*. London: Falmer Press.

Marshall, C. (1997b). *Feminist critical policy analysis II: A perspective from post-secondary education.* London: Falmer Press.
Marshall, C. (2000). Policy mechanisms for education gender equity in Australia. *Education Policy, 14*(3), 357-384.
Marshall, C., & Gerstl-Pepin, C. (2005). *Re-framing educational politics for social justice.* Boston: Allyn & Bacon.
Marshall, C., & Anderson, G. L. (1995). Rethinking the public and private spheres: Feminist and cultural studies perspectives on the politics of education. In J. Scribner & D. H. Layton (Eds.), *The study of education politics: Politics of education association yearbook, 1994* (pp. 169-182). London: Falmer Press.
Marshall, C., & Andre-Bechely, L. (2008). Feminism and education politics: No longer for women only. In B. S. Cooper, J. G. Cibulka, & L.D. Fusarelli (Eds.) *Handbook of education politics and policy.* (pp. 283-310). New York, NY: Routledge.
Marshall, C., & Young, M. (2006). Gender and methodology. In L. Smulyn (Ed.), *Handbook on gender and education.*
Marshall, C., Patterson, J., & Rogers, D. (1996). Caring as Career: An Alternative Model for Educational Administration. *Educational Administration Quarterly, 32*(2), 271-294.
Marshall, C., Mitchell, D, & Wirt, F. (1989). *Culture and education policy in the American states.* London: Falmer Press.
Mawhinney, H. B. (1997). Institutionizing women's voices, not their echoes, through feminist policy analysis of difference. In C. Marshall (Ed.), *Feminist critical policy analysis I: A perspective from primary and secondary schooling* (pp. 216-38). London: Falmer Press.
McFadden, A. H., & Smith, P. (2004). *The social construction of educational leadership: Southern Appalachian ceilings.* New York, NY: Peter Lang.
Noddings, N. (1984). *Caring: A feminine approach to ethics and moral education.* New York, NY: Teachers College Press.
Stivers, C. (1991). Toward a feminist perspective in public administration theory. *Women and politics, 10*(4), 49-65.
Stromquist, N. P. (1997). Gender policies in American education: Reflections on federal legislation and action. In C. Marshall (Ed.), *Feminist critical policy analysis I: A perspective from primary and secondary schooling* (pp. 54-72). London: Falmer Press.
Titus, J.J. (2000). Engaging student resistance to feminishm: "How is this stuff going to make us better teachers?" *Gender and Education, 12*(1), 21-37.
Tyack, D., & Hansot, E. (1982). *Managers of virtue: Public school leadership in the U.S., 1890-1980I.* New York, NY: Basic Books.
Weiler, K. (1988). *Women teaching for change, gender, class & power.* South Hadley, MA: Bergin & Garvey.
Weiler, K. (1993). Feminism and the struggle for a democratic education: A view from the states. In M. Arnot & K. Weiler (Eds.), *Feminism and social justice in education: International perspectives.* Bristol, PA: The Falmer Press.
Weis, L. (Ed.). (1988). High school girls in a de-industrializing economy. In *Class, race, & gender in American education* (pp. 183-208). Albany: State University of New York Press.

Weis, L. (1993). White male working-class youth: An exploration of relative privilege and loss. In L. Weiss & M. Fine (Eds.), *Beyond silenced voices: Class, race, and gender in United States schools* (pp. 237-258). Albany: State University of New York Press.

Weis, L. (1997). Gender and the reports: The case of the missing piece. In C. Marshall (Ed.), *Feminist critical policy analysis I: A perspective from primary and secondary schooling* (pp. 73-90). London: Falmer Press.

Willett, C. (2002). Parenting and other human casualties in the pursuit of academic excellence. In A. Superson & A. Cudd (Eds.), *Theorizing Blacklash: Philosophical reflections on the resistance to feminism* (pp. 119-131). New York, NY: Rowman & Littlefield.

Yates, L. (1993) Feminism and Australian state policy—Some questions for the 1990's. In M. Arnot & K. Weiler (Eds.), *Feminism and social justice in education* (pp. 167-85). London: Falmer Press.

SCENIC OVERLOOK

Chapters 1 and 2

Guidelines for Discussions and Reflection

For school leaders:

1. In what ways is the author's personal story similar or different than your experiences?
2. What were some life-altering events that influenced the author's ability and willingness to lead for social justice?
3. What questions do you have for the author?
4. What have been your own formative experiences related to gender?

For those preparing school leaders:

1. In what ways is the author's personal story similar or different than your experiences?
2. What were some life-altering events that influence how you prepare aspiring school leaders to lead for social justice?
3. What experiences do you share with aspiring school leaders that illustrate issues of sexism, counter hegemony and activism?

4. What have been your own formative experiences related to gender and leading
5. What have been your own formative experiences related to gender and academia?

Catherine Marshall's chapter invited the reader to gain a deeper understanding of how literatures and behaviors deemed appropriate by dominant structures attempted to suppress her intellect and imaginative possibilities. Marshall's efforts to lay bare the powers that attempt to silence women's issues are still at the heart of her work, research and activism. Although current dominant discourses seem to afford women in educational leadership positions new spaces to examine the intersections of gender and power, not enough has changed since the 1970s to dismantle the masters' house.

In the next chapter, 40 years after Catherine Marshall took the stage, Christa Boske invites the reader to consider her lived realities as an educational leader from the next generation of women in academia. The chapter encourages the reader to consider the realities facing those who promote social justice issues in schools as well as in academia. Such experiences were internalized as symbols of hope, grounding Christa's work as an activist early on.

CHAPTER 2

A TIME TO GROW

Workplace Mobbing and the Making of a Tempered Radical

Christa Boske

The biggest disease today is not leprosy or tuberculosis, but rather the feeling of being unwanted, uncared for, and deserted by everybody. The greatest evil is the lack of love and charity, the terrible indifference toward one's neighbor.

—Mother Teresa

Clearly, there are groups of children who experience being ostracized within our American public schools due to racial identity, sexual identity, class, language, immigration status, ability, and other differences (Ladson-Billings, 1994; Noguera, 2008; Oakes, 1985; Small & Newman, 2001; Lugg, 2003). When children from historically marginalized groups are compared to their White middle-class counterparts, children who are marginalized experience higher rates of being identified as needing special education services, as well as significantly lower standardized achievement scores, allocation of educational resources, and lower expectations (Alexander, Entwisle, & Olsen, 2001; Banks, 2006; Delpit, 1995; Kozol,

2005; Jencks & Phillips, 1998; Ortiz, 1997). Children served in America's inner-city schools endure wider social conditions, living under oppressive circumstances (Epstein & Dauber, 1991; McLaren, 1998). The education of children from oppressive conditions is becoming increasingly important to countries around the world (Banks & McGee Banks, 2003).

It is not fair to make the statement that all children who live in oppressive conditions attend "bad "schools. However, it is legitimate to report that urban education in the United States tends to perpetuate the belief that those who have been historically marginalized have the inherent inability to achieve in school (Gould, 1996; Ladson-Billings, 1998; Lipman, 2004; Spring, 1980). Developing models of school practice that reflect on the worth and equality of those who have been marginalized is critical to constructing systems of change in education (Gonzalez, Moll, & Amanti, 2005). Developing *ourselves* as agents of change requires a "moral vision and ethical norms ... to account for and transform existing forms of dogmatism, oppression, and despair" (Laible, 2000, p. 686). Leading for socially just practices requires us to listen to those who are underrepresented and to look within ourselves, heightening our awareness and understanding of lived realities.

The duty of public education is to end oppression for children with these lived experiences (Dewey, 1916/1944; Freire, 1970). According to Mezirow (1990), we need to provide children with plans to take action. Fulfilling such responsibility, as outlined by Freire, suggests that schools understand the complicities of wider social forces, which create educational barriers within American schools. The notion of looking within is the first step to leading toward a school leader's transformation that has the potential for systemic educational reform (Cross, Bazron, Dennis, & Isaacs, 1989). The possibilities for systemic educational reform are more imaginable when the leader is committed to the process (Hillard, 1991; Stout, 1986), and has internalized the skills of reflective practice (Kottkamp, 1990; Osterman & Kottkamp, 1993; Schon, 1983).

This discussion seeks to extend the understandings about relationships between knowledge of self and promoting social justice, specifically for children and families from historically disenfranchised groups. Although reflecting on school practices is often encouraged in preparation programs (Barnett, et al., 2000; Gray & Smith, 2007; Ketelle & Mesa, 2006; Scribner et al., 1999; Sergiovanni, 2001; Smith & Piele, 2006), exploring beliefs, core values, and the influence of assumptions on school practices is also important to understanding what it means to be a leader (Brown, 2004; Cross et al.., 1989). Self-study has become a focal
point for practitioners pursuing a better knowledge of their particular practice and the work of those with a concern for teaching, leading, and learning in similar fields (e.g. reflection, action research, teacher research,

participant research, and practitioner research) has been influential in shaping how self-study is perceived and conducted (Hamilton et al., 1998).

The focus of this study centered on personal narrative; reflecting on my personal journey was considered a primary task (also see James, Dunning, Connolly, & Elliot, 2007). I considered reflection as a primary task because the process encourages intentional thoughtful examinations that deepen personal awareness and understanding (see Clandinin, 1995; Halen Faber, 1997; Hamilton, 2002; Terrell & Lindsey, 2009). I examined the affects of developmental contours of childhood experiences, which afforded me opportunities to witness hegemonic beliefs within my family, church, and school. These experiences inspired me to lead for social justice by addressing oppressive systemic school practices. Questioning oppressive school practices that perpetuated inequity and injustice was considered by many in my life as questionable, even dangerous. These experiences as well as others shared throughout this discussion illustrate the intersection of promoting issues of social justice and creating counter-hegemonic narratives.[1]

The purpose of this self-study was to gain a deeper understanding of how my lived experiences influenced my beliefs, will, and school practices; especially within inner-city schools. This self-examination increased an awareness of the social dynamics related to lived experiences challenging hegemonic structures and institutional metanarratives.[2] The creation of my narrative revealed significant events that contoured identity as a leader. Examining these issues afforded me the opportunity to investigate issues of privilege and power in leading for social justice (Brown, 2004; McLaren & Kincheloe, 2007).[3] This method of inquiry is underexplored and in need of further investigation (Terrell & Lindsey, 2009).

LOOKING WITHIN

How, or if, we choose to overcome oppression in American schools presents serious challenges. More recently, with influence from the social sciences, a growing number of scholars contend we live in a story-shaped world (Bruner, 1986, 1990; Polkinghorne, 1988; Sarbin, 1986; Somers, 1994; Taylor, 1989; Tooms, 2007). This position suggests that our lives are storied and identity is narratively constructed. Understanding the complicities of identity includes the examination of wider forces (social, cultural, political, and economical circumstances) (Gardner, 2001). Examining how people develop a sense of self and how self interacts with others and the world in which they live is called *social constructionism* (Gergen, 1999, 1965; Smith & Sparkes, 2008). The interactions between self and others provides people with a context to understand the roles they play in the world in which they live (Stryker & Burke, 2000). Smith (1998) notes that *personal heritage* (race, class, religion, gender, ability, immigration status, sexual orientation and other categories) influences how we see ourselves and how we relate to others.

Both theories are concerned with how people understand self, others, and interact with society at large. Cross et al. (1989) refers to this theory as cultural proficiency. This theory informs school leaders of how their core values, beliefs, and assumptions are influenced by the contexts in which we live and work (Terrell & Randall, 2009). Looking inward is not independent of school practices, policies, or the larger society. Milner IV (2007) placed race and culture at the core of self-examination. The guiding principles of cultural proficiency focus on, *To what extent, if any, do our values and beliefs align with what we do?* (Cross et al., 1989). This guiding framework encourages school leaders to examine and understand how personal beliefs about educating children and families from a myriad of contexts (Shapiro & Stefkovich, 2005).

Through the process of cultural proficiency, school leaders examine to what extent they hold themselves accountable to meet the multiple needs of the school communities they serve and how their identities shape their efforts on a daily ongoing basis. This reflective process encourages school leaders to look within, enhancing the demand to confront vulnerabilities, preconceived notions, assumptions, and prejudices (Terrell & Randall, 2009). Engaging in authentic dialogue regarding relationships between self awareness and practice make changes to their school practices and encourage school communities to dialogue about larger social issues. These issues include the negative perceptions, discriminatory practices, and assumptions associated with serving children and families in inner-city schools (Brown, 2002; Cross et al., 1989).

Reflection on practice and self-study are becoming increasingly important regarding the scrutiny between beliefs and school practices (Barnes, 1998; Whitehead, 1995). One means of constructing knowledge and finding meaning is through personal reflection. This study examines childhood experiences and to what extent, if any, those experiences influence my work in inner-city schools. In the following discussion, I consider my work within a residential treatment center as a coordinator, school social worker, and school leadership positions in inner-city schools.

DEVELOPING AN INFORMED PERSONAL PERSPECTIVE

Self-study involves an in-depth examination, and in this case, the examination focused on my leadership development (Schein, 1989; Schon, 1983; Wheatley, 1994). As the purpose demands analysis and personal reflection, I followed a self-study methodology used in studies seeking personal narrative (Brown, 2004, 2005). Self-study provides a methodology that encourages scholars to address issues in pursuit of gaining a deeper understanding dissonance between internal beliefs and practices (Russel & Korthagen, 1995). I sought to examine to what extent, if any, my commitment to promote educational equity through collective action. Primary data was drawn from personal journal entries, formal documents, and official documents (test data, letters, and other forms of data) from previous places of employment. I also considered my responses to guiding questions throughout my lived experiences. The secondary data included: (a) responses to my clinical supervisors; and (b) communication between school community members and myself regarding the role we play in educating children from emerging majority populations.

FANNING THE FLAME: AHA MOMENTS AND THE BEGINNING OF SOCIAL JUSTICE QUESTIONS

Often times, I was asked during interviews for school leadership positions, "Where does your passion for social justice stem from?" This examination provided the opportunity to explore the development of counter-narratives throughout childhood. My experiences in church, relationships with family members, and friendships/working relations with peers shaped my understanding of what it meant to live with people different than me. The church taught me that Christians were superior to all other forms of religion. Family relatives informed me that White people were superior to all other races of people, including intelligence, education, and economics. Family relatives and teachers enlightened me regarding gender identity and what it means to be a girl. And finally, peers and church teachings informed me that heterosexuality is "normal" and anything else is "abnormal."

My first experience in understanding the influence of metanarrative was in the Catholic Church. When I was eight years old, I attended Catholic religious classes after school at St. Michael's because we attended what many considered the "poor public schools." Sister Ann, the nun responsible for our religious growth, informed the children that we were "only to associate with Catholics because God favored Catholics." She continued by outlining the church's expectations for forming friendships, dating, and ultimately marriage. Sister Ann stated that "all the children of the world were going to hell if they were not raised Catholic." I raised my hand and asked, "But if a kid was born in India or Africa and their family didn't know about being Catholic, why would God punish them? I thought God loved everybody." Sister Ann replied, "God loves Catholics, not Jews or Lutheran or Muslims ... just Catholics. You will be friends with only Catholics ... marry a Catholic ... and raise your children Catholic." Thus, at an early age that holding different perspectives than members of my church was not encouraged.

A second significant experience in understanding racial dominance was in elementary school. Early in elementary school, I learned "God did not intend for people with different skin colors to be together", and in this case, to marry and have children. I was informed "God made people with different skin colors in order to separate us from each other" because "people with the same skin color should be with people like them." Later in elementary school, I recall extended family members using derogatory terms to describe racial groups as well as aligning racial identity with their specific behaviors. Relatives identified "Blacks as lazy" and "always being on welfare." In mid-sentence, my grandmother whispered the word *Black* when she referred to neighbors down the street. Although I asked relatives to stop using hurtful language, they continued to do so. I was either asked to leave the room "if I couldn't handle it" or I was informed "I just didn't understand because I didn't grow up with *them*."

Another life-altering episode occurred in middle school when I learned what it meant to be a "real" girl. I was encouraged to curl my hair, participate in "girl" activities, like boys, and carry a purse. I remember quickly brushing my hair and running out the door as a child, but now as a "real" girl, I had to contend with the dreaded curling iron. I recall being active in sports, playing softball and quarter-backing for our neighborhood football team because I "threw like a guy." But as a "girl," I needed to discover new gender appropriate activities like gymnastics or dancing or cheerleading. I recall wanting to play the drums in band. I was informed drums were a "boy's" instrument. I chose to play the alto saxophone in hopes this instrument was enough to pass as a "real" girl. I was also encouraged to "like boys" and someday get married. I told people at the age of 10 "I was not going to get married to a boy or have children by birth, because I planned to adopt children from around the world." I was discouraged to fulfill my "life plan." I realized at an early age I was *different* than other girls my age.

High school was the arena where the words *faggots* and *dykes* became dangerous. I worked at a local fast food restaurant. My supervisor, a high school peer, asked me one day, "What the hell are you doing with those dykes?" I asked what the word *dykes* meant. He answered me with, "Well, they all play softball together ... have sex with each other ... all of them...so they were nothing but dykes." I told my supervisor they were my friends and they were kind to me. He replied, "If I see you with them again, I am going to tell everyone that you're a dyke." Upset, I shared this experience with my family. Their overarching concern was my reputation.

If I continued *these* friendships, what would my people think? I was encouraged to focus on my *other* groups of friends.

Similar beliefs were also upheld within my Big Ten college sorority. Accusations made by sorority sisters accused me and my friend of being dykes. Our sorority's national headquarters sent an executive board member to investigate me and my friend for being identified as dykes. We were interviewed separately for over an hour. The national representative asked both of us to step into the room. She "determined through her investigation we were dykes." The representative informed us she possessed the authority to "use her executive power to take away my friend's presidency and my vice-presidency." She identified our alleged sexual identity as "not being appropriate for sorority life." We were told to "pack up our belongings and leave immediately because dykes like us were not allowed to live here." We both refused to leave the sorority, requesting a copy of the "evidence" as well as the policy allowing sorority members to be ostracized because of their perceived sexual identity. The representative grew frustrated with both of us. She informed the sorority of the findings from her investigation and eliminated our executive positions. Neither the representative nor the university sorority council addressed us after the investigation. We assumed the sorority could not deny us housing due to accusations drawn from what we perceived as an interrogation. Neither of us shared this experience with our families. Because we understood an accusation such as this would devastate our faithful Catholic families who identified as LGBTQ "life styles" as unacceptable.

THE TIPPING POINT TO ANOTHER CAREER

As an aspiring graphic artist in college, I was required by a professor to create a laundry detergent advertisement depicting a suburban housewife in her thirties, with two children, and a family dog, washing clothes with a smile on her face. The professor informed me this type of laundry detergent "brought the woman joy because she had more time for her duties as a wife and mother." When I asked him about the power of visual medium and perpetuating social roles for men and women, he became frustrated. He demanded "I do what I was told." I informed the professor "I could not look at myself in the mirror or go to bed at night knowing I promoted products that influence how people view themselves." I was not interested in perpetuating oppressive gender norms through advertisements. He informed me "there is no room for social justice in advertising. You have obviously chosen the wrong field." He continued noting, "You'll be fired from your job if you do not follow societal norms." When I spoke with classmates about the remarks, they made comments such as, "there's good money in advertising" or "you need to do what you are told or you don't get paid." I simply could not "sell my soul" for a paycheck. I wanted to find a career that challenged human oppression.

Eventually I found social work was a natural fit between my passion to challenge human oppression and mobilize communities. At first, my parents were not pleased with my desire to change my career path; this was painful as parent approval was important. My newly chosen career path did not align with their dream for me. I felt the need to defend my stance. I received a full academic scholarship for the following school year.

Through my studies, I was reminded of a long-standing history in American schools. This long-standing history included the challenge of providing equitable educational opportunities to all children across the country due to national origin, gender, language, and class. The Civil Rights Movement (as cited in Carson, 2003), Title IX, Education Amendments (as cited in Sadker & Sadker, 1994), and *Lau v. Nichol* (as cited in Nieto, 2004) prohibit discriminatory practices according to national origin, language, and gender. Education was perceived as the ideal vehicle for social mobility for all American citizens. I discovered a correlation between national origin and socioeconomic groups. While the majority of children living in poverty were White, a disproportionate number of children from Black/Latino/a and First Nation People lived below the poverty line (U.S. Department of Commerce, Bureau of the Census, 2004). Disparities such as these were not visible topics in schools. Often times, educators considered issues of national origin, gender, language, class, and federal mandates as irrelevant to schooling children. Educators' indifference to addressing these complex societal issues played a significant role in my call to action—to work within inner-city school communities and promote just practices for historically disenfranchised populations.

I was offered my first position at a nonprofit residential treatment center for boys as a residential counselor. I was the first woman and White person to be hired on the school campus. All off-campus professionals, including therapists, teachers, psychologists, and directors were White; however, all subordinate positions, similar to mine, were held by Black and Latino men.

The campus was located within ten miles of three metropolitan areas surrounded by mounds of dirt, barbed wire fencing, and weeds. Each young man who resided in the program was transferred from juvenile detention centers across the country. The majority of residents were identified as wards of state. Parents/guardians either chose to give up their parental rights or were forced to give up their parental rights to the state. Residents lived realities including incarceration for rape, sexual assault, armed robbery, drug dealing, theft, attempted murder, and/or physical assault. The community at large did not want the residents to leave the campus or attend their public schools. They feared for the safety of teachers and public school students. The campus director noted, "We are doing everything we can to keep the boys out of jail, but this is their destiny."

The on-campus teachers had preconceived notions regarding the destinies of the residents. One teacher noted, "These boys are lucky if they stay alive by the time they are nineteen. There is no hope for these boys." Another teacher said, "I don't know if you know this, but these boys just go in and out of jail. They are a mess and a menace to society." I did not understand why an organization would perpetuate oppressive practices by limiting the residents' life experiences. I thought the mission and vision of the organization included words such as *empowerment* and *community mobilization*. I was under the impression people who chose to work in social services were committed to eliminating oppression. And yet I felt I needed to defend my actions.

I decided to present my inquiry to the campus director. I wanted to examine the impact of current policy and pedagogical practices within the campus school. I was perceived as an "outsider" by the director, psychologists, teachers, and community members. People who challenge the practices within the institution were not welcome. Many believed "there was no hope for 'these' boys." Members of the larger community were threatened by my "new scholarly song," which departed from societal metanarratives and "seeking understanding" (Bell, 1992, pp. 144, 146).

When I marketed my inquiry as a means of increasing the organization's financial status through increased community engagement, the director gave me his approval. Although the permitted me to conduct the needs assessment, I did not receive assistance through the process. The needs assessment needed to be conducted "outside" of my work day. I was not reimbursed for mileage nor allotted funds for surveys or assistance in compiling the data.

I wondered, "If I did not present my inquiry as benefiting the institution financially, would my inquiry supported on the premise of improving the lived experiences of the residents?" Unfortunately, I think my requests would have been rejected. Knowing this, I learned in order to improve the circumstances of those who faced oppression, those with power needed to believe they too were gaining something from the advancement of those who were considered subordinates (see Bell, 1980; Castagno & Lee, 2007). This realization would influence the way in which I worked with larger systems, especially concerning the institutional practices that perpetuated the marginalization of others. As Ladson-Billings (1998) explained, "we have to take bold and sometimes unpopular positions" (p. 22) to bring the sensitive topic of racism to the forefront and address the convergence and divergence of interests in school policy and practice.

All of the people within the school community and community at large were White, English speaking, Christian, and middle class professionals. They asked questions about the purpose of my inquiry and how their insight would be utilized. I found myself helping teachers, school leaders, community members, and business owners reflect on the power of creating a sense of belonging and community. In regards to teachers, we spoke of student outcomes. When speaking to school leaders, we discussed school-parent-community relations. When I spoke with community members, we discussed creating a community who looked after their "brothers and sisters." Although negotiation and convergence were difficult to achieve, the task at hand was not impossible (King, 1963).

No one expressed interest to address the wider social forces influencing the residents' lived experiences. Each group was interested in their own agendas. I shared the findings from the needs assessment with leaders from the residential treatment center. The boys were identified by the school and larger community as "Black and Mexican gang-bangers" (members of gangs). Community members were afraid of being physically harmed by the boys; meanwhile, the boys feared being harassed by the community members.

To create a *win-win* situation, I realized the community's self-interests must be addressed. We needed the community to know we were "listening" and "addressing" their concerns. Making genuine connections between the campus and the larger community would provide opportunities for meaningful relationships between the residents and the community.

We examined the curriculum, student expectations, and making real-world connections through problem-based learning strategies. Several colleagues expressed their beliefs that "these boys could not learn." I shared the boys' painful stories and lived experiences. Their stories "moved" my colleagues and made "these boys real people." The process of listening to the lived realities of the children, as well as our imagined possibilities for the organization, led to a commitment for human advocacy. The commitment evolved into work with Habitat for Humanity, the Humane Society, several nursing homes (visiting with residents, feeding the elderly, and being certified as volunteers), food pantries, political organizations, environmental groups, and mentor-mentee apprenticeships.

Such vision promoted our grassroots-based movement to advocate for social change and exercise the power of collective voices. Within six years, the unit transformed from a revolving door (two or three boys returning to jail each month) to graduating three residents from high school. Two received full merit scholarships to a big ten university (with special provisions and assistance provided to support them through their studies) and a donation from a mentor for a full scholarship to a cooking school in a major metropolitan area. One of 18 residents returned to jail for physical assault within the next two years. Their stories and lived experiences provide a glimpse for me about the power of articulating a vision and mobilizing a historically disenfranchised community. My activist stance of leading for social justice was inspired by my outrage at the unmet needs of children who face and live oppression on a daily basis.

INDENTIFYING AS A TEMPERED RADICAL

The nation's deepening racial and ethnic texture, with increased in the number of English Language Learners and Black/Latino/a students in schools, created a space for me to identify social justice as imperative to American education in the twenty-first century (see Marshall & Oliva, 2006). In order to improve race relations, as well as reconsider the influence of hegemonic practices in schools, I challenged how schools educated children. I encouraged discussions with teachers, school leaders, parents, students, and community members. These discussions focused on how schools determined the knowledge, skill sets, and attitudes necessary for meeting the needs of increasingly diverse school populations. In-depth examinations regarding cross-cultural interactions and oppressive school practices were critical to the process. Within each organization in which reform occurred, being a member of the organization and forming meaningful relationships with school members was essential. I discovered an emerging identity as a tempered radical.

Tempered radicals are individuals who belong to organizations, but are seen as outsiders because their values, beliefs, and/or agendas are misaligned to those of the dominant culture (Meyerson, 2001). They feel their social identity put them in the spotlight because of difference, which could include race, sexual identity, class, religion, language, gender or other. They struggle with how to "fit" in the larger community even though their differences seem to be at odds with the larger organization (Meyerson, 2001; Tooms, 2007). Although they are members of the organization, their desire to change the organization from the inside out creates tension between members of the dominant culture and the tempered radical. They are committed to making such change, which they identify as fundamentally different than the dominant culture of the organization (Meyerson & Scully, 1995). They navigate their way through the complicities of organizations in order to make change—often moving from conformity to protest.

I consider myself a tempered radical, a catalyst for promoting individual and systemic transformation in schools (see Meyerson, 2001). I was knowingly at odds with the dominant culture of professionals within inner-city schools (predominantly White, middle-class, English speaking, Christian teachers in inner-city schools and White, English-speaking, middle/upper class, Christian mean as school leaders). Many times, throughout my childhood and career, I was harassed for questioning hegemonic practices. Actions to promoting humanity, critical thinking, and cultural responsiveness were often resented by people with whom I lived and worked.

I found myself subjected to a steady range of hostile ploys and communications, which is what Leymann (1990) describes as workplace mobbing. Originally, it was associated with the behavior of small birds combining to defend a nest; later, "mobbing" was linked to the workplace by Heinz Leymann, a Swedish psychologist who conducted studies in the 1980s regarding the affects of psychological harassment at work. Leymann steered away from the term *bullying* because the term suggested physical connotations. He frames mobbing as a form of social isolation. Terms such as "mobbing" and "bullying" overlap with variations in interpretation in different countries. In English-speaking countries, the term mobbing refers to a group of social eliminators who focus their efforts on a single target. The term *workplace mobbing* emerged to characterize **the desperate need for organizational members to eliminate and debilitate a threatening target** (Davenport, Schwartz, & Elliot, 1996). The social elimination is carried out by people who have fallen into believing an alleged offense. In some cases, mobbing of coworkers is devastating, leading to issues with employment, health, personal relations, and livelihood (see Westhues, 2004).

Leymann's (1990) contributions regarding workplace mobbing suggest it can be played out without outward violence in addition to unfriendly acts, intimidation, undermining the target's self-confidence, and group solidarity against the target who questions hegemonic practices. Because I was sought to disrupt power structures in my workplace, I was publicly harassed, denied merit pay increases, overlooked for promotion, and in some cases, my employment was threatened. I was asked to document my claims of impropriety with data while colleagues were permitted to state opinions as facts. On one school campus, faculty members wanted to ensure any "new" school practices were not in violation of union policies. I felt the need to protect myself by continuing to document information to help the organization determine if school practices were aligned with the school's mission. When pressured to conform to "traditional" school practices, I used data and research to make a stance for activism. Although data collection was time consuming, the process itself as well as sharing the findings was a process that seemed to influence how we made decisions. When I had data to support my claims and allies willing to take a stance, members of the dominant culture slowly started to "let go" of their tight reins.

Other times, faculty members informed me I would be "carefully watched." My willingness to address issues of race and racism on school campuses was "threatening" to the traditional ways in which the educational system operated. I received threatening anonymous notes asking me "which side am I on" in addition to complaints in which "I listened to the children and families too much." I was informed by union workers "I needed to reconsider who my mentors were" because my mentors were Black, rather than White.

I was not only isolated in the schools I served with White faculty and school leaders, but I was also an "outsider" to many of my peers during my graduate studies. Many of my peers led suburban and rural schools expressing their desire to continue to work in predominantly White, middle class, English speaking, and Christian communities. They noted their discomfort in working with children who did not share similar backgrounds. Children with whom they could not identify were perceived as "those kids" who "have all these problems." Several colleagues "sold their souls" for six-figure salaries and lofty titles informing us of unethical practices like "busing Mexican children away from campus during state testing" and "diagnosing Black children as recipients of special education because they didn't know what else to do with them." Addressing each of these issues during class ostracized me from the majority of my peers.

Similar scenarios of mobbing occurred within academia. One university supervisor inquired about my personal life. The supervisor asked me about a ring on my finger. I continued to focus on the agenda for the meeting. After the supervisor requested the information 10 more times, the supervisor asked, "So, who is he?" When I replied with "her name is ...", the supervisor left the table. Upon the supervisor's return, I was informed I would lose my job if anyone knew I was a dyke because "this is a conservative Christian community and we don't accept these kinds of things." After informing the supervisor of the university policy regarding the nondiscrimination policy for sexual identity, the supervisor informed me, "It doesn't matter what that policy says. I am telling you what will happen to you."[4]

Recognizing the context for the possibility of workplace mobbing is essential to understanding situations in which social elimination can take place. Westhues (2004) identified ten specific clues that contextualize opportunities for workplace mobbing (p. 15):

1. *A popular, high-achieving target:* The target pursued by the group performs average or above average, is respected, and is considered popular within some social circles.

2. *Lack of due process:* Standard procedures, policies, fairness, and other processes are altered for the target. The target experiences the making of rules by eliminators as they move forward.
3. *Odd timing:* The eliminator takes the target by surprise through unscheduled, unannounced, unexpected moments in an attempt to catch the target off-guard.
4. *Resistance to external review:* The eliminator(s) penalize the actions of the target and possibly overturn possibilities by people in higher positions of authority.
5. *Secrecy:* Eliminators prefer to keep their actions more confidential and private. Targets also prefer to keep the social elimination private in order to avoid "pubic shaming" (p. 15).
6. *Unanimity:* Members within the organization come to consensus regarding the need to socially eliminate the threatening target.
7. *Fuzzy charges:* Accusations and/or charges are placed on the target to justify social elimination. The accusations, rather valid or not, collectively add up to the alleged necessity to ostracize the target. The alleged infractions become "completely obvious" to social eliminators (p. 15).
8. *Prior marginalization:* The target is marginalized, ostracized, and "treated with contempt before offenses are cited for grounds for expulsion and humiliation" (p. 15). The steps to eliminate the target have been informally processed.
9. *Impassioned rhetoric:* The target is subjected to name-calling and the group's compelling interest to *destroy* the target. The target is associated with adjectives such as "appalling, preposterous, hideous, repugnant, and vicious" (p. 15).
10. *Back-biting:* The target is the center of gossip and rumors to further the social elimination process.

Such rumors and storytelling discredit the target as well as humiliate the target.

However, not all targets are subjected to social elimination," take the bait" from social eliminators, or internalize attempts to publicly humiliate them (see Westhues, 2004, 2005). I contend we investigate the intersections of Meyerson's (2001) *tempered radicalism* and Leymann's (1990) *workplace mobbing* to further understand how targets transform themselves into tempered radicals. The intersections of these two concepts suggests some targets have a "fire in their belly", which they use to confront the actions of social eliminators in an effort to promote humanity.

WORKPLACE MOBBING, TEMPERED RADICALISM, AND SCHOOL LEADERSHIP

I walked into school leadership positions with high ideals and guiding principles that encouraged me to advocate for *all* children. The harsh reality was that many educators with whom I worked did not share the same core values or principles. I identified as a relatively young, White, English speaking, woman who grew up in a working class family as a first generation college student. I was a parent of a Latina adopted child and identified outside of work as a LGBTQ person with the same-sex partner of many years. Many colleagues shared their assumptions regarding my personal background, including, but not limited to being a married heterosexual who was raised in an educated Christian family. Many of my colleagues also assumed we shared similar cultural values regarding race, gender, class, language, ability, and other areas of difference. Their hegemonic beliefs influenced how they understood me as a school leader, social worker, colleague, friend, and neighbor. Because "I looked like them," they thought we led similar lives, shared similar beliefs, and acted in similar ways. The majority of my colleagues identified as White, middle class, Christian, English speaking, and heterosexual. Educators considered anyone "outside" of their identifiers as "abnormal," especially when considering the influence of race.

Understanding the impact of social construction and biological concepts of race was critical to how I responded to issues related to race, ethnicity, and national origin (see Smedley, 1998). At first, assumptions about "who I was" because of my physical appearance, provided me with opportunities to be "included." However, once I shared my beliefs and practices, many colleagues chose to put forth effort to eliminate my efforts to address issues of race and racism in schools. In response to such efforts, I responded by forming meaningful relationships with colleagues who were "targets" themselves. Once I subjected myself to the possibilities of being humiliated and socially eliminated from the organization, other "targets" took notice of my actions. I was asked to meet with "targets" in more excluded locations to discuss cultural interactions and oppressive school practices. Together, we addressed oppressive school practices in an effort to honor students, family members, and our community.

In an effort to overcome the culture of institutions involved in workplace mobbing, the mechanisms that foster mob mentality must also be addressed (see Westhues, 2004, 2005). Yamada (2004) contends in addition to "developing fair legal standards and ajudicatory mechanisms," we need to recognize when "mob mentality has taken over and the pertinent institution is too weak to withstand it, heaven help those who are on the receiving end, for they may be doomed" (p 400). In each situation, I considered the consequences associated with addressing hegemonic practices and the risk-taking associated with addressing social eliminators.

I was often asked by aspiring school leaders, faculty, parents, and children, "So, where do you start?" The size of the problem seems quite large when considering the affect of hegemonic practices on beliefs, practices, and understanding the world. I encouraged people to look within. I emphasized deconstructing how beliefs, attitudes, and lived experiences highly regulate the way we see ourselves, who we serve, and the world in which we live (see Gergen, 1999). I initiated this examination by offering colleagues opportunities to look within and address conflicts between culture and school. The crippling effect of recognizing discriminatory practices seemed to paralyze educators from considering what role they played in perpetuating oppression. I shared the lived experiences of children and families who endured oppressive practices in schools. I supported their lived realities with data centered on detailed accounts of invalid disciplinary actions, declining graduation rates, increased student absences, and oppressive pedagogical practices.

It was imperative I address oppressive conditions as they occurred in the workplace, which provided a context for people to understand how actions taken perpetuated oppressive conditions. I provided several examples of real-life circumstances presented throughout my career as a school leader. These issues are categorized as addressing hegemonic school practices and workplace mobbing as a tempered radical (Appendix A). The issues presented in each situation addressed the need to acknowledge the tension between cultures of schools, serving diverse communities, and looking within. At the heart of each experience was an opportunity to take action and address oppressive practices. Advocating for equity-oriented practices promoted human advocacy within each organization, which should be at the heart of what we do as school leaders (see Marshall & Oliva, 2006).

Parents, support staff, and children shared experiences of "having doors closed on them" and "not feeling welcomed in schools." Parents reported teachers and school leaders using racial slurs in front of their children, and in many cases, blaming children's racial identity for "not making annual yearly progress on standardized testing." Latina support staff shared an "unwritten rule" of not being allowed to enter the school office or drink from the water cooler. Only White teachers were welcome in the school office. Children also shared stories of human oppression. They noted teachers perceived them as "worthless" and identified themselves as attending "ghetto schools" and "living without hope."

Such beliefs and attitudes perpetuate discriminatory practices in schools and lead to more painful lived experiences by children and their families. Confronting these situations often led to stressful and challenging conversations with faculty members. Whether I was new to the organization or serving several years, there were consequences, both positive and negative, for every action taken. Although consequences for addressing the needs of children and families often led to unchartered territory, confronting oppressive hegemonic school practices was essential to making systemic change.

As a culturally proficient school leader, I internalized advocacy as a means of social justice for children and families from historically disenfranchised groups. Many teachers complained I spoke "too often" or "too nicely" to students and their families. They assumed my duty was to "punish 'those' bad kids," not work with them. I found comfort in having mentors who shared a commitment to address oppressive school practices. Because of their support, and forming alliances with other tempered radicals, I am convinced our shared core values and beliefs provided a foundation from which to transform oppressive school-wide practices.

In order to move organizations forward, I realized the need for allies. Because the dominant culture threatened the possibility of promoting social justice in schools, individual culturally proficient colleagues often felt isolated. By putting my agenda in the forefront, over time, allies introduced themselves as "people who believed in what I was doing" or "were trying to do the same things." Each culturally proficient professional worked within schools with extreme caution, often describing their daily interactions as "walking on pins and needles" or "waiting for the hammer to fall." What we discovered throughout our alliance was the common shared belief that student success was central to our role.

POWER AND PRIVILEGE

Not all of my mentors identified as being culturally proficient, nor were they interested in addressing oppressive school practices. Making concerted efforts to challenge hegemonic practices to promote the needs of *all* children was not exercised in schools, especially schools led by predominantly White principals. Even in two schools led by principals and/or assistant principals who were Black and/or Latino/a, confronting stereotypes regarding race, class, gender, sexual identity, language and so on, were considered "risky" business. Their responses surprised me. I assumed school leaders, especially school leaders who were members of historically disenfranchised groups, addressed issues of human oppression in similar ways. I was wrong. After dialoguing about their positions to advocate for historically disenfranchised groups, I learned about positions of power and privilege.

My White privilege provided me a space to address White colleagues who denied the existence of economic achievement gaps as well as racial achievement gaps. School leaders noted that as "Black/Latino/a persons, if we go and promote opportunities for Blacks or Hispanics, White teachers just think we are standing on our soap boxes." A Black school leader noted, "If you go out there, looking like one of them, their heads will turn by the words coming out of your mouth, but you have their attention." A Latino school leader said, "We need White people as allies; otherwise, we aren't moving anywhere. This is all part of their White privilege." Although some of my colleagues identified addressing the social and political forces that continue to impact our schools as "courageous," our actions were long overdue in this country. I was informed by Black/Latino/a/Asian teachers and school leaders that "I wasn't really White." They identified my beliefs, values, and actions as counter-narratives because I publicly addressed issues of race, class, gender, sexual identity, ability, as well as other areas of equity. I was also asked by many White teachers and students, "Whose side am I on?" One White male middle school student asked me, "Why do you like Black people so much?"

I did not feel it was imperative to choose sides. I did not perceive my beliefs as promoting Black struggles. I simply could not imagine living in a country with the quest for freedom knowing that people from historically disenfranchised groups continued to experience hatred and discrimination. I thought it was imperative to address the lived realities and struggles of children and their families because school cannot proclaim to have their best interests at heart when specific populations continue to experience oppression.

By offering opportunities to address the influence of race, class, gender, language, and immigration status were offered to all school members, the detailed accounts of lived experiences became points of reference from which I learned. Members of historically disenfranchised groups engaged in dialogues regarding oppressive conditions. White educators who did not identify as culturally proficient identified me as "*their* champion." These specific White teachers considered me a "traitor" to my race, while members of historically disenfranchised groups were increasingly participating in discussions about the injustices endured by their children in school.

The belief to empower children and families who were disenfranchised was viewed as contrary to the cultural norms of the schools I served, so it was considered a problem. If I attempted to break the mold of traditional school practices, I needed to continue to reflect on my current practices, dialogue with other school leaders about crossing over borders (cultural, classed, gendered, geographic, sexually oriented, other). This type of practice embraces difference and challenges traditional school practices that perpetuate the marginalization of children and families from historically disenfranchised groups (see Saldivar, 1997).

Making personal investments in families and the community at large through home visits, advocating for parents, and promoting school practices that honored the lived experiences of those we served was important to addressing hegemonic practices. Through the examination of pedagogical and system-wide practices, we considered how to meet the diverse needs of *all* learners. One means of addressing these issues was initiating professional development opportunities that fostered discussions regarding human oppression, which led to the creation of the Multicultural Task Force.

The Multicultural Task Force specifically focused on reflective practice (considering dissonance between beliefs, lived experiences, and school practices). We engaged parents and community members on their own terms. We listened to the social conditions and needs of the broader community. All discussed initiatives were aligned with the school improvement plan, meeting the needs of the school community as well as the broader community. We discussed the realities of desegregating our discipline and academic achievement data, as well as reflecting on current pedagogical practices. The findings suggested that the school's practices resulted in high rates of Black/Latino/a children receiving special education services, disproportionate numbers of Black/Latino/a children sent out of class for disciplinary actions, low student expectations, preference for English speaking students, and negative perceptions of children and families served.

Using data to convey the influence of reflective practice seemed to challenge the existing power structure in schools. Educators found it difficult to argue that 2,335 children were sent out of class in six months, missing an average of 140,100 minutes of classroom instruction. In one school, 78% of the discipline referrals were addressed to Black students. The total percentage of Black students in the school was only 38%. This finding was eye-opening for teachers. I also collected narratives from students, parents/guardians, teachers, and community members regarding their lived experiences in school. Listening and reflecting on community narratives afforded educators opportunities to listen to painful stories as well as the realities faced by those served. In three years, this school decreased discipline referrals by over 80%. School members addressed practices that reproduced social inequities and blamed children and their families for the ills of society. The school transformed itself to a community that promoted human advocacy.

Listening to the struggles and painful realities of children and families can be quite overwhelming. The daily challenges they face and our role to promote just practices sometimes seems insurmountable. Self-study allowed for the discovery of leading with courage and passion. Leading as a culturally proficient educator provides opportunities to promote systemic responsiveness that addressing human oppression. Uncovering human oppression can lead to a wide range of feelings, such as frustration, stress, fear, excitement, and other intense emotions. Identifying myself as a tempered radical provided me with a framework to understand the consequences associated with creating a counter-narrative and challenging society's metanarratives. Addressing challenges in strategic ways has the potential to make powerful changes for historically disenfranchised populations within our nation's schools.

Looking within to acknowledge the existence of personal cultural assumptions is the first step to addressing human oppression. I realize that I cannot begin to expect aspiring school leaders with whom I work to take risks if I do not have the courage to become introspective and change my practices. If I allow time and intellectual guidance for aspiring school leaders to engage in the journey toward cultural proficiency, they too may discover their authentic selves (see Cross et al., 1989). Promoting an authentic self provides opportunities for aspiring school leaders to engage in understanding the social construction of difference (see Gergen, 1999), as well as insight regarding the influence of wider social forces influencing America's educational system (see Grant & Sleeter, 2009; Marshall & Oliva, 2006). Through this journey, we might foster an internal accountability within school leadership programs. This internal accountability might include examining to what extent programs address human oppression, politics of education, and historical cultural misconceptions embedded in the fabric of our nation's wider social forces (see Marshall & Gerstl-Pepin, 2005; McLaren & Kincheloe, 2007). Opportunities such as these might provide spaces for candidates to address the complex struggles for power within educational arenas. These complex struggles include understanding that power shapes who gets what, when, and how.

The journey of becoming a culturally proficient school leader involves those who prepare them to provide intellectual guidance. Intellectual guidance might include candidates reconsidering their role from managing schools to engaging school communities. Shields and Edwards (2005) propose a change in the system's leadership style from managerial to dialogic (p. 63). Creating an atmosphere that encourages understanding is essential to developing a strong sense of self (see Elson, 1986). An essential part of the learning process is having someone with whom students can question their beliefs and practices (Shields & Edwards, 2005; Shields, LaRoque, & Oberg, 2002).

IS IT WORTH IT?

How we lead matters. Looking within shapes how we understand ourselves in an effort to promote humanity in schools. It appears this reflective study inspired me to confront blindness, privilege, power, and inequities that systemically influence how schools meet the needs of all children. Creating a counter-hegemonic narrative encouraged me to question and hold suspect to proclaimed societal truths. By engaging in courageous, meaningful, reflective dialogue, I was encouraged to articulate what I thought, felt, and witnessed in schools. Although my actions were considered *dangerous* by many in my life, articulating my values and beliefs provided a space for me to discover the power of alliances. Aligning with practitioners who identified as culturally proficient created a unified force within each school system. This unifying force enhanced the lives of historically disenfranchised populations by acknowledging and addressing oppressive school practices. At times, I underestimated the synergy of this unification in addition to the significance of impacting episodes that fostered my determination to imagine possibilities. As Laible (2000) asserts, "a loving espistemology," I am consciously working toward engaging in socially just practices that widen the way in which I understand and respond to the voices of those who have been underserved. My hope is that sharing personal journeys such as this encourages each of us to grapple with what it means to lead, realizing that all journeys begin from within.

What emerged from painful mobbing experiences were opportunities that fostered the emergence of a tempered radical. This journey created a space for me to understand and appreciate the emotional and physical strains of those who have historically struggled with inequities, as well as those who continue to sacrifice themselves in the struggle to eliminate human oppression. I realize the fight isn't over. Our nation continues to experience tumultuous times, twisting civil rights into civil wrongs, by engaging in human oppression. We are reminded that the struggle to care for our children and families continues. Caring for our children and families involves a commitment that considers people throughout their lives.

There is a value in caring for others and addressing ways to fundamentally improve the lived experiences of those who have been ostracized, especially children within our nation's schools. As Freire (1970) reminds us, social change will occur for oppressed groups when they "create a new situation, one which makes possible the pursuit for fuller humanity" (p. 29). As a scholar preparing twenty-first century school leaders, I take this charge seriously. I am responsible for reconsidering how I contribute to perpetuating oppressive practices that lead to unjust experiences. Leading for social justice is an emotional journey, requiring insight, hard work, and courage. Engaging our hearts and minds to transform schools into communities of care is what I hope for when I pass the torch to the next generation of school leaders.[5]

NOTES

1. For the purpose of this discussion, hegemony is the belief that one social group is dominant over another, which is often aligned with cultural dominance such as, race, gender, sexual identity, gender class and so on (Jonathan, 2002).
2. For the purpose of this chapter, metanarratives are societal beliefs that are often perceived as universal truths (Vavrus, 2002).
3. The internal accountability of this reflective process, encourages the examination of situations in which school leaders take responsibility for enforcing just and democratic ideals (Firestone & Shipps, 2005).
4. Over the next several months, the supervisor contacted me via phone. The person called at 8:00 a.m. asking me why I was "late", because I "usually arrived fifteen minutes earlier." The same supervisor made frequent 'drop-bys" and asked, "What are you writing? You know you need to publish if you want to make it here." The supervisor was seen walking by a Gay Straight Alliance meeting at UCEA to "check on me." Another time the same supervisor informed me, "Do what I tell you to do, no questions asked because I have the upper administration in the palm of my hand, kid."
5. In honor of Shel Silverstein's *The Missing Piece Meets the Big O*, I would like to acknowledge Autumn K. Tooms, who helped me to realize that I, as the *missing piece,* do not need a *piece* to complete me. My *circle*, Autumn, encourages me to develop my own momentum and never stop rolling.

APPENDIX A: ADDRESSING HEGEMONIC SCHOOL PRACTICES AND WORKPLACE MOBBING AS A TEMPERED RADICAL

Addressing Hegemonic Beliefs and Practices	*Addressing Workplace Mobbing*
A White male middle school teacher working in a predominant Black/Latino/a inner-city school announced during a formal teacher evaluation, "I don't know why the hell we work with these kids anyway. They are only going to get as far as a mobile home."	Three White male high school union members from a predominantly impoverished inner-city school informed me I was "hanging around the wrong people" because my mentors were Black. I was told that if I continued to allow them to mentor me, then I would be ostracized by the White teachers.
A White female elementary teacher yelled at students behind closed doors stating, "You're completely stupid! What's wrong with you?"	A White male graduate student informed me I was a "White racist because I didn't support the Whites like I should."

A White male eighth grade teacher in a predominantly Latino/a inner-city school denied a student to use the bathroom. The student came to the office with tears in his eyes whispering, "I wet my pants."

Two White female middle school teachers teaching in an inner-city school announced schools should "send Black kids back to Africa where they belong."

An inner-city high school Latina assistant principal announced, "These kids are worthless."

An inner-city White male superintendent noted during a leadership meeting, "America's official language is English. The parents and kids need to learn our language if they want us to teach them. There will be no exceptions."

A Black female middle school principal raised her voice at an eighth grade male student in the presence of a group of middle school girls. The principal yelled, "If you weren't such a *faggot*, you wouldn't have these problems."

A White male university school leader made a racial joke during a faculty meeting and used the word *nigger*.

A White male colleague made a racial joke after interviewing a candidate who identified as an American Indian. He said, "Well, we better not hire that person because I'm afraid I will get Tommy-hawked in the middle of the hallway."

An upper level administrator informed me "my pedagogical practices for examining race and racism do not belong at this university and are not aligned with our leadership program. You are to address only the standards we tell you to address."

A White male upper level administrator informed me "some teachers were complaining that they feel expected to spend time with the students after school. They see you spending time with them and now they feel guilty. You need to stop going outside and talking with parents and students. Let them leave the area and go home."

A White school leader stated privately in an unscheduled afterschool meeting, "I know there is something wrong with you and I am going to find out what it is." This occurred after documenting the person was not fulfilling weekly obligations as a coordinator. The person informed me I was a "private person, so I must be gay." The person insinuated "being gay" was synonymous with being a "pedophile.

A White male supervisor used the terms "dyke and faggot" in addition to derogatory racial comments in the workplace.

White male colleagues stated during a public meeting regarding curricular activities their thoughts regarding international programming. The first colleague stated, "If we wanted to go to Mexico, we could just go 20 miles north of here." Another colleague proceeded by stating, "We have nothing to learn from the Mexicans."

A White male supervisor informed me to "lower my standards because I was making my colleagues look bad. They cannot keep up with you and they are not interested in your social justice work. There is no place for social justice in this program."

REFERENCES

Alexander, K. L., Entwisle, D. R., & Olsen, L. S. (2001). Schools, achievement and inequality: A seasonal perspective. *Education Evaluation and Policy Analysis*, *23*(2), 171-191.
Banks, J. (2006). *Race, culture, and education*. New York, NY: Routeledge.
Banks, J. A., & McGee Banks, C. A. (2003). (Eds). *Handbook of research on multicultural education*. San Francisco: Jossey-Bass.
Barnes, D. (1998). Looking forward: the concluding remarks at the castle conference. In M. L. Hamilton (Eds.), *Reconceptualizing teaching practice: Self-study in teacher education* (pp. ix–xiv). London: Falmer Press.
Barnett, B. G., Basom, M. R., Yerkes, D. M., & Norris, C. J. (2000). Cohorts in educational leadership programs: Benefits, difficulties, and the potential for developing school leaders. *Educational Administration Quarterly*, *36*(2), 255-282.
Bell, D. A. (1980). *Brown v. Board of Education* and the interest-convergence dilemma. *Harvard Law Review*, *93*(3), 518-533.
Bell, D. A. (1992). *Faces at the bottom of the well: The permanence of racism*. New York, NY: Basic Books.
Brown, E. (2002). The (in)visibility of race in narrative constructions of the self. In J. Loughran & T. Russell (Eds.), *Improving teacher education practices through self-study* (pp. 145-160). London: Routledge Falmer.
Brown, K. (2004). Leadership for social justice and equity: Evaluating a transformative framework and andragogy. *Educational Adminstration Quarterly*, *42*(5), 700-745.
Bruner, J. (1986) *Actual minds, possible worlds*. Cambridge, MA: Harvard University Press.
Bruner, J. (1990) *Acts of meaning*. Cambridge, MA: Harvard University Press.
Carson, C. (2003). *Civil rights chronicle: The African-American struggle for freedom*. Lincolnwood, IL: Legacy.
Castagno, A. E., & Lee, S. J. (2007). Native mascots and ethnic fraud in higher education: Using tribal critical race theory and the interest convergence principle as an analytic tool. *Equity and Excellence in Education*, *40*, 3-13.
Clandinin, D. J. (1995). Still learning to teach. In T. Russell & F. Korthagen (Eds.), *Teachers who teach teachers: Reflections on teacher education* (pp. 25-31). London: Falmer Press.
Cross, T., Bazron, B., Karl, D., & Mareasa, I. (1989). *Toward a culturally competent system of care* (Vol. 1). Washington, DC: Georgetown University.
Davenport, N., Schwartz, R. D., & Elliot, G. P. (1996). *Mobbing: Emotional abuse in the American workplace*. Ames, IA: Civil Society.
Dewey, J. (1916/1944). *Democracy and education: An introduction to the philosophy of education*. New York, NY: The Free Press.
Elson, M. (1986). *Self psychology in clinical social work*. New York, NY: W.W. Norton.
Epstein, J. L., & Dauber, S. L. (1991). School programs and teacher practices of parent involvement in inner-city elementary and middle schools. *The Elementary School Journal*, *91*(3), 289-305.

Firestone, W. A., & Shipps, D. (2005). How do leaders interpret conflicting accountabilities to improve student learning? In W. A. Firestone & C. Riehl (Eds.), *A new agenda for research in educational leadership* (pp. 81-100). New York, NY: Teachers College Press.
Freire, P. (1970). *Pedagogy of the oppressed*. New York, NY: Herder and Herder.
Garner, P. (2001). *Teaching and learning in multicultural classrooms*. London: David Fulton.
Grant, C. A., & Sleeter, C.E. (2009). *Making choices for multicultural education: Five approaches to race, class, and gender* (6th ed). Hoboken, NJ: Wiley & Sons.
Gergen, K. (1999). *An invitation to social construction*. Thousand Oaks, CA: Sage.
Gonzalez, N., Moll, L. C., & Amanti, C. (2005). *Funds of knowledge: Theorizing practices in households, communities, and classrooms*. Mahwah, NJ: Erlbaum.
Gould, S. J. (1996). *The mismeasure of man*. New York, NY: W.W. Norton.
Gray, D. L., & Smith, A. (2007). *Case studies in 21st century school administration: Addressing challenges for educational leadership*. Thousand Oaks, CA: Sage.
Halen-Faber, C. (2002). Encouraging critical reflection in preservice teacher education: A narrative of a personal learning journey. *New Directions for Adults in Continuing Education, 74*, 51-60.
Hamilton, M. L. (2002). Change, social justice and re-liability: Reflections of a secret (change) agent. In J. Loughran & T. Russell (Eds.), *Improving teacher education practices through self-study* (pp. 176-189). London: RoutledgeFalmer.
Hamilton, M. L., & Pinnegar, S. (1998). Conclusion: The value and the promise of Self-study. In M. L. Hamilton (Ed.), *Reconceptualizing teaching practice: Self-study in teacher education* (pp. 234-246). London: Falmer. Press.
Hilliard, A. (1991). Do we have the will to educate all children? *Educational Leadership, 40*(1), 31-36.
Jencks, C., & Phillips, M. (1998). *The Black-White test score gap*. Washington, DC: Brookings Institution.
Ketelle, D., & Mesa, R. P. (2006). Empathetic understanding and school leadership preparation. *Leadership Review, 6*, 144-154.
King, M. L. (1967). *Where do we go from here: Chaos or community?* Boston: Beacon.
Ladson-Billings, G. (1998). Just what is critical race theory and what's it doing in a nice field like education? *International Journal of Qualitative Studies in Education, 11*(1), 7-24.
Ladson-Billings, G. (1994). *The dreamkeepers: Successful teachers of African-American children*. San Francisco: Jossey-Bass.
Laible, J. (2000). Loving epistemology: What I hold critical in my life, faith, and profession. *International Journal of Qualitative Studies in Education, 13*(6), 683-692.
Leymann, H. (1990). Mobbing and psychological terror at workplaces. *Violence and Victims, 5*, 119-126.
Lipman, P. (2004). *High stakes education: Inequality, globalization, and urban school reform*. New York, NY: Routledge-Farmer.
Lugg, C. (2003). Sissies, faggots, lezzies, and dykes: Gender, sexual orientation, and a new politics of education? *Educational Administration Quarterly, 39*(1), 95-134.

Kottkamp, R. B. (1990). Means for facilitating reflection. *Education and Urban Society, 22*(2), 182-203.
Kozol, J. (2005). *Shame of the nation: The restoration of apartheid schooling in America.* New York, NY: Crown.
Marshall, C., & Oliva, M. (2006). *Leadership for social justice: Making revolutions in education.* Boston: Pearson.
Marshall, C., & Gerstl-Pepin, C. (2005). *Re-framing educational politics for social justice.* Boston: Pearson.
McLaren, P. (1998). *Life in schools: An introduction to critical pedagogy in the foundations of education.* Reading, MA: Addison Wesley Longman.
McLaren, P., & Kincheloe, J. L. (Eds.). (2007). *Critical pedagogy: Where are we now?* New York, NY: Peter Lang.
Meyerson, D. E. (2001). *Tempered radicals: How people use difference to inspire change at work.* Boston: Harvard School Press.
Meyerson, D. E., & Scully, M. (1995). Tempered radicalism and the politics of ambivalence and change. *Organizational Science, 6*(5), 585-600.
Mezirow, J. (1990). *Fostering critical reflection in adulthood: A guide to transformative and emancipatory learning.* San Francisco: Jossey-Bass.
Milner IV, H. R. (2007). Race, culture, and research positionality: Working through dangers seen, unseen, and foreseen. *Educational Researcher, 36*(7), 388-400.
Nieto, S. (2004). Puerto Rican students in U.S. schools: A troubled past and the search for a hopeful future. In J. A. Banks & C. A. McGee Banks (Eds.), *Handbook of research on multicultural education* (2nd ed.) (pp. 515-541). San Francisco, CA: Jossey-Bass.
Noguera, P. A. (2008). *The trouble with Black boys: And other reflections on race, equity, and the future of public education.* San Francisco: Jossey-Bass.
Ortiz, A. A. (1997). Learning disabilities occurring concomitantly with linguistic differences. *Journal of Learning Disabilities, 30*(3), 321-332.
Oakes, J. (1985). *Keeping track: How schools structure inequality.* New Haven, CT: Yale University Press.
Osterman, K. F., & Kottkamp, R. B. (1993). *Reflective practice for educators: Improving schooling through professional development.* Newbury Park, CA: Corwin Press.
Polkinghorne, D. (1988) *Narrative knowing and the human sciences.* Albany: State University of New York Press.
Russel, T., & Korthagen, F. A. J. (1995) (Eds). *Teachers who teach teachers: Reflections on teacher education.* London: Falmer Press.
Sadker, M. & Sadker, D. (1994). *Failing at fairness: How America's schools cheat girls.* New York, NY: Charles Scribner's Sons.
Saldivar, J. D. (1997). *Border matters: Remapping American cultural studies.* Berkeley: University of California Press.
Sarbin, T. (ed.) (1986) *Narrative psychology: The storied nature of human conduct.* New York, NY: Praeger.
Schein, E. (1989). *Organizational culture and leadership: A dynamic view.* San Francisco, Jossey-Bass.
Schon, D. A. (1983). *The reflective practitioner.* New York, NY: Basic Books.

Scribner, J. P., Sunday-Cockrell, K., Cockrell, D. H., & Valentine, J. W. (1999). Creating professional communities in schools through organizational learning: An evaluation of a school improvement process. *Educational Administration Quarterly, 35*(1), 130-160.

Sergiovanni, T. J. (2001). *The principalship: A reflective practice perspective* (4th ed.). Needham Heights, MA: Allyn & Bacon.

Shapiro, J. P., & Stefkovich, J. A. (2005). *Ethical leadership and decision making* (2nd ed.). Mahwah, NJ: Erlbaum.

Shields, C. & Edwards, M. (2005). *Dialogue is not just talk: A new ground for educational leadership*. New York, NY: Peter Lang.

Shields, C. M., LaRoque, L. J., & Oberg, S. L. (2002). A conversation about race and ethnicity: Struggling to understand issues in cross-cultural leadership. *Journal of School Leadership, 12*(2), 116-137.

Small, M. L., & Newman, K. (2001). Urban poverty after the truly disadvantaged: The rediscovery of the family, the neighborhood, and culture. *Annual Review of Sociology, 27*, 23-45.

Smedley, A. (1998). *Race in North America: Origin and evolution of a worldview*. Boulder, CO: Westview Press.

Smith, S. C., & Piele, P. K. (2006). *School leadership: Handbook for excellence in student learning*. Thousand Oaks, CA: Corwin Press.

Smith, B., & Sparkes, A. C. (2008). Contrasting perspectives on narrating selves and identities: an invitation to dialogue. *Qualitative Research, 8*(1), 5-35.

Somers, M. (1994). The Narrative Constitution of Identity: A Relational and Network Approach. *Theory and Society, 23*, 635-649.

Spring, J. (1980). *Educating the worker-citizen: The social, economic, and political foundations of education*. New York, NY: Longman.

Stout, R. (1986). Executive action and values. *Issues in Education, 4*(3), 198-214.

Taylor, C. (1989) *Sources of the self: The making of the modern identity*. Cambridge, MA: Harvard University Press.

Terrell, R. D., & Randall, L. B. (2009). *Culturally proficient leadership: The personal journey begins within*. Thousand Oaks, CA: Corwin Press.

Tooms, A. K. (2007). The right kind of queer: "Fit" and the politics of school leadership. *Journal of School Leadership, 17*, 601-630.

U.S. Department of Commerce, Bureau of the Census. (2004). *Income, poverty, and health insurance coverage in the U.S., 2003*. Washington, DC: U.S. Government Printing Office.

Vavrus, M. J. (2002). *Transforming the multicultural education of teachers: Theory, research, and practice*. New York, NY: Teachers College Press.

Westhues, K. (Ed.) (2005). *Winning, losing, moving on: How professionals deal with workplace harassment and mobbing*. Lewiston, NY: The Edwin Mellen Press.

Westhues, K. (Ed.) (2004). *Workplace mobbing in academe: Reports from twenty universities*. Lewiston, NY: The Edwin Mellen Press.

Wheatley, M. J. (1994). *Leadership and the new science*. San Francisco: Berrett-Koehler.

Whitehead, J. (1995). Educative relationships with the writings of others. In T. Russel & F.A. J. Korthagen (Eds), *Teachers who teach teachers: Reflections on teacher education* (pp. 113-129). London: Falmer Press.

Yamada, D. (2004). The role of the law in combating workplace mobbing and bullying. In K. Westhues (Ed.), *Workplace mobbing in academe: Reports from twenty universities* (pp. 388-403). Lewiston, NY: The Edwin Mellen Press.

SCENIC OVERLOOK

Chapters 2 and 3

Guidelines for Discussions and Reflection

For school leaders:

1. When have you experienced being "other?" What happened? How did this experience shape your identity? Map the stages/steps in your own development related to being identified as "other."
2. Discuss when your values were in contraction with the larger system. Describe what happened. How did this experience shape your identity? Map the stages/steps in your own development related to your values being in contradiction to larger systems.
3. How do you think people who live on the margins due to race, class, sexual identity, language, religion, ability, and gender interplay with the larger school community?
4. What school practices and/or school policies support and/or protect children, families, and professionals who live on the margins? Provide examples of school practices and/or school policies.

For those preparing school leaders:

1. When have you experienced being "other?" What happened? How did this experience shape your identity? How did this experience influence your school practice?
2. As a scholar preparing school leaders, have your values been in contraction with the larger system. What happened? How did the experience shape your identity?
3. How do you support aspiring school leaders in gaining a deeper understanding of marginalization and its interplay with the larger school community?
4. What is your experience in addressing school policies that support and/or protect the rights of children and families, especially for people who live on the margins? To what extent does your preparation program prepare aspiring school leaders to address such issues? What experiences are afforded to aspiring school leaders to respond to the systemic needs of those they serve throughout your preparation program?

Christa Boske's chapter invited the reader to bridge personal selves with a deeper understanding of what it means to fight the good fight. Leading for social justice is more than considering the influence of larger contexts and complaining about assumptions made. Fighting the good fight suggests school leaders seize opportunities to promote positive societal trends that begin from within and transcend throughout school practices.

In the next chapter, Catherine Lugg presents herself as a member of the tail-end boomer and mid-era gay rights generation. Her scholarly assumptions regarding the multidimensional analyses of educational policy caused friction with her older colleagues. Catherine Lugg's authentic voice interplays with both primary and secondary sources in a gracious effort to document her personal history and courage to address LGBTQ issues with the historical.

CHAPTER 3

WHAT'S A NICE DYKE LIKE YOU EMBRACING THIS POSTMODERN CRAP?

Catherine A. Lugg

It was possible, for the most part, to assume that the heterogeneous sexual minority population was comprised substantially of male, affluent WASPs; it was possible to conclude mistakenly that all was well in the lives of this nation's nonheterosexual population but for the exception of majoritarian sexual orientation bias.

Francisco Valdes,
on the early gay rights legal scholarship (1998, p. 1417.

Much of the early research on gay and lesbian liberation embraced tightly defined social categories, which were clear, concise, and wildly inaccurate (see Hutchison's critique, 1997). These categories (for example, one was either gay or straight; a woman or a womyn; etc.) excluded many individuals who could not and/or would not be locked into logic-tight binaries. But for many early scholars and activists, sexual orientation and identity were to be neat—that is, one was clearly gay or straight—or male or female for that matter (see Eisenstein, 1988; MacKinnon, 1989).

Although this early work did establish important political and research foundations on a landscape that was bereft of any queer-positive information and praxis, by design, it was largely exclusionary (Hutchinson, 1997, 1999, 2000, 2001; Valdes, 1995, 1997, 1998; Wilchins, 2004). These exclusive stances could and did cause endless heartache for those who did not meet the embedded assumptions of the early gay-liberation movement ("gays" were to be White and largely male, as well as of a certain age and class—see Valdes, 1998).

The author of the historical essay is a tail-end member of the boomer-generation and thus, historically, should be considered as a member of the mid-era gay rights generation (late 1970s—early 1980s). Yet, I came out both professionally and personally into an era marked by postmodernity (the early 1990s), a time that posits all identity is inherently unstable. Furthermore, my training as an educational policy scholar was deeply influenced by critical legal studies, critical race theory, and feminist legal theory. Consequently, my scholarly assumptions are that regardless of the policy issue involved, race, class, gender, and now sexual orientation (as well as age, dis/ability and religion) are "at play" within the policy process—sometimes explicitly, more often, implicitly. I also personally identify as "queer" instead of "lesbian" or "gay" because of the term's inclusive nature (covering lesbian, gay, bisexual, trans, intersexual and queer questioning people), as well as its provocative political stance. Historically, calling someone "queer" is to hurl a vicious slur—literally "fighting words" (Faderman, 1995). But the term was embraced in the 1990s by both LGBT activists and queer theorists. That said, these political and theoretical stances do cause friction with older colleagues and friends who claim I am ignoring or minimizing gay and lesbian issues, or less politely—that I have sold out to the academically fashionable.

But at first, my research agenda did not address issues of queer rights, the politics of education and educational policy. Instead, I focused on right-wing political movements in the United States in general, and the Protestant Right in particular, as to how they shaped and reshaped policy affecting public schools.

In this chapter, I present a historical overview of the queer rights movement in the United States, from the late 1940s to today, weaving in snapshots of my own life into the narrative. Readers who wish more historical information should consult Tables 3.1 and 3.2 that appears at the end of this article. Additionally, I illustrate how intersectional and multidimensional analyses can uncover the ways that shifting/multiple identities shape the policies and practices of U.S. public schooling by drawing on the work of scholars and activists who acknowledge the intersections and multidimensionality of our constructed and assembled identities (Valdes,

Hutchinson, Yoshino, and Wilchins). I also draw from the earlier work of social scientist Erving Goffman, who examined how stigmatized populations navigated their social worlds. I conclude this article by exploring the notion of *differentiated citizenship* and what implications it may hold for public school policy and the politics of education.

IN THE BEGINNING (1940S-1969)

We were all so closeted and it was so illegal to be queer. You could be put in jail, put in mental hospitals!

Merrill Mushroom,
on being a queer youth in the 1950s (in Sears, 1997, p. 27)

In the beginning of the modern queer rights movements, there was the Stonewall rebellion—or so the story goes. Yet, by making June 1969 the "starting point" of the contemporary queer rights movements, much of the critical organizing work by the early "Homophile" organizations that established greater basic awareness, education and understanding is completely over-looked (D'Emilio, 2002). In particular, the Mattachine Society, which was founded by Harry Hay in late 1950, took the radical stance that "homosexuals" comprised a legitimate minority group like any other historically marginalized population (D'Emilio, 1983). Drawing on his years as an activist for the Communist Party, USA,[1] Hay employed classic Marxist analyses to underscore his belief that "homosexuals" were no more diseased, sinful or criminal than any other part of the general population. Hay argued that the social, economic, legal, medical and political obstacles that confronted "the homosexual" were rooted in prejudice, and prejudices, since they were not rational, could be eradicated through greater education and awareness, as well as political activism (Scagliotti & Schiller, 1986). Consequently, Hay organized Mattachine to combat the massive ignorance and prejudice of the times, fight police entrapment of gay men in the court system, as well as engage in nascent political activism (Alwood, 1996; D'Emilio, 1983). In the 1950s, Mattachine members provided research subjects for Evelyn Hooker's path-breaking psychological research demonstrating that queer people were not, by definition, mentally ill. By 1965, Mattachine members organized the first pro-gay protest in front of the White House, decrying the gay-ban in federal employment (Bullough, 2002; D'Emilio, 1983).

That said, the post World War II era was the height of what legal researcher Bill Eskridge has called the *Kulturkampf,* or the cultural war against homosexuals (1994). Homosexuality was repeatedly equated with both moral and political subversion (Johnson, 2004), hence the era's slur, "Commie, pinko, queer" (D'Emilio, 1983; Faderman, 1994). Same-sex consensual sexual behavior was banned in all 48 and then 50 states, making queer people, by definition, criminals (Eskridge, 1994, 1999; Leslie, 2000). Furthermore, homosexuality and bisexuality were seen as forms of severe mental illness—a dangerous diagnosis in an era rife with involuntary civil commitment laws (Freedman, 1987; Goffman, 1963). Queer people who could not pass as nonqueer were frequently spirited off to mental institutions where psychiatrists employed a variety of supposedly therapeutic treatments including medication, electroshock, and occasionally lobotomy, in society's quest to eradicate queer identity (D'Emilio, 1983; Freedman, 1987; Scagliotti & Schiller, 1986; Terry, 1999).

In U.S. public schools, employees suspected of "queer tendencies" could be and were dismissed from their positions without legal recourse (Blount, 1998; 2005; Faderman, 1994; Harbeck, 1997; Kepner, 1998; Lugg, 2003b). In Florida, beginning in the late 1950s, a full-scale witch-hunt of suspected queer educators stripped of both their jobs and their professional licenses, without legal recourse (see Eskridge, 1994; Kepner, 1998). Furthermore, public school teachers and administrators were to be on the watch for any "homosexual tendencies" in either students or their colleagues. Single teachers, particularly single male teachers, were subjected to intense public and administrative scrutiny and marriage became to the "de facto" qualification for both male and then increasingly, female educators (Blount, 1998, 2005; Lugg, 2003b).

Given the multiple oppressions and legal restrictions across areas of identity, not surprisingly, the vast majority of the early gay rights activists (and Mattachine's members) were White men (D'Emilio, 1983), who held far more political and economic power than other queer constituencies. Furthermore, while there was a lesbian organization, Daughters of Bilitis (DOB), it was more focused on basic education and outreach than political and legal activism when compared to Mattachine (Faderman, 1994). That said, both Mattachine and DOB were largely organized around a simple dichotomy—you were either "gay," a "family member," "choir member," "member of the women's softball team," "friend of Dorothy," (all code for queer) or you were not. Activists, working at the height of the Cold War hysteria or *Kulturkampf* against queers, employed this simple, if flawed, dichotomy to organize, resist, and push for greater sexual liberation. While these early activists had numerous biases, they established the foundation for what was to come. All that was needed was a spark.

Conflagrations and Fragmentations (1969-1980)

We are the Stonewall girls
We wear our hair in curls
We wear no underwear
We show our pubic hair ...
We wear our dungarees
Above our nelly knees! (Drag queens singing in a Rockettes-style "kick-line" while directly confronting the New York City police during the first night of the Stonewall Rebellion, in Duberman, 1994, pp. 200-201)

And yet, in the beginning, there was the Stonewall Rebellion (Duberman, 1994; Marotta, 1981; Teal, 1971). Located in the heart of Greenwich Village, *The Stonewall Inn* was a gay bar, notorious for both its seemingly outlandish clientele as well as its perpetually sticky floors. But the Stonewall was one of the few places where queers could somewhat safely congregate, somewhat free from police harassment and somewhat free of Mafia shakedowns (Duberman, 1994; Teal, 1971). The rebellion began late on June 27, 1969, when the New York City police department attempted to raid the bar, arresting patrons for "disorderly conduct," historically code for being queer (see Eskridge, 1994). Instead of being quietly and docilely led away to the waiting "Paddy Wagons," the bar's patrons fought back, led by drag queens of color.[2] Patrons, who vastly out-numbered the cops, beat police officers and smashed their patrol cars. The police called for reinforcements but the rioters fought them to a standstill. For the next five nights, queer people battled the police in response to the recent raid as well as to years of endless police harassment. By the time the rebellion was suppressed, a radically different vision of queer rights was born (D'Emilio, 1983; Duberman, 1994; Jay, 1999; Marotta, 1981; Teal, 1971). As poet Alan Ginsberg noted at the time, "they've lost that wounded look that fags all had 10 years ago" (in Jay, 1999, p. 75).

Two new activist organizations quickly emerged from the rebellion: The radical Gay Liberation Front (GLF), which advocated for the liberation of all oppressed people everywhere; and the Gay Activist Alliance (GAA), which focused solely on gay rights. While GLF was more egalitarian in outlook, it collapsed after a few years, fragmenting into pieces as competing agendas and ideologies tore the organization apart (Marotta, 1981). The GAA, which still exists (and there is a New Jersey chapter in Morris County), had more political success by its tight focus on securing gay rights. GAA members "zapped"—or publicly confronted with television cameras rolling—NYC Mayor John Lindsay, TV host Dick Cavett, and the homophobic NYC Board of Education (Marotta, 1981). Inspired by GAA's media successes, other gay activists targeted the 1970 American Psychiatric Association's (APA) annual convention, for sponsoring a session on aversion therapy, that is, conditioning queer people to hate, loathe and fear their orientation and identity (Scagliotti & Schiller, 1986). The activists effectively shouted down that particular session and urged APA to stop talking *about* queer people and start talking *with* queer people (Bullough, 2002; Marotta, 1981).

For the next few years activists like long-time Mattachine member Frank Kameny and DOB member Barbara Gittings attended the APA conventions as participants in queer-affirming sessions. The supposed science that determined queer people, by definition, were mentally ill collapsed under nearly 30 years of data demonstrating that presumption was utterly false. The political pressure by activists also helped (Bullough, 2002). By 1973, APA had reversed its stance on homosexuality and bisexuality as inherent mental pathologies, removing homosexuality, bisexuality and lesbianism from its list of mental disorders. In response to this changed medical status, 22 states repealed their bans on consensual sodomy, while two more had their bans overturned by their state supreme courts (see Lugg, 2003a; 2006). During the 1970s and into the early 1980s, and in roughly half the U.S. states, queers went from being medically pathological, morally sinful, and inherently criminal, to merely sinful, and only in some quarters (Lugg, 2003a).

The 1970s also witnessed the emergence of "gay" scholarship. Researchers and artists like Martin Duberman, John D'Emilio, Audrey Lorde, Toby Marotta, Kate Millet, and Adrienne Rich drew on their impressive scholarly skills as they wrote their lives into their work. And yet, with this flowering of gay activism and scholarship came tensions and disruptions. In an era of greater social and political liberation, queer activists of various organizations were not going to automatically defer to White gay men as they had in the past (Frye, 1981). In particular, lesbian activists, who were and were not part of the larger women's movement, no longer tolerated the sexism of their gay male peers or the homophobia of the women's movement (Jay, 1999; Seidman, 2003). Lesbian separatists withdrew into all-lesbian enclaves in the hopes of developing a new, "womyn-centered" society (Frye, 1981; Jay, 1999; Marotta, 1981; Vaid, 1995). Lesbian-separatists advocated for changing the spelling of women to womyn, to exemplify the decentering of men in their new society (see Frye, 1981). Similarly, transgendered activists, after being politically and emotionally scalded by lesbian activists and gay men, retreated into their own organizations (Duberman, 1994; Jay, 1999). Identity and identities were fragmenting into multiple pieces and directions, and the old reliable dichotomies of "gay" or "straight" began to collapse.

Thanks to the visibility of gay rights activists, a few public school teachers began to venture from their closets instead of being hurled from them by homophobes (Harbeck 1997). Yet, the political and legal environments were particularly hostile towards "gay school teachers" given the cultural mythology surrounding the supposed "recruitment" by queer teachers of vulnerable youth into immorality (Harbeck, 1997; Lugg, 2003b). Consequently, queer educators were generally fired or pressured into resigning if their orientation became public knowledge (Lugg, 2003a; Shilts, 1982). And if they sued their districts in a bid to keep their positions, queer litigants generally lost legal cases and then their positions (Harbeck, 1997; Lugg, 2003a; 2006). Not surprisingly, although queer people were increasingly visible throughout the 1970s, queer educators working in public schools overwhelming kept their identities hidden and remained largely invisible (Blount, 2005).

This greater visibility and public awareness of queer people and our issues also energized a nascent Protestant Right, which took direct aim at our social movement. Comprised largely of White Protestants who were Biblical literalists (Detwiler, 2000; Oldfield, 1996; Shupe & Stacy, 1982; Wilcox, 1996), the growing Protestant Right of the 1970s had a host of political grievances: the activism and success of the African American civil rights movement, school desegregation, legalization of abortion, the Constitutional ban on governmentally-sponsored prayer in public schools, and the possible ratification of the Equal Rights Amendment (Diamond, 1995; Haberman, 2005). However, their greatest political vitriol was aimed at queer people, who represented a seemingly direct affront to their theological beliefs. While initially derided as politically opportunistic televangelists—thanks to the involvement of TV preacher Jerry Falwell—the Protestant Right would gain national political power by the 1980s.

MY GROWING AWARENESS (1960S-1980S)

My name is Harvey Milk and I'm here to recruit you.
                            —1978 (in Blasius & Phelan, 1997, p. 451)

I was born the year that John Kennedy was assassinated, in March of 1963. Thanks to the strategic placement of the playpen in front of my parents' TV set, my earliest memory is of Jack Ruby killing Lee Harvey Oswald. At the time, my rural Appalachian town was notable for having cable TV, thanks to the ingenuity of local residents who had formed a television cooperative in the early 1950s.[3] My parents were terrific news junkies, so current events were to be observed by the household and then discussed at the very next family meal.[4] While I was not raised by TV, it was a critical component of my political education, as were newspapers and news magazines. This was tightly supervised by my parents and their parents, since they belonged to opposing political parties—and strongly disagreed on almost everything except Baptist theology.[5] So, my understandings of sexuality and identity were largely formed by: the Baptist church, public TV, and broadcast news reports.

By the early 1970s, I had a firm grip on human reproduction thanks to my mom reading to me, and then giving me, various age-appropriate books. As the decade unfolded, her great and frequently voiced fear was that she would become a grandmother much too early. I earnestly assured her that was highly improbable, but did not go into details as to why. Sexual orientation was a highly uncomfortable and little discussed topic, particularly for rural folks. For example, when the local and much beloved school-marm's partner died, I vividly remember the town's adults worrying: "What would Miss Case do?" The partners had been together for over 50 years and they were in their 90s. The great fear was that Miss Case would not survive without her partner. And she did not, dying a short time later. But the entire matter was discussed in hushed and oblique tones, as the vast majority of the town's residents quietly paraded to Miss Cases' home to pay our solemn but collective respects.

During the late 1970s when I was in high school, I was both aware and completely unaware of my own identity because I was working so very hard to pass as nonqueer to be like everyone else—or so I assumed. Only much later, would I discover that feeling was typical for a queer kid of my generation and religious upbringing. We were taught by a homophobic society to be selectively blind to ourselves in hopes that we would turn out "normal" (D'Emilio, 1983; Sears, 1997). School itself was boring and a chore, and extra-curricular activities made it only somewhat more palatable (band, choir, basketball and track, in order of importance). High school was something I had to endure, like going to the dentist, but I knew that I was going to college and *then* life would be much better.

In 1977, the election of Harvey Milk as an "out gay man" to the San Francisco Board of Supervisors utterly fascinated me and I eagerly devoured all manner of news on Milk and San Francisco because both seemed so wonderful. Other gay rights news was far more troubling. I was horrified as were my parents by Anita Bryant's hateful campaign (Save Our Children) in Dade County Florida, against queer people. Bryant, who was a former Miss America, and a television salesperson for the Florida orange-growers, was popular in conservative circles for her "wholesome" musical acts. She was also fast becoming the darling of the nascent Protestant Right given her homophobic crusade (McGarry & Wasserman, 1998). My parents' long-standing attitude toward all bigotry was that it was "stupid" to be so hateful. In my parents' world view, since hate was equated with stupidity, hate and hateful people could and should be vigorously (and to be honest, viciously) mocked. I vividly remember watching a spoof of Bryant on the Carol Burnett television show, which was a completely over-the-top patriotic/religious musical extravaganza. Burnett was made-up to be Bryant, complete with a gaudy corsage of oranges (the fruit—not the blossoms), tweaking Bryant's role as a pitch woman for the Florida orange growers. The entire show ended with Barnett lifting her arms to the heavens and singing, "and we'll all be happy and gay!" which had the television audience howling and my parents crying with laughter. Given my adolescent faith in the power of TV, Carol Burnett, and humor to change people's hearts and minds, I firmly believed everything was going to be okay for queer people.

In 1978, the assassinations of Milk and Mayor George Mascone shattered those adolescent assumptions. I had vaguely known that queers were routinely victims of extreme violence and that this violence was American as apple pie and Chevrolet. I chanted "Smear the queer" just as loudly as my friends from the band section during football games in support of "our guys." And violence against queers escalated throughout the 1970s (D'Emilio, 2002). Milk's assassination, followed by his killer's partially successful "Twinkie defense" (mental impairment due to the consumption of junk food prior to the act—see Epstien, 1983; Shilts, 1982), showed me exactly how America valued its queer citizens. Unfortunately, that lesson was going to get even starker.

THE REAGAN/DYING ERA: BEHOLD, A PALE HORSE (1981-1988)

And I looked, and behold a pale horse:
And his name that sat on him
was Death, and Hell followed with
him. And power was given unto
them over the fourth part of the
earth, to kill with sword, and with
hunger, and with death, and with
the beasts of the earth. (Revelation 6:8, in Shilts, 1987, p. 3)

The election of Ronald Reagan as U.S. president exemplified a major shift in U.S. public policy. Former President Jimmy Carter had carefully, if uncomfortably, courted LGB communities (trans people were beyond the political pale at this time), and even tepidly campaigned against the homophobic Briggs initiative, which would have banned queer and queer-positive employees from working in California public schools (Epstein, 1983; Shilts, 1982). By contrast, Reagan owed his election partially to the Protestant Right, a political constituency that despised queers as de facto religious heretics (Diamond, 1998). What little political access queers had gained at the federal level with Carter evaporated in January of 1981.

At the beginning of the Reagan era, I headed off to music school, which I hoped would be wonderfully new, free, and exciting. It was, but there were a few drawbacks. No one was "openly gay" although rumors abounded, and some of us were terrible at passing as nonqueer. The vast majority of us remained deeply closeted, hiding in the metaphorical attic with the lights out and a blanket thrown over us for good measure. Furthermore, since I was majoring in *music education*, the gendered expectations were stifling. Female music majors were expected to focus on our energies at the elementary level, ideally becoming general music teachers. Men were strongly encouraged to focus on the high school level, since elementary music was seen as a "career killer" for them. In high school, I had loved band and dearly wanted to be an instrumental music teacher at the secondary level. I deeply resented being steered towards the elementary level. I dug in my heels and responded to the increasing faculty pressure by being a chronic cut-up and clown. The more the faculty insisted that we all become "professional" (gender appropriate and closeted), the more my friends and I cut class, hung out, played pool, smoked (which was a flunking offense for singers and wind instrumentalists), and focused our energies on smuggling booze into the dorms for the weekend parties.

In the summer of 1983, I received an urgent phone call from my brother David, who was then working as a lab technician for the Wistar Institute in Philadelphia. The Institute was researching a new disease that appeared to be sexually-transmitted, but no one was positive of how this "bug" was picked-up. The great concern was that this new disease was absolutely lethal: If you contracted it, you would die, period. David was adamant that if I were sexually active I was to insist that my (male) partner use a condom. This was my introduction to AIDS. Given my brother's insistence, I started scouring news reports about AIDS—but there was little reporting at that point (Alwood, 1996). According to the scant reporting, it appeared to affect only gay men, injection drug abusers, and Haitian immigrants (Gross, 1993; Shilts, 1987), so while I was concerned for my few gay friends, I was not too worried about myself. Back at school, AIDS was rarely mentioned, although I did worry about the young men who came out as soon as they graduated. By the mid-1980s, I was in graduate school for music where I generally resided in self-imposed musical isolation and political oblivion.

Meanwhile, AIDS galloped across the American landscape. Even in the early 1980s when it was called Gay Related Immune Deficiency (or GRID), the disease *did not* discriminate against particular social groups if given the opportunity (Shilts, 1987; Silin, 1995). Nonqueer women, their children, and hemophiliacs also contracted the disease, quickly shattering the myth that only gay men could get the disease. Thousands of people perished, sometimes in particularly gruesome ways thanks to the collapse of their immune systems (Shilts, 1987). Many patients suffered from Karposi's sarcoma (a disfiguring form of cancer) and AIDS-related anorexia, meaning AIDS was a visible illness (Alwood, 1996; Gross, 1993; Shilts, 1987). For gay men who had long hid their orientation, AIDS "outed" them to their friends, family members and occasionally, their employers, sometimes with devastating results (Alwood, 1996; Gross, 1993).

In the case of Rock Hudson, who had long played a hunky heterosexual heart-throb in movies and on television, his declining health status became fodder for tabloid and eventually mainstream news in 1985 (Alwood, 1996; Gross, 1993; Shilts, 1987). Rumors about his queer orientation had been splashed across the tabloid headlines for decades, although the mainstream press declined to pursue the abundant evidence (Gross, 1993; Shilts, 1987). Since Hudson currently had a role on the popular TV show *Dynasty*, his was a familiar face to millions of Americans. By the summer of 1985, it was a face that was clearly dying. Gaunt, mottled, and visibly frail, Hudson had appeared that July with his former movie co-star, Doris Day, in a press conference to promote her new television show, which was to be shown on the Christian Broadcast Network. Both Day and the reporters covering the event were shocked by his appearance (Shilts, 1987). At the time, Hudson's publicist claimed he was in "perfect health," but that transparent lie only fueled the explosion of speculation of the news media regarding his health status and orientation (Alwood, 1996). By the end of the month, his doctor ended the rampant and occasionally lurid speculation by simply stating, "Mr. Hudson is being evaluated and treated for complications of Acquired Immune Deficiency Syndrome" (Shilts, 1987, p. 582). By that time, over 6,000 Americans had died from AIDS and other 12,067 had been diagnosed (Shilts, 1987).

Prior to the revelation of Hudson's diagnosis, the reporting on AIDS had been largely nonexistent (Alwood, 1996; Gross, 1993; Shilts, 1987). Similarly, the federal government had been silent, withholding acknowledgment of the crisis as well as funds to fight the exploding epidemic (Shilts, 1987). With Hudson's diagnosis and revelation that yes indeed, he was a gay man who had AIDS; AIDS became mainstream news for the first time since the epidemic began (Alwood, 1996). It had taken four years and over 6,000 deaths, from when the epidemic first began to send Americans to their doctors back in 1981, for the media to finally report on one the most horrific epidemiological events of the 20th century (Shilts, 1987).

President Reagan, who had known Hudson for decades and who, prior to Hudson's public diagnosis, had yet to even mention AIDS, finally did so in September of 1985, when he empathized with parents who did not permit their children to attend school with "kids with AIDS" (in Alwood, 1996, p. 234). His comment was in reaction to two community school boards in Queens trying to ban children with AIDS (or who lived with someone with AIDS) from attending their public schools (Schwarz & Schaffer, 1985).[6] This would be Reagan's last comment until events forced him to mention it more directly amid the 1987 media swirl regarding the Surgeon General's Report on AIDS (Vaid, 1995).

Reagan's silence on AIDS was consistent with his administration's orientation regarding public health funding in general, and funding that might, however indirectly, benefit "militant homosexuals" in particular (Gross, 1993; Shilts, 1987; Valdes, 1998). A major component of the Reagan electoral coalition was the Protestant Right, who viewed out queers as mortal threats to the existence of their faith and by extension, the United States, since they believed the United States was God's chosen land (Diamond, 1998). With the emergence of AIDS as a deadly disease, many prominent leaders of the Protestant Right coupled AIDS, and queers with the supposed fallen moral status of the United States. As the Reverend Jerry Falwell opined:

> When you violate moral, health and hygiene laws, you reap the whirlwind. You cannot shake your fist in God's face and get by with it. (in Shilts, 1987, p. 347)

Conservative commentator and Reagan speech writer Patrick Buchanan demonstrated a similar level of understanding and compassion when he wrote, "The poor homosexuals—they have declared war upon nature, and now nature is exactly awful retribution" (in Shilts, 1987, p. 311). *National Review* editor and godfather of the American Conservative movement, William F. Buckley, advocated that AIDS patients be tattooed so that all Americans would know of their diseased status (Alwood, 1996). This trope of *the immoral and diseased queers* was quickly picked-up and amplified by the mainstream press (Alwood, 1996; Gross, 1993; Shilts, 1987).[7]

The U.S. Supreme Court stepped into this whirling climate of fear and loathing and issued a major decision affecting queer rights. The case was *Bowers vs. Hardwick*, and it involved the constitutionality of Georgia's blanket ban on consensual sodomy. Hardwick, who had been repeatedly harassed and possibly gay-bashed by the arresting officer, (see Thomas, 1992) was arrested in his own home for consensual sodomy with a male houseguest.[8] The Supreme Court, in a 5-to-4 decision, ruled that the Georgia statute was constitutional. In upholding the law, the court stated that there was no constitutional right to "homosexual sodomy" (*Bowers v.*

Hardwick, 1986, at 190-191). Nor did queer people have a right to privacy if "homosexual conduct occurs in the privacy of the home" (at 195-196). To add further insult to injury, the court had no opinion as to remainder of the Georgia consensual sodomy law. So far as the Supreme Court was concerned, laws barring consensual sodomy did not pertain to heterosexuals (Dayoff, 2001; Murdoch & Price, 2001; Thomas, 1992).

The *Hardwick* decision was a huge blow for queer people in the United States (Eskridge, 1999; Murdoch & Price, 2001). For professionals who needed state licenses (like teachers and administrators, but also doctors, dentists, beauticians, electricians, etc.), the Hardwick decision meant that their continued employment was at-risk if their nonqueer status became known. Most states ban convicted criminals from holding a state professional license. In the law review literature queers were known as statutory criminals or statutory felons (depending on state law), since one's legal status was tied to identity (Dayoff, 2001; DuBuisson, 2006; Leslie, 2000; Murdoch & Price, 2001). If a person was open about their sexual and/or gender identity, they risked not only being fired, but having their licensure revoked (Lugg, 2003a, 2003b, 2006).

For queer teachers and administrators, the hysteria over AIDS and the *Hardwick* decision were a devastating one-two punch. The climate was even more hostile for queer educators than it had been in the 1970s. Furthermore, the conflation of AIDS and sexual orientation, led to legislative proposals that all public educators be tested for the virus that caused AIDS (HIV). If an educator tested positive for the virus, they were to be dismissed (Blount, 2005). While these efforts failed, they did nothing to reduce the level of hysteria.

Public school students who suffered from HIV/AIDS also encountered enormous discrimination and hatred (Brier, 2006; Silin, 1995). The experiences of Ryan White, who was barred from his Kokomo public school district for over a year, riveted the nation's attention. White, who had hemophilia, contracted AIDS from a tainted blood product—a common fate for many hemophiliacs of the 1980s (Shilts, 1987). In 1985, after an extended bout in the hospital, Ryan's parents requested that he be permitted to return to school. The district refused and in turn the Ryan family sued, eventually winning and Ryan returned to his school (Johnson, 1987). However, the school and community environments were so toxic (complete with name-calling, most frequently, "queer," and finally with a bullet through the family's front window), that only a year later they relocated to another, far more welcoming, Indiana community. Ryan White's school experiences, which were televised across the United States, horrified many Americans, but they underscored the fear and loathing of that era.

IN YOUR FACE WITH *NO* DISGRACE (1986-1990S)

> Education concerning AIDS must start at the lowest grade possible as part of any health and hygiene program.... There is now no doubt that we need sex education in schools and that it must include information on heterosexual and homosexual relationships. The threat of AIDS should be sufficient to permit a sex education curriculum with a heavy emphasis on prevention of AIDS and other sexually transmitted diseases. (Koop, 1986, p. 31)

While President Reagan remained largely silent during the AIDS crisis, he did order the U.S. Surgeon General, C. Everett Koop, to begin work on a comprehensive report on AIDS during his 1986 State of the Union address (Shilts, 1987). Back in 1981, when Koop was nominated by Reagan, he was considered a safe choice for Surgeon General, given his fundamentalist religious background and activist background in anti-abortion politics. Feminists and queer rights activists strenuously objected to his nomination, but the Senate easily confirmed Koop's appointment. Acting on Reagan's 1986 request, Koop spent much of the early part of that year interviewing scientists and medical personnel. But much to the surprise of his religious brethren and queer activists, this report was largely grounded in science—not ideology (Shilts, 1986; Vaid, 1995). Bypassing the administration's policy review process, Koop issued a bluntly-worded report that specifically addressed AIDS, how it was contracted, and measures that individuals and the United States could take to stop its transmission. Furthermore, Koop ensured that this report was sent to every household in the United States. For an administration that had devised a "Just say no" response to what it perceived were social and moral vices, the explicit Surgeon's General Report on AIDS (1986) was a reality-based slap in the face.[9]

The Surgeon's General Report was also a reality slap for the United States. By advocating that, "Education concerning AIDS must start at the lowest grade possible," Koop had legitimized sexuality education in public schools, something the Protestant Right had loathed and mobilized against since the 1960s (see Martin, 1996). What the report did was legitimize serious—not hysterical—discussion on AIDS prevention and treatment in the general public and mass media (Shilts, 1987). While some Protestant Right activists latched on to the Report in their calls for mandatory and massive AIDS testing (Vaid, 1995), the Surgeon General's Report on AIDS actually rejected that stating, "The procedure could be unmanageable and cost prohibitive. It can be expected that many who test negative might actually be positive due to recent exposure to the AIDS virus and give a false sense of security to the individual and his/her sexual partners concerning necessary protective behavior" (Koop, 1986, p. 33). The Surgeon General's Report on AIDS stressed that it was certain behaviors (like unprotected anal sex and sharing needles) that placed individuals at risk, not their identities. Given his out-maneuvering of the Reagan administration in getting the Report published and then distributed, Koop became an unlikely hero to queer activists (he was after all, still a Protestant fundamentalist). Nevertheless, activists latched on to the report's straight-forward medical advice and call for explicit AIDS education, both which ran counter to Reagan administration nostrums (Vaid, 1995).

But activists had been radicalized by both the Reagan administration's deadly negligence in responding to AIDS (Gross, 1993; Vaid, 1995), and the U.S. Supreme Court's decision in *Hardwick* (Eskridge, 1999; Gross, 1993; Murdoch & Price, 2001). The separatism that had divided gay men and lesbians vanished as they focused their energies to collectively battle against a hostile power—their own federal government (Faderman, 1995). New activist organizations flowed from the AIDS crisis including the Gay Men's Health Crisis (GMHC), which focused on serving and advocating for clients with AIDS. From GMHC, came a splinter group, Act-Up or the Aids Coalition to Unleash Power. Act-Up members directly and publicly confronted politicians, health and business and industry officials who they perceived as not responding appropriately to the crisis (Faderman, 1995; Gross, 1993). Much like the earlier GAA zaps of the 1970s, Act-Up staged media-savvy events, from blockading the FDA, to dropping a house-sized condom on notorious homophobe and U.S. Senator Jesse Helms' home in 1991 (Thompson, 1994). Act-Up also generated the most iconic symbol of the era: a black shirt, with a pink triangle emblazoned on the front with white lettering underneath simply stating "Silence=Death" (McGarry & Wasserman, 1998).

One tactic that this new generation of queer activists embraced was that of "outing" or of publicly revealing a "closeted" queer's identity (Gross, 1993). This tactic was highly controversial within various queer communities, since the disclosure was both involuntary and widely publicized. But unlike the McCarthyite witch hunts of the 1950s and 1960s that focused on the lowly civil servant or teacher,[10] the outings of the 1990s targeted politicians and celebrities (Gross, 1993). And no one outed with more enthusiasm or righteous anger than Michelangelo Signorile. Signorile, who had been a gossip columnist, and cut his political teeth in Act-Up. With many of his friends sick and dying, he was not going to be polite in taking closeted queers with real cultural power to task:

> These monster columnists are oppressing us each in their spaces—and half the time they're gay or lesbian themselves! But that doesn't stop them from deeming us invisible, making homophobic remarks or schmoozing and worshiping the people who are killing us.... I say to them, and to every other

writer, columnist, artist, designer, etc., who's whirling with the oppressors: I realize you're oppressed just like the rest of us (which is why you're hiding in the first place). But don't react to it by oppressing us. It's much easier for you to break the chain of homophobia than it is for me. You are in enormous positions of power. Use that. This is a crisis!
SOMETHING HAS TO BE DONE AND IT HAS TO BE DONE FAST. AND YOU ARE IN THE POSITIONS TO DO IT. Be part of the solution instead of part of the problem. If not, then get the fuck out of our way. Because we're coming through and nothing is going to stop us. And if that means we have to pull you down, well, then, have a nice fall (Signorile, 1993, pp. 72-73).

Signorile went on to out billionaire Malcolm Forbes and, most famously, then-Pentagon spokesman and current NBC reporter Pete Williams (Signorile, 1993). At the time of Williams' outing, the U.S. military had a total ban on queer personnel (Shilts, 1993). A military person suspected of being queer could be hauled before an investigatory committee, questioned at length about their personal life, and if deemed "queer" during a hearing, given a dishonorable discharge—which barred them from ever collecting veterans' benefits. Most people who were charged with "homosexuality" opted for an administrative discharge, since the regulations tilted heavily in favor of the prosecution. Those accused of being queer would simply not win if the matter went before a military hearing, and upon conviction, they faced possible jail time (Shilts, 1993). Furthermore, if the queer military person in question had received educational benefits while in-service, the Pentagon was suing for repayment of those educational expenses (Shilts, 1993). That the Pentagon's chief spokesman was a gay man at a time when the military was conducting all-out witch-hunts against personnel suspected of being queer, represented the height of hypocrisy (Alwood, 1996; Gross, 1993; Signorile, 1993).

Signorile's highly visible efforts at outing encouraged other activists and activist organizations to out well-known politicians and media celebrities as well (Alwood, 1996). In particular, OutPost, a possible off-shoot of Queer Nation (see Gross, 1993), ran an outing campaign mimicking the Absolut vodka ads under the theme "Absolutely Queer." And with tongue planted firmly in its organizational cheek, each poster claimed that "Cleaner Closets Today Mean a Better Tomorrow" (Gross, 1993, p. 84). Posters outing Jodie Foster, Merv Griffen, kd lang, Pete Williams and Greg Louganis sprang up all over Manhattan (Gross, 1993).[11] Queer activists across the United States took their cues from this campaign, and began busily outing their closeted sisters and brothers, particularly if they worked for, worked with, or were related to professional homophobes (for example, John Schlafly, son of conservative icon Phyllis Schlafly and Congressman Steve Gunderson, who had a poor record on queer rights—see Gross, 1993)

This generation of activists also embraced the word "queer," which, historically, had been the most vicious of slurs. One of the critiques of the older gay rights movement was it only represented gay White men of a certain class. Consequently, the general public stereotyped all queers as being gay, White men, with sizeable disposable incomes—a patent falsehood (Hutchinson, 1997, 1998, 2000, 2001, 2005; Valdes, 1995, 1997, 1998). Groups like Queer Nation strove to be diverse across the board and embraced the word "queer" for both its provocative power and inclusive nature (Faderman, 1995). Members of Queer Nation and similar activist-minded groups also sought to provoke and perhaps enrage what they saw as the larger, more complacent, and isolationist gay and lesbian communities (Faderman, 1995; Gross, 1993; Signorile, 1993). These activists were sick of polite and patient politics and simply were not going to take any crap or attempts at mollification—by anyone, queer or nonqueer (Faderman, 1995).

This is when, at the very beginning of the outing movement, that I gathered up my miniscule courage and came out, first and most importantly to myself, and then ever-so-slowly to the rest of the world.[12] I had been gently prodded for a few years by a sympathetic colleague, Nancy, whose sister was a lesbian. Nancy happily began supplementing my reading with works by Mary Daly, Olga Broumas and Adrienne Rich, who were far more interesting than St. Thomas Aquinas or tomes on flute pedagogy and church music. But the final push that got me out of the closet was the murder of a cousin—a shocking and horrific act that forced me to sit down and take a hard look at my life. In the harsh light of John's murder, I asked myself a very simple question: "If I died tomorrow, could I say I've ever loved anyone?" The answer was "no." That realization was intolerable. And so, a sequence of changes began. Out with the gravity-defying, Iowa "big hair," in with a short hair cut. Out with the wardrobe full of recital dresses, in with more sensible, comfortable and *less expensive* attire. Out with the music career, in with a doctoral program in educational theory and policy. Out with endless slogging over music history and music theory, in with happily obsessing about politics, policy and history. Out with teaching flute lessons every Saturday morning, in with trolling the university library every weekend for various historical queer books and journal articles. Out with trying to live my life as it *should be*, in with living my life *as it is*. Out with living in Des Moines, Iowa, which had on-going and scary gay-bashings, in with living in State College, Pennsylvania, which had on-going and scary gay-bashings (oh well). This entire process took about eight years, from when I started being gently nudged (Fall

1988), to coming out to myself (July 1990), to coming out professionally (Fall 1996).

Like many of my queer compatriots at Penn State, I largely used my doctoral program to help me come out. I began to read anything and everything related to queers and queer history to learn that: (1) I was not and had *never* been alone; (2) Queers and queer activism had a long history; (3) Homophobia and hatred towards queer people also had a long history; and (4) We all have some measure of power to change our very own corners of the world. Perhaps what was most profound was the new awareness of how deeply ingrained the lies about queer people are in the United States (D'Emilio, 1983), and particularly how these lies shape public education (DuBuisson, 2006; Silin, 1995). In a happier vein, I began to seriously date for the first time in my life. Because of the sheer terror that had kept me completely "in the closet," I had largely missed out and/or escaped much of the adolescent "rites of passage." At age 27, I quickly made up for over a decade of missed developmental experiences.

Yet, the final the mask of passing with supposed nonqueer respectability had yet been pried off my face (see Goffman, 1959, 1963). While I would not out-right lie, I continued to hedge on revealing personal information. But this became an increasingly complex chore, largely because I would never exactly remember how much information I had told to whom. On occasion, this confusion would cause me to inadvertently out myself. During this time (1991-1996), I was being "selectively out," or "covering" my orientation in many instances—not lying, but not exactly dissuading people if they thought I was nonqueer either (Yoshino, 2002).

Furthermore, at the beginning of my research career (1991), I was not out professionally, although I had completely changed fields. I did not feel safe to be "out" to colleagues—much less pursue an avowedly queer research agenda, although I was reading as much queer history as I could get my hands on. Instead, I took an oblique tact, focusing my initial work on various right-wing political movements, the politics of education and public school policy (Lugg, 1996). Since the political right-wing strenuously objected to queers and queer civil rights, as well as making queer erasure a central component of their public school agenda (Herman, 1998; Lugg, 1998), it was an indirect way of working on what I cared most about. Eventually, that final mask would fall away too, once I moved to a state with strong civil rights protections for queers—New Jersey. Given the green-light by a sympathetic and supportive new colleague, in the fall of 1996 I happily embraced queer work as part of my research agenda.[13]

QUEERING THEORY (1990S-2000S)

"We're here, we're queer, get used to it!"
"We're here! We're queer! We're absolutely FABULOUS!"—Queer rights chants of the 1990s.

Given the high-energy and media savvy of the 1990s queer rights activists, the academy began to embrace an explicitly queer approach to theorizing (Pinar, 1998). From literature and sociology, to law and education and beyond, queer understandings of every aspect of human existence was examined and re-examined from various queer lenses. Influenced by postmodernity (Sullivan, 2003; Wilchins, 2004), the central assumption is that all identity is socially constructed, that is race is a social construction, gender is a social construction, and sexual orientation is a social construction and so forth (see Sullivan, 2003; Wilchins, 2004). That said, how these various identities are perceived in a racist, sexist, homophobic, classist, etc., country can have very real consequences (Hutchinson, 1997, 1999, 2000, 2001; Valdes, 1995, 1997, 1998; Wilchins, 2004). Furthermore, queer theory posits that we have multiple identities that respond to and with the specific social context of the moment (Wilchins, 2004), as well as interact with each other (Hutchinson, 1997, 1999, 2000, 2001; Valdes, 1995, 1997, 1998). In some cases, race is more prominent than orientation, in other situations class is the most important component of identity, in others, it is the intersection of race and gender, for example, the lived experiences of women of color (Crenshaw, 1991; Harris, 1990; Hutchinson, 1997, 1998, 2000, 2001, 2005; Valdes, 1995, 1997, 1998). The practical implications are that our very understandings of whom we see ourselves to be are constantly being negotiated and re-negotiated in highly dynamic and interactive environments (Wilchins, 2004). Thus, to a large extent, identity is always up-for-grabs.

The death of neat identity dichotomies triggered by queer theory's and postmodernity's ascendancies not only rattled nonqueer academics' scholarly cages (Wilchins, 2004; Yoshino, 2002), but disturbed every day relationships. In the span of one week, two fellow and nonqueer doc students and I each managed to "flunk" the identity test, when we tried to participate in various student organizations. Over a shared lunch, we discovered that Barbara had been told she was not Native American enough, Marie was informed she was not African American enough, and similarly I was not lesbian enough to "really belong" to our respective student groups. Obviously, other aspects of our respective identities were sociologically "drowning out" what our would-be compatriots assumed to be our only defining feature. Of course, each of us, like every other human being had multiple dimensions to our identities (Hutchinson, 1997, 1998, 2000, 2001, 2005; Sullivan, 2003; Valdes, 1995, 1997, 1998; Wilchins, 2004).

But at that time and place, identity, at least at the organizational level, was tightly dichotomous. You either *were* one specific identity—or you *were not*. Holding multiple identities at once was too threatening to those schooled on having one, solitary and *essential*, identity. At least the three of us shared a good laugh about our supposed deficits.

At that time, I found queer theory to have insightful and creative explanatory power in how human beings made decisions ranging from voting behavior to artistic taste (Lugg, 1999). I loved how it could turn common-place understandings inside-out and upside-down, its inclusivity (lesbian, gay, bisexual, trans, intersexual people all are included), its fierce anti-essentialism (particularly Queer Legal Theory, see Valdes, 1995) and its assumption that all identity is multifaceted and unstable (Pinar, 1998; Sullivan, 2003). But my enthusiasm also led to real-life disruptions. In the spring of 1996, a dear friend and colleague, who had long considered herself a radical lesbian-feminist, was appalled by my theoretical "dalliances" and asked me, "What's a nice dyke like you embracing this postmodern crap?" She saw the advent of queer theory, and "queer-dom" in general, as tangible threats to her long-standing identity. To a point, she was correct. Consequently, our friendship ruptured beyond all repair. I was clearly *not* a lesbian—by her definition, so I could no longer be her friend. It was a hard lesson to learn that I had firmly landed in her *"not"* category and that theory *really* matters.

Queer theory, as well as any scholarship on queer people, came late to educational research when compared to fields of literature and history. As William Pinar explained in 1998, "Homophobia (not to mention heterosexism) is especially intense in the field of education, a highly conservative and often reactionary field" (p. 2). When queer activism finally found its way into U.S. public schools, beginning in the 1990s, teachers and administrators were ill-prepared and largely hostile towards student demands for a Gay-Straight Alliances (GSAs), or that the prom be desegregated vis-à-vis queers, or that dress codes be revisited (Woog, 1995). The research found and continues to find public schools to be violently hostile towards queer students and contemptuous of queer adults, with adults ignoring or even on some occasions sanctioning the emotional and physical abuse of queer children (Kosciw & Diaz, 2006; Kozik-Rosabal, 2000; Pascoe, 2007; Walters & Hayes, 1998).

And yet, beginning in the 1990s, the federal government unintentionally opened up a space for queer children attending U.S. public schools, where they could address issues of orientation, if at times, in a highly circumscribed fashion. In 1990 in *Board of Education v. Mergens*, the U.S. Supreme Court upheld the Constitutionality of the Equal Access Act. Enacted in 1984, this federal law requires that any public school that maintains a "limited public forum," must allow student-initiated noncurricular clubs to meeting during noninstructional time. Originally, the law was intended to protect the formation of student Bible clubs, but it was so broadly written that it basically permitted any student-initiated club so long as it did not disrupt the orderly running of the school (MacGillivray, 2004). To some extent, I would argue that *the EAA was unintentionally queered by the U.S. Supreme Court*, which would be a classic queer theory reading of the law.

Consequently, Gay Straight Alliances or GSAs are noncurricular clubs that have sprung up across the United States in the wake of the *Mergens* decision (Kosciw & Diaz, 2006; MacGillivray, 2004). Like other school-based clubs, they are protected by the federal Equal Access Act of 1984. GSA's have been highly controversial since their inception, largely because they are federally protected, *queer-positive* student clubs (Lugg, 2003b; Pascoe, 2007; Rehder, 2001). Furthermore, school districts that have tried to ban the clubs out-right have run into a legal buzz-saw, repeatedly losing in federal court (Lugg, 2006). For a brief time, the Salt Lake City public school district tried to ban all student-related noncurricular activities, but that eliminated football—a politically problematic stance. Furthermore, in the case of Salt Lake City, Utah, the students who were lobbying for the GSA eventually restructured the organization into a curricular-related club, which made it impossible to ban (see Lugg, 2003b).

However, for all of their appeal for providing queer students "safe-space," school-related queer clubs have their drawbacks. They are frequently seen as only for White students (Hong, 2001; McCready 2001), or in some cases, only White women (Pascoe, 2007). Consequently, the politics of "one solitary identity" still is a play in many public schools. Furthermore, some states have responded to the advent of GSAs by requiring students get parental permission to join any extracurricular organization (Johnson, 2007; Lugg in press). These laws technically do not target GSAs, however, given the high degree of parental disapproval and/or violence targeting their queer children, requiring parental permission might well be an effective means to further limit the popular student appeal of GSAs (Johnson, 2007; Lugg, in press).

At the close of the twentieth century, there had been numerous improvements to the status of queer U.S. citizens, with some states enacting civil rights protections in their state constitutions, and some states amended their public school codes to protect queer kids who attended public schools (Lugg, 2006). Additionally, many municipalities enacted "domestic partnership" ordinances, which provided limited legal protections for queer partners. And with the introduction of antiretroviral medications in 1996, AIDS was becoming less lethal disease, although its management remains highly complex. Yet, queers would retain our legal stigma as we moved into the new century. This essay now turns towards a brief discussion of contemporary politics vis-à-vis queer Americans, the politics of education, and some concluding observations.

CONCLUSION: QUEERS AND THE POLITICS OF DIFFERENTIATED CITIZENSHIP

> [The] ... public school entrance is often reported as the occasion of stigma learning, the experience sometimes coming very precipitously on the first day of school, with taunts, teasing, ostracism, and fights. (Goffman, 1963, p. 33)

Currently, the legal status of U.S. queer citizens largely depends upon the state in which we reside. While the U.S. Supreme Court decriminalized all consensual sodomy in 2003, in *Lawrence v. Texas*, not a single state that formerly criminalized consensual sodomy has repealed these unconstitutional laws. As a result, queer identity remains criminalized in 14 states (Lugg, 2006). Furthermore, none of these states have revised their public school codes to comport with *Lawrence*, meaning that queer educators risk their licenses if they publicly come out, since they would become "statutory criminals" (see DuBuisson, 2006; Leslie, 2000; Lugg, 2006). Additionally, these un-reconstructed laws make it very difficult for any sympathetic nonqueer educator to directly address queer issues in their public school classrooms since they could be accused of "promoting criminality" (Lugg, 2003b; 2006).

By contrast, other American states have moved in more progressive directions. In 2003, the Massachusetts' state supreme court ruled that the state could not discriminate against same sex marriages, although it also ruled that the marriage requirements only pertained to in-state residents. This nonresident ban was lifted in 2008 by newly elected governor Deval Patrick. The state of Connecticut's supreme court also invalidated its civil union law, noting that a separate legal status for gays and lesbians was untenable under the Connecticut constitution. Furthermore, in May of 2008, the California state supreme court, in a 4-3 decision, ruled that that state's referendum banning same-sex marriage violated the state's constitution. This decision was promptly overturned by a state-wide constitutional referendum in November 2008. The entire matter is now before the California supreme court--again. At present, while "gay marriages" cannot be conducted in New York, the state now recognizes marriages contracted elsewhere as does New Mexico. Additionally, New Jersey, New Hampshire, and Vermont have a civil union mechanism for same-sex partners, while Oregon, Washington, DC, Washington State, Maine and

Hawaii have some form of domestic partnership available for same-sex partners (see HRC, 2008).

Nevertheless, at the federal level, the Defense of Marriage Act (1996)—which forbids federal recognition of same-sex marriages, civil unions, and/or domestic partnerships—remains in force, at least for now.[14] This law also allows individual states to ignore these relationships if they are not sanctioned by a specific state in question. On a practical level, this means I am currently paying an "out queer" federal tax penalty for covering my partner on my state benefits health plan. The federal government counts these benefits as additional earned income since it refuses to recognize our civil union granted by our home state. Furthermore, since the federal government and individual states can abrogate our legal contract because we are queer, we could be denied hospital visitation rights in queer-hostile states. This is a real concern since we visit my partner's family in South Carolina every winter, because South Carolina still criminalizes queer identity. If we had a child, one of us could be denied recognition as a parent in queer-hostile states, literally making one of us a "legal stranger" to our child (see Polikoff, 1990; Richman, 2002), although these parental rights would be recognized in our home state. And finally, if my partner were a non U.S. citizen, she would not be able to apply for citizenship by dint of our civil union, since again, the federal government does not see the civil union as a valid legal contract (Pfitsch, 2006).

One way to explain the current political and legal environment for queers is to point out these structural inequalities force queers into a lesser form citizenship—or a form of *differentiated citizenship*. While current political theorists (Kymlicka, 1995; Young, 1900; 2000) have a quite different conception of differentiated citizenship—where historic difference is positively attributed under the law—drawing on U.S. history and case law, many U.S. citizens have experienced second, third or even bottom-tier citizenship rights when compared to those held by propertied, non-queer, White, males who happened to be Protestant (Eisenstein, 1988; Irons, 1999; Kairys, 1998; Leslie, 2005; MacKinnon, 1989). For purposes of this discussion, *differentiated citizenship is a hierarchy of political and legal rights based on group characteristics (like being female or being Muslim) that have been historically stigmatized in the United States.*

The current regime of differentiated citizenship for queers largely plays out on a largely dichotomous basis. You are either one specific identity--or you are not (Crenshaw, 1991; Harris, 1990; Hutchinson, 1997, 1998, 2000, 2001, 2005; Valdes, 1995, 1997, 1998; Yoshino, 2002). For queers, this means regardless of any other aspect of our identities, embracing the label of "the queer," because of its historic stigma (see Goffman, 1963), will override most, if not all, other signifiers of identity (see Hutchinson, 1997; 2005).[15] Additionally, with the variation in laws and regulations concerning queers, the degree of significance changes from state-to-state. To be really concrete, being queer person in South Carolina, a state that officially hates queers to this day, is far more perilous than being queer person in Vermont, which has specific civil rights protections.

Although queer identity has been de-pathologized by various medical and psychological associations, and recently decriminalized by the U.S. Supreme Court, the lesser-citizenship is imposed for religious reasons. The on-going political battles involving "gay marriage" exemplify that point. Opponents repeatedly invoke quasi-religious to full-blown religious arguments in justifying this specific curtailment in civil rights. But marriage in the United States, to be valid, is a civil matter--not religious. While one can be married by a divine, if one does not hold a state-issued marriage certificate, religion-only marriages, by definition, are legally invalid. Additionally, millions of nonqueer Americans have been married in civil or religion-free ceremonies, including Protestant Right stalwarts Sarah and Todd Palin (Stritof & Stritof, 2008). Nevertheless, because queer Americans are viewed by many individuals in the larger public as religious heretics (see Diamond, 1998), we are subject to real curtailments of civil rights and liberties, as well as verbal and physical assaults if we "step out of our place" (see Thomas, 1992; Pascoe, 2007). Like other Americans who experience differentiated citizenship, we are constantly stereotyped and stigmatized by a culture that has historically viewed us as threats to the very health of the nation state (D'Emilio, 1983; Diamond, 1998; Johnson, 2004).

Queer children are particularly endangered by a society that loathes queers, and in some locales, this hate is state-sanctioned (see Lugg, 2006). Many public schools continue to maintain dangerously homophobic and occasionally lethal environments. Queer kids experience the highest rates of assaults, verbal taunts, bullying, and the like, with transgendered children at the greatest risk for ill-treatment in public schools (Arriola, 1998; Brittenham, 2004; Kosciw & Diaz, 2006; Pascoe, 2007; Robson, 2001). Teachers and administrators can also display reactions ranging from honest cluelessness, to dangerous indifference, to overt hostility towards their queer students (Kozik-Rosabal, 2000; Kumashiro, 2002; Lipkin, 2004; Lugg, 2003b, 2006; Pascoe, 2007). Originally, I was going to address the February 2008 murder of Lawrence King by a classmate while at his Oxnard, CA public school in this essay. However, I find that I remain paralyzed with rage. Perhaps in time I will find the words. Using a fast Queer Legal Theory analysis, however, I will note the lack of press coverage of his February 2008 murder (when compared to the crucifixion of Matthew Shepard 10 years ago), is probably due to Larry's multiple identities at play: child of color, poor, gay and possibly transgendered. His identities were far more complex, dynamic and nuanced than what the typical media narrative could fathom.

Queer public school employees, while unlikely to be beaten or assaulted at work, still face incurring the wrath of their communities and school boards (Fraynd & Capper, 2003; Lugg, 2003a; Tooms, 2007). Even in ostensibly progressive states, there is enormous pressure on queer school personnel to remain closeted for fear of igniting a local political backlash (DuBuisson, 2006).[16] Furthermore, public school leaders feel very constrained regarding their identities, so they remain closeted and largely silent in hopes of being "The Right Kind of Queer"—never, *ever* seen or heard as a public queer (Tooms, 2007). Ironically, queer educational leaders could exercise the power they hold to improve the lives of the queer children in their buildings. Yet the fear of receiving the "pink triangle" stigma keeps many silent and complicit with their own oppression and oppressors (Fraynd & Capper, 2003; Tooms 2007; see Signorile, 2003 for a more general discussion). Consequently both the official and hidden public school curricula, as well as the larger political and legal environments, will continue to enforce many norms of differentiated citizenship vis-à-vis queers within the public school's walls.

That said, since the late 1940s, there have been numerous steps in making public schools and the larger U.S. culture less officially hostile for queers. And in general, queers are no longer routinely jailed, thrown out of school and/or thrown into mental institutions—though these occasionally still happen. The political climate is far less hostile and this is real progress. However, a less hateful climate still does little in the way in promoting meaningful equity and social justice for queers on a daily basis. My queer sisters and brothers remain endangered, our lives subjected to the whims of the ever-shifting political winds. Until the vast majority of nonqueer Americans are willing to relinquish the advantages that differentiated citizenship provides them, the United States and U.S. public schools will be oppressive-to-dangerous places for queers.

ACKNOWLEDGMENT

This chapter originally appeared in *The Journal of School Leadership* (volume 16, issue 2.)

Table 3.1. Timeline of Major Events in U.S. Queer History

Year	Event
1948	Harry Hay begins to theorize regarding the political status of "the homosexual." Begins to seek out like-minded queers to form an organization.
1948	*Sexual Behavior in the Human Male* published by Alfred Kinsey.
1950	The Mattachine Society is founded by Harry Hay and Chuck Rowland. It is the first "homophile" organizations of the modern era. Daughters of Bilitis (DOB) is founded in 1955 by Del Martin and Phyllis Lyon.
1953	*Sexual Behavior in the Human Female* published by Alfred Kinsey
1957	The adjustment of the male overt homosexual. *Journal of Projective Techniques, 21*, 18-31, by Evelyn Hooker. This is the first published research article demonstrating that there was no mental pathology related to orientation.
1965	First pro-gay picket of the White House.
1969	Stonewall Rebellion. GLF and GAA are quickly formed.
1970s	Roughly half the states throw out their laws banning sodomy.
1973	LGB identity is depathologized by the American Psychiatric Association
1977	Harvey Milk is the first out gay man to be elected to major political office in the United States.
1977	Ballot initiatives pass in several locales banning legal protections against discrimination for queer people.
1978	California Proposition 6 is defeated.
1978	Harvey Milk is assassinated 3 weeks after leading the fight against Proposition 6.
Late 1970s	AIDS comes to the United States.
1980	Ronald Reagan elected President. Age of conservative national governance begins
1980s	Two states include gay men, lesbians and bisexuals in their civil rights statutes.
1985	Rock Hudson dies from AIDS.
1986	Surgeon General's Report on the AIDS epidemic.
1986	The U.S. Supreme Court rules in *Bowers v. Hardwick* that states are free to criminalize consensual sodomy. These laws have historically criminalized queer identity.
Late 1980s	The outing closeted queers begins.
1993	President Clinton signs the military gay ban known as "Don't ask, don't tell."
1990s	Six states add specific civil rights protections for LGB people.
1990s	Five states have their sodomy laws judicially invalidated; three more states repeal these laws.
Mid-1990s	Gay-Straight Alliances (GSAs) grow in popularity. These are queer positive public school student groups. They are protected under the 1984 Equal Access Act.
1996	Protease Inhibitors are made available. Their advent greatly reduces the death rate from AIDS.
1996	President Bill Clinton signs the "Defense of Marriage Act."
1996	The U.S. Supreme Court, in *Roemer v. Evans*, rules that queers cannot be stripped of their civil rights merely because they are a despised class.

(Table continues on next page)

Table 3.1. (Continued)

1998	Matthew Shepard is crucified.
1999	California passes a statewide "domestic partnership" bill.
2000	Vermont permits partnered queers to form legal partnerships under the rubric of "civil unions."
2000s	Seven states pass civil rights protections for LGB or LGBT people.
2000s	Three states have their sodomy laws judicially invalidated; One more state repeals its laws.
2003	The U.S. Supreme Court, in *Lawrence v. Texas*, invalidates all laws banning consensual sodomy in the United States.
2003	The Commonwealth of Massachusetts sanctions same-sex marriage.
2003	New Jersey passes a statewide "domestic partnership bill.
2005	Connecticut passes a statewide civil union bill.
2006	The New Jersey Supreme Court invalidates the domestic partnership bill as violative of the equal protection clause of the state constitution. The legislature then passes a civil union law.
2007	The State of Washington passes a statewide domestic partnership law.
2008	Lawrence King is murdered by a classmate.
2008	The California Supreme Court permits "gay marriage" which is then repealed by a statewide ballot initiative.
2008	The Connecticut Supreme Court throws out Civil Union legislation and sanctions same-sex marriage.
2008	New Hampshire passes a civil union bill.
2008	Oregon and Maryland pass a domestic partnership bill.

Table 3.2. Queer Histories, Artifacts, and Film Documentaries Consulted

Alwood, E. (1996). *Straight news: Gays, lesbians, and the news media*. New York, NY: Columbia University Press.

Blasius, M., & Phelan, S. (Eds.). (1997). *We are everywhere: A historical sourcebook of gay and lesbian politics*. New York, NY: Routledge.

Blount, J. M. (2005). *Fit to teach: Same-sex desire, gender and school work in the twentieth century*. Albany: State University of New York Press.

Blount, J. M. (2003). Homosexuality and school superintendents: A brief history. *Journal of School Leadership, 13*(1), 7-26.

Blount, J. M. (1998). *Destined to rule the schools*. Albany: State University of New York Press.

Brier, J. (2006). "Save our kids, keep AIDS out:" Anti-AIDS activism and the legacy of community control in Queens, New York. *Journal of Social History, 39*(4), 965-987.

Bullough, V. L. (2002). *Before Stonewall: Activists for gay and lesbian rights in historical context*. Binghamton, NH: Harrington Park Press.

D'Emilio, J. (1983). *Sexual politics, sexual communities: The making of a homosexual minority in the United States, 1940-1970*. Chicago: University of Chicago Press

(Table continues on next page)

Table 3.2. (Continued)

D'Emilio, J. (2002). *The world turned: Essays on gay history, politics, and culture*. Durham, NC: Duke University Press.

Duberman, M. (1994). *Stonewall*. New York, NY: Plume.

Epstein, R. (1983). *The times of Harvey Milk*. United States. Black Sand Productions.

Eskridge, Jr., W.N. (1994). Democracy, Kulturkampf, and the Apartheid of the closet. *Vanderbilt Law Review, 50*, 419-443.

Faderman, L. (1991). *Odd girls and twilight lovers: A history of lesbian life in twentieth-century America*. New York, NY: Penguin Books.

Freedman, (1987). "Uncontrolled desires": The responses to the sexual psychopath, 1920-1960. *Journal of American History, 74*(1), 83-106.

Gross, L. (1993). *Contested closets: The politics and ethics of outing*. Minneapolis: University of Minnesota Press.

Jay, K. (1999). *Tales of the lavender menace: A memoir of liberation*. New York, NY: Basic Books.

Johnson, D. K. (2004) *The lavender scare: The Cold War persecution of gays and lesbians in the federal government*. Chicago: University of Chicago Press.

Kepner, J. (1998). *Rough news-daring news: 1950s' pioneer gay press journalism*. New York, NY: Harrington Park Press.

Marcus, E. (1992). *Marking history: The struggle for gay and lesbian equal rights, 1945 - 1990*. New York, NY: Harper Collins.

Marotta, T. (1981). *The politics of homosexuality*. Boston: Houghton Mifflin.

McGarry, M., & Wasserman, F. (1998). *Becoming visible: An illustrated history of lesbian and gay life in twentieth-century America*. New York, NY: Penguin Books.

Milk, H. (1978). The hope speech. In M. Blasius & S. Pehlan, *We are everywhere: A historical sourcebook of gay and lesbian politics* (pp. 51-53). New York, NY: Routledge.

Murdoch, J., & Price, D. (2001). *Courting justice: Gay men and lesbians v. the Supreme Court*. New York, NY: Basic Books.

Scagliotti, J., & Schiller, G. (1986). *Before Stonewall: The making of a gay and lesbian community* [Motion picture]. United States: Before Stonewall.

Sears, J. T. (1997). *Lonely hunters: An oral history of lesbian and gay southern life, 1948-1968*. Boulder, CO: Westview Press.

Shilts, R. (1982). *The mayor of Castro Street: The life and times of Harvey Milk*. New York, NY: St. Martin's Press.

Shilts, R. (1987). *And the band played on: Politics, people and the AIDS epidemic*. New York, NY: St. Martin's Press.

Shilts, R. (1993). *Conduct unbecoming: Gays & lesbians in the U.S. military*. New York, NY: St. Martin's Press.

Signorile, M. (1993). *Queer in America: Sex, the media, and the closets of power*. New York, NY: Random House.

Teal, D. (1971). *The gay militants: How gay liberation began in America, 1969-1971*. New York, NY: St. Martin's Press.

Terry, J. (1999). *An American obsession: Science, medicine and homosexuality in modern society*. Chicago: University of Chicago Press.

Thompson, M. (1994). *Long road to freedom: The Advocate history of the gay and lesbian movement*. New York, NY: St. Martin's Press.

Weiss, A., & Schiller, A. (1988). *Before Stonewall: The making of a gay and lesbian community*. Tallahassee, FL: Naiad Press.

NOTE

1. Hay was eventually thrown out of the CPUSA for being queer. At the time, BOTH the CPUSA and the U.S. federal government viewed homosexuals as a security risk, because of their supposed vulnerability to blackmail. Ironically, the CPUSA hated queers as much as the FBI of J. Edgar Hoover, whose own sexual orientation was indeterminate (see Johnson, 2004).
2. Generally, the police used great violence in raiding gay bars. Trans men and women tended to be beaten as well as sexually assaulted, and gay and lesbian patrons were beaten and sometimes sexually assaulted. Those who were later charged with disorderly conduct had their names, where they were arrested, their home addresses, and places of employment published in their local newspapers, an invitation for future vigilante violence. Furthermore, since identity was equated with criminality, queers and little legal recourse if they were abused by police officers or other "concerned citizens" (Duberman, 1994; Eskridge, 1994; Jay, 1999; Marotta, 1981; Scagliotti & Schiller, 1986; Teal, 1971)
3. This cooperative still exists, having survived for over 50 years.
4. My youngest brother and I were probably the only elementary students who watched nearly all of the congressional Watergate hearings, from start to finish. Our mother insisted that we watch history unfold. While some of it was ungodly boring (particularly for an 8-year-old and 10-year-old), I remember vividly watching Barbara Jordon verbally "peel" a hapless Nixon-era flunky. The only person I had seen so thoroughly berate an individual for "screwing up" was my mother's mother—who was a career English teacher. The low-pitched and slowly presented verbal paddling was painfully familiar. Needless to say, I was completely impressed by Jordon.
5. My mother's family members were "Jeffersonian Democrats" and union members. My father's family were small businessmen and "good government" Republicans. My father's father firmly believed FDR was the closest thing to the Anti-Christ that the United States had seen. By contrast, my Grandmother Pearson, who was a widow and career educator, attended the 1936 Democratic convention. She also graces the cover of "Fit to Teach" (see Blount, 2005). Where they all could agree was on religion: All were members of the First Baptist Church (American Baptist Convention) of Knoxville, PA. The church is long defunct.
6. Parents in these community districts later sued the city for the right to ban students with AIDS. They eventually lost the court case (see Schwarz & Schaffer, 1985).
7. An AIDS magazine or *zine* that appeared in the early 1990s confronted the stigma of AIDS head-on. It's name? *Diseased Pariah News* (see McGarry & Wasserman, 1998, p. 237).
8. Hardwick was most likely entrapped by a rabidly homophobic police officer. Legal scholar Kendall Thomas demonstrates that Hardwick's arrest was the culmination of ongoing harassment by the arresting officer (Thomas, 1992). Furthermore, the houseguest in question was a closeted and married public school teacher from North Carolina, who pleaded

guilty to a reduced charge, paid the fine, and fled back home with his certification in tact (see Murdoch & Price, 2001).
9. The reaction from movement conservatives was predictable. According to Shilts, "Anti-feminist leader Phyllis Schlafly decreed that the sex-ed recommendations represented little more than a call to institute grammar school sodomy classes. Anti-abortion groups went about the business of withdrawing their previous awards to Koop. President Reagan observed his ritualistic silence, though the PHS officials who had approved the report's printing without White House clearance quickly found themselves exiled to bureaucratic Siberia" (1987, p. 588).
10. And the U.S. military continues to hunt queers to this day, under the rubric of "Don't Ask, Don't Tell" (see Lugg, 2003b).
11. The Foster poster text read, "Oscar Winner. Yale Graduate. Ex-Disney Moppet. Dyke." The Griffin poster's text was, "Casino magnate, 'Jeopardy' creator. Ex talk-show host. Fag" (see Gross, 1993, p. 84).
12. Some queer people refuse to be out "on the job," but I was completely radicalized by Signorile who spoke at Penn State in the spring of 1994. In particular, he took White, queer graduate students to task, hammering home the point that we would have enormous privilege and access during our careers. Consequently, we have a duty exploit that privilege to make the world better for *all* of our queer brothers and sisters. As he said, "What's the point of having power if you refuse to use it?"
13. While I was out at work and in my research, I did not come out in the job interview. I was later told by multiple supportive colleagues that doing so would have sunk my candidacy. After I was hired, there was little my less-than-sympathetic colleagues could do. Although I've had a few professional bumps at Rutgers, including a protracted fight over tenure involving my queer research agenda, these headaches have not been with my immediate school, which has been supportive-to-fabulous over the past 12 years. As I now tell anyone who will listen, I get paid a lot of money by the state of NJ to obsess about queers, public schooling and U.S. politics. I seriously doubt anyone has a better job.
14. Presidential Candidate Barak Obama stated he supported a repeal of DOMA, since it was punitive. That said, President Obama has remained mum on this point. He is a most uncomfortable political position, given that his own parents' marriage was illegal in several states at the time they were married. Several courts, including the recent Connecticut supreme court decision, have noted the similarities between state bans on same-sex marriage and the old bans on inter-racial marriage.
15. This presents an acute dilemma for queers of color who can be viewed as betraying their racial and/or ethnic brethren if they come out (see Hutchinson, 1997, 1999, 2000, 2001; Valdes, 1995, 1997, 1998; Wilchins, 2004).
16. In over 12 years of working at Rutgers, I have had numerous queer administrators as students. Yet no one dared or dares to be out professionally. I am not surprised, but am depressed at the ongoing reality of administra-

tive practice in the NY metro when compared with the ideals established in the NJ Law Against Discrimination.

REFERENCES

Alwood, E. (1996). *Straight news: Gays, lesbians, and the news media*. New York, NY: Columbia University Press.

Arriola, E. R. (1998). The Penalties for puppy love: Institutionalized violence against lesbian, gay, bisexual and transgendered youth. *The Journal of Gender, Race & Justice, 1*, 427-470.

Blasius, M., & Phelan, S. (Eds.). (1997). *We are everywhere: A historical sourcebook of gay and lesbian politics*. New York, NY: Routledge.

Blount, J. M. (2005). *Fit to teach: Same-sex desire, gender and school work in the twentieth century*. Albany: State University of New York Press.

Blount, J. M. (2003). Homosexuality and school superintendents: A brief history. *Journal of School Leadership, 13*(1), 7-26

Blount, J.M. (1998). *Destined to rule the schools*. Albany: State University of New York Press.

Brier, J. (2006). "Save our kids, keep AIDS out:" Anti-AIDS activism and the legacy of community control in Queens, New York. *Journal of Social History, 39*(4), 965-987/

Brittenham, K. (2004). Equal protection theory and the Harvey Milk High School: Why anti-subordination alone is not enough. *Boston College Law Review, 45*, 869-904.

Bowers v. Hardwick, 478 U.S. 186 (1986).

Bullough, V. L. (2002). *Before Stonewall: Activists for gay and lesbian rights in historical context*. Binghamton, NH: Harrington Park Press.

Crenshaw, K. W. (1991). Mapping the margins: Intersectionality, identity politics, and violence against women of color. *Stanford Law Review, 43*, 1241.

D'Emilio, J. (1983). *Sexual politics, sexual communities: The making of a homosexual minority in the United States, 1940-1970*. Chicago: University of Chicago Press

D'Emilio, J. (2002). *The world turned: Essays on gay history, politics, and culture*. Durham, NC: Duke University Press.

Dayoff, A. D. (2001). Sodomy laws: The government's vehicle to impose the majority's social values. *William Mitchell Law Review, 27*, 1863-1894.

Detwiler, F. (2000). *Standing of the premises of God: The Christian Right's fight to redefine American's public schools*. New York, NY: New York University Press.

Diamond, S. (1995). *Roads to dominion: Right-wing movements and political power in the United States*. New York, NY: Guilford.

Diamond, S. (1998). *Not by politics alone: The enduring influence of the Christian Right*. New York, NY: Guilford.

Duberman, M. (1994). *Stonewall*. New York, NY: Plume.

DuBuisson, E. (2006). Teaching from the closet: Freedom of expression and out-speech by public school teachers. *University of North Carolina Law Review, 85*, 301-348.

Eisenstein, Z. R. (1988). *The female body and the law.* Berkeley: University of California Press.
Epstein, R. (1983). *The times of Harvey Milk.* Black Sand Productions.
Eskridge, W. N., Jr. (2001). The constitution of equal citizenship for a good society: The relationship between obligations and rights of citizens. *Fordham Law Review, 69,* 1721-1751.
Eskridge, W. N., Jr. (1999). *Gaylaw: Challenging the Apartheid of the closet.* Cambridge, MA: Harvard University Press.
Eskridge, W. N., Jr. (1994). Democracy, Kulturkampf, and the Apartheid of the closet. *Vanderbilt Law Review, 50,* 419-443.
Faderman, L. (1991). *Odd girls and twilight lovers: A history of lesbian life in twentieth-century America.* New York, NY: Penguin Books.
Fraynd, D. J., & Capper, C. A. (2003). "Do you have any idea who you just hired?!?" A study of open and closeted sexual minority K-12 administrators. *Journal of School Leadership,13,* 86-124
Freedman, (1987). "Uncontrolled desires": The responses to the sexual psychopath, 1920-1960. *Journal of American History, 74*(1), 83-106.
Frye, M. (1981). Lesbian feminism and the gay rights movement: Another view of male supremacy, another separatism. In M. Blasius & S. Pehlan (Eds.), *We are everywhere: A historical sourcebook of gay and lesbian politics* (pp. 499-510). New York, NY: Routledge.
Goffman, E. (1959). *The presentation of self in everyday life.* New York, NY: Anchor Books.
Goffman, E. (1963). *Stigma: Notes on the management of spoiled identity.* New York, NY: Touchstone Books.
Gross, L. (1993). *Contested closets: The politics and ethics of outing.* Minneapolis, MN: University of Minnesota Press.
Haberman, A. (2005). Into the wilderness: Ronald Reagan, Bob Jones University, and the political education of the Christian Right. *The Historian, 67*(2), 234-53.
Harbeck, K.M. (1997). *Gay and lesbian educators: Personal freedoms, public constraints.* Malden, MA: Amethyst.
Harris, A. P. (1990). Race and essentialism in feminist legal theory. *Stanford Law Review, 42,* 581-615.
Harris, N., Dyson, M. R. (2004). Safe rules or gays' schools? The dilemma of sexual orientation segregation in public education. *University of Pennsylvania Journal of Constitutional Law, 7,* 183-218.
Herman, D. (1998). *The antigay agenda: Orthodox vision and the Christian right.* Chicago: University of Chicago Press.
Hong, A. H. (2001). There are no gay Koreans. In K. K. Kumashiro (Ed.), *Troubling intersections of race and sexuality: Queer students of color and anti-oppressive education* (pp. 109-111). Lanham, MD: Rowman & Littlefield.
Human Rights Campaign. (2008, June 3). Relationship recognition in the U.S. Retrieved from http://www.hrc.org/documents/Relationship_Recognition_Laws_Map.pdf
Hutchinson, D. L. (1997). Out yet unseen: A racial critique of Gay and Lesbian Legal Theory and political discourse. *Connecticut Law Review, 29,* 561-645.

Hutchinson, D. L. (1999). Ignoring the sexualization of race: Heteronormativity, Critical Race Theory and anti-racist politics. *Buffalo Law Review, 47,* 1-116.

Hutchinson, D. L. (2000). "Gay rights" for "gay Whites"? Race, sexual identity, and equal protection discourse. *Cornell Law Review, 85,* 1358-1391.

Hutchinson, D. L. (2001). "Intersectionality," "multidimensionality," and the development of an adequate theory of subordination. *Michigan Journal of Race & Law, 6,* 285-317.

Hutchinson, D. L. (2005). The majoritarian difficulty: Affirmative action, sodomy, and Supreme Court politics. *Law and Inequality, 23,* 1-93

Irons, P. (1999). *A people's history of the Supreme Court.* New York, NY: Penguin Press.

Jay, K. (1999). *Tales of the lavender menace: A memoir of liberation.* New York, NY: Basic Books.

Johnson, K. (2007, March 17). Utah sets rigorous rules for school clubs, and gay ones may be target. *The New York Times.* Retrieved from http://www.nytimes.com/2007/03/17/education/17utah.html?ex=1331784000&en=25a20fdf6f61b10b&ei=5090&partner=rssuserland&emc=rss.

Johnson, D. K. (2004) *The lavender scare: The Cold War persecution of gays and lesbians in the federal government.* Chicago: University of Chicago Press.

Johnson, S.D. (1987). Factors related to intolerance of AIDS victims. *Journal for the Scientific Study of Religion, 26*(1), 105-110.

Kairys, D. (1998). Introduction. In D. Kairys (Ed.), *The politics of law: A progressive critique* (3rd ed.) New York, NY: Basic Books.

Kepner, J. (1998). *Rough news-daring news: 1950s' pioneer gay press journalism.* New York, NY: Harrington Park Press.

Koop, C. E. (1986). *Surgeon general's report on acquired immune deficiency syndrome.* Washington, DC: U.S. Public Health Service Public Affairs Office.

Kosciw, J. G., & Diaz, E. M. (2006). *The 2005 National School Climate Survey: The experiences of lesbian, gay, bisexual and transgendered youth in our nation's schools.* New York, NY: Gay, Lesbian and Straight Education Network.

Kozik-Rosabal, G. (2000). "Well, we haven't noticed anything bad going on," said the principal. *Education and Urban Society, 32*(3), 368-389.

Kumashiro, K. (Ed.). (2001). *Troubling intersections of race and sexuality. Queer students of color and anti-oppressive education.* Lanham, MD: Rowman & Littlefield.

Kymlicka, W. (1995) *Multicultural citizenship: A liberal theory of minority rights.* Oxford, Clarendon Press.

Lawrence v. Texas, 539 U.S. 558 (2003).

Leslie, C. R. (2000, Winter). Creating criminals: The injuries inflicted by "unenforced" sodomy laws. *Harvard Civil Rights-Civil Liberties Law Review, 35,* 102-181.

Leslie, C. R. (2005). The importance of *Lawrence* in the context of the Supreme Court's historical treatment of gay litigants. *Widener Law Review, 11,* 189-220.

Lipkin, A. (2004). *Beyond diversity day.* Lanham, MD: Rowman & Littlefield.

Lugg, C. A. (1998, May). The religious right and public education: The paranoid politics of homophobia. *Educational Policy, 12*(3), 267-283.

Lugg, C. A. (1996). *For God and country: Conservatism and American school policy.* New York, NY: Peter Lang.

Lugg, C. A. (1999). *Kitsch: From education to public policy.* New York, NY: Falmer Press.

Lugg, C. A. (2003, January). Our straight-laced administrators: LGBT school administrators, the law, and the assimilationist imperative. *Journal of School Leadership, 13*(1), 51-85.

Lugg, C. A. (2003, February). Sissies, faggots, lezzies and dykes: Gender, sexual orientation and the new politics of education. *Educational Administration Quarterly, 39*(1), 95-134.

Lugg, C. A. (2006, January & March) Thinking about sodomy: Public schools, legal panopticons and queers. *Educational Policy, 20*(1-2), 35-58.

Lugg, C. A. (in press). Letting the bullies win? The politics of educational choice and the politics of stigma at the intersection of queer youth. In T. C. Pedroni (Ed.), *Educational markets and the dispossessed: Agency, identity, and subalternity in unsettling educational times.* Albany: State University of New York Press.

MacGillivray, I. K. (2004). *Sexual orientation & school policy: A practical guide for teachers, administrators and community activists.* Lanham, MD: Rowman & Littlefield.

MacKinnon, C. A. (1989). *Toward a feminist theory of the state.* Cambridge: Harvard University Press.

Marcus, E. (1992). *Marking history: The struggle for gay and lesbian equal rights, 1945-1990.* New York, NY: Harper Collins.

Marotta, T. (1981). *The politics of homosexuality.* Boston: Houghton Mifflin.

McCready, L. (2001). When fitting in isn't an option, or, why Black queer males at a California high school stay away from Project 10. In K. K. Kumashiro (Ed.), *Troubling intersections of race and sexuality: Queer students of color and anti-oppressive education* (pp. 37-53). Lanham, MD: Rowman & Littlefield.

McGarry, M., Wasserman, F. (1998). *Becoming visible: An illustrated history of lesbian and gay life in twentieth-century America.* New York, NY: Penguin Books.

Milk, H. (1978). The hope speech. In M. Blasius & S. Pehlan (Eds.), *We are everywhere: A historical sourcebook of gay and lesbian politics* (pp. 51-53). New York, NY: Routledge.

Murdoch, J., & Price, D. (2001). *Courting justice: Gay men and lesbians v. the Supreme Court.* New York, NY: Basic Books.

Oldfield, D. M. (1996). *The Right and the righteous: The Christian Right confronts the Republican Party.* Lanham, MD: Rowman & Littlefield.

Pascoe, C. J. (2007). *Dude you're a fag!* Berkeley: University of California Press.

Pfitsch, H.V. (2006). Homosexuality in asylum and Constitutional law: Rhetoric of acts and identity. *Law & Sexuality, 15,* 59-89

Pinar, W.F. (1998). Introduction. In W. F. Pinar (Ed.), *Queer theory in education* (pp. 1-47), Mahwah, NJ: Erlbaum.

Polikoff, N. D. (1990). This child does have two mothers: Redefining parenthood to meet the needs of children in lesbian-mother and other nontraditional families. *Georgetown Law Review, 78,* 459-575.

Pollack, J. (1994). Lesbian/gay role models in the classroom: Where are they when you need them? In L. Gerber (Ed.), *Tilting the tower: Lesbians teaching queer subjects* (pp. 131-141). New York, NY: Routledge.

Rehder, T. (2001). Discussion and expression of gender and sexuality in schools. *Georgetown Journal of Gender & the Law, 2*(2), 489-509.

Richman, K. (2002). Lovers, legal strangers, and parents: Negotiating parental and sexual identity in family law. *Law and Society Review, 36,* 285-318.

Robson, R. (2001). Our children: Kids of queer parents & parents & kids who are queer: Looking at sexual minority rights from a different perspective. *Albany Law Review, 64,* 915-948.

Roemer v. Evans, 517 U.S. 620 (1996).

Scagliotti, J., Schiller, G. (1986). *Before Stonewall: The making of a gay and lesbian community* [Motion picture]. United States. Before Stonewall.

Schwarz, F.A.O., Shaffer, F.P. (1985). AIDS in the classroom. *Hofstra Law Review, 14,* 163-191.

Sears, J. T. (1997). *Lonely hunters: An oral history of lesbian and gay southern life, 1948-1968.* Boulder, CO: Westview Press.

Seidman, S. (2003). *The social construction of sexuality.* New York, NY: W.W. Norton.

Shilts, R. (1982). *The mayor of Castro Street: The life and times of Harvey Milk.* New York, NY: St. Martin's Press.

Shilts, R. (1987). *And the band played on: Politics, people and the AIDS epidemic.* New York, NY: St. Martin's Press.

Shilts, R. (1993). *Conduct unbecoming: Gays & lesbians in the U.S. military.* New York, NY: St. Martin's Press.

Shupe, A.,& Stacey, W. A. (1982). *Born again politics and the moral majority: What social surveys really show.* New York, NY: The Edwin Mellon Press.

Signorile, M. (1993). *Queer in America: Sex, the media, and the closets of power.* New York, NY: Random House.

Silin, J.G. (1995). *Sex, death and the education children: Our passion for ignorance in the age of AIDS.* New York, NY: Teachers College Press.

Stritof, S & Stritof, B. (2008). Todd and Sarah Heath Palin marriage profile. About.com. Retrieved from http://marriage.about.com/od/politics/p/sarahpalin.htm.

Sullivan, N. (2003). *A critical introduction to queer theory.* New York, NY: New York University Press.

Teal, D. (1971). *The gay militants: How gay liberation began in America, 1969-1971.* New York, NY: St. Martin's Press.

Terry, J. (1999). *An American obsession: Science, medicine and homosexuality in modern society.* Chicago: University of Chicago Press.

Thomas, K. (1992). Beyond the privacy principle. *Columbia Law Review, 92,* 1431-1516.

Thompson, M. (1994). *Long road to freedom: The Advocate history of the gay and lesbian movement.* New York, NY: St. Martin's Press.

Tooms, A. (2007). The right kind of queer: Fit and the politics of school leadership. *Journal of School Leadership, 17*(5), 601-630.

Valdes, F. (1995). Queers, sissies, dykes, and tomboys: Deconstructing the conflation of "sex," "gender," and "sexual orientation" in Euro-American law and society. *California Law Review, 83,* 3-377.

Valdes, F. (1997). Queer margins, queer ethics: A call to account for race and ethnicity in the law, theory, and politics of "sexual orientation." *Hastings Law Journal, 48*, 1293-1341.

Valdes, F. (1998). Beyond sexual orientation in Queer Legal Theory: Majoritarianism, multidimensionality, and responsibility in social justice scholarship or legal scholars as cultural warriors. *Denver University Law Review, 75*, 1409-1464.

Walters, A. S., & Hayes, D. M. (1998). Homophobia within schools: Challenging the culturally sanctioned dismissal of gay students and colleagues. *Journal of Homosexuality, 35*(2), 1-24.

Weiss, A., & Schiller, A. (1988). *Before Stonewall: The making of a gay and lesbian community.* Tallahassee, FL: Naiad Press.

Wilchins, R. (2004). *Queer theory, gender theory: An instant primer.* Los Angeles: Alyson Publications.

Wilcox, C. (1996). *Onward Christian soldiers? The Religious Right in American politics.* Boulder, CO: Westview.

Woog, D. (1995). *School's out: The impact of gay and lesbian issues on America's schools.* Boston: Alyson Publications.

Yoshino, K. (2002). Covering. *Yale Law Journal, 111*, 769-939.

Young, I.M. (1990). *Justice and the politics of difference.* Princeton, NJ: Princeton University Press.

Young, I.M. (2000). *Inclusion and democracy.* New York, NY: Oxford University Press.

SCENIC OVERLOOK

Chapters 3 and 4

Guidelines for Discussions and Reflection

For school leaders:

1. Compare your reactions to the author's understanding of the importance of the modern queer rights movement.
2. What is your understanding of queer theory? To what extent does queer theory apply to your role as a school leader? Support your claims.
3. What polices and school practices are in place within your school district to support children and/or family members who identify as queer? If policies and school practices are in place, what is the impact on student learning? If not, why are policies and school practices not in place?

For those preparing school leaders:

1. What are your experiences with the queer rights movement?
2. How do these experiences influence how you understand the queer rights movement? How do you incorporate queer theory in your courses?

3. How do aspiring school leaders respond to queer issues facing children, families, and educators in the twenty-first century?
4. How does your preparation program encourage aspiring school leaders to address the lived experiences of children and/or family members who identify as queer?

Catherine Lugg's chapter considered the multidimensional analyses of U.S. public schooling educational policy and the queer rights movement. She navigated the reader through the interplay of her personal identity and the queer rights movement, uncovering the intersections and multidimensionality of identities as well as school policies and practices.

In the next chapter, Gaetane Jean-Marie also explores personal identity as her "fire in the belly" leads her to critique without fear, pushing the boundaries as a Black academe. The author encourages the reader to reconsider the influence of critical pedagogy in an effort to address issues of social justice in school leadership.

CHAPTER 4

"FIRE IN THE BELLY"

Igniting a Social Justice Discourse in Learning Environments of Leadership Preparation

Gaetane Jean-Marie

In my role as a faculty of educational leadership, preparing thoughtful educational leaders for today's schools necessitates ongoing critical reflection on my pedagogical practices to advance social justice (Glickman, 1993). Viewing my classroom as a micro-society, I seek to create a community of learners who engage in activity, discourse, and reflection with the purpose of deepening aspiring leaders' knowledge, cultivating critical thinking, and heightening their sensitivity toward the enactment of social justice across local, regional, and global context (Facione, 2007; Jean-Marie, Normore, & Brooks, 2009; Levitt, 2008).

In this chapter, through an analysis of my evolution as an educator and scholar, I explore how I prepare educators, whether preservice teachers during graduate school or aspiring and practicing school leaders to engage social justice issues in a committed, sustained and creative way. This paper further discusses how I strive to ignite "fire in the belly" (Mer-

Bridge Leadership: Connecting Educational Leadership and Social Justice to Improve Schools
pp. 97–119
Copyright © 2010 by Information Age Publishing
All rights of reproduction in any form reserved.

chant & Shoho, 2006) in support of social justice as an educator and scholar (i.e., from my teaching experience in graduate school to a scholar in a leadership preparation program). Fire in the belly, a term coined by a college dean who was a participant in Merchant and Shoho's (2006) study:

> comes from the capacity to recognize the injustice but also having cultivated a kind of basic self-confidence and a basic self-assurance. We don't develop a fire in the belly about social injustice in the absence of the cultivation of a strong philosophical base, a sense of competence, and a sense of security in the individual. It involves self-examination; it involves teaching—not just to skills, or to knowledge—but to the development of the total human being. And I can't imagine that you can educate leaders without attending to that. (p. 98)

For me, the fire in my belly for social justice started to evolve in my early educational experience as an immigrant to the United States and when I was searching for a path to pursue in my career trajectory.

As a framework for this paper, I chronicle three periods that have been vital to my development as an intellectual and signify my profound commitment to social justice (see Figure 4.1), the impetus for the fire in my belly. These include *resistance*, *transformation* and *activism* as pivotal to my formation as an educator and scholar.

In the first period, resistance (i.e., resisting the call to teach), I focus on my early educational experience as an immigrant from Haiti and my initial exposure to teaching in an educational program. In the second

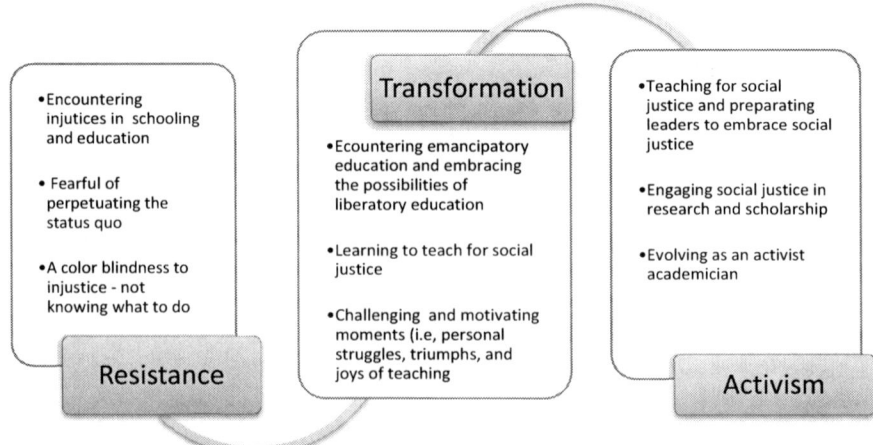

Figure 4.1. Social justice conversion process.

period, transformation (i.e., toward emancipatory pedagogy), I discuss my encounter with Freire's and other critical and feminist theorists' writings and their influence on the fundamental philosophical base of my teaching. In the last period, activism (i.e., a social justice framework), I share how teaching for social justice is part of a quest to eradicate inequities in schools, a responsibility I could not abdicate after my doctoral graduate school experience. Further, to advance teaching for social justice as part of my activism, I consider how engaging in research is an integral part in my efforts to develop school leaders to meet the needs of all learners.

RESISTING THE CALL: LIFE IN SCHOOLS AND THE EARLY BEGINNINGS OF MY TEACHING JOURNEY

In reflecting on my career trajectory, it conjures up memories of my adolescent years in the late 1970s as a newcomer to America whose family fled a poverty-stricken, third world country - my native home, Haiti. My family, similar to immigrant families who migrated to the States, was in search of sanctuary, opportunity and freedom on the shores of America to have a life experience full of hopes and dreams. As I navigated through a Western educational system, I was a representation of "other," "different," "foreigner"; and thirty years later, I have not divorced myself from the fabric of my Haitian ancestry. Still today, I maintain an accent and hold dear to my cultural customs (i.e., speaking my native language, cooking ethnic dishes and celebrating Haitian traditions such as Haiti's Independence Day on January 1st).

When I migrated to the United States, I dreamed of achieving the American dream. I did not know exactly what that was at the age of seven but I believed that education was the great equalizer. I firmly believed that doing well in school was the key to success. But, it was not that easy. I remember being marginalized because I was different, had an accent and felt like an outsider by teachers and classmates, not all. But, I was one of the lucky ones who encountered less prejudice because of the few teachers who saw my potential and encouraged me to do well. So, I did. But, there was always that nagging feeling when I saw classmates who were not provided with assistance and guidance to overcome their obstacles. There was a pervasive belief that some children are destined to fail; many teachers and administrators' demeanor reflected this perception about the "kids they gave up on". As an adolescent, I struggled with accepting how America, *my America* would elevate some students and marginalize others. If you were smart or demonstrated some proclivity toward intelligence, teachers eagerly called on you in class and heralded your academic success. This was not the America I believed as the land of opportunity and espoused the fundamental American values of equity, liberty and democracy (Quantz, Cambron-McCabe, & Dantley, 1991). There was something wrong about an educational system that negated educational equity for all. Very early on, I was learning that schools privileged some and marginalized others who were deemed a product of their environment and destined to fail in life. But, I rejected such a notion because as an immigrant, I believed everyone can learn and had a right to a quality education. My strong belief about equal educational opportunity was the beginning of the fire in my belly about social justice, though I did not know it then.

Those early schooling experiences cemented for me my resistance toward the teaching profession. Further, the teaching profession was not enticing because I saw too many teachers give up on students. Echoing Lewis' (1990) sentiments, if we do not use education to transform society, we use it to maintain the status quo (if not intentionally, then by default), which is not a neutral position either (p. xxi). Fortunately for me, along my educational path since second grade in New Jersey, I had three wonderful teachers (i.e., Mrs. Bell in third grade, Ms. Lemon in forth grade and Mrs. Gardner in eighth grade) who compensated for the "ineffective ones" I would later encounter. As I progressed throughout elementary grades and on to middle and high school, I saw many Black boys drop out (or pushed out); many were smart but felt disconnected to school (i.e., regularly suspended, disengaged in class or had blank faces when the teacher called on them). In retrospect, these experiences evoke feelings of helplessness and anger about the inequities perpetuated in schools. The notion that schools elevated some and left others behind was always problematic for me. Unlike many aspiring teachers who enter the teaching profession today because a teacher influenced them, I rejected teaching as a possible career choice because I did not want to perpetuate educational inequity. Certainly, there are teachers who had similar experience but entered the teaching profession to make a difference along the lines of instruction for social justice. However, at that particular moment in my life when I was contemplating my future, I remember vividly standing in the school hallway thinking, I did not want to become a teacher.

My evolution as an educator took a circuitous route, even to arriving at this juncture in my professional career as a faculty of educational leadership. I best characterize my entry to the field of education as one who stumbled into teaching. As I previously mentioned, I resisted going into the teaching profession because of a deeply held belief that schools did not provide equal opportunity for all. However, the more I tried to distance myself from the teaching profession, the more I felt a tug to go in that direction. I started teaching during my sophomore year of undergraduate study in a precollege program at a local university in an inner-city. I was hired as a teaching assistant to work with "at-risk" (a term I no longer use because it represents deficiency and have replaced it with marginalized, disenfranchised, living on the margins) students from Grades 7-9; the program also included 10th-12th graders. This was simply an opportunity to earn money during the remainder of my undergraduate study. As a political science major and English minor, I had my sights set on law school and did not intend to go into teaching.

Although I had my sights on a different career trajectory, I was again exposed to the disparities of inner-city children in the educational system, now as an adult. The experience at precollege further revealed the devastating effects of inequitable educational opportunities in urban school districts. I am reminded of Walker and Dimmock (2005) who argue that the challenges accompanying the education of diverse groups and ways to provide worthwhile, socially responsible, and equitable education are both exhilarating and alarming. Despite the resources and academic programs that were in place at precollege, some students were more difficult to reach and just disconnected in school. Too often schools have treated students as empty vessels who need to be filled with knowledge and by the time they are provided with alternative programs, they are already preconditioned or wired to traditional approaches of teaching and learning (i.e., didactic, rote and banking concept) that a reconditioning is needed to validate students' experiences and build on their cultural knowledge (Wink, 2000). Greene (1998) insightfully states, "students must be enabled to, at whatever stages they find themselves to be, to encounter curriculum as possibility. The curriculum ought to provide a means for learners to understand their world (i.e., life experiences) so they can articulate the themes of their existence and to reflect on those themes" (p. 19). hooks (1994) asserts that the classroom is the most radical space of possibility but schools do the contrary which typically is to confine learners to a rote, assembly-line approach to learning.

Reflecting further on my teaching experience at precollege, I struggled to find effective approaches to engage students, a sentiment that permeated among program staff and administrators. Although the program provided rigorous academic programs and cultural enrichment activities, precollege did not have the tremendous impact we had hoped to achieve. We had success with some but not enough students. Consequently, more accountability systems were implemented to exert pressure on students to learn. The increased pressure placed on students caused many to drop out of the program. In many ways, we continue to fail students when schools adopt the deficit perspective suggesting that students are to be blamed for their failure (Tillman, Brown, Campbell-Jones, & Gonzalez, 2006). Consequently, I became dismayed by the little difference I could make in the lives of young people. Similar to precollege, schools struggle to help students self-actualized and many teachers lose the confidence to educate students to be thoughtful, active citizens (Giroux, 1998). My disillusionment with public education increased and inevitably, I concluded that teaching was not my calling.

After undergraduate school while still working at precollege, I decided to pursue a masters' degree in criminal justice as I contemplated law school. However, toward the end of my masters' degree, I had the opportunity to go to law school to get a joint degree but that was short-lived. After I graduated with my masters, I realized that I did not want to work with adolescents after they became entrenched in the criminal justice system. I felt a tug toward the teaching profession but for a long time I did not heed to the voice inside me. I would continue to struggle with my resistance during graduate school in North Carolina in pursuit of my doctorate, the beginning of my transformation.

TOWARD EMANCIPATORY PEDAGOGY: LEARNING TO TEACH FOR SOCIAL JUSTICE

My first encounter with Freire's (2000) writings in *Pedagogy of the Oppressed* greatly influenced my engagement with learning and teaching, and transformed my view of education. Jackson (2007) contends that "teaching can never be divorced from the critical analysis of how society works, and teachers must challenge learners to think critically about the social, political and historical realities within which they inhabit the world" (p. 203). Jackson further iterates that in order to motivate learners to engage in critical discussions, teachers must also be critical analysts who challenge the status quo. Wow, I did not get this in my criminal justice program in graduate school. However, it was narrowly introduced in undergraduate! Further, I did not encounter the kinds of texts such as those by Michael Apple (1995) *Education and power*, Maxime Greene (1978) *Landscapes of learning*, bell hooks' (1994) *Teaching to transgress*, to name a few books that opened me to a new world about education and the possibility it holds. I wished I had encountered these kinds of writings as an undergraduate student.

Levitt (2008) who draws from Foucault's critical writings on various social institutions (e.g., schools) postulates that education involves inquiry, dialogue, and debate to clarify ideas or regimes of truth. According to Levitt, Foucault believed that one must "engage in analysis, reflection, and change—applied not only to others, but to oneself, as well" (p. 48). As I reflect on my educational career path to this present juncture, my experience can be summarized as a conversion of passive consumer of educational thought to "emancipatory pedagogy" (Habermas, 1972). As a passive consumer of educational thought, I was well-schooled in the banking system of education, memorizing information and regurgitating it as a demonstration of the knowledge I gained from what was deposited, stored and used at a later date (Freire, 2000; hooks, 1994). But, I wanted more than technical knowledge.

Similar to Giroux's productive knowledge, *technical knowledge*, according to McLaren (1998) is that which can be measured and quantified, which is what permeates classroom teaching. Another form of knowledge is *practical knowledge* which is about understanding the way people construct institutions and how they communicate and give meaning to their social lives (McLaren, 1998). For me, my urge to understand the world better and improve it was very much related to my immigrant background and what I understood about suffering and poverty. I felt a social responsibility to my ancestors, youth and future generations to share what I was learning. As early as eighth grade, I thought about teaching but rejected it because I believed education, if inequitable, privileged some and marginalized others who did not display eagerness toward learning. My own experience as a student of a Western educational system was grounded in technical and practical knowledge. Both the technical and practical knowledge posited by the German social theorist, Jurgen Habermas are passive and that neither would set me on my intellectual journey to become a critical thinker.

However, a third knowledge posited by Habermas (1972) is *emancipatory knowledge* which is based on increased self-awareness and transformation of experience. In other words, knowledge is gained by self-emancipation through reflection leading to a transformed consciousness or 'perspective' transformation. Initially, this kind of knowledge was introduced in undergraduate school when I took courses on the history of Africa to learn about my African ancestry and contemporary literary writers. It provided a foundation for learning about social justice, equality, and empowerment (hooks, 1994; James, 1993; McLaren, 1998;). However, emancipatory knowledge was reintroduced and reinforced during my pursuit of a doctoral degree in cultural studies and educational leadership. Shortly after completing my master's degree in criminal justice, I applied to graduate school in North Carolina with a heartfelt desire to make a difference in society. I was not entirely certain what laid ahead but I was optimistic about my future.

I encountered transformative education and developed knowledge and understanding about critical theory and pedagogy (Foster, 1986; Giroux, 1988; Lerner, 1997) in my graduate courses. It was during this period that I was beginning to find the language for what was to become the core of my philosophical belief: a social justice orientation. My social justice formation began in undergraduate school but it was in graduate school I learned that learning could be liberatory (Freire, 1998; hooks, 1994). My professors in graduate school provided frameworks for me to examine hard questions regarding the intersection of social class, race, and gender; they challenged me to think seriously about pedagogy in relation to the practice of freedom (Freire, 1998; 2000; hooks, 1994; McLaren, 1998). My professors reignited and fermented the fire in my belly (Merchant & Shoho, 2006), and encouraged me to learn (unlearn/relearn) and critique without fear. They helped push the boundaries of what I knew as I grappled with my "outsider-within" (McDemmond, 1999) status as a Black emerging scholar in academe. They approached the classroom environments as open spaces where students from diverse cultural experiences could engage in discourse, understand the fluidity of a complex society and bridge gaps through cultural understandings. I learned through them what hooks (1994) explicates about her insights, strategies, and critical reflections on pedagogical practice. She asserts, "teaching is a performative act. And it is that aspect of our work that offers the space for change, invention, spontaneous shifts, that can serve as a catalyst drawing out the unique elements in each classroom (p. 11). Through this perfomative act, my professors helped me become more engaged and an active participant in learning, an activist process that I was being oriented to and one I wanted to reciprocate.

Not only did I yearn to practice this kind of activism in pedagogy (James, 1993), I was also beginning to embrace the teaching profession as part of my destiny. Seeing how my professors approached teaching from a standpoint that sought to educate for critical consciousness (hooks, 1994) and ignite activism in pedagogy (James, 1993), I knew I could help my students uncover the underlying political, social, cultural and economic foundations of the larger society (McLaren, 1998). With this recognition, the period of my graduate school provided me rich opportunities to learn and enrich my understanding about critical pedagogy, to gain greater personal awareness through reflection, and to develop a passion to engage in praxis as an agent of social change.

FROM STUDENT TO TEACHER: LEARNING TO TEACH FOR DIVERSITY AND SOCIAL JUSTICE

As I was increasing my understanding about emancipatory pedagogy in graduate school, my professors encouraged me to put into practice my new found knowledge by teaching one of the undergraduate courses offered in the department. In teaching an upper level foundation course, *The Institution of Education*, I sought to create an open, inclusive classroom environment which was invigorating but at times difficult because students expected this course to be value-neutral. However, the assigned readings sought to stimulate and challenge students to expand their experiential base. As Bickford (2008) asserts, "new knowledge has the potential to create outrage. To harness that outrage and motivate action for social justice is an appropriate goal for educators, and follows in the footsteps of seeing education as a crucial tool in producing an informed and activate citizenry" (p. 142). Realizing that students needed an outlet to express their thoughts, I used journals so that students could reflect on their experiences and pose questions to themselves and me. They also engaged in action-research projects (i.e. an assignment on poverty included eating on a $1 daily budget for a few days) to help them link theory to practice. Further, these activities were for the purpose of encouraging students to take an active rather than a passive role in their self-development, and advance critical analyses of racism, sexism and classism, and other markers of difference.

However, for many students this was their first time exploring multifaceted critical social issues (i.e. equity and access, social justice, affirmative action etc.) and their implications for educational practice. Similarly, I was learning from my students on how we can explore a democratic process about teaching and learning as they encountered texts that pushed them beyond their comfort zone. In assessing students' experiences from my first teacher education course in fall, 2001, which was predominantly White, several students revealed the following in an assignment that asked them to reflect on their experiences in this course:

> This class has made me more open to challenge my train of thinking. It has made me more aware of how we must challenge not only our methods of teaching children but ourselves as potential teachers.

> I don't feel like "learned" is a good word to describe what I've gotten out of this class over the course of the semester. Almost all the issues we discussed I was already aware of, but my understanding of the depth of some of the topics definitely increased.

> This class has helped me to really think about education: what it is, what my responsibilities will be as a teacher, how society affects it, how politics come into play. I have sometimes thought about some of these things, but never really thought why things are the way they are and if they are right or wrong.

> Although I might have learned more about educational issues in this class, I have learned the most about my role in society.

> This class not only has taught me things about teaching, but it has also taught me about myself and challenged my way of thinking. It challenged my beliefs and caused us to move beyond the "how" of everything and look at the "why." Why do I do, feel and believe the things I do?

It would be erroneous to suggest that all my students were receptive to the critical issues discussed in class. Many of my White students resisted, became defensive, or simply disengaged from the process of critical inquiry. As a woman of color in a predominantly White university, my students' resistance did not surprise me. As hooks (1994) posits, "the choice to work against the grain, to challenge the status quo, often has negative consequences" (p. 201). Initially, I struggled to find a space where engagement and criticality were welcomed features of the classroom discourse. There was a dissonance between the students who I taught and the course content. No matter how I structured my course syllabus in an honest effort to disclose through course objectives and student learning outcomes, the evaluations usually criticized the amount of time spent discussing race or more precisely "bashing Whites".

At times, I developed a hypersensitivity to these tensions and consistently had to adjust my "mask" to fit the classroom environment, as Paul Dunbar avers in *We Wear the Mask* (1993):

> We wear the mask that grins and lies,
> It hides our cheeks and shades our eyes,—
> This debt we pay to human guile;
> With torn and bleeding hearts we smile,
> And mouth with myriad subtleties.
>
> Why should the world be over-wise,
> In counting all our tears and sighs?
> Nay, let them only see us, while
> We wear the mask.
>
> We smile, but, O great Christ, our cries
> To thee from tortured souls arise.
> We sing, but oh the clay is vile
> Beneath our feet, and long the mile;
> But let the world dream otherwise,
> We wear the mask!

However, there were momentary lapses in the adjustment process of my mask where a rage flooded my being. I would admit to myself that separating the essence of who I am from what I do is not possible. In that moment when the rage was present, I managed to readjust the mask and transcend this emotional storm. The transcendence enabled me to see through the fog, the haze and the rage to students' potential and possibility for developing a critical consciousness and struggling for social justice. For that, I am thankful because it allowed the more empowering feelings of care and nurture to emerge and dominate my classroom in order that the potential and the possibility for change might evolve (Noddings,

2002). Truly believing in the possibility of change, I persisted in my efforts to help my preservice teachers take an active role in self-development, and give voice to new ways of thinking about education, teaching and learning. In the course of one semester it was difficult to observe the transformation in students' thinking about the various issues examined in class. However, students' reflections provided a snapshot of their growth.

While teaching another undergraduate course that same year (2001) for freshmen Teaching Fellows, Brandy (pseudonym for a student) shared her thoughts about the kind of impact the course had on her. She wrote:

> One night a week, I return to my dorm room with my thoughts racing with confusion, happiness, sadness, anger and complacency. Sometimes I feel like crying; other times, I feel as if I am well on my way to understanding. And yet, with all these contradicting emotions and thoughts, I find myself eager to return to the same class the very next week. As this spring semester has flown by, I feel that the seminar in Teaching Fellows has been one of the most beneficial of all my classes. I accredit these most complex thoughts and feelings to the assigned readings and to the sincere discussions that are evoked by the text. If I had to characterize this semester with one word, it would have to be "awareness". I feel that the issues raised and discussed in class have made me more aware and which made me truly think about the teaching profession in a more critical manner.

For Brandy, the classroom was a safe place for her to further explore her thoughts about schooling and education which challenged her to interrogate the teaching profession more closely. Similar to hooks (1994), I conscientiously work to make my classroom a "democratic setting where everyone feels a responsibility to contribute, a central goal of transformative pedagogy" (p. 39). Sharing was not relegated only to my students but also to me as the instructor of the class. My willingness to share my thoughts and feelings about the topic under discussion was to create a climate of openness and intellectual rigor. I also felt it was important that no student would be invisible; so I called on different students all the time although some resented having to make a verbal contribution. If a student did not want to participate, I moved on to the next student and always reminded the class that I will call on all students. Participation was an important aspect of the course. Over time, students felt they were part of a classroom community where they felt free to talk and talk back. Engaged in mutual participation, I was learning from my students, listened, and observed in class and in their reflective journals their struggles of giving up old ways of thinking, knowing and learning new approaches. Together, we "surrendered to the wonder of re-learning and learning ways of knowing that went against the grain" (hooks, 1994, p. 44).

For Brandy, as her comfort level increased over the course of the semester, she participated more in class and her reflection revealed the growth she experienced by the end of the semester:

> The articles have brought to my attention many problems and issues that need to be addressed and need solutions. And every class I sit and almost laugh at the notion that 30 or so educators-to-be, sit and try to come up with solutions that have been plaguing education as we know it. Then, I think, this is how problems are solved and solutions are reached ... As I have been given much, almost too much to think about this semester, I feel extremely lucky to have the opportunity to discuss and bring to attention issues and problems I would've not have otherwise thought of prior to this class. I leave this class with such mixed emotions; but for once, I am thankful for being so indecisive. I have learned that we may never know the right answers but that does not mean we quit searching.

This student's reflection depicts how she grappled with encountering multiple perspectives in an effort to become mindful of her actions on the world in order to gain new knowledge, cross cultural barriers and encounter multiple perspectives that generate new possibilities (Greene, 1988). Years later, I still read students' reflections from my very first two courses because they represent the radical change in my pedagogy. My exposure to Freire, hooks, Giroux, Gramsci, McLaren, Collins, West, educational theorists and philosophers in my graduate program, and further study on my own about revolutionary African American literary women writers transformed the way I teach. Furthermore, it has re-ignited my passion for ideas, critical thinking and the dialogical exchange I have with students (Freire, 2000; hooks, 1994; McLaren, 1998). Toward the completion of my doctoral studies, I reflected deeply on whether I wanted to pursue academe as a faculty member or stay on the current path as a full-time administrator in higher education.

Teaching is a noble profession; however, hooks' (1994) elucidation of engaged teaching is that it is taxing to the spirit; but it is also an expression of political activism. This revelation confirmed that I was embarking on the right path; therefore, I made the decision to pursue a tenure track position at The University of Oklahoma-Norman campus.

POLITICAL ACTIVISM: DEVELOPING LEADERS AND ENGAGING IN RESEARCH FOR SOCIALLY JUST SCHOOLS

The discussion to this point provides a glimpse of my circuitous journey to the teaching profession in academe. Unlike many educational scholars who followed the traditional path to the teaching profession and later enter academe, I did not. As previously discussed, I resisted the path of teaching but while pursuing a different career path, I felt a tug pushing me further into teaching. In addition to my early teaching experience in a precollege program, the university classroom was truly my training ground for what was to become my passion and an expression of my political activism. After the completion of my graduate studies, I accepted a tenure-track faculty position in a graduate program in educational leadership. To date, much of my research and teaching in a leadership preparation program are influenced by my orientation to critical pedagogy and theory which laid the foundation for my commitment to social justice (Merchant & Shoho, 2006).

As a faculty of educational leadership, I continue to explore social justice leadership development of aspiring school leaders through the integration of inquiry and reflection to interrupt persistent inequities in schools. Given the increasingly abrasive and polarized American society today, school leaders are faced with increased challenges (i.e. fewer resources, lack of funding, limited teachers and classrooms) to meet the needs of all learners. Therefore, it is incumbent upon leadership preparation programs to address issues of social justice to help aspiring school leaders develop a sophisticated understanding of diversity, to critically evaluate oppressive social patterns and institutions, and to work more democratically to create just and inclusive practices and social structures (Adams, Bell & Griffin, 2007).

Whether it is in my graduate courses, Curriculum Development and Theory, Administration and Organizational Theory, Leadership in a Postmodern World, or Visionary Leadership, I engage concepts and frames of thinking to help aspiring school leaders understand and critically analyze the political, social, economic and educational inequities perpetuated in schools. As Dantley and Tillman (2006) argue, "leadership for social justice interrogates the policies and procedures that shape schools and at the same time perpetuate social inequalities and marginalization due to race, class, gender and other markers of otherness" (p. 19). Important to my pedagogical practices is using multiple strategies to facilitate my teaching to help aspiring school leaders develop the knowledge, skills, dispositions, and commitment to provide a socially just educational environment for all students (Tillman, Brown, Campbell-Jones, & Gonzalez, 2006). Some of these strategies include visiting schools, posing potential and real-life dilemmas encountered by school leaders, meetings with school leaders on leadership principles and styles, and tapping the expertise and wisdom of current and past school leaders who regularly visit my classes as presenters. I also rely on presentations from students, peer-reviews and critiques of research papers, collaborative learning for class related research projects, and technology integration in the form of on-line interaction and discussions.

My introduction to teaching in an inner-city precollege program was a precursor to the work I am deeply engaged in today as a faculty of educational leadership. During my years at precollege, many of the inner-city students struggled to experience success and as a result, they dropped out of the program. For every student who did not stay in the program, I experienced a personal loss because of the bleak future that lied ahead of them, and I felt powerless about changing their circumstances. According to Glickman (2005), a "true democracy must have an educated citizen and to be truly educated—rather than indoctrinated- one must learn in a democratic environment" (p. 493). If education is to empower students, how is it that we continue to fail students? As Quantz, Cambron-McCabe and Dantley (1991) contend, "empowerment is the critical assessment of society and a commitment to illuminating the cultural and society trappings that deny equity and justice and to a commitment to advancing a more active democracy" (p. 7).

Teaching for social justice and infusing it in my courses is about attending to the injustices inner-city children and disenfranchised students encounter in schools (Adams, Bell & Griffin, 2007; Darling-Hammond, French, & Garcia-Lopez, 2002). It is a commitment to fight for the success of all students rather than accept that their failure is inevitable. Preparing thoughtful educational leaders for today's schools include helping aspiring leaders understand the multiple levels and impact of bias in society and helping them to be introspective about their entrée into social justice leadership (Rodriguez & Baum, 2006).

Teaching for social justice can be daunting when it is not integrated in the structure and curriculum of an educational leadership program. Often, it is pursued in isolation by faculty who have an interest in and/or engage in research on social justice. On the nights I taught a class, on my drive home afterwards, I would replay in my mind how class went that evening. Where did we get stalled in our discussions and what might I need to clarify or further explore in the next class? Were there students who did not participate and what was the basis of their silence? By then, my adrenaline would escalate because I wanted to help my students make the connections and apply what we examined to their school practices. But there were moments when the subject matter was too heavy for them and again, I would leave class reflecting on how things went on that particular evening. If they were stuck on a particular issue, I followed-up with the class through email before the next class meeting. When we reconvened I would start class by "checking in" to inquire what questions they may have had from the previous class. We would probe deeper into a particular subject before proceeding with the discussion topic for that class period.

I learned a long time ago that the curriculum needs to be fluid to allow for those teachable moments. Teaching for social justice is not something I can check off as "they got it"- let's move on to the next topic! For many in-service teachers and administrators, they have had limited experience in interrogating social justice issues. Recognizing that some students may not have had marginalizing experiences, they may be challenged and or resistant to discussions and examinations about social justice. Developing a sensitivity or appreciation for social justice is a process. In order to prepare school leaders to respond to the demanding and cultural challenges that schools have to contend with (Black & Murtadha, 2007), Merchant and Shoho (2006) argue that faculty in leadership preparation programs must be intentional in moving the discourse of social justice beyond classroom discussions to experiences that enable students to recognize and combat inequities in our school system.

Three weeks into one course, *Leadership in a Post-modern World*, we were beginning to delineate what social justice was and grapple on its importance for disrupting inequities in school systems that are reluctant to change. Students were assigned readings from Marshall and Oliva's (2006), *Leadership for Social Justice* and other readings (Furman and Shields, 2005; Normore & Jean-Marie, 2008) to situate social justice and leadership for social justice. For some, the concept was evasive and I remember us teasing out its core meanings (i.e., access, equity, democracy, distribution of resources, etc). But, we did not remain on the periphery of examining theoretical constructs and abstract meanings of social justice. Our class discussions were followed by "action or application" oriented activities and projects to build on our examination of social justice as a process. For example, students were asked to make observations on inequities of the communities in which they work (Hafner, 2006), conduct an equity audit (Scheurich and Skrla, 2003) to take stock on how their schools are meeting learners' educational needs, and unpack policies and practices that perpetuate the status quo (e.g., privileging some and marginalizing others). For those in administrative positions, I challenged them to raise critical issues in meetings with their colleagues and district leaders. At times, we would strategize in class on how to approach a particular issue that was being considered in their district (e.g., mock debates). These action/application oriented practices and projects guide leaders to reflect on and critique the every day practices of schooling, what Capper (1993) views as a process of deconstruction to reconstruction. As Hafner (2006) poignantly reminds me, when engaging students in these kinds of action/application oriented practices, "there lies hope – hope that schools, as social structures, might generate and reinforce policies and practices that clearly demonstrate a commitment to social justice" (p. 188). In essence, my classroom community is a nurturing place for educational leaders to explore and begin to deepen their commitment to social justice. I view this kind of work as political activism to move the discourse of social justice to deeply embedded practices. This political activism is not only reflected in my teaching but also in my scholarship.

My scholarly inquiry began in my graduate studies at both Rutgers University and the University of North Carolina-Greensboro. While my graduate courses were a source of knowledge to broaden the scope of my understanding about critical theory, social justice, democracy, philosophy and moral education, my research courses were another source of knowledge for exploring and examining theoretical constructs in my interest on women and educational leadership. Simultaneously as a doctoral student in educational leadership and cultural studies, I pursued a post-baccalaureate certificate in women's studies. These joint pursuits provided an opportunity to examine the intersection of feminist theories, critical race theory, and educational leadership. The absence of women, in particular the experiences of Black women in mainstream literature was a void I wanted to fill in the research literature. My exposure to Anna Julia Cooper, Septima Clark, and Mary Church Terrell as teacher activists working for social justice documented in the work of Collins, 1990/2000; Giddings, 1984; Guy-Sheftall, 1995; and Hine, 1990 have broadened my landscapes of learning (Greene, 1978). As a result of these works, I developed the yearning to learn about leadership for social justice through the voices and experiences of women of color, past and present.

As several scholars on feminist and Black feminist theory (e.g., Blackmore, 1999, Collins, 1990/2000; Hine, 1990; hooks, 1999; Shakeshaft, 1989) lament, the omission of women in educational leadership obscures the contribution women have to offer the educational field. Their scholarship has greatly influenced women's epistemology and the ways leadership is conceptualized and practiced. A further glaring omission which consequently influenced the direction of my dissertation research is the experiences of African American women leaders, particularly in historically Black colleges and universities (hereafter, HBCUs). My qualitative dissertation focused on the leadership discourses of African American women administrators (i.e., presidents, deans, vice chancellor and president, and senior administrators) in HBCUs in one southern state. Among the findings were revelations of how African American women of the segregation and desegregation era have been actively involved in political movements that sought to improve the material conditions of the Black community, and how they have transcended the barriers of racism, classism and sexism in the fight for equality of opportunity and social justice.

This seminal work influenced the direction my scholarship would take as an emerging scholar.

When I started the professoriate at The University of Oklahoma in 2002, I embraced the opportunity to advance my research in a university climate that fostered high, scholarly inquiry. As I reflect on my scholarship over the past seven years, three areas of research dominate the focus of my scholarly engagement (i.e., *women and educational leadership, social justice issues and urban school reform*).

In the area of *women and educational leadership*, my work focused on both the higher education and secondary education context. I continued to pursue my research on women leaders in academe but with a particular focus on female secondary school administrators. Although there has been an increased presence of women leaders in education, there remains a disproportionately low representation of women in secondary education. As research suggests, 54% of secondary school teachers are females but only 26% serve as secondary principals (Eckman, 2002). Research also suggests that school districts are not tapping into an underutilized resource (i.e. recruitment of women and people of color) to cultivate a leadership pool that would more closely reflect the current and future demographics of American schools. Extending the research of Young and McCleod (2001) who studied twenty aspiring and practicing female principals, of whom nearly all were White and only four were secondary principals, I conducted a qualitative study that examined the leadership experiences of a diverse group of female secondary school leaders (i.e., race, ethnicity, teaching experience, administrative experience, urban & suburban school districts) in one south-western state. The central premise of the research focused on how leadership experiences for each principal evolved over time in terms of how leadership roles were impacted by their leadership-orientation, gender, and race. While I was the primary researcher to collect data, this research project involved collaboration with a colleague in the analysis stage

In a second study on high school principals, in collaboration with a senior researcher and a practitioner in a leadership organization, we investigated how female principals teased out complex gendered views of leadership to bridge the gaps between community-school in urban, suburban and rural school communities. This study brought 16 female secondary principals together as co-researchers and together determined the study's directions and formulated interview questions for nine participants who provided the primary data for the overall study. Their insights helped address Walker and Dimmock's (2005) call to examine the particularity and diversity of cultural and contextual conditions within which leadership takes place. The study sheds light on how female principals carve out their own leadership visions in a variety of contexts.

Limited to the participants in this study, we began to unearth numerous similar and dissimilar ways in which female high school principals negotiate school community relationships and their own interpretation of effective leadership.

Overall, these research studies have contributed to the knowledge base about women in educational leadership. They have also resulted in publication in several peer-reviewed journals and book chapters. I have also presented at conferences that focused on women's issues (e.g., Women in Educational Leadership Conference, National Women's Studies Association) in addition to presenting at the annual conferences of the American Educational Research Association (AERA), University Council for Educational Administration (UCEA), and the College of Education Research Conference, Florida International University. Relatedly, I have integrated these studies in my graduate courses to disseminate and advance knowledge about the role of women in educational leadership.

A second branch of my research agenda focuses on the contexts in which *educational leaders conduct the business of educating children for a more socially just future* (i.e., equity and access, social justice). This is pursued through my research on female school leaders in public schools and higher education. In these lines of research, an additional element focused on how these school leaders' socialization processes unfold in the context of social justice in educational leadership. As schools are becoming increasingly diverse and educational reform has focused on standards-based and high-stakes testing, it is important to examine what leadership theories and practices guide school leaders in their decision-making. In the first study on female high school principals, one of the findings focused on four female principals' leadership practices that embraced social justice, democratic schooling, and issues of equity. This line of inquiry is an area I continue to develop in my courses and in my scholarship.

From my dissertation research, I have also published manuscripts that focused on one of the findings pertaining to issues of social justice (i.e. social justice project rooted in community). Specifically, these manuscripts have appeared in *The Educational Forum, Advancing Women in Educational Leadership, the Journal of Women in Educational Leadership, and the International Electronic Journal for Leadership in Learning*. The findings from both studies provide opportunities to facilitate and promote discussion on how beliefs are enacted to promote action-oriented leadership practices in support of social justice.

The third area of my research agenda, *urban school reform*, is the least developed yet promising. My work on urban education consists of a co-authored chapter and qualitative studies on female leaders of which urban high schools were part of my unit of analysis. Further, while a faculty at Florida International University, I was involved in data analysis of an ethnographic study conducted at a high poverty, high-minority urban high school which investigated how racial dynamics and race relations influenced leadership activity in the school. Since my return to the University of Oklahoma in 2007 on the Tulsa campus which is nested in an urban community, I have been actively involved in local school districts through relationships forged with district leaders and graduate students in the educational leadership program who are school administrators and teachers in neighboring districts. These relationships and connections to local school districts have created opportunities to pursue research on urban school reform. For example, a promising research is the community schools project called Tulsa Area Community Schools Initiative (TACSI) in which I have been actively involved with colleagues in my program area. As a research team, we have developed a longitudinal research design for TACSI that uses integrated methods to measure the implementation and effectiveness of the community school model. The research design will test the efficacy of the community school model for changing learning conditions and performance outcomes within TACSI schools. TACSI's community school initiative is a part of a national reform effort to improve the educational outcomes of disenfranchised and/or marginalized children. Another initiative is the work with district leaders on the utilization of an inquiry process to implement and evaluate the FOCUS program, a restructuring of teaching and learning to improve the educational attainment of high-challenged learners. With these research undertakings, the opportunities to pursue my research on urban school reform are possible.

As I enter the next phase of my professional career as a tenured associate professor, my interest is to further develop my research strand on urban school reform with a continued focus on leadership for social justice. In addition to my research, my involvement in professional organizations such as AERA's SIGs, *Leadership for Social Justice, Leadership for School Improvement, and Urban Learning, Teaching & Research* supports this focus. As I continue to develop this area of research, my commitment is to infuse curriculum with my research to help develop well-adjusted school leaders who embrace socialization processes, diversity, and social justice in leadership preparation and training to meet the needs of diverse student populations.

CONCLUSION

Much of this paper centered on my nontraditional journey into the teaching profession, and how I came to critical pedagogy and developed a commitment to social justice. As an immigrant, my early experiences with issues of inequity and marginalization had an impact on my outlook about schooling and education in a Western society. These experiences became part of the impetus that ignited the fire in my belly to fight for social justice rather than accept things as "just the way things are." However, teaching for social justice was a conversion process—for example, *resistance-transformation-activism* in which I surrendered to the call to teach. Through my conversion, I developed specific knowledge and concrete, practical skills to help my former preservice teachers, and now aspiring and practicing school leaders of educational leadership to define for themselves what it means to be efficacious in exploring and confronting social justice in their practitioner settings. Also, engaging in research informs my teaching and activities (i.e., infuse social justice in my teaching to expand the awareness and knowledge of aspiring and practicing school leaders).

As I reflect on my role in academe, hooks (1994) sums what continues to be my motive operandi that fuels my commitment to advance social justice:

> The classroom, with all its limitations, remains a location of possibility. In that field of possibility we have the opportunity to labor for freedom, to demand of ourselves and our comrades, an openness of mind and heart that allows us to face reality even as we collectively imagine ways to move beyond boundaries, to transgress. (p. 207)

As an educator and researcher whose activism is grounded in emancipatory action, I continue to build a repertoire of strategies so through shared knowledge and experience with aspiring and practicing school leaders, we can work toward social justice to achieve equity and opportunity for all learners.

REFERENCES

Adams, M., Bell, L. A., & Griffin, P. (2007). *Teaching for diversity and social justice* (2nd ed.). New York, NY: Routledge.

Apple, M. W. (1995). *Education and power* (2nd ed.). New York, NY: Routledge.

Bickford, D. M. (2008). Using testimonial novels to think about social justice. *Education. Citizenship and Social Justice, 3*, 131-146.

Black, W. R., & Murtadha, K. (2007). Toward a signature pedagogy in educational leadershippreparation and program assessment. *Journal of Research in Educational Leadership, 2*(1). Retrieved from http://www.ucea.org/JRLE/issue_2007_2_1.php.

Blackmore, J. (1999). Troubling women: Feminism, leadership and educational change: The upsides and downsides of leadership and the new managerialism. In C. Reynolds (Ed.), *Women and school leadership: International perspectives* (pp. 49-72). Albany: State University of New York Press.

Capper, C. A. (Ed.). (1993). Administrator practice and preparation for social reconstructionist schooling. In *Educational administration in a pluralistic society* (pp. 288-315). Albany: State University of New York Press.
Collins, P. H. (1990/2000). *Black feminist thought: Knowledge, consciousness, and the politics of empowerment.* New York, NY: Routledge.
Darling-Hammond, L., French, J., & Garcia-Lopez, S. P. (Eds.). (2002). *Learning to teach for social justice.* New York, NY: Teachers College.
Dantley, M. E., & Tillman, L. C. (2006). Social justice and moral transformative leadership. In C. Marshall & M. Oliva (Eds.), *Leadership for social justice: Making revolutions in education* (pp. 16-30). Boston: Allyn & Bacon.
Dunbar, P. L. (1993). *The collected poetry of Paul Laurence Dunbar* (J. M. Braxton, Ed.). Charlottesville: University Press of Virginia.
Eckman, E. W. (2002). Women high school principals: Perspectives on role conflict, role commitment, and job satisfaction. *Journal of School Leadership, 12*(1), 57-78.
Facione, P. A. (2009). Critical thinking: What it is and why it counts. *Insight Assessment.* Available: http://www.insightassessment.com/pdf_files/what&why2006.pdf
Foster, W. (1986). *Paradigms and promises: New approaches to educational administration.* New York, NY: Civitas Books.
Freire, P. (2000). *Pedagogy of the oppressed* (New rev. 20th anniversay ed.). New York, NY: Continuum.
Freire, P. (1998). *Pedagogy of hope.* New York, NY: Continuum.
Furman, G. C., & Shields, C. M. (2005). How can educational leaders promote and support social justice and democratic community in schools? In W. A. Firestone & C. Riehl (Eds.), *A new agenda for educational leadership* (pp. 119-137). New York, NY: Teachers College.
Giddings, P. (1984). *When and where I enter: The impact of Black women on sex and race in America.* New York, NY: William Morrow.
Giroux, H. A. (1988). *Teachers as intellectuals: Toward a critical pedagogy of learning.* New York, NY: Bergin & Garvey Paperback.
Glickman, C. D. (1993). *Renewing America's schools: A guide for school-based action.* San Franciso: Jossey-Bass.
Greene, M. (1978). *The landscape of learning.* New York, NY: Teachers College.
Greene, M. (1988). *The dialectic of freedom.* New York, NY: Teachers College.
Gross, S., Sernak, K., MacDonald, T., Brown, L., & Blanco, R. (2005). *Cultivating ethical leadership for promoting authentic learning for all.* Paper presented at the 10th Annual Values and Leadership Conference, Penn State University, State College, Pennsylvania, October.
Guy-Sheftall, B. (Ed.). (1995). *Words of fire: An anthology of African American feminist thought.* New York, NY: The New Press.
Habermas, J. (1972). *Knowledge and human interests* (J. J. Shapiro, Trans.) London: Heinemann.
Hafner, M. H. (2006). Teaching strategies for developing leaders for social justice. In C. Marshall & M. Oliva (Eds.), *Leadership for social justice: Making revolutions in education* (pp. 167-193). Boston: Pearson.
Hine, D. C. (Ed.). (1990). *Black women in U.S. history.* Brooklyn, NY: Carlson.

hooks, b. (1999). *Ain't I a woman: Black women and feminism.* Cambridge, MA: South End.
hooks, b. (1994). *Teaching to transgress: Education as the practice of freedom.* New York, NY: Routledge.
Jackson, S. (2002). Freire re-viewed. *Educational Theory,* 57, 2, 199-213.
James, J. (1993). Teaching theory, talking community. In J. James & A. Y. Davis (Eds.), *Spirit, space & survival: African American women in (White) academe* (pp. 118-138). New York, NY: Routledge.
Jean-Marie, G., Normore, A. H., & Brooks, J. (in press). Leadership for social justice: Preparing 21st century school leaders for a new social order. *Journal of Research on Leadership and Education.*
Lewis, H. M. (1990). Introduction. In M. Horton (Ed.), *The long haul* (pp. xix-xxi). New York, NY: Doubleday.
Lerner, M. (1997). *The politics of meaning.* New York, NY: Addison-Wesley.
Levitt, R. (2008). Freedom and empowerment: A transformative pedagogy of educational reform. *Educational Studies, 44,* 47-61.
Marshall, C. & Oliva, M. (Eds.), *Leadership for social justice: Making revolutions in education.* Boston: Allyn & Bacon.
Merchant, B. M., & Shoho, A. R. (2006). Bridge people: Civic and educational leaders for social justice. In C. Marshall & M. Oliva, *Leadership for social justice: Making revolutions in education* (pp. 85-108). Boston: Pearson.
McDemmond, M. (1999). On the outside looking in. In W. B. Harvey (Ed.), *Grass roots and glass ceilings: African American administrators in predominantly White colleges and universities.* New York, NY: State University.
McLaren, P. (1998). *Life in schools: An introduction to critical pedagogy in the foundations of education.* New York, NY: Longman.
Noddings, N. (2002). *Educating moral people: A caring alternative to character education.* New York, NY: Teachers College.
Normore, A. H., & Jean-Marie, G. (2008). Female secondary school leaders: At the helm of social justice, democratic schooling and equity. *Leadership and Organizational Development Journal, 29*(2), 182-205.
Quantz, R. A, Cambron-Mcabe, N., & Dantley, M. (1991). *Preparing school administrators for democratic authority: A critical approach to graduate education.*
Scheurich, J. & Skrla, L. (2003). *Leadership for equity and excellence: Creating high-achievement classrooms, schools, and districts.* Thousand Oaks, CA: Corwin.
Shakeshaft, C. (1989). The struggle to create a more gender inclusive profession. In J. Murphy & K. Seashore Louis (Eds.), *Handbook of research on educational administration* (2nd ed., pp. 99-118). San Francisco: Jossey-Bass.
Tillman, L. C., Brown, K., CampbellJones, F., & Gonzalez, M. L. (2006). Transformative leadership for social justice: Guest editors' introduction. *Journal of School Leadership, 16,* 122-125.
Walker, A., & Dimmock, C. (2005). Leading the multiethnic school: Research evidence on successful practice. *The Educational Forum, 69,* 291-304.
Wink, J. (2000). *Critical pedagogy: Notes from the real world.* New York, NY: Addison Wesley Longman.

Young, M. D., & McLeod, S. (2001). Flukes, opportunities, and planned interventions: Factors affecting women's decisions to become school administrators. *Educational Administration Quarterly, 37,* 462-502.

SCENIC OVERLOOK

Guidelines for Discussions and Reflection

For school leaders:

1. Where do you place yourself according to Figure 4.1? What experiences led you to this place on the continuum? Support your position.
2. How do you move from learning about social justice to leading for social justice? Discuss your understanding.
3. What is your reaction to the Paul Dunbar's "We Wear the Mask?" How does your reaction compare to the author's reaction?
4. How do your personal experiences compare to the author's experiences in committing to social justice? Support your position.

For those preparing school leaders:

1. Where do you place the students in your preparation program according to Figure 4.1? Where do you place yourself? Where would you place your colleagues? What experiences led you to any of these places on the continuum?
2. How do you move students from learning about social justice to leading for social justice?

3. What is your reaction to the Paul Dunbar's "We Wear the Mask?" How does your reaction compare to the author's reaction?
4. How do your personal experiences compare to the author's experiences in committing to social justice as a scholar who prepares school leaders for the twenty-first century?

We now conclude Section I, or Looking Inward, and begin our journey across the Leadership Bridge to Section II, Looking Outward.

THE LEADERSHIP BRIDGE

CHAPTER 5

LEADING JUSTLY IN A COMPLEX WORLD

Carolyn M. Shields

There is growing recognition nationally and internationally that educational leaders need to know how to exercise just leadership in contexts of diversity, contexts that are rapidly changing, in part, because of the forces of globalization. In American schools, for example, students from White, African American, and Latino families, increasingly find themselves in classrooms with students from Asia, the Middle East, and Africa—many of whom have experienced severe hardship in their home countries. Thus, there is a persistent need for discussion about how to lead justly in diverse schools that are ever more reflective of the global population. For example, creating appropriate learning environments for children who may have spent their last few years living in a refugee camp with no opportunity for formal schooling will require different resources, curricula, and pedagogies from those used for other groups of students, yet, this not part of the knowledge base of many school administrators. Leading justly is itself a complex task—one that requires educational leaders to constantly address questions related to equity, inclusion, and quality. It requires, as Foster posited over two decades ago, that leadership "be critically educative; it can not only look at the conditions in which we live, but it must also decide how to change them" (1986, p. 185).

Justice-oriented educators need to become aware of which conditions are inequitable and need to be changed; to consider not only of how to raise test scores and ensure that all students are meeting the standards established for adequate yearly progress (AYP) under legislative mandates, but how to create schools in which all children feel welcome, and are fully included in the academic, social, and emotional activities of the school. In addition, educators have a responsibility to help students develop global curiosity, global understanding and awareness, and a sense of citizenship—not only locally but globally.

In this chapter, I argue that to be a socially just educational leader in this age of globalization requires educational leaders to reflect carefully on what it entails to successfully lead in complex and diverse contexts. First, I submit that a transformative leader needs to understand some of the complexities of globalization, including the ways in which it affects—both negatively and positively—cultures, communities, and communication. I then make the argument that being a socially just leader is not a role one can exercise silently and in private, but that it often also necessitates that one take a courageous stance as a public intellectual.

I will argue that to be a socially just educational leader in American schools requires a new way of thinking about the purposes of schooling, focusing on more than students' achievement on standardized tests, both self-awareness and understanding the interconnectedness of a world marked, in part, by global disparity, by economic challenge, and by political upheaval. Indeed, I firmly believe that hope for a better future for all lies in more robust and more equitable education globally. Others (see for example Cohen, 1989; Hayward, 2000; Noddings, 2005) support this position and note that North American educators too often live in isolation from knowledge and understanding of the issues faced by the rest of the world, issues that impinge on their ability to successfully educate students from diverse sociocultural backgrounds who comprise ever larger proportions of the student bodies in their own schools.

Despite the pressing need for global understanding, there is evidence that few programs in educational leadership make diversity, disparity, globalization, and social justice central considerations (Marshall, 2004; Knight, 2004). This situation must change. If we are to address their intellectual isolation, educators will need to develop and inculcate what I can only call "global curiosity"—a profound interest, and sense of involvement, in the inextricable interconnectedness of the modern world.

The purpose of this chapter, therefore, is twofold: first, to help educational leaders reflect on some of the complexities of globalization as it informs the role of a socially just educational leader, and second, to help them consider more fully how these ideas may best be enacted by transformative leaders who take a stance as pubic intellectuals. In my concluding comments, I will also address some implications of these two themes for leadership preparation programs.

THEORETICAL GROUNDING

Before I address the impact of globalization on cultures, communities, and communication, let me address, as Harding (1996) argues we should, my own standpoint, both experientially and theoretically. My career has been shaped by first hand experiences in many countries, by the influence of many thoughtful and caring individuals, and by academic theories related to democratic and transformative leadership, leadership for social justice, spiritual leadership, moral and ethical leadership, and many other perspectives.

SOME PERSONAL INFLUENCES

In the past few years, I have had the opportunity to visit a school operated in a dirt hardened back yard for street children in Rawalpindi, Pakistan, and have only begun to understand the challenges associated with educating these children when attending school prevents them from earning what amounts to a few pennies a day (often through begging)—pennies that make the difference between having an evening meal and going to bed hungry. I have had numerous conversations about how, although child employment in many countries contravenes the UN Rights of the Child, it may also keep a child away from a life of prostitution and provide sustenance for a family. I have talked with educators in remote Muslim communities in Thailand who are convinced that permitting children access to the internet will destroy their traditional values and way of life—already threatened by virtue of their minority status in the country. And I have visited schools in Fiji, South Africa, and elsewhere, that, although sparsely equipped with print materials or other educational resources, are rich in parental support and in which teachers and students enthusiastically embrace learning.

For me, leading justly in a complex world requires doing one's utmost to ensure equitable education for both male and female students in all countries, to provide adequate teacher and leadership training in all countries, and to support the impartial distribution of adequate and appropriate educational resources—especially in countries in which graft and corruption divert much needed funds away from schools and classrooms. It must also, however, begin at home—making North American educators and their students more aware of diverse and disparate material conditions throughout the world and cognizant of their responsibility to the wider global community.

SOME ACADEMIC INFLUENCES

Many educational leaders focus on theoretical perspectives related to transactional (Burns, 1978) or transformational (Leithwood & Janzi, 1990) leadership—theories that are firmly grounded in Western organizational perspectives. In contrast, I have chosen to emphasize transformative leadership (Quantz, Rogers, & Dantley, 1991; Weiner, 2003; Shields, in press)—leadership that begins with questions of justice and democracy related to the wider social context, that critiques inequitable practices, and that offers the promise not only of greater individual achievement but of a better life lived in common with others. Transformative leadership inextricably links education and educational leadership with the wider diverse social context within which it is embedded and it recognizes, with Freire (1998), "that education is not the ultimate lever for social transformation, but without it transformation cannot occur" (p. 37). Because it looks beyond the schoolhouse walls to consider broader national and global contexts (including socioeconomic and cultural arenas), transformative leadership offers the possibility of critically assessing both the negative and positive aspects of globalization.

In similar fashion, Western approaches to leadership that purport to be objective are often considered to be sterile and irrelevant to cultures in which spiritual values play a major role (Smith, 1999). Thus, I seek to highlight theories of leadership that attend to a balance among the intellectual, emotional, and spiritual (e.g., Hunter, 1998; Palmer, 1998; Shields, Edwards, & Sayani, 2005) and that encourage leaders to embed, rather than deny, the values of the cultures within which they work. Kincheloe and Steinberg (1995) posited that education should be "just, optimistic, empathetic, and democratic" (p. 2). These elements provide a scaffold for education that is more equitable, holistic, participatory, and that opens opportunities for future possibility. Combined with the theories of leadership identified above, these components offer guidance for educational leaders who are cognizant of the social disparities that negatively affect the ability of children to succeed in educational organizations; they suggest the importance of critical democratic leadership (see also Portelli, 2001), and offer some hope for education that carefully attends to diverse perspectives and needs, balances critique with promise, and hence, has the potential to be relevant to both local and global contexts.

Let me be clear. In my mind, the goal of introducing global perspectives into leadership preparation programs is not simply one of enhanced understanding of complex issues. Indeed, openness and understanding are simply starting points, in that I believe our goal, as transformative leaders, must be to take action to redress wrongs and enhance justice both locally and internationally. It is to the nature of globalization and to the need for global understanding and socially just action that we now turn.

THE COMPLEXITIES OF GLOBALIZATION

Globalization is sometimes seen as the solution to the extensive global disparities in quality of life indicators such as life expectancy, access to healthcare, access to education, average annual income and so forth. At other times, it is seen as the problem, exacerbating inequities in the name of capitalism and profit. And yet, an examination of some themes often associated with globalization suggests its many tensions and conflicting perspectives—all of which suggest that reality is more complex and nuanced than we often realize.

Dr. Surim Pitsuwan, Secretary General of ASEAN (an association of 12 SE Asian Nations), in a recent keynote address (April, 2008), decried the disparities in average annual per capita income among ASEAN countries (from $270 to $50,000) and argued that although globalization has had many positive economic impacts in some areas of the world, and has "floated many yachts," it has not "floated all the boats." He concluded that the only way to address such disparity is through a greater emphasis on education and excellence in educational leadership.

These disparities are also reflected in the central metaphor of Friedman's (1999) book about globalization, *The Lexus and the Olive Tree*. The Lexus—a luxury vehicle built by Toyota that often costs over $50,000 US represented consumerism, acquisition. For Friedman, the Lexus symbolized capitalism—the globalizing economic drive for profit and the role of privatized forces for rapid economic development. The olive tree, on the other hand, represented those elements in our traditions and cultures that root us, anchor us, identify us, and locate us in this world (p. 31). The tree reminds us of the need for belonging, intimacy, connectedness, and preservation of those aspects of local culture that matter. These metaphors emphasize the tensions inherent in globalization—a force that is neither inherently positive nor totally negative. Such tensions raise numerous questions about competitiveness, communication, culture and community. Scholars (see for example, Apple, 2001; Giroux, 2005) tell us, for example, that sometimes the corporate focus is so unerringly on capitalism, profit, and economic competitiveness, it can lead to disconnection from questions of human dignity, and social responsibility. In turn, this outcome accentuates the need for equilibrium and poses the challenge of how best to create an equitable balance among competing forces.

CAPITALISM AND COMPETITIVENESS

WalMart is considered by many to be an exemplar of the negative impact of globalization—lost jobs at home and a concomitant manufacturing of goods "offshore" in substandard conditions for substandard wages. But in a more balanced consideration, it can also remind us of some positive elements of globalization. Jobs in one country correlate with additional employment elsewhere (even though the shift generally capitalizes on low minimum wages and the persistence of poor working conditions in developing countries). In 2008, when the case of former employee Deborah Shank came to international attention, the outcry against large multinational corporations was intense and immediate. Deborah, an overnight shelf stocker from Missouri, had been compensated by a trucking company for the severe injuries she had received when her van was crushed by a large truck. When WalMart realized she had received compensation for medical expenses from both their insurance company and a settlement from the trucking company, they sued, asking (as was their technical legal, if not moral, right) for her family to reimburse their insurance company. Deborah was severely brain injured and unable, not only to work, but to care for herself; and, despite the minimal compensation, covering the costs of her care had led her husband to the brink of bankruptcy. Hence, when the story broke, public furor exploded against the corporation, seen as focusing on the economic bottom line, with no compassion for the welfare of its employees. Despite the ultimate change of policy, the incident generally reinforced WalMart's image as an insensitive globalizing force.

On the other hand, the speed with which public opinion was mobilized by the major international news media and the rapidity with which Wal-Mart changed its position is indicative of the way in which rapid communication may be seen as a positive force of globalization. It is unfortunate, of course, that WalMart had not seen the dehumanizing implications of its action without public pressure. At the same time, the fact that major news companies combined with millions of messages from ordinary people to achieve a positive result in less than a week is encouraging.

It is not just retail corporations or multinationals that risk falling into the trap of competitiveness, legalism and dehumanization, but educational organizations as well. The use of standardized test scores for international comparisons and rankings that neglect contextual differences is only one example. Far too often, educators deal with students and their needs by appealing to rules and policies rather than to practices that address students' real needs. For example, opportunities for vouchers and school choice seem to respond to the public call for increased parental choice, but may, at the same time, neglect the declining enrolment and concomitant loss of student funding suffered by schools in which parents may be less able to take advantage of the choice options. In today's accountability climate, with high stakes testing and school rankings, it is easy for administrators to lose sight of the moral purposes of education and to unintentionally fall prey to the forces of the global market place. Too often choices are made to accept corporate sponsorship by makers of soft drinks or junk food that, while providing needed funds for academic resources, may also be contributing to the growing phenomenon of youth obesity. Regardless of parental pressure on the one hand, or mounting economic challenges on the other, must never sacrifice the humanizing and empowering goals of education to the "bottom line." The economic virtues of the Lexus and the traditional values of the olive tree must continually be held in a tenuous balance.

EXPANDED COMMUNICATION

We saw, in the illustration of WalMart, the potential of rapid global communication networks to influence policy. In some cases, as in the foregoing, such influence is positive. But we must always be cautious about the possible deleterious impact of global communication as well. One excellent example of the kind of global communication made possible (and necessary) by increasing globalization is that of the on-line open access encyclopedia Wikipedia in which people are free to post information, to challenge, question, to ask for retraction or deletion but in which ultimately the weight of consensus that we have attained a reasonable accurate account wins the day. There is no doubt that this, and similar communication tools, have made information available to any one able to access the internet and particularly to many whose access to information through print media is severely limited. Yet, the very glut of information, its accessibility, and the immediacy with which it is available raise additional questions. How do we know if the information is biased or incorrect? Who decides what should be included, what should be omitted or deleted and on what basis? How do we ensure that people use their access ethically—without posting slander or deliberate falsehoods? Indeed, the more information there is available, the greater our responsibility to examine it carefully.

This is particularly important because the nature of the information we receive is in large part determined by the power (and economic backing) of those who can control and manipulate information dissemination. In the documentary movie, *Control Room,* about the role of media during the second Gulf war, begun in 2003, Samir Kheder, senior producer for the Al Jazeera satellite news network, states, "You do not wage a war without rules, without media, without propaganda" and throughout the video, one becomes aware of how the "news" is manipulated by both sides to serve patriotic purposes. Kheder emphasizes what Americans have come to accept, that "American media were highjacked by some people in the administration ... to elevate fear" related to weapons of mass destruction. He then goes on to suggest that too often the media are "there to defend the values of the people" rather than to present unbiased perspectives on the news. This view, while not new, is worth emphasizing. What we often come to accept as "truth," is shaped in certain ways by those with the power to tell a particular story or to highlight certain perspectives. To be sure, all choices about what to communicate are subjective, but making deliberate choices to include or exclude based on the message one wants to communicate rather than attempting to present a well-rounded account is particularly dangerous. This issue must be addressed in public schools by teaching students to develop criteria for accepting or rejecting the proliferation of opinion and material found in blogs, My Space, Facebook, Wikipedia, and "mainstream" media outlets.

The discussion of the role of the media during the Iraq war is reminiscent of Janis' (1977) *Groupthink*—a book in which he demonstrated the dangers of consensus through an analysis of incidents such as "Pearl Harbor" and the "Bay of Pigs." Groupthink, a term coined in the 1950's by William Whyte, has come to refer to a rationalized way of thinking in which people who are deeply involved in a cohesive group permit the goal of unanimity to override any examination of alternative perspectives.. Janis acknowledges that cohesion is necessary for organizations to work together but also warns of the dangers of consensus driven decisions. A more recent example is the way in which the Bush administration and Congress all decided to pursue an invasion of Iraq without solid evidence of weapons of mass destruction.

Although groupthink is not new, globalization has the power to enhance the spread of particular kinds of information, to garner public opinion, and hence, may increase the chances of groupthink. If we are careful to introduce new, different, and sometimes conflicting perspectives and information that certainly increase complexity, we will also be able to reduce the potential for faulty decision making and simplistic solutions.

In education, the tendency to groupthink is obvious in many ways. Sometimes school leaders are afraid to step away from the group, to challenge, for example, the inappropriateness of ranking schools based on standardized test data without consideration of the student body, prior levels of achievement, or gains made during a given year. They permit aggregate and average scores to mask the discrepancies and challenges posed when data are disaggregated. This pressure to seek a consensual solution must often be challenged if leaders are to make decisions that result in socially just solutions.

Here, I must aver that consensus is a powerful tool in an administrator's lexicon; however, it is important to recognize that consensus does not always bring about desirable or equitable ends. Fennimore (1997) investigated a commonly advocated form of consensus known as conflict resolution or mediation and concluded that attempting to create a win-win situation in a situation in which there is inherent inequity may make participants feel good, but likely does little to redress the underlying situation of inequity. She gave the example of a situation that arose in a school when students in a magnet program were being educated in smaller classes and with many more educational resources than children in the regular classes in the same school. Parents objected to the unequal distribution of resources and a court case ensued. In this case, a win-win solution resulted—one in which although the original inequitable resource distribution was maintained, some modifications to each program were accepted. Despite the appearance of compromise in which the magnet program received minimally fewer resources and class size in the regular program was slightly reduced, the greater political power of the "magnet" parents won the day. If the playing field is inequitable at the outset, a win-win solution may simply perpetuate, if not exacerbate inequities.

Sometimes, educators have become so used to the need for solidarity and consensus that groupthink seems to lead to cowardice. Thus, even when they are aware of alternatives, educational leaders may be afraid to say too loudly, for example, that there are other goals worthy of consideration than those assessed by standardized tests. In many cases, even when there is a strong sense that something is not right, educators may not have workable alternatives, and once again, instead of admitting a lack of knowledge, may resort to responses such as deficit thinking, blaming the family or students' situations, or calling for remedial placement of students (rather than remediation of pedagogical practices and changes to school structures and environments). These latter responses to increased global communication—groupthink and cowardice—must be eschewed if we are to lead justly.

COMMUNITIES IN FLUX

The rapid expansion of means of communication and information sharing has undoubtedly had a significant impact on the meaning of community. Where it used to be a term grounded in a particular place, we now have virtual communities—communities of scholars, bloggers, friends—facebook, my space, and so on. In 1887, in a now famous and often translated work, Tonnies explored the polarized nature of community by using the gemeinshaft (roughly: "local") gesellschaft (roughly: "cosmopolitan") (see for example, Tonnies, 1957). In many parts of the world with easy access to communication, globalization has almost eliminated this polarization and the local aspect of community has been replaced by new and competing perspectives and values. In those communities, some people still look with longing to a mythical past time when people in a community shared similar hopes, dreams, and values. At the same time, as stated earlier, globalization affects communities unequally and some remain relatively untouched by, even isolated from, the explosion of information technology. For them, gesellshaft is still far from a daily reality.

The message is that we can no longer assume that when people come together in a common space they share common values, common information and traditions, or beliefs about the definition and framing of problems or their solutions. Neighbors, both Christian, may have very different perspectives on controversial social issues such as abortion or gay marriage. One Muslim woman may choose to wear the traditional hijab, while another may reject any head cover, instead opting for more western garb. Making assumptions about people's beliefs, while never appropriate, has become increasingly problematic in this era of globalization. We can no longer assume that the neighbors who look like us share our values and perspectives; our intellectual and emotion community is as likely to consist of people in another country as those who live on our street. The norms and assumptions of previous communities must be re-examined through the use of democratic deliberation based on new norms of respect, openness to difference, a willingness to embrace conflict and disagreement and learn from one another.

Likewise, in educational organizations, we cannot assume homogeneity, but rather difference. Public schools have become one of the places in which people from different races, linguistic and cultural backgrounds, class and socioeconomic status, and religious beliefs regularly come together. In recognition of this situation, two decades ago, scholars began to write about the need for educational leaders to create "communities of difference" (Furman, 1998; Shields, 2003) in which traditional norms, beliefs, values, and practices may no longer be assumed. Instead of being able to build on a core of shared tradition, the new core is a belief in the need for absolute regard for all people (Starratt, 1991), the value of diverse perspectives in shaping the new norms and practices of the community, and the need for strong relationships and extensive dialogue to accomplish the goal.

An educational leader in a school with a diverse student population from many cultures may need to engage in extensive reflection and deliberation about what kind of social activities are appropriate for the new mix of students. When an outstanding student is the star of the school debating team, extensive communication with parents about the nature of the activity may prevent an unpleasant surprise when a parent states that, due to religious beliefs, the child may not go out of town unsupervised to participate in a state final competition. More importantly, educational leaders will need to carefully examine the pedagogy and curriculum of their schools to ensure that the diverse backgrounds and perspectives of their students are welcomed and included, that the former Eurocentric approach to teaching is replaced with one that is more conducive to democratic deliberation, critique, and reflection.

New forms of community require new ways of thinking. Leaders in national and state governments as well as educational leaders will need to ensure that policies and practices take account of the ever more diverse population. This is particularly important because a diverse group of electors is rarely fully represented in governing bodies; for example, school leaders often find themselves responsive to elected boards that continue to be comprised primarily of White, middle class members, while, at the same time, being responsible to a large and extremely diverse school community. This situation, and many others, suggests that courageous leadership is required—especially in situations in which there are power imbalances and inequities or in which difficult questions must be raised and addressed. Leaders must be prepared to carefully and critically assess each situation and to determine an appropriate and equitable strategy in which multiple voices are heard and perspectives considered.

CULTURES IN CONFLICT

There is no doubt that culture is an integral part of community. However, as we saw in the previous section, community is no longer (if it ever really was) based on a shared culture, but is grounded in multiple and sometimes competing cultures. To emphasize the role of globalization in the multiplication of diverse cultural perspectives, I have chosen to discuss culture as a separate entity.

As Friedman's metaphors suggested, we need to hold traditional values and new approaches in some sort of tenuous tension. At the same time, it is important to determine which of the older values are worth preserving. Sometimes, traditional values can lead us to forge bonds and develop communities that exclude, and often harm, others. One global example might be the ways in which the Afghan Taliban was so focused on promoting a particular ideology that it destroyed historic giant Buddhas. Another might be the ways in which certain communities have developed such an anti-American backlash that many innocent people are hurt during attacks on luxury hotels worldwide. Although the backlash is prompted by those who reject the excesses and spread of capitalism throughout much of the world, the wanton killing of victims is an ill conceived attempt to protect traditional values. Benjamin Barber (1995) in a book called *Jihad vs McWorld* also captures these tensions and argues that capitalism runs wild when it is disconnected from what he calls "the humanizing constraints of the democratic nation-state" (p. xii). The need is to determine how to address the tensions that are inherent in our interconnected global economic and political systems in a world of national, regional, ethnic and religious divisions and still maintain a strong connection to our common humanity.

These global tensions do not only reflect economic or political situations. Similar attitudes are evident in our educational organizations. Too often we talk about welcoming diversity and providing support for all students, but if it appears that English-language learners are preventing a school from attaining AYP, they quickly become the scapegoats and the school community begins to take steps to relegate these students to other schools and different communities. Too often we hear disparaging remarks about students from non middle-class, non-Caucasian backgrounds, suggesting that *they* chose to come to this country and hence it is solely their responsibility to *adapt* to our norms and to learn "the American way." The situation is complex. There is no doubt that many newcomers may have actively chosen America as their new country, believing that the relocation offers new opportunities and advantages to their children. These immigrants (those whom Ogbu, 1992, might call "voluntary minorities") came, knowing that their children will be exposed to Western cultures, Western curriculum, and that the language of instruction will be English. But they also come, hoping that they contribute something meaningful to their new country. Others, who are long standing American citizens (African Americans, and others) of course originally came less voluntarily and have suffered repression and oppression from the outset.

In most countries, indigenous people (Maori, Mayan, Native American, etc,) still experience unequal socioeconomic outcomes (lower wages, poorer health and less health care, lower levels of education, and so on) than those in dominant power positions. In fact, in the past, educators worldwide made what is now widely perceived to be the mistake of requiring all indigenous children to reject their home languages and to speak only English. With the loss of language has come, not only a loss of culture, but considerable dislocation in social and economic circumstances as well. The concomitant belief of the dominant middle class was, for too long, a belief that Native Americans, for example, were incapable of governing themselves and needed to be granted special status under the watchful "guardianship" of the federal government. At the time, education was often conceptualized as a means of civilizing the "savages," of eliminating their ethnicity and their culture, and making them as "White" as possible. The reasons for the inequality are complex, but generally stem from those in power (often the conquerors) taking a deficit approach to the indigenous populations. We must take care not to reintroduce similar practices for those who have chosen to make our home, their home, as well.

An important aspect of leading justly in a complex world requires us to consider the impact of globalization on the identity development of all students, helping them to balance the cultures and traditions from which they come and the needs of the new community. Because all are changed when they encounter new perspectives, we must take care, as we are introducing new ways of thought or action to students not to devalue the values and practices of their homes. We also must take care not to essentialize students' cultures and hence, to make unwarranted assumptions about what they are or are not able to do. The issue is considerably more complex than it first appears, because our tendency is to think of cultures that seem exotic (and often distant) as homogeneous. Too often educators are told, for example, things like "Native American children are good with their hands," or "Asian children are good at math"—both bold and inaccurate generalizations, of course.

We must also take care not to jump to conclusions when students' approaches or speech patterns are different from those we have normally encountered. For example, one of my international doctoral students speaks with the directness that is the norm in his culture. On one occasion he knocked on the door of my colleague to keep a previously established appointment, and asked his question about his programmatic research requirement. Her reply to him was that he was always "rude" and made her feel defensive—a reply that bothered him tremendously for days. His culture demands respect for those in authority, but because his speech cadences were different from his domestic peers, the professor misrecognized his approach. Although for this student who is proficient and fluent in English, operating in a second language did not appear to be a complicating factor, second language learners often do appear more direct, and less nuanced—not out of lack of respect, but because of linguistic limitations. It is incumbent upon us, as educational leaders, to be aware of the dangers of what Taubman calls the fictional identity register—one that "imprisons the subject" (1993, p. 291) in an identity created by others' perceptions and understandings. Making unwarranted assumptions about any aspect of identity—race, ethnicity, culture, class, religion or spirituality—can be both alienating and objectifying.

As educational leaders whose students increasingly reflect the global (rather than local) community, and bring multiple perspectives to each conversation, how do we help teachers and students to learn skills of critique and discrimination, to sort myth from reality and opinion from "truth"? The challenging task is to help students to be both critical of, and open to, new ideas and indeed, to have the agency to shape identities that will be both different from those of their parents and yet connected to the traditions of their communities and countries. To do this, we must help educators and students to overcome their fear of the "Other," to avoid pathologizing that which they do not understand, and to develop deep respect for difference. In other words, we must determine how to balance the allure of the Lexus with the important roots provided by the olive tree and to help others to do the same.

To successfully address the challenges related to capitalism, communication, community, and culture, I will argue, in the next part of this chapter, that educators need to become both transformative leaders and public intellectuals.

TRANSFORMATIVE EDUCATIONAL LEADERS AS PUBLIC INTELLECTUALS

Educational leaders can no longer ignore the ways in which the forces of globalization act—both for good and for ill. In fact, it is apparent that to advance Foster's (1986) conception of leadership that is "critically educative," that looks at the "conditions in which we live," and decides "how to change them" (p. 185), educational leaders will need new strategies. Standing on principle and arguing against child labor when one realizes the importance to the family income of a 10 year old boy working in his father's copper shop in Pakistan, pounding designs into decorative pots with an awl and a small nail, suddenly seems very hollow. Arguing that newly arrived, and perhaps undocumented, immigrant parents must come into the school to register their children seems somehow inappropriate. And yet, persistent questions remain. In this section I argue that to successfully address such complex questions, socially just educational leaders need to develop four dispositions and skill sets: an awakening of global curiosity, the ability to establish strong, dialogic relationships; a transformative approach to leadership; and a willingness to take a stance as a public intellectual.

AWAKENING GLOBAL CURIOSITY

In their local contexts, educational leaders must be supported as they challenge inequities in policies and practice and they must learn how to engage others in the difficult and challenging conversations required to effect justice more globally. A recent example makes the point graphically. A graduate student (already a respected educational leader) enrolled in my introduction to educational administration course seemed surprised when much of the conversation about leadership roles focused on equity and social justice. At one point, we spent considerable time discussing a pedagogical strategy (outlined by Bigelow, 1998) that helped students become aware of the depressed conditions in developing countries—conditions that in North America often lead to lower prices for imported commodities than for those manufactured at home. In frustration she burst out, "Why do we have to talk about these things? Students won't even enjoy shopping any more!" The student's relatively isolated and privileged position in society had made her oblivious to the material realities and needs of people in developing countries, in part because she had not had any first hand experiences, either through international travel or through prolonged interaction with people from other countries or cultures. Her outrageous response emphasizes the urgency of helping leaders understand the complex issues related to the interconnected nature of society.

I believe that the first step toward leading justly is, therefore, reaching out—seeking understanding of complex issues. We need to understand that simply cracking down on the Afghan opium trade will enrich the drug lords, but leave the peasant farmer with no means of sustenance. However, in this still very tribal country, providing the farmers with alternative sources of sustenance—perhaps grape vines or wheat—and finding ways to help stabilize the markets may be a more successful strategy. Arguing against the recent law outlawing corporal punishment, the traditional means of classroom management exercised by many teachers in overcrowded and under-resourced South African classrooms may seem morally right. But unless we provide alternative pedagogical and classroom management strategies, teachers report increased frustration and lack of control in crowded classrooms of 50-60 students (Nkukwana, 2006, p. 1). Closer to home, arguing for increased parental choice in schooling may seem "democratic," but at the same time, may exacerbate inequities in schooling, especially continuing to marginalize and disadvantage children from minoritized families. Here developing the disposition I have identified as "global curiosity" is an essential starting point. Interestingly, curiosity is also one of the traits that President Obama (2009), in his inaugural address, identified as one of the "true things" to which we need to return if we are to fulfill our "duties to ourselves, our nation, and the world, duties that we [must] not grudgingly accept but rather seize gladly."

DEVELOPING DIALOGIC RELATIONS

The second necessary disposition is something I have called "dialogic relationships"—getting to know others whose lived realities differ from one's own and developing strong, personal and relationships with them. Such relationships require more than simply learning about others; they entail meaningful and personal interaction among individuals and groups who hold different values, dissimilar beliefs and understandings, and who are willing to respectfully engage and learn from each other. Buber (1970) describes such relationships as "I-Thou" relationships, necessarily based on mutual respect.

In some ways, dialogue is both the very act of developing respectful and meaningful relationships and the vehicle for so doing. It is important here to explicate what I mean by dialogue, especially because a frequent critique of "too much talk" is that it rarely leads to socially just action. Freire (1998) acknowledges this misunderstanding, saying that

> dialogue cannot be blamed for the warped use sometimes made of it—for its pure imitation, or its caricature. Dialogue must not be transformed into a noncommittal "chewing the fat." (p. 249)

Here I am using the concept of dialogue ontologically; it is not simply talk, but a way of life, living in openness to the rich diversity of the world (Shields & Edwards, 2005). This use of dialogue is consistent with the work of both Freire and Bakhtin, two scholars who consistently posit the centrality of dialogue. Freire states that:

> It is meaningful precisely because the dialogical subjects, the agents in the dialogue, not only retain their identity, but actively defend it, and thus grow together. Precisely on this account, dialogue does not *level* them, does not "even them out," reduce them to each other...On the contrary, it implies a sincere, fundamental respect on the part of the subjects engaged in it. (1998, p. 248)

Here Freire is clear that those who participate in dialogue "grow" together, not in the sense of becoming more alike, but certainly in terms of new respect and understanding. For Baktin, dialogue is life itself—necessary for existing fully, for understanding, and for making decisions. He writes:

Everything ... gravitates toward the dialog, toward dialogical opposition, as the center point. Everything else is the means, the dialogue is the end. One voice alone concludes nothing and decides nothing. Two voices is the minimum for life, the minimum for existence. (1973, p. 213)

The message is that living dialogically necessitates moving beyond talk; it requires starting from new and deeper understandings of those who are different from ourselves, but it also requires action—collective action grounded in our dialogic relationships. In other words, socially just leaders understand that talk without action is empty and that critique without positing alternate and workable solutions is both vacuous and dangerous. Thus, I argue in the next section that leading justly in an era of globalization obliges educators to adopt a theory of leadership that emphasizes transformation.

ADOPTING A TRANSFORMATIVE APPROACH

To lead justly in the complex contexts of globalization, requires, in short, leadership that begins with questions of justice and community; leadership that not only critiques inequitable practices but offers the promise of both greater individual achievement and of a better life lived in common with others. Transformative leadership goes well beyond attending to improving the school as a whole or to raising test scores in order to meet jurisdictional expectations. It acknowledges, with Bourdieu (1977) and many others, that education is a field of struggle and therefore must attend to issues of power, conflict, and tension. And, perhaps most importantly, it focuses on implementing change to redress inequities.

For the past few years, I have been a coinvestigator in an international study intended to explore educators' conceptions of social justice and socially just leadership. Frequently, dedicated educators in high needs schools spoke passionately about finding new pedagogical strategies to ensure that all students in their schools met the specified academic benchmarks. When we asked these educators what their role might be, and what social justice would be like, should they move to a more homogeneous school with a higher average socioeconomic status, many seemed baffled. They scratched their heads and generally replied with words suggesting that all students have needs and they would try to meet whatever needs they identified.

Although a good school leader must address students' learning needs as they are identified—it seems to embody a thin conception of social justice. For me (and my coresearchers, see for example Mohan, Shields, Ibrahim, 2008), a more robust conception of socially just leadership would involve the leader helping students of privilege to understand their social position, helping them to develop not only a global curiosity, but a more global sense of responsibility. Leading justly involves recognizing how one's own position and lifestyle may contribute to exacerbating or alleviating global disparity—and this is the case whether one is in a high needs or more affluent school. It requires, as demonstrated by Westheimer and Kahne (2004) that if we want to educate students for social justice, we will need to initiate programs that not only foster individual responsibility, or participatory citizenship practices, but justice-oriented approaches.

One strategy often purported to increase awareness is the "internationalization" of education. Too often, however, this is limited to the recruitment of some international students or the addition of a reading from a country outside our own. Yet, when international students appear in our classrooms, how often do we consider the opportunity one of mutual learning and exchange? Most common is the approach that assumes they have little background knowledge and that they have come to absorb what we have to offer. We rarely take the time to learn from them—especially if it requires that we make an effort to understand their expression—as they often struggle to express themselves in a second language. We rarely take time to consider their prior situations, their specific learning needs, or how they can contribute to our understanding of a global community. We rarely encourage the introduction of new perspectives from different traditions that might enrich our understanding.

A transformative approach to educational leadership requires that we recognize that even though we cannot alleviate all injustice or all material disparity, we must do what we can both to challenge unjust practices and to overcome inequity, and to teach others to do the same. Transformative educational leaders need to act with courage and conviction to bring about the promise of education as apprenticeship that teaches students, as Maxine Greene (1988) states, to be "citizens of the free world—having the capacity to choose, the power to act to attain one's purposes, and the ability to help transform a world lived in common with others."

TAKING A POSITION AS A PUBLIC INTELLECTUAL

I have become increasingly convinced that a transformative educational leader must take the courageous path of being a public intellectual—involving oneself in the life of the wider community, seeking opportunities to contribute questions, critique, and ideas—but also ensuring the creation of spaces in which we can learn from one another. It is not enough to understand; it is not enough to empathize; we must act. This is neither an easy nor necessarily a popular role. By the term "public intellectual," I suggest (with Bourdieu & Passeron, 1977; Said, 1994; and others) that because educational leaders enjoy a social location of power and privilege, our very position requires that we take seriously our responsibility to speak to, and act for, the public good. To do so requires that we have a well-developed understanding of society based on the "possibility of more equal, respectful, and mutually beneficial ways of community life" (Green, 1999, p. vi). As public intellectuals, we must carefully identify areas where current structures, polices, and practices may be working well and those where change is urgently needed.

Bourdieu and Passeron (1977) argued that "the primary contribution of social scientists to society is to illuminate the mechanisms of domination and to show how these mechanisms reproduce social inequities, thus making the social sciences inherently critical" (p. 29). Said (1994) similarly explained that "the intellectual is an individual endowed with a faculty for representing, embodying, articulating a message, a view, an attitude, philosophy or opinion to, as well as for, a public" (p. 9). He added that taking a critical stance

> Cannot be played without a sense of being someone whose place it is publically to raise embarrassing questions, to confront orthodoxy and dogma (rather than to produce them), to be someone who cannot easily be co-opted by governments or corporations, and whose raison d'être is to represent all those people and issues that are routinely forgotten or swept under the rug. (p. 9)

For scholars, being a public intellectual may need to begin with a challenge to dominant research paradigms that often require a stance of assumed "objectivity" or neutrality—the careful detaching of oneself from any suggestion of research guided by a moral purpose or from what have come to be known as activist or advocacy approaches to research. For practicing school leaders, speaking out about injustice is perhaps even more difficult because educational leaders are often valued by boards and districts for their ability to present a united front and to keep the school and district from "bad press." Those who choose to speak out often find that the work is very lonely. An exemplary school principal who participated in a recent focus group related to leadership for social justice observed that "you need to have a table to bring it [the conversation] to." She explained that as a principal focused on social justice, participating in the group was the first time she had had an in-depth discussion of how to promote social justice. She asked:

> Who would I call if I had a question? I don't know. I think it's an issue of critical mass and also ... there has to be a table to bring it to. There has to be an audience to argue it with. There have to be people to have a dialogue,

and right now they are all the test score people. (Mohan, Shields, Ibrahim, 2008, p. 8)

Educational leaders who are dedicated to leading justly in a complex world must stop working in isolation; develop deeply dialogic communities in which we focus on how to move an equity agenda forward; and enact transformative practices. As public intellectuals, we must learn to speak out about globalization. Too often, however, even if the "table" exists and conversations are enjoined about leading justly, the dialogue is restricted to local and national issues.

Here, I am arguing that for educators to be public intellectuals in this era of globalization, we need an expanded discussion that moves beyond national borders and boundaries and considers the inextricably interconnected nature of humanity. I also posit, of course, that we need to go beyond dialogue to action, despite the fact that sometimes, the very complexity of our contexts and the tensions inherent in making difficult choices seems overwhelming.

At times, we are so afraid of being "politically incorrect," of making the "wrong" decision, that we fail to act at all. Sometimes, the easiest course of action is inaction. Yet, this is often inconsistent with leading justly. This is not, however, to suggest that any action is always better than inaction; acting swiftly to comply with the provisions of a punitive discipline policy may, for example, be inequitable. Responding positively to a call to arms may lead to the irony of engaging in warfare in a misguided attempt to "promote democracy." Instead, together, we must wrestle with the diverse perspectives derived from our dialogic relationships and, acknowledging that our insight and hence our decision, may still be imperfect, determine the best action we can take in a given situation. Taking care not to essentialize or pathologize, to include the voices and perspectives of those who may be affected by a given decision, and to examine our motives, we must act.

CONCLUSION: LEADING JUSTLY IN A COMPLEX WORLD

In this chapter, I have argued that "global curiosity"—an insatiable desire to constantly learn more about the complex interrelationships of the local and the global is essential for educational leaders who want to lead justly in this complex world. I have also argued that, because talk without action is reprehensible, global responsibility must accompany global curiosity—examining the situation and then determining when, where, and how to act.

I have suggested that, among other issues, leaders will need to attend to the ways in which capitalism, consumerism, and rapidly expanded means of communication impinge on the ways in which we think about both community and cultures in new and often more complex ways. Further, I have demonstrated that these forces not only influence economic or political arenas, but social and educational ones as well, albeit in different ways in distinct contexts. To address these new realities, I have also suggested that educational leaders will need to develop strong dialogic relationships, to adopt transformative leadership practices, and to take a stance as a public intellectual. These are not predilections that may be acquired in a vacuum but instead will require a rethinking of both the content and scope of leadership preparation programs.

Effective preparation programs for global leadership will need to be grounded firmly in conversations about global disparities and inequities, about the integral interrelations between the local and the global, and about the tensions and paradoxes inherent in globalization—all of which have the potential to alleviate, but too often exacerbate, disparity and inequity. Such programs will increase their emphasis on the centrality of dialogic relations, focusing on helping educators to develop relationships with those whose backgrounds and cultures are different from their own. This may well require that programs in educational leadership increase the participation of international students and reduce the central focus on state standards. It may require that the traditional fundamentals of curriculum (law, finance, administration) be balanced with courses focused on transformation, dialogue, and global awareness. Further, new educational leadership preparation programs will emphasize the futility of individualism and competition, the loneliness of working in isolation, and the dangers of excessive compliance with the status quo.

The forces of globalization are inexorable—with considerable potential either to oppress and marginalize or to liberate and empower individuals, groups, and even nations. North American educators and students must comprehend the ways in which developed nations continue to repress those who are less fortunate and we must acknowledge our responsibility. Then, as Said (1994) argued, the public intellectual must act

> on the basis of universal principles: that all human beings are entitled to expect decent standards of behavior concerning freedom and justice from worldly powers or nations, and that deliberate or inadvertent violations of these standards need to be testified and fought against courageously. (p. 9)

Those of us who have the resources and the power to influence the negative impacts of globalization must not delay. We must never hear another educator put the enjoyment of shopping over the rights of other human beings to freedom and justice. We must join together as engaged and committed public intellectuals, working not only for the good of every individual in our local school system, but for the common good of society as well.

REFERENCES

Apple, M. (2001). *Educating the "right" way: Markets, standards, god, and inequality.* New York, NY: Routledge Falmer.

Bakhtin, M. (1973). *Problems of Dostoevsky's poetics.* Ann Arbor, MI: Ardis.

Barber, B. (1995). *Jihad vs. McWorld.* New York, NY: Ballentine Books.

Bigelow, B. (1998), The human lives behind the labels: The global sweatshop, Nike, and the race to the bottom, In W. Ayers, J. A. Hunt, & T. Quinn (Eds.), *Teaching for social justice* (pp. 21-38). New York, NY: Teachers College Press.

Bourdieu, P., with Passeron, J. C. (1977). *Reproduction in education, society and culture.* London: Sage.

Buber, M. (1970). *I and thou* (W. Kaufman, Trans.). New York, NY: Charles Scribner & Sons.

Burns, J. M. (1978). *Leadership.* New York, NY: Harper & Row.

Cohen, J. (1989). *Teaching beyond the borders: A review of the global studies Latin America Unit.* Retrieved from ERIC database. (ED308126)

Fennimore, B. S. (1997) When mediation and equity are at odds: Potential lessons in Democracy, *Theory into Practice, 36,* 59-64.

Foster, W. (19869). *Paradigms and promises.* Buffalo, NY: Prometheus.

Freire, P. (1998). *Pedagogy of freedom: Ethics, democracy, and civic courage.* Lanham, MD: Rowan & Littlefield.

Freire, P. (2000). Education for critical consciousness. In A. M. A. Freire & D. Macedo (Eds.), *The Paulo Freire reader* (pp. 80-110). New York, NY: Continuum.

Friedman, T. L. (1999). *The Lexus and the olive tree.* New York, NY: Random House/Anchor.

Furman, G. C. (1998). Postmodernism and community in schools: Unraveling the paradox. *Educational Administration Quarterly, 34*(3), 298-328.

Giroux, H. A. (2005). The terror of neoliberalism: rethinking the significance of cultural politics. *College Literature, 32*(1), 10-19

Green, J. M. (1999). *Deep democracy: Diversity, community, and transformation.* Lanham, MD: Rowman & Littlefield.

Greene, M (1988). *The dialectic of freedom.* New York, NY: Teachers' College Press.

Harding, S. (1996). Rethinking standpoint epistemology: What is strong objectivity? In E. F. Keller & H. Longino (Eds.), *Feminism and science.* Oxford, England: Oxford University Press.

Hayward, F. M. (2000), *Internationalization of U.S. higher education* (Preliminary status report). Washington, DC: American Council on Education. Retrieved from http://www.acenet.edu/bookstore

Hunter, J. C. (1998), *The servant.* Rocklin, CA: Prima Publications.

Janis, I, (1977). *Groupthink: Psychological studies of policy decisions and fiascos*. Boston: Houghton Mifflin
Kincheloe, J. L., & Steinberg, S. R. (1995). The more questions we ask, the more questions we ask. In J. L. Kincheloe & S. R. Steinberg (Eds.), *Thirteen questions* (2nd ed.). New York, NY: Peter Lang.
Knight, J. (2004), Internationalization remodeled: Definition, approaches, and rationales, *Journal of Studies in International Education, 8*(1), 5-31.
Leithwood, K., & Jantzi, D. (1990). Transformational leadership: How principals can help to reform school cultures. *School Effectiveness and School Improvement, 1*(4), 249-280.
Marshall, C. (2994). Social justice challenges to educational administration: Introduction to a special issue. *Educational Administration Quarterly, 40*(1), 3-13
Mohan, E., Shields, C. M., & Ibrahim, G. (2008, November). *Bringing social justice "to life": Educational leaders' perspectives on practicing social justice*. Paper presented at the annual conference of the University Council for Educational Administration, Orlando, FL.
Nkukwana, J. G. (2006). *Educational reforms and their impact on leadership*. Unpublished paper, Walter Sisulu University, Butterworth, Eastern Cape Province, South Africa.
Noddings, N. (Ed.). (2005). *Educating citizens for global awareness*. New York, NY: Teachers College Press.
Obama, B. H. (2009), Inaugural address. *Chicago Tribune*. Retrieved from http://www.chicagotribune.com/news/politics/sns-ap-inauguration-obama-text,0,7494603.story?page=2.
Ogbu, J. (1992). Understanding cultural diversity and learning. *Educational Researcher, 21*(8), 5-14.
Palmer, P. J. (1998). *The courage to teach: Exploring the inner landscape of a teacher's life*. San Francisco: Jossey-Bass.
Pitsuman, S. (2008, April). Keynote address delivered at the opening ceremony of the International Conference on Leadership in Diversity and Globalization, Phulet, Thailand.
Portelli, J. P. (2001). *Erosion of democracy in education: Critique to possibilities*. Calgary, Alberta, Canda: Detsileg.
Quantz, R. A., Rogers, J., & Dantley, M. (1991). Rethinking transformative leadership: Toward democratic reform of schools. *Journal of Education, 173*(3), pgs. 96-118.
Said, E. W. (1994). Representations of the intellectual. In E. W. Said (Ed.), *Representations of the intellectual: The 1993 Reith lectures* (pp. 3-17). London: Random House.
Shields, C. M. (2003). *Good intentions are not enough: Transformative leaderships for communities of difference*. Lanham, MD: Scarecrow.
Shields, C. M. (in press), Leadership: Transformative. In E. Baker, B. McGaw, & P. Peterson (Eds.), *International encyclopedia of education* (3rd ed.). Oxford, England: Elsevier.
Shields, C. M., & Edwards, M. M. (2005). *Dialogue is not just talk: A new ground for educational leaders*. New York, NY: Peter Lang

Shields, C. M., Edwards, M. M., & Sayani, A. (Eds.). (2005). *Inspiring practice: Spirituality and educational leadership*. Lancaster, PA: Pro>Active.
Smith, L. T. (1999). *Decolonizing methodologies: research and Indigenous peoples*. Dunedin, NZ: University of Otago Press.
Starratt, R. J. (1991). Building an ethical school: A theory for practice in educational leadership. *Educational Administration Quarterly, 27,* 185-202.
Stromquist, N. P., & Monkman, K. (2000), *Globalization and education: Integration and contestation across cultures*. Lanham, MD: Roman & Littlefield.
Taubman, P. (1993). Separate identities, separate lives: Diversity in the curriculum. In L. Castenall & W. Pinar (Eds.), *Understanding curriculum as a racial text: Representing identities and difference in education* (pp. 289-307). Albany: State University of New York Press.
Tonnies, F. (1957). *Of sociology: Pure applied and empirical*. Chicago: University of Chicago.
Weiner, E. J. (2003). Secretary Paulo Freire and the democratization of power: Toward a theory of transformative leadership. *Educational Philosophy and Theory, 35*(1), 89-106.
Westheimer, J., & Kahne, J. (2004) What kind of citizen? The politics of educating for democracy, *American Educational Research Journal Summer, 41*(2), 237-269.

SCENIC OVERLOOK

From the Leadership Bridge

Guidelines for Discussions and Reflection

For school leaders:

1. How do you lead justly in diverse schools? Provide personal experiences.
2. To what extent do you believe issues of globalization influence the makings of a socially just educational leader? Support your claims.
3. To what extent do the author's complexities of globalization influence your understanding, ability, and/or willingness to engage in such practice?
4. Map your stages/steps in developing yourself as a public intellectual. How will you foster the development of a transformative approach to school leadership? What will it mean for you to identify as a public intellectual?

For those preparing school leaders:

1. How do you encourage aspiring school leaders to lead justly in increasingly culturally diverse schools? How does your preparation program support such efforts?

2. To what extent does your preparation program address issues of globalization on schools?
3. To what extent does your program consider the influence of globalization in creating socially just educational leader?
4. How do you understand the complexities of globalization? To what extent does this understanding influence your ability and/or willingness to engage in such discussions/experiences with students?
5. How have you developed as a public intellectual?
6. How do you foster the development of a transformative approach to school leadership for aspiring school leaders?

We now move to Section II: Looking Outward.

SECTION II

LOOKING OUTWARD

CHAPTER 6

THE MISEDUCATION OF A PROFESSOR OF EDUCATIONAL ADMINISTRATION

Learning and Unlearning Culturally (Ir)relevant Leadership

Jeffrey S. Brooks

This chapter focuses on issues that confront educational leadership instructors who conduct their work abroad and suggests that approaching work from a perspective of culturally relevant pedagogy (Ladson-Billings, 1992) can help overcome some of these issues—both in transnational and domestic contexts. Primary data for this paper is derived from my experience teaching organizational leadership to graduate students at a university in the Philippines, and to a lesser extent my experiences teaching the same subject at universities in the United States. These teaching experiences highlight the necessity of understanding social justice as a culturally relevant phenomenon with context-specific political and social dynamics rather than as a set of abstract principles that can be applied to understand or guide leadership as something that can be generalized to multiple situations and locales. Building on the work of Hafner (2006) and Ladson-Billings (1995) I argue that this demands a re-thinking of how we engage students and conceptualize leadership both internationally and domestically, and I explore several instructional methodologies that hold promise for deepening students' understanding of social justice. Based on these data, I suggest that educational leadership is to some extent a local and global phenomenon and that this realization should urge researchers to reconsider research methodologies and the knowledge bases that undergird their work so as to be culturally relevant to a local and global audience.

DANGEROUS MINDS IN EVERY SCHOOLHOUSE

Gloria Ladson-Billings (1998) begins an article on culturally relevant pedagogy and teacher assessment by evoking the film *Dangerous Minds*. Ladson-Billings explains that the film, in which a White teacher "saves" the "class from hell" (p. 255)—comprised wholly of students of color—is an example of cultural and racial bias. Further, she contends that the film, and others of its ilk, go beyond bias and are better characterized as a dangerous admixture of ignorance, missionary zeal, and insensitive, uncritical and discriminatory teaching behaviors that assume students of color are disadvantaged, deficient, and need a "White" shining knight to save them from themselves. While *Dangerous Minds* is Hollywood contrivance (though based on a true story), a growing body of empirical evidence (see Rovai, Gallien & Whiting, 2005 for a useful overview) suggests that Ladson-Billings' critique extends beyond celluloid and is playing out in classrooms across the United States. Moreover, while Ladson-Billings' appraisal centers on racial dynamics of African American students oppressed by a White Anglocentric curriculum, culture of course extends beyond race. While in the United States racism may be one of the most obviously problematic manifestations of cultural oppression, it is hardly the only one. To be sure, students are implicitly and/or explicitly deemed culturally irrelevant if they deviate from the dominant culture in terms of issues related to gender, religion, sexuality, social class, language, economics, socioeconomics, learning style, and many other areas of difference. Sadly, despite scattered and infrequent success stories, it is hard to argue against the contention that the public schools of the United States are providing a second-rate education to students who are not members of the dominant middle/upper class of White America (Delpit, 1996; West, 1993). Indeed, it seems rather than an education based on engaging lessons that facilitate learning and matriculating through curricula that communicate possibility, students are often afforded a vigorous miseducation fraught with stereotypes, exclusion and marginalization that delegitimizes their culture rather than celebrating it. They are indoctrinated into and then repeatedly abused by a system that tells them what they know is invalid, their way of looking at the world is subsufficient and that they are a failure-waiting-to-happen rather than a success-in-the-making. The message is this: your culture is irrelevant, and by extension, *you* are irrelevant—this school system is designed to persecute you rather than help you reach your potential. This is a school system founded on culturally irrelevant pedagogy.

Students receive the messages of culturally irrelevant pedagogy vis-a-vis explicit and implicit messages. Among implicit lessons are those taught through a hidden curriculum of rules, instructional techniques, and forms of assessment that are either insensitive to, or do not value, the way that students' culture—which was acquired and internalized long before they set foot in a school and influences the way they learn and respond to formal education. The lessons of the hidden curriculum teach students from a cultural minority that anything other than mainstreamness is improper and will be assessed as a downward deviation from excellent, and possibly even from average (Apple, 1979). Acting in any way other than the way of dominant folk lacks taste, intelligence, and perhaps most importantly, culture (Ogbu, 1978). This anti-difference quality existed long before 1954, when *Brown versus Board* ordered the desegregation of U.S. public schools (Kluger, 2004). Recent scholars point out that schools are "resegregating" at an alarming rate and others argue that while desegregation happened at the school level, in terms of a redistribution of students of color, have never truly segregated (Spring, 2006). Spring, for example, argues that the United States has simply progressed through stages of marginalization rather than move beyond it. First-generation segregation was the pre-Brown era, when schools were clearly separate and unequal. Second-generation segregation was institutionalized through curricular tracking of various kinds, manifest in the prevalence of students of color in special education programs, a concurrently high number of White students in advanced course offerings and teacher promotion systems structured in a way that means in many instances that low-performing (read: students of color) are taught by the least experienced teachers. Resegregation of schools, the widening of the achievement gap based on color and the emergence of publicly-funded chapter schools may ultimately suggest a form of Third-generation segregation. Again, while my example focuses on race, these multiple forms of oppression are mirrored for students with nearly any nonmainstream characteristics.

Even as I type these words, I can hear many of my colleagues, students and friends: "But I don't want schools like that and I work hard to create educational experiences that *are* culturally relevant, that strive to celebrate individual difference and to teach liberation instead of oppression! I understand critical theories that interrogate and dismantle hegemony! I know that something new is needed! I will make it happen! I'm not part of the problem—I'm part of the solution!" A few years ago I would have led the chorus. But now I ask, skeptically, both of myself and my colleagues ... *really?* Such rhetoric sounds great, plays well to sympathetic audiences...and it's exactly what sensitive and progressive educators, no matter their color or culture, are taught to say and think about this issue in Colleges of Education and in some cases by their peers in schools. Yet how is it that schools seem to be increasingly intolerant rather than tolerant, that students and schools "fail" at an unprecedented rate, and that for all the innovations in critical theory developed by brilliant minds in our field, we are left with schools that don't look much different than they did a century ago (Tyack & Cuban, 1985)? How is it that we are so bad at translating passionate and noble intent into tangible actions that produce better educational processes and outcomes?

These questions are among the most important any educator might consider, and I try to keep them at the heart of my work as a teacher, researcher, and servant in my position as a professor of educational leadership at a large public university. What I have come to realize, however, is that there is a distance between conceptual awareness and empirical action. I have heard for more beautiful speeches about education than I have witnessed beautiful education in schools, and unless we accept the responsibility to actively bridge this distance the insights of critical theory and culturally relevant pedagogy are useless. In this chapter, I aim to explain and explore the evolution of my understanding of what some of the issues I've discussed so far really look like in practice by reflecting on steps and missteps I have taken in my thinking and work. More specifically, I use certain ideas from culturally relevant pedagogy literature and a few from critical theory as a way to make sense of my (r)evolution as an academic. In a sense, some of this may seem like it's nothing new; but, as someone who believes deeply in the transformative potential of both critical theory and culturally relevant pedagogy, I urge you to think carefully about your own work bridging the gap between thought and action as you read the following pages of this book. To help prompt you to engage the ideas here and make them your own, I will pose each of the level-one headers in the chapter as questions that hopefully we will consider together. So, at the onset, please accept this introduction as an invitation to join me in a dialogue of ideas and action toward the end of helping us both reflect on how we can be what we think. My belief is that it is ultimately more important how **YOU** answer each of these questions than how I answer them.

WHAT KIND OF CONVERSATION WILL WE HAVE?

The purpose of this chapter is to urge both of us (you and I) to reflect on our dispositions, knowledge and espoused values and consider whether we operate as educators from a pedagogy of cultural relevance or irrelevance. To attend to this goal, I followed a biographical methodological approach used in studies seeking to investigate similar phenomena (Shields, 2005; Shields, LaRocque, & Oberg, 2002; Shields & Edwards, 2005; Waite, Nelson, & Guajardo, in press). My friend Autumn Tooms and I have also worked with this technique in another research project (Brooks & Tooms, in press). Primary data for this chapter are derived from my experience teaching organizational leadership in the Philippines (I am a U.S.-based educational leadership professor). These data are then critiqued through a conceptual framework grounded in culturally relevant pedagogy. Ultimately, these teaching experiences highlight the necessity of understanding educational leadership as a culturally relevant phenomenon with context-specific political, economic, legal and social dynamics rather than as a set of abstract and universal principles. Building on the work of Hafner (2006) and Ladson-Billings (1995), I argue that this demands a re-thinking of how instructors engage students and concepts as responsible and committed teachers of leadership. I explore several instructional methodologies and epistemologies that may hold promise for deepening students' understanding of leadership, and ultimately their understanding of educational leadership principles and practice (Marshall & Oliva, 2006). Based on these reflections and analyses, I suggest that culturally relevant educational leadership (a) is a glocal phenomenon, meaning a meaningful integration of the local with the global, (b) begins with each student's culture and knowledge rather than a curriculum or the instructor's culture, and (c) that leaders must focus on the cultural relevance of education for multiple stakeholders, including students, professional educators (e.g. teachers, counselors, administrators, etc.), and non-professional educators (e.g. families/guardians, community leaders, policymakers, etc.). The recursive and iterative nature of this project demands that all of this be woven together rather than discretely organized into a more traditional and linear format.

ARE YOU UNLEARNING YOUR MISEDUCATION?

The Ladson-Billings article I mentioned at the onset of this chapter is one in a series of works on culturally relevant pedagogy where she and others have argued that a fundamental disconnect between teaching and student cultures and subcultures is the root of a differentiated, unequal and inequitable education for people of minority cultures in the United States (e.g. Delpit, 1996; Ladson-Billings, 1992, 1995, 1998; Ogbu, 1978). In essence, these authors state that education from a culturally irrelevant pedagogical orientation amounts to intellectual colonialism that strips students of their humanity rather than helping attain their goals and dreams (Ladson-Billings, 1997). While the core of Ladson-Billings' argument is centered on specific conditions affecting the education of African-American students in the United States, the case against culturally irrelevant pedagogy is applicable internationally as scholars seek to teach and conduct research in cross-cultural contexts, as I will demonstrate in a subsequent section. But first, it is important that I discuss some of the ways that scholars in educational leadership have grappled with some issues similar to those Ladson-Billings and her colleagues have investigated.

Scholars have examined how cultural relativism relates to the conceptualization and practice of educational leadership (see Capper, 1993 for an excellent collection of such studies). Researchers have also investigated school leaders' capacity to influence the culture of schools (Deal & Peterson, 1999; Fullan, 2001) and the way that cultures and subcultures influence leadership practice (Brooks & Jean-Marie, 2007). However, few have used Ladson-Billing's framework as a means to deconstruct and reflect on the possibility that those who prepare and train leaders may in fact be party to the miseducation of leaders and administrators by providing them with culturally irrelevant instruction and curricula.

CULTURALLY (IR)RELEVANT PEDAGOGY: WHAT IS YOUR PERSONAL HISTORY?

In order to ground a subsequent critique of my own experience teaching educational leadership in the Philippines, it is important to explain my personal teaching philosophy and some of the instructional techniques I have used. My teaching philosophy is based on the belief that educational leadership, policy, and foundations theories and concepts can and should be integrated to help shape relevant experiences for aspiring researcher-practitioners, regardless of the level of education (P-20) in which they seek to lead and regardless of whether their leadership is formal or informal. Accordingly, my courses incorporate: (a) resources from educational policy sources such as local, state, federal and international-level policies and statutes, (b) classic and cutting-edge empirical and conceptual educational leadership research, and (c) multidisciplinary theoretical and empirical studies that can deepen our understanding of multifaceted and often interrelated educational phenomena. Further, I actively seek out materials written by scholars and leaders representing and serving diverse populations, and I include works that urge students to consider their positionality with respect to issues of social justice. To me, diversity means diversity of race, ethnicity, gender, social class, sexual orientation, religion, epistemology, economic status, geography, language, and learning styles, among other characteristics.

When I use the term social justice, I have to admit that I have yet to discover an entirely fulfilling definition that fully encapsulates what I mean, but I can advance the following propositions that guide my thinking about justice[1]:

1. Justice *and* social justice are important for educational leaders to consider and ultimately practice. This distinction recognizes the individual and collective dynamics of justice.
2. Justice is about equity, equality, access, and many other interrelated subfactors.
3. Justice and social justice have been studied in all the social sciences, in law, philosophy and in other fields such as peace studies and conflict resolution. Educational leaders have much to learn from this work.
4. Justice and social justice are fluid concepts that evolve over time and change from situation to situation—injustice can never be "eradicated," as it constantly reforms and comes from another angle when dismantled in one place or situation.
5. It is important to know that justice exists as both an abstract concept and a set of concrete factors that affect people on a day-to-day basis.
6. Leadership for justice is an action and/or advocacy-oriented approach to education that seeks to positively influence educational, political and social forces that impact a child's life.

Certainly, it is difficult to include such a plurality of perspectives and meaningfully complement these ideas into every aspect of a single course, but I try my best with my limited understanding of the concepts. However, I also recognize that selecting quality course materials does not necessarily yield meaningful course experiences.

In terms of instruction I seek to develop in-course activities that challenge and broaden students' perspectives of salient issues, increasing their capacity to critically analyze topics through a variety of methods and conceptual frameworks, and examine their discrete role as empowered actors in the policy processes that shape educational issues at local, state, federal, and international levels. For example, here I have assigned students to interview and present critiques of the perspectives of local and state-level stakeholders, write literature reviews in the form of policy briefs on topics chosen by local educators, critical reflection assignments, and empirical investigations of local, state, national and international phenomenon.

Additionally, I have found Hafner's chapter (2006) "Elements of Social Justice Education Practice" (p. 177), particularly helpful in terms of helping me think about how to design course activities. She advises that instructors of leaders for social justice should:

1. Balance the emotional and cognitive components of the learning process through teaching that pays attention to personal safety, classroom norms, and guidelines for group behavior.
2. Acknowledging and supporting the personal (the individual student's experience) while illuminating the systemic (the interactions among social groups) through teaching that calls attention to the here-and-now of the classroom setting and grounds the systemic or abstract in an accumulation of concrete, real-life examples.
3. Attend to social relations within the classroom through teaching that helps students name behaviors that emerge in group dynamics, understand group process, and improve interpersonal communications, without blaming or judging each other.
4. Utilize reflection and experience as tools for student-centered learning through teaching that begins from the student's world view and experience as the starting point for dialogue or problem-solving.
5. Value awareness, personal growth, and change as outcomes of the learning process through teaching that balances different learning styles and is explicitly organized around goals of social awareness, knowledge, and social action, although proportions of these three goals change in relation to student interest and readiness.

In terms of in-class activities, I employ a combination of cooperative learning and experiential learning in my courses, and often ask students to develop and teach problems-based learning (Brooks, 2006; Jackson & Kelley, 2002) modules as a complement to other assignments. These strategies reflect my belief that adult learners bring a rich and varied set of professional and personal experiences to their studies (Baumgartner, 2001). As such, instruction should be challenging, immediately relevant, and constructively build on previous experience and knowledge. All that being said, the most wonderful teaching philosophy is weak if it can't bear the weight of reality; mine has developed, and I hope improved, but it has also been found wanting in many respects and it evolves as I constantly design and evaluate the success and failure of various course elements.

MALIGAYANG PAGDATING SA PILIPINAS (OR…WELCOME TO THE PHILIPPINES)

In 2007, I spent 5 months in the Philippines after winning a grant to support fieldwork and a semester of lecturing at Capitol University in Cagayan de Oro City (CDO) on the island of Mindanao. Before this period, I had traveled abroad a bit, but never worked as a teacher outside of the United States. At that point I had taught educational leadership at the university-level for 4 years, with some success, as evidenced through peer and student evaluations. I arrived in CDO on a blistering June morning and was soon thereafter assigned to teach organizational leadership in the Graduate School at Capitol University. My students were 16 Filipinos/as and one male Korean student from various degree programs. The Korean student in my class did not speak English, the language of instruction at the university, and was accompanied by an interpreter. In the Philippines, the path to school leadership does not go through the university. Instead, people become principals through one of two routes: they are either appointed by a school division superintendent, or by a Barangay Captain (something like a neighborhood mayor). This means that K-12 educational leadership is seldom taught, and is even less frequently an area of interest among Filipino scholars. So, I had few educators in my class, and more students from business, nautical studies, and engineering. Additionally, there were few indigenous resources from which I could draw. The leadership books I found in local stores and on bookshelves were predominantly from the United States, and were either penned by mass-market leadership gurus like Joseph Maxwell[2] or were black market educational administration texts with content over thirty years old. None of these seemed a great fit to me. I asked the Dean of the Graduate School to advise me as to what materials they commonly used to teach courses, and after she showed me her library and a few previous syllabi, which used a great deal of photocopied and free-access Internet materials, I was confident that I could design a relevant and challenging course.

I designed the course loosely around Peter Northouse's (2007) *Leadership: Theory and Practice* and planned to follow that up with Marshall and Oliva's (2006) *Leadership for Social Justice: Making Revolutions in Education*. I was certain these materials would give the students a good foundation in both classic and cutting-edge educational leadership concepts. The plan as to use many of the collaborative and experiential learning activities I had success with in courses I taught in the United States. We would study the largely technical and abstract Northouse perspectives on theory and use the self- and organizational evaluation surveys at the end of his chapters to prompt reflection. Then, I thought, I would really get the students going by having them read the social justice book, which I was sure would be inspiring and a big hit, as it was with so many students in the United States. Then my abstract plans hit the concrete of reality. Since I felt I didn't understand the cultural or even professional contexts in which these students practiced I decided to have them write PBL scenarios that we would analyze using the various theories we would discus in the course.

At the beginning of the semester, I learned that students had no books, and most had little money to spend on books. This was simply not a realistic expectation. To put it in perspective, the Northouse book cost around U.S.$60, plus shipping, for a paperback copy. At the time I taught the course this amount converted to approximately 2,900 Philippine Pesos. As I conducted the research part of my work in the city I soon discovered that the average teacher in Cagayan de Oro made around 3,000 Pesos *per month*. This salary often was an entire family's sole source of income. It was completely unreasonable for me to require the book, so instead I ordered a few extra copies and left them in the library so students had access to them. At the beginning of the semester, this seemed to work well, but even the fact that I could order additional copies of such high-priced books made me, and my students, acutely cognizant of the fact that in many ways, I was very much "the other" in this classroom.

For the most part, the semester went extremely well. Even though many said I intimidated them at the beginning of the semester, we developed a fine set of class norms and engaged in many activities the students later explained were memorable and useful. For example, after reading a chapter on team leadership and working through some problem-based learning modules we coconstructed, we went outside and analyzed the school's basketball team during a scrimmage. This sort of nonlecture exercise seemed to appeal to students, many of whom explained that they were used to sitting through hours and hours of lectures.

As the semester wore on, and I went deeper into my research in the city's schools I began to realize more about the day-to-day social, economic, political and organizational conditions in which my students worked and lived. I slowly understood the highly hierarchical nature of Filipino society, where subordinates are rarely, if ever, encouraged or allowed to question those "above" them in the organization and/or family. In large segments of Filipino society, this deference to authority is a virtue, a way to show respect. Further, cultural values such as *bahala na* (this-too-shall-pass attitude), *amor propio* (dignity), *hiya* (sense of shame), the importance of the extended family and the *barkada* (gang of friends), *bayanihan* (working together), and many others. Therefore, it shouldn't have surprised me when the first stumbling block of the semester came when we studied transformational leadership.

This is hugely oversimplified, but basically transformational leadership centers on charismatic leaders inspiring authentic change through shared decision making and the empowerment of subordinates (Northouse, 2006). Vision, missions, and the like come from the theory's lexicon and represented a real challenge to students, many of whom held deeply-rooted values related to deferring to authority out of respect and who preferred silence to broadcasting controversial opinion. On the day we discussed the theory, there was a very large hush in the room. Finally, a student spoke up and said, "look, if I did this—from my position—I would be fired." A principal I spoke with in my fieldwork put a more dire spin on the same issue when he explained the consequences of questioning or speaking out in opposition to superiors: "if I did that, I'd either be fired … or killed." This experience with transformational leadership, an engaging but ultimately not what I would characterize as a confrontational theory of leadership, suggested to me that much of what I might teach them via the Marshall and Oliva book on leadership for social justice was likely to be at best a look at an American curiosity and at worst an irresponsible instructional decision on my part. This book focuses on leadership conceived as advocacy and activism. Instead of digging into that book deeply, I did what I should have done the first class session, I shut up and listened to my students—and asked the class which leadership topics we had covered, or neglected, they would like to investigate. After developing a list of topics, which included issues mainly focused on organizational dynamics such as culture, structure, efficient processes, and communication we explored each drawing from salient literature more situated in an ethos of understanding rather than advocacy, and instead used these initial discussions to ask them what advocacy and activism might look like based on their understanding of Filipino culture. In the next section, I review a few more detailed constructs drawn from the culturally relevant pedagogy literature and critique my experience in light of these constructs.

HOW MIGHT CULTURALLY RELEVANT PEDAGOGY INFORM EDUCATIONAL LEADERSHIP?

Culturally relevant pedagogy is "a theoretical model that not only addresses student achievement but also helps students to accept and affirm their cultural identity while developing critical perspectives that challenge inequities in schools (and other institutions) perpetuate" (Ladson-Billings, 1995a, p. 469). Culturally relevant pedagogy emphasizes several propositions:

1. *Culturally relevant pedagogy is focused on academic and nonacademic success.* Banks and Banks (1995) suggest that "despite the current social inequities and hostile classroom environments, students must develop their academic skills. The way those skills are developed may vary, but all students need literacy, numeracy, technological, social and political skills" (p. 160). Importantly, while academic skills are at the heart of this orientation toward education, it also makes clear that these skills must be relevant inside and outside of the classroom. Success, then, is not limited to strictly classroom success, but also to success more broadly conceived as enhanced quality of life, which also includes economic, social, and political prosperity.

2. *Culturally relevant pedagogy demands a critical, deep and ongoing understanding of self, other and context as the foundation of education.* This means that for education to be culturally relevant, teachers and students must begin their work together by reflecting on their own culture, values, knowledge and situations and by seeking to understand the culture, values, knowledge and situations of the other people with whom they will co-construct their education, and the multiple contexts in which they will learn and teach. Culturally relevant pedagogy, then, is simultaneously about learning visible curricula and unlearning hidden curricula. Students and teachers bring intentional and unintentional attitudes, dispositions, and biases to their educational practice.

3. *Culturally relevant pedagogy is a constructivist approach to education.* Culturally relevant pedagogy assumes that knowledge is coconstructed by educators and educators as they learn in context. This has implications for both instruction and curricula. Certain instructional approaches such as problems-based learning (Brooks, 2008) and cooperative learning (Banks & Banks, 1995) hold more promise for promoting coconstruction than didactic approaches such as lectures. Curricula should be flexible, relevant and adaptable rather than monolithic and static. There is no immutable base of knowledge for the culturally relevant educator. Further, as constructivism suggests an approach to education that prizes an assimilation of existing knowledge with extant knowledge through higher order critical thinking. Put differently, this approach is about teaching *with* students, not *at* them; there is no single knowledge base, but multiple knowledge bases that continually evolve as

new information and experiences challenge and extend existing information and experiences.
4. *Culturally relevant pedagogy stresses the importance of the immediate and long-term usefulness of education.* Since culturally relevant pedagogy is founded on prior knowledge of students and teachers, it is of immediate use in that it builds on what is already there in a manner that allows students to meaningfully and progressively enhance current perspectives and knowledge. Additionally, since culturally relevant pedagogy is grounded in a critical perspective toward the assimilation of that which is new and that which is old, it equips students and teachers alike with a set of skills and dispositions oriented toward lifelong learning.

Each of these propositions must be understood not as normative dicta, but as specifically contextualized and idiosyncratic manifestations germane ultimately to *particular* student-teacher relationships, situations, and contexts. While culturally relevant pedagogy is rooted in constructivist ontology, the propositions nonetheless acknowledge the teacher's discrete influence in shaping their relationships with students, and also their influence in shaping students' relationship with the base of knowledge that undergirds curriculum and instruction in a given course or educational situation. Further, in translating this pedagogy into concrete instructional practice, Ladson-Billings found that "culturally relevant teaching must met three criteria: (a) an ability to develop students academically, (b) a willingness to nurture and support cultural competence, and (c) the development of a sociopolitical consciousness" (Ladson-Billings, 1995a, p. 483).

Ladson-Billings' work is, importantly, a critical perspective on education. She recognizes that status-quo educational practice will perpetuate a deeply-rooted cultural hegemony that stands only to perpetuate inequities rather than ameliorate them. Like Freire (1970), Ladson-Billings calls for an end to "banking" concepts of education that emphasize the supremacy of the teacher as dispenser of knowledge and instead demands a move toward the development of conscientizacão, which "refers to learning to perceive social, political, and economic contradictions, and to take action against the oppressive elements of reality" (Freire, 1970). Put differently, culturally relevant teaching focuses on: (a) teaching *with* rather than *at* students; (b) understanding that cultural differences between and among teachers and students demand an approach to instruction that is sensitive to needs, traditions, and mores of individual students, as well as cultures and subcultures within an educational setting, (d) recognizing that due to power and cultural dynamics embedded in the teacher-student relationship, the teacher is always "the other" (Ladson-Billings,

1995a, p. 470; Young, 1999) and; (c) both the process and the outcomes of education and achievement.

SO WHAT? *OR*, HOW CAN WE DISCUSS, REFLECT ON, AND EXTEND THESE IDEAS?

I came to feel that many of the theories I presented in my teaching experience in the Philippines, if not the manner in which I presented them, were culturally irrelevant. First, I found that much of my understanding of leadership, and the way I taught it, was context-specific to the United States. This forced me to recognize that quite a lot of the way U.S. scholars talk about social justice and leadership in the literature with which I was familiar assumes protection of the U.S. legal and educational systems, which in some ways provides certain basic protections and rights for activist-leaders, free speech and basic human rights. Moreover, many theories assume U.S. cultural and behavioral norms associated with public education, history and society in the United States. Many concepts I taught simply weren't applicable, and in fact if the students I worked with at Capitol University did some of the things I suggested and have seen my students do in U.S. schools, they might suffer tremendous consequences.

My experience teaching in the Philippines taught me that many educational leadership scholars in the United States feel comfortable speaking as though the findings and orientation of their work has global application when in fact they are limited by national, state, and local context-specific dynamics. Absolutist terminology abounds, when a more prudent and context-specific language is required. In addition to the Filipino cultural values previously articulated, I realized when I visited the schools in my Philippines study that there was a whole set of issues I had read about but wasn't prepared well to teach in relation to social justice practice *in situ*: student, teacher and administrator poverty, disease, transportation issues, facilities issues, theft and lack of instructional resources, severe school overcrowding, nepotism, corruption, language, gender, class, postcolonialism, and inequity issues, all in a cultural milieu that I was only able to grasp in part because I had read cultural anthropology work in addition to educational leadership literature. All applied theories of social justice, and possibly all theories of leadership, are ultimately emic, rather than etic—though we often pretend that the opposite is the case.

As I reflect on my experiences teaching educational leadership in the Philippines, I am struck by my need to continue to learn and expand my understanding of many interrelated concepts and practices. I am more in tune with the notion of glocalization, which holds that we all work and live in two simultaneous and reciprocal spheres, one local and the other global (Brooks & Normore, in press). They influence one another and are influenced by a variety of other dynamic and ever-shifting factors. My time in the Philippines also made clear to me that teaching educational leadership demands instruction from a culturally relevant pedagogical perspective, one that begins with student experiences rather than curriculum, that encourages the organic development of a personalized understanding of leadership practice, and one that incorporates diversity on a global level rather than marginalizing individuals by promoting a narrow theoretical understanding of leadership.

ACKNOWLEDGMENT

A previous version of this chapter was presented at the 2008 Annual Convention of the University Council for Educational Administration. I thank my Auburn University colleagues in the Friday Research Group for their support and critique of this work. This research was in part supported by a grant from the J. William Fulbright Foundation, Council for International Exchange of Scholars & United States Department of State (PL. 87-256, #7162). I thank these organization, the faculty and students of Capitol University, and the Philippine-American Educational Foundation for their support of this work.

NOTES

For a more fully developed discussion of these points, see my two chapters in the book: Bogotch, I., Beachum, F. Blount, J., Brooks, J. S., & English, F. W. (2008). *Radicalizing educational leadership: Toward a theory of social justice*. Rotterdam, The Netherlands: Sense Publishers.

Please note that I have nothing against Maxwell's work, I find more technical texts that extend students' conceptual understanding of leadership theory more appropriate for graduate work.

REFERENCES

Apple, M.W. (1979). *Ideology and curriculum*. Routeldge and Kegan Paul: Boston.

Baumgartner, L. M. (2001). An update on transformational learning. In S. B. Merriam (Ed.), *The new update on adult learning theory* (pp. 15-24). San Francisco: Jossey-Bass.

Bogotch, I., Beachum, F. Blount, J., Brooks, J. S. & English, F. W. (2008). *Radicalizing educational leadership: Toward a theory of social justice*. Rotterdam, The Netherlands: Sense Publishers.

Brooks, J. S. (2006). Problem-based learning. In F. W. English (Ed.), *Sage encyclopedia of educational leadership and administration* (pp. 806-807). Thousand Oaks, CA: Sage Publications.

Brooks, J. S., & Jean-Marie, G. (2007). Black leadership, white leadership: Race and race relations in an urban high school. *Journal of Educational Administration, 45*(6): 756-768.

Brooks, J. S., & Normore, A. H. (in press). Educational leadership: A glocal perspective. *Educational Policy.*

Brooks, J. S., & Tooms, A. K. (in press). A dialectic of social justice: Learning to lead through reflection and dialogue. *Journal of School Leadership.*

Capper, C.A. (Ed.) (1993). *Educational administration in a pluralistic society.* Albany: State University of New York Press.

Deal, T.E. & Peterson, K.D. (1999). *Shaping school culture: The heart of leadership.* San Francisco: Jossey-Bass,

Delpit, L. (1996). *Other people's children: Cultural conflict in the classroom.* New York, NY: The New Press.

Fullan, M. (2001). *Leading in a culture of change.* San Francisco: Jossey-Bass.

Hafner, M. M. (2006). Teaching strategies for developing leaders for social justice. In C. Marshall & M. Oliva (Eds.), *Leadership for social justice: Making revolutions in education* (pp. 167-193). Boston: Pearson.

Jackson, B. L., & Kelley, C. (2002). Exceptional and innovative programs in educational leadership. *Educational Administration Quarterly, 38*(2), 192-212.

Kluger, R. (2004). *Simple justice: The history of Brown vs. Board of Education and Black America's struggle for equality.* New York, NY: Vintage Books.

Ladson-Billings, G. J. (1998). Teaching in dangerous times: Culturally relevant approaches to teacher assessment. *The Journal of Negro Education, 67*(3), 255-267.

Ladson-Billings, G. J. (1997). *The dreamkeepers: Successful teachers of African-American children.* San Francisco: Jossey-Bass.

Ladson-Billings, G. J. (1995a). Toward a theory of culturally relevant pedagogy. *American Education Research Journal, 35,* 465-491.

Ladson-Billings, G. J. (1995b). Toward A critical race theory of education. *Teachers College Record, 97,* 47-68.

Ladson-Billings, G. (1995c). But that's just good teaching! The case for culturally relevant pedagogy. *Theory into Practice, 34*(3), 159-165.

Ladson-Billings, G. (1992). Liberatory consequences of literacy: A case of culturally relevant instruction for African American students. *The Journal of Negro Education, 61*(3), 378-391.

Ogbu. J. (1978). *Minority education and caste: The American system in cross-cultural perspective.* San Diego, CA: Academic Press.

Rovai, A. P., Gallien, L. B., & Wighting, M. J. (2005). Cultural and interpersonal factors affecting African American academic performance in higher education: A review and synthesis of the research literature. *The Journal of Negro Education, 74*(4), 359-370.

Shields, C. M., & Edwards, M. M. (2005). *Dialogue is not just talk: A new ground for educational leadership.* New York, NY: Peter Lang.

Shields, C. M., LaRocque, L. J., & Oberg, S. L. (2002). A conversation about race and ethnicity: Struggling to understand issues in cross-cultural leadership. *Journal of School Leadership 12*(2), 116-137.
Spring, J. (2006). *American education* (12th ed.). Boston: McGraw Hill.
Tyack, D., & Cuban, L. (1995). *Tinkering toward utopia: A century of public school reform*. Cambridge, MA: Harvard University Press.
Waite, D., Nelson, S. W., & Guajardo, M. (in press). Teaching and leadership for social justice and social responsibility: Home is where the struggle starts. *Journal of Educational Administration and Foundations*.
West, C. (1993). *Race matters*. New York, NY: Vintage Books.
Young, M. D., & Brooks, J. S. (2008). Supporting graduate students of color in educational administration preparation programs: Faculty perspectives on best practices, possibilities, and problems. *Educational Administration Quarterly, 44*(3), 391-423.
Young, M. D. (2000). Considering (irreconcilable?) contradictions in cross-group feminist research. *International Journal of Qualitative Studies in Education, 13*(6), 558-588.
Young, M. D. (1999). Multifocal educational policy research: Toward a method for enhancing traditional educational policy studies. *American Educational Research Journal, 36*(4), 677-714.

SCENIC OVERLOOK

Chapters 5 and 6

Guidelines for Discussions and Reflection

For school leaders:

1. Discuss and compare your understanding of culturally irrelevant pedagogy. How do you see this play in classrooms and school systems?
2. How do you see issues of culturally relevant phenomenon impact students' lives?
3. How does the author's experience with culturally irrelevant pedagogy compare to your lived experiences?
4. What are your feelings/thoughts as you read the author's experiences about the impact of dominance and its affect on perpetuating culturally irrelevant pedagogy?

For those preparing school leaders:

1. How do you understand culturally irrelevant pedagogy? How do you support such understanding throughout your courses?
2. How do aspiring school leaders understand how this plays out in classrooms and school systems? How do you support students in addressing such issues in the schools they serve?

3. How does your program address cultural relevancy throughout students' course work?
4. How does the author's experience with culturally irrelevant pedagogy compare to your lived experiences?
5. What are your feelings/thoughts as you read the author's experiences about the impact of dominance and its affect on perpetuating culturally irrelevant pedagogy? How often are issues such as this discussed with faculty in your preparation program?

Jeffrey Brooks' chapter confronted educational leadership's work abroad, suggesting we consider what it means to work from a culturally relevant framework. He offers his lived experiences as a scholar working at a university in the Philippines. Jeffrey Brooks encouraged scholars who prepare school leaders to consider how we engage students' internationally as well as domestically in issues of social justice.

In the next chapter, Colleen Larson and Teboho Moja recognize the importance of encouraging aspiring school leaders to engage with an increasing global society. The authors examine the findings from a 9-year study abroad program in South Africa, which inspire us to become more active in building bridges between home communities, global citizenship and leading for social justices issues worldwide.

CHAPTER 7

INDIVIDUAL TRANSFORMATION FOR GLOBAL IMPACT

Increasing Global Citizenship Through Study Abroad

Colleen L. Larson and Teboho Moja

In a recent *New York Times* article, "Cum Laude in Evading Bandits" Nicolas Kristof (2009), challenges universities to transform conventional approaches to education by getting students out of classrooms and beyond the borders of their own country and comfort zone. He writes:

> If colleges provide credit for dozing through an introductory Spanish class, why not give credit for a "gap year" in a Bolivian village? If students can learn about microfinance while sitting comatose in 9 A.M. lectures, couldn't they learn more by volunteering with a lender in a Bangladesh slum?

As awareness of our increasing global interdependence grows, leaders everywhere are recognizing the importance of encouraging international travel for the purpose of creating a greater appreciation of and tolerance for people beyond our borders. Disturbing acts of terrorism and clashes between nations and people illuminate the eminent danger of failing to understand the perspectives of people who are often deeply divided along racial, ethnic, religious, and class lines. These cultural divides are increasingly problematic in a world that is evermore connected through international commerce, communication systems, and travel. However, opportunities for more interaction do not always lead to greater understanding or connection. As deeply held values, beliefs and perspectives collide, multicultural, racial, and ethnic misunderstanding often fuels greater alienation. Kofi Annan, the Secretary-General of the United Nations asserts that one way we can address our global failure to understand one another is through education, broadly, and through the increasing use of traveling to and studying in other countries, specifically. He believes that study abroad programs are "more important than ever," saying:

> Clearly, we need to use education to advance tolerance and understanding. Perhaps more than ever, international understanding is essential to world peace—understanding between faiths, between nations, between cultures. We need each other as friends, as allies, as partners in a struggle for common values and common needs. (p. 2)

Annan's call for a greater attention to global education in the aftermath of 9/11, particularly to developing countries, motivated the U.S. Senate to unanimously declare 2006 as the "Year of Study Abroad." This resolution enhanced the visibility and importance of study abroad in the United States and set the stage for further efforts to expand study abroad opportunities through schools and universities. Annan, believes that in a global context of growing intolerance and conflict, study abroad experiences are critical to the effective education of today's youth. Further, he suggests that such programs can play an important role in enhancing cultural understanding, tolerance, and global cooperation.

This growing interest in encouraging travel to and study in developing countries arises within a societal context in the United States where just 28% of its citizens hold valid passports. Of this small percentage of people who travel abroad, the vast majority seek travel to England, Italy, France, or Spain. Similarly, the majority of European citizens seek travel to other European or U.S. destinations only. This means that people living in the United States as well as in other industrialized nations have considerably less exposure to and experiences with the developing nations within Africa, the Middle East, Asia, South America, Central America, or Australia. The low percentage of U.S. citizens who travel internationally, and particularly to developing countries, illuminates a large gap in the global experiences of people living in industrialized nations.

Over the past 10 years, the United States has seen a gradual increase in the number of citizens traveling to developing countries; however, much of this increase can be attributed to stricter passport policies post 9/11. Newly nationalized U.S. citizens who regularly visit family and friends in the country of their birth also contribute to the increased numbers of people traveling to developing countries, and men and women serving in the military, not surprisingly, go to developing countries. However, they rarely have a choice in where they will travel. Finally, students are increasingly, getting passports and they are traveling to emerging nations through university programs—so study abroad program are encouraging students to travel to places where the vast majority of U.S. citizens do not choose to go on their own.

The American Association of State Colleges and Universities sees a significant role for higher education to play in educating its citizens for membership in a global society. They remind us that:

> While the events of September 11 have underscored the need for strong homeland security and national defense, they have also powerfully reminded the nation of its inextricable relationships with the world community, as well as the vital importance of better awareness and understanding of its global neighbors ... higher education institutions, as primary agents of intellectual and cultural exchange, must maintain and enhance their international outlook in the world that is emerging.... If today's educated people are to be able to move comfortably in many different cultures, they must have the advantage of global education. (American Association of State Colleges and Universities Report, 2001)

Today, university sponsored study abroad programs are taking students to developing nations in growing numbers, however, traveling to developing nations through university sponsored programs is relatively new. Study abroad programs today have departed considerably from the dominant model that was established long ago for language immersion purposes. Given that these new programs are underpinned by considerably different purposes than earlier study abroad programs, universities have much to learn about how to design these programs well. Kofi Annan (2001) argues that, to be effective, programs that are designed to enhance global understanding must strike at the heart of the problems we face in becoming a global community, saying:

> None of us is born intolerant of those who differ from us. Intolerance is taught and can be untaught—though often with great difficulty. But prevention is far preferable to cure. We must work to prevent intolerance from taking hold in the next generation. We must build on the open mindedness of young people, and ensure that their minds remain open.... Clearly, we need to use education to advance tolerance and understanding. Perhaps more

than ever, international understanding is essential to world peace—understanding between faiths, between nations, between cultures. (p. 1)

Annan calls on universities to develop international programs that advance global tolerance and understanding. Former President Clinton saw both an economic advantage in encouraging studying abroad as well as an opportunity to expand global awareness and cooperation through education. He noted that 500,000 international students are studying in the United States at the postsecondary level, saying:

> These students not only contribute some $9 billion annually to our economy, but also enrich our communities with their cultures, while developing a life-long appreciation for ours. The goodwill these students bear for our country will in the future constitute one of our greatest foreign policy assets. Today the defense of U.S. interests, the effective management of global issues, and even an understanding of our Nation's diversity require ever-greater contact with, and understanding of people and cultures beyond our borders.

International and national leaders alike, then, agree that we need educational opportunities that can enhance multicultural understanding and cultivate better global citizens. However, study abroad programs have not always been designed to increase tolerance, enhance global understanding and encourage global citizenship.

In this paper, we examine some of the purposes underpinning study abroad programs and explore how these purposes shape not only the design of the programs, but the activities provided for the students within them. Given the importance of study abroad to the education of America's youth and given our limited and relatively recent insight into how to design these programs to enhance multicultural understanding and global citizenship, in this paper, we examine one program that is designed for these purposes, and in the final section, we discuss how this program is playing out in the experiences of the students who have participated in it. Through the stories they tell, we get greater insight into the experiences and activities that enhanced their understanding of social justice, increased their multicultural understanding, and created stronger commitments to global citizenship.

ACADEMIC TOURISM OR GLOBAL CITIZENSHIP?

Over the past 60 years, the intended outcome of study abroad programs has been quite narrow and easily articulated as it almost exclusively focused on language immersion for the purpose of becoming fluent in a foreign language. However, in recent years, study abroad programs have

Figure 7.1. A continuum of study abroad program/purposes.

flourished in universities across the United States and the purposes of these programs have become quite varied.

In this paper, we suggest that the majority of study abroad programs sponsored by U.S. universities today exist on a continuum (see Figure 7.1 below), emphasizing different purposes and offering students different kinds of learning opportunities. Although we discuss these programs at the polar ends of the spectrum, most programs exist at some point along this continuum. At one end of this spectrum, study abroad programs emphasize academic tourism in both their purposes and outcomes. These programs encourage students to spend a part of their academic program abroad, often two to three weeks during summer or winter breaks, allowing students to earn academic credit while visiting another country. The content of the specific course of study may or may not actually connect to the country being visited. These programs successfully encourage students to travel abroad and register for classes that they could often take without traveling abroad. A primary purpose of these programs is to encourage students to travel beyond the borders of their own country. Program activities focus on formal coursework, typically, with a professor from their home university. Activities may also include visits to popular tourist sites, places of historical significance, museums and parks, and popular restaurants for experiencing local cuisine. Billed as part academic, part vacation, these programs, typically, provide enticing opportunities for international travel, particularly, for students who have not traveled abroad previously. These programs often take students to major international cities like Paris, London, or Rome—and enable them to progress in their programs of study.

In contrast to programs that emphasize academic tourism, study abroad programs at the other end of this spectrum are rooted in concerns for advancing issues of social justice and increasing global citizenship. These programs are designed to help students understand and confront the social, political and economic inequities in the country and communities they visit as well as examine the normative policies and practices of developed countries that either enhance or limit opportunities for people in emerging nations. For example, our program in South Africa began soon after Apartheid had ended and the first democratic election in which Blacks could vote made Nelson Mandela the first Black President of South Africa. Through this program, we wanted to help students understand the atrocities and injustices of Apartheid, and follow this fledgling democracy as it struggled to create greater equity and opportunity for its majority Black population through social and educational reform.

Programs that are designed to increase multicultural understanding and enhance global citizenship, like this one, emphasize the importance of participating in the life world of people living in the host country. These programs, too, offer a 3-week to a yearlong experience; however, the design of these programs departs dramatically from those that feature academic tourism as their primary purpose.

Study abroad programs concerned with issues of social justice and global citizenship emphasize learning about the issues and challenges facing the host country and its people. In programs designed for these purposes, educators build in many opportunities for students to get to know both the country and its people. The academic component of the program, typically, helps students to understand the historical, cultural, and political challenges facing the host country. In these programs, immersion in the country and with people who live socially, culturally, and economically different lives within it is a critical part of the learning experience. Through these encounters, students begin to understand the challenges to and importance of creating a more socially just society, not only in the host country, but in the United States as well.

In the sections that follow, we share the experiences we have had and what we have learned about developing a study abroad program rooted in concerns for advancing social justice and increasing global citizenship. When individuals become active in issues of social justice, their willingness to confront and interrupt injustice both at and home and abroad grows. We wanted a program that would increase our students' willingness, confidence and capacity to interrupt inequity and encourage them to become global citizens who care about and act upon injustice not just in the United States, but also in South Africa and beyond. The United Nations Educational Scientific and Cultural Organization (UNESCO) has identified global citizenship as a key educational goal, which is critical to sustainable development. In fact, UNESCO and other conferences sponsored by the United Nations regularly includes an emphasis on enhancing global citizenship through education as a theme.

There are various definitions of global citizenship used in different disciplines, however, all of them share a genuine concern for human beings beyond the self and a strong interest in working for the greater sustainability of the world. The Okanagan Academic Planning Team at the University of British Columbia defined a global citizen as one who is: "willing to think beyond boundaries of place, identity and category, and recognize[s] all humans as their equals while respecting humanity's inherent diversity. Within their own sphere of influence, global citizens seek to imagine and work towards a better world" (UBC 2005). This is the vision of global citizenship guiding the development of our program.

In traveling throughout South Africa, we transport students to a life world well beyond the one they know. During their time in South Africa, they have opportunities to interact with and develop an understanding of people who are often very unlike them. However, over the years, we have found that without attention to adult learning theory and human behavior, well-intentioned efforts to address issues of race, ethnicy and poverty can backfire as students resist the uncomfortable and distressing dissonance that may arise when encountering clashes between their own life world and that of the people they meet in South Africa. Through our experience in developing this program over the past decade, we have come to believe that study abroad programs can achieve the education goals articulated by Kofi Annan, however, most programs are not designed to advance these purposes. Therefore, if universities want to offer study abroad programs that have the power and potential to enhance tolerance and understanding and increase global citizenship, they will have to create programs that are, specifically, designed to achieve those ends.

Designing Study Abroad for Enhancing Global Understanding and Citizenship

The program featured in this study is one of several NYU study abroad programs to South Africa. This program is underpinned by the belief that study abroad ought to be mutually beneficial to those visiting the country and to those hosting them. Therefore, from the very beginning of the application process, students are encouraged to consider how they will give back to the country that is contributing to their development as global citizens. This emphasis has grown stronger in the later years of the program as our own understanding about education for global citizenship has increased. Initially, the giving back was in the form of gifts for our hosts and the children we visited in schools, such as pens, paper and crayons. However, over the years, "giving back" has taken a decidedly different, more personal and longer lasting turn. Students are now teaching lessons in classrooms, volunteering in orphanages and schools, preparing a brai[1] for new South African friends and acquaintances, and teaching English to interested members in an ethnic community to name a few. Additionally, our program has adopted a school in South Africa, built a library, which they did not have, and each year works with the educators to develop the programs and increase the resources available to the educators and students in the school.

Our program is specifically designed for graduate students who wish to develop a global perspective on social and educational policy issues in South Africa. We do not claim to fully prepare our students for global citizenship within the brief time that we have with them, but rather we are intentional about beginning a process that engages them in thinking about the meaning of social justice and their role as global citizens.

In the next section, we discuss what we have learned about the value of using personal narratives to increase students capacities to understand: how they have come to believe what they do about racial, ethnic, and class others; how narrow or biased perspectives give way to more culturally and globally sophisticated structures through new experience; and how this transformation in perspective enables students to see themselves as global citizens in a broader community.

The Role of Personal Narrative in Creating Global Citizens

Researchers recognize the value of personal narrative for understanding how people make sense of human experience (Bruner, 1990). Robert Coles (1989) notes that it is only through stories that we can fully enter another's life. Through personal narrative, we can penetrate cultural barriers, give voice to human experience, and understand human intention and action. Over the years, we have seen the very different reactions that students have had to their experiences in South Africa and we have come to understand that negative, fearful or defensive reactions to new experiences are often rooted in prior experiences and in deeply held perspectives. In seeing their discomfort, we reflected on the program by asking ourselves three questions: How do U.S. students make sense of their experiences in a developing country like South Africa? What attitudes, beliefs, prejudices or judgments do they bring to this experience, and how can study and research in a developing country encourage personal transformation and growth?

The transformative theory of adult learning as discussed by Jack Mezirow (1991) provided a valuable framework for understanding our students' experiences in the program and offered guidance for redesigning the program based upon what we were learning from our students.

Mezirow asserts that transformation and change in personal attitudes, beliefs, and judgments about others is shaped and limited by language and culture, as well as by prior experience. As adults, we make sense of all new life experience through the lens of prior experience, or said differently, our personal narrative. This insight was particularly important to us as professors who were taking students from the western world to a developing country, South Africa. This trip transports students to the other side of the world and places them in a country that differs markedly from anything most of them have experienced previously. If our interpretations of racial, cultural, and class others is limited by our own prior experience, as Mezirow suggests, we knew that we had to pay attention to how students were responding to and making sense of what they were seeing and experiencing. This insight helped us to see the importance of sharing personal narratives in the program so that we had better insight into how students were making sense of their experiences in South Africa. We wanted to embrace a learning process that would help students to understand where their own perspectives on issues of race, poverty, equity and social justice came from, and remain open to the different perspectives that they would inevitably encounter in their interactions with classmates and the people of South Africa.

Mezirow argues that meaning perspectives, which are not unlike paradigms (Kuhn, 1962) or schemas (Valian, 1998), are "concepts, beliefs, judgments and feelings" (p. 223) that unconsciously shape our interpretations of new experiences. He states that these meaning perspectives, or generalized sets of habitual expectations, act as "conceptual codes that form, limit and even distort how we think, what we believe, and how we feel. These perspectives also impact "what, when and why we learn" (p. 34).

In adult learning, growth and change occurs when our meaning schemes, or conscious and unconscious tacit belief systems, are challenged through new experiences and transformed through reflection and critical discourse. This component of adult learning theory suggests that if study abroad programs are to encourage transformation and growth, opportunities for reflection and critical discourse about experiences that directly challenge prior belief systems must be built into the design of the program.

Mezirow also found that a new belief, or a perspective transformation, occurs when individuals become aware of problematic gaps between their deeply held beliefs and convictions and new experiences that call those beliefs or convictions into question. He notes that a transformation in perspective occurs only when there is a conscious recognition of the difference between an old perspective that no longer makes sense (given new experiences) and a new perspective that is actively embraced. This shift in perspective is most likely to occur when new experiences can no longer be integrated comfortably into the existing belief system, often creating discomfort and considerable distress.

As adults grow and gain in experience, they typically seek to resolve contradictions in their perspective schemes, which allows them to embrace more culturally and globally sophisticated structures and integrate new experiences. Mezirow explains that a perspective transformation is often a precondition for meaningful change in behavior. Specifically, this means that many students in study abroad programs may have to face preconceived beliefs about racial, ethnic, and class others before they are can embrace more culturally and globally sophisticated perspectives and become capable of participating a broader global community. In the next section, we provide an overview of the program and the processes we use to increase students capacities to become more open and active citizens in a global community.

THREE PHASES OF THE STUDY ABROAD PROGRAM

From its inception, our study abroad program has been offered in the summer, however, the program extends well beyond the four weeks that are actually spent in South Africa due to preprogram and postprogram activities. This program brings doctoral and masters students who are interested in social and educational reform, leadership and advocacy, politics and policy studies, and international education together. The program is divided into three major sections: the preprogram preparation, immersion program in South Africa, and the postprogram follow-up. The purposes and processes used in each phase is discussed below.

Preprogram Preparation

In the preprogram phase, we focus on several key issues: introducing former students of the program to prospective students; recruiting a diverse and politically engaged student group; immersing students in relevant cultural readings, films, music and art prior to travel; introducing students to issues of social justice and awakening them to the historical, social, political and economic context of South Africa by suggesting South African writers, activists, poets and filmmakers; and, inviting students to South African events such as films, art exhibits, and African food festivals taking place across NYC.

Program planning and preparation for the study abroad in July begins in the Fall semester when we bring students who have recently returned from S. Africa together with students who are thinking about going the following year. This meeting is mutually beneficial to both the returning students and to the prospective students. Students who are returning from their study abroad experience are, typically, balancing many emotions. On the one hand they are still excited about the experience that they have had and on the other hand, they often struggle with their reentry into their own wealthy society and privileged lives after experiencing a world where so many have so little. Students are often stunned to find that sharing their experience with friends, family, and significant others is not always easy or appreciated by those who have not shared the experience. Therefore, we have found that by creating this opportunity to talk with interested students about their experiences, returning students find an interested audience, which both groups find valuable and emotionally rewarding. Through these preprogram activities, prospective students can also better assess whether or not they want to study in South Africa.

Another important preprogram activity is having students take relevant course work for increasing their awareness of equity and social justice issues in South Africa prior to studying abroad. Students are encouraged to take a course on international perspectives on educational reform with Professor Moja where they can choose to study the educational system in South Africa in greater depth or a course on the politics of multiculturalism in communities with Professor Larson. This course introduces students to multiple perspectives in multicultural misunderstanding and helps them to develop a language for talking across racial, ethnic, and cultural difference. Although neither of these courses is required for participating in the study abroad program in South Africa, many students who take either course end up being interested in learning more about issues of equity and social justice in education and choose to learn more about these issues by going to South Africa.

From the very beginning, when students express an interest in going to South Africa, they are told that this study abroad program differs from many others at NYU in that it requires home stays and volunteer work in poor communities. Therefore, students who are not comfortable with the idea of working in poor communities or with getting to know the people who live in them do not select this program of study. Having made mistakes in the past, it is very important to us that we select the best students for this program and its purposes and that the students also have sufficient information to select the best program for them.

Another important feature of our study abroad program is our concerted effort to regularly select a racially and ethnically diverse student group to take to South Africa. Because issues of race and ethnicity are so central to daily life in South Africa, we have found that when we have a diverse group, our students are forced to confront difficult racial and ethnic issues within the group as well as with the people of South Africa. In a racially mixed group, students become more aware of racial injustice because they experience it, often for the first time from a multicultural perspective. For example, they experience the racial caste system that is still visible in everyday interactions in many parts of South Africa. They see, for example, how the Black students in the group are often served their food last whenever Whites are seated at the table. Students of mixed race are struck by the realization that in this country, people of mixed race are legally classified as "coloured." They also see how shocked South Africans are to see a racially and ethnically mixed group of people socializing together in public.

Having a racially and ethnically mixed group is also important because students experience South Africa in very different ways and their experiences are often based on the color of their skin. Many White students, for example, experience what it is like being a part of a minority race for the first time by being in a country where just 13% of the population in South Africa is White, whereas, Black students have just the opposite experience. Therefore, bringing a diverse student group together is vital to making conversations about issues of race both within the group and within this country far richer.

Another important component of our preprogram is bringing the group of students together soon after they are selected for the program in March to give them the syllabus for the course and to get them started on readings and seeing films that will help orient them to South Africa. This gives students 3 months to prepare for their trip and time to immerse themselves in the rich and robust literature of South Africa. Many students who travel to South Africa have never read a book by a South African writer nor have they seen a film based on life in South Africa. For us, an important component of study abroad is having students read voraciously and learn vicariously about the country they are visiting through the voices, experiences of the people engaged in the struggle to move this country out of the injustices of apartheid and into a vibrant and thriving democracy.

Because we spend just 1 month is South Africa, we want students to spend their time there with the people of South Africa. Therefore, having students read and see movies, including those that illuminate issues of inequity and document important fights for social justice, prior to going to South Africa is a critically important. In addition to the syllabus with required course readings and assignments, students are given a list of books and films and they are encouraged to read broadly and watch as many of the movies as they can prior to their trip. This assignment provides students with a needed knowledge base from which to begin their experience in South Africa.

Program Immersion in South Africa

During the 4 weeks we spend in South Africa, the program evolves around several pivotal activities that are designed to enhance students' awareness of and insight into issues of social and educational reform in South Africa. These central components include: a focus on the individual and the collective, daily journals and reflections, presentations by key policymakers in South Africa, travel throughout the country, evening Indaba sessions by the fireplace, youth group volunteering opportunities, and inquiry into and research critical issues of equity and social justice, such as access to education, AIDS in communities, and biracial identity in South Africa to name a few. In this section, we examine these immersion experiences in greater depth.

Once we are in South Africa, the program begins with a focus on "who are you?" and "who am I? Following the advice of John Dewey, we have come to believe that education for global citizenship must be grounded in both the personal narratives and lived experiences of the students. This process requires examining who we are individually first. The concept of race and issues of privilege and inequity are put on the table at our first session together in South Africa. We ask students: When did you first become aware of race, ethnicity, or class and how has race, ethnicity, or class affected your life? We often begin this process by telling students our own stories first.

Teboho shares a powerful story of being raised in South Africa as a Black woman under apartheid. She points out that being born Black in South Africa under the apartheid system meant that from the very beginning, she was destined for a life of oppression, injustice and discrimination. She recalls:

> The dividing line amongst my people was between those who chose to accept the apartheid system and live by the rules of the oppressor and those who questioned it and chose to make a contribution to changing the system. In high school, I chose to get involved in the struggle for change, questioning the injustices of our society and the brutal treatment of those who opposed the system. When a university student, an activist against injustice and apartheid, was expelled, my fellow students and took to the streets to protest against the system Our resistance was met with brutal police force and introduced me to tear gas when the first canister was fired and just missed hitting me by a few inches. That was a defining moment for me to use education as a mechanism to address issues of injustice in society. Since that time, in every institution of higher education I attended or taught in, I have been actively involved in struggles toward change. It took 1 year at NYU before I decided to find a way to teach students about the struggle in South Africa and help them understand through experiential learning the effects of an unjust society. I was working with my colleague, Colleen, who shared the same social justice values and concerns that I had, and we believed that we could design a program that would help students to see a society in transition. This was a society that was moving from a legalized system of social injustice to a society that would embrace difference and strive

toward achieving greater equity and opportunity for all people. We were aware that the atrocities and the injustices of the past could not be undone, but we wanted our students to meet people in South Africa who were moving ahead with their lives and who were determined to improve their life chances through education and through the numerous projects that were being started by ordinary members of the society. Our students were very interested in and motivated to learn about equity and opportunity in South Africa so that was encouragement enough to try to design a program that would help them to understand inequity and injustice, using South Africa as a laboratory, and help them to engage more deeply with issues that are of global concern.

Coming from a very different standpoint, Colleen recalls that her first awareness of race occurred when she was 10 years old. Growing up in a small and predominantly White mid-Western community in the United States, she recalls reading a story in the local newspaper about a Black postal worker who could not find housing for his family in the town where her family lived. Without a car, he had to take a bus, traveling 25 miles to the city to work each morning and then walking another two miles from the nearest bus stop to the post office.

> I remember feeling so sad and truly upset that nobody in my city would rent a home to this man and his family. He had to quit his job because he couldn't continue the daily commute. This was in the 1960s, and every night I remember seeing Martin Luther King speaking on the news or people marching for basic civil rights like being able to ride a bus or eat in a diner or attend a school, or buy a home. I couldn't understand how White people could treat others so badly just because of the color of their skin. And I remember thinking that all of these marches took place in the south, so I thought, oh—that is where all of the racist people live.
>
> I grew up in a fairly liberal, democratic family so when I read that article in our paper, I was hurt and angry to find out that people in my own city, my neighbors were also racist and believed that Blacks and Whites should not live in the same city, much less the same neighborhood. I remember that my father tried to explain that White people lived in our town and Blacks lived in the neighboring town. He said that that was just the way it had always been and that some people wanted to keep it that way. But as a child, I felt the injustice in that. Also, I realized for the first time that even though adults were supposed to teach children right from wrong, they did not always do the right thing.
>
> So growing up in the sixties, I was very aware of social justice issues. In high school, I had some very good humanities teachers who encouraged me to learn more and write about my passionate interest in social justice issues. I wanted to interview the only Black teacher in the school about what he experienced growing up and what he experienced working in a White school system. I was thrilled when he agreed to talk with me. I found his

story so compelling and so did the teachers and students in my class. That is when I learned about the importance and power of personal narrative to change what people think and believe.

In college, I remember I had a bulletin board in my dorm room with quotes I loved about justice issues and my favorite one was Martin Luther King's quote, "Injustice anywhere is a threat to justice everywhere." To me that meant that it wasn't ok to care about women's issues or Black issues only. I joined the National Organization of Women and joined the movement to pass the equal rights amendment in the 70s, and then I became interested in working for greater democracy in the workplace in the 80s and 90s. So when I met Teboho at NYU and we began talking about equity issues and South Africa and her desire to take students there to focus on issues of social and educational reform, I knew that I had found a kindred spirit.

After we share our stories, students begin to open up and tell stories about their own experiences. This narrative process reveals stark differences in the lived experience of race, ethnicity, gender and class and awakens students to the power of their own past experiences as well as to those of others. Many students have never shared their stories in a racially mixed group. This process also allows students to hear the compelling stories of students who do not share their racial, ethnic or class background. By beginning with personal stories of race and ethnicity, students can more easily understand one another's differences in how they make sense of equity issues and understand why they each react differently to their experiences in South Africa.

Once students have shared and discussed their individual stories, we ask them to consider: Who are we as a group? In this discussion, we talk about how we want to "be with one another" over the next month. This is important because these students spend a lot of time with one another, so we discuss what we need to know about one another and how we each want to be treated within the group. Finally, we discuss who we are as a diverse group newly situated in a country where race and class remains a highly visible and dominant organizing framework. We have found that establishing a foundation from which we can communicate with one another is critical to the success of the study abroad experience. Only after students have shared and discussed their own experiences, beliefs and feelings about race and class and after they have discussed what they want and need from one another do we begin examining education and social reform issues in South Africa.

Throughout the course, we continually revisit this process of sharing individual stories and personal perspectives in light of new experiences encountered in South Africa. Over the years, we have learned that if students are to develop their capacities to understand others and talk across difference, issues of racial and ethnic tension or discomfort must be kept on the table and openly discussed from the very beginning of the program to the very end. Students often encounter feelings of personal dissonance around issues of race and ethnicity in South Africa and this discomfort always holds either the potential for transformation to a more culturally inclusive perspective or deeper entrenchment in narrow beliefs and perspectives, which are grounded in prior experience.

Another way we encourage students to move beyond unexamined views of equity and social justice is to keep them actively engaged in writing a daily journal throughout the entire month they spend in South Africa. All students are told to bring a journal with them. They begin writing in this journal on the first day of their trip and continue writing until the day they leave the county. This process helps students to capture the many feelings and experiences that they are confronting each day. We find that students use these journals to write about feelings and experiences that they willingly share with one another as well as experiences and feelings that they do not share. Nevertheless, journal writing provides an opportunity for students to capture what Denzin calls, the "epiphanic moments" or those encounters that challenge what they believe to be true and also reflect upon what they are feeling and how they are responding to these experiences. The students submit their journals to the professors several times during their stay in South Africa and at the end of the program. We read these journals to see how students are making sense of their experience and to identify any issues that may be important to talk about in a large group.

We have found that the personal narratives that students record in their journals, are more easily shared around a fireplace and in dimly lit room than they are in the light of day. Therefore, over the years we moved our discussion of issues arising in the journals from our scheduled seminar in the morning to an evening session, which we call Indaba.

Weekly Indaba sessions provide an important opportunity for students to process what they are experiencing and feeling in South Africa. The *indaba*, a Zulu word that means gathering by the fireside to discuss serious issues, provides both professors and students a planned time to talk informally about the study abroad experience. There is no formal or set agenda for these sessions. The purpose is to discuss and reflect upon whatever the students feel a need to talk about. Typically, these issues come from experiences or encounters that students have had over the week, or from critical issues raised in the students' journals.

In Indaba sessions, potato chips are consumed, drinks are poured and everyone huddles around a fire, as students open up and reveal their frustrations, confusions, and surprising as well as satisfying insights about what they are experiencing in South Africa. This is a place where difficult topics are discussed, deep feelings are shared and new insights emerge. What we came to appreciate over the years is the importance of building open and informal time like this into the schedule. Students need opportunities to process what they are experiencing and they benefit by listening to the perspectives of others on what they are feeling and how they are making sense of their experience. The students also benefit by having a facilitator to step in and help them talk through issues that may be divisive and difficult for the group to discuss on their own.

In the past, we made the mistake of over planning and filling students time with too much activity and too little down time to process all that was being absorbed during the study abroad experience. Without time, for critical reflection and conversations, students have too little support and insufficient opportunity to move from entrenched beliefs to new and more inclusive perspectives regarding issues of social justice and global citizenship.

Another major component of the study abroad experience involves an inquiry project focusing on an issue relevant to social and educational transformation in South Africa. Students are encouraged to choose a social or educational policy issue that is of interest to them and to connect with people from South Africa who can provide insight into that issue. This process of interviewing others forces students to interact with and talk to the people of South Africa on important issues. For example, students have studied equity between White and Black schools, political art, women and AIDS, orphaned children, the colored or biracial experience, and Whites in South Africa today to name a few. Through this inquiry project, we encourage students to examine complex issues from multiple perspectives by talking with people who have different experiences with and perspectives on the issue they hope to understand.

In the last few years, we have also encouraged students to consider suggesting an alternative to the inquiry paper. This alternative assignment is a relatively new option and requires students to create some project that can be shared with people in the United States to increase their knowledge about and understanding of South Africa. Students have designed educational units on South Africa and presented them in elementary and secondary schools across the country. This project helps to spread the lived realities and stories of South Africa to U.S. children and youth and, hopefully, motivates the next generation to travel to South Africa and to other destinations one day.

Throughout the program we also invite key policymakers, leading scholars, political activists, musicians and artists in South Africa to talk with our students and share their experiences and perspectives on social and educational transformation. This component of the program grounds students in the complexities of educational and social reform and awakens them to the complicated notion of what social justice means in South Africa today. For example, in a land where health, education and employment agencies are all struggling for government support, difficult choices are being made about where money will be spent. How do government officials, for example, make choices between building and staffing new schools or providing medicine to people who are dying of AIDS? The experiences of key policymakers and political activists in this country helps students to understand first-hand how people have experienced apartheid and the journey toward social justice as well as the difficult choices that policymakers must make when deciding which social justice issues deserve attention and how limited dollars ought to be spent.

Another important component of this study abroad experience is traveling throughout the country during our month in South Africa. South Africa is rich in cultural and ethnic diversity and boasts eleven official languages. Therefore, we want to ensure that students experience life in Cape Town, Johannesburg and Pretoria, which are all major but very different cities with very different histories in South Africa, as well as life in small rural village communities like Venda. Venda is a former bantustan, or Black homeland, 1 of 10 territories assigned to the Black majority under Apartheid. This helps to explains why White people are still a curiosity here and why locals are less accustomed to seeing visitors from other countries than are South Africans who live in the larger cities.

In Venda, students participate in home stays with families in one of the villages. A day is also spent participating in the local Chief's program which often includes presiding over an initiation ceremony celebrating boys or girls transition into adulthood, attending a wedding, or participating in a meeting of local Chiefs on the needs of their communities. During these stays, students have valuable opportunities to experience life in a small rural village and interact with families and people in the broader community.

Volunteer work is also encouraged and organized throughout the students stay in South Africa. Linking with an active student organization in Pretoria, students spend free afternoons working in a variety of NGOs or helping out in local schools or orphanages. We have found that these valuable opportunities help students to break away from the comfort of their group and encourages them to take greater risks to talk to the people of South Africa, and experience first hand the struggle to achieve greater equity and social justice at the individual, community, and institutional level.

Finally, students also have a long weekend free. We call it YOYO, which means, you are on your own. When students first hear about this, many are terrified. "You are leaving us?" Nevertheless, we encourage students to organize and travel beyond the South African borders to gain confidence in their abilities to navigate new places and to seize opportunities to learn about South Africa's neighboring countries. Students typically go off in groups of two or five or even rent a van for seven or eight people and travel to Swaziland, Botswana, and Mozambique to name a few. Others choose to spend this time doing additional volunteer work with NGOs, local orphanages or schools. Students return from these weekends feeling proud, confident and invigorated by all that they managed to experience and achieve on their own. This experience alone has made several students from each group each year decide to extend their stays in Africa at the end of the program and travel across Africa with greater excitement and confidence.

Postprogram Activities

Postprogram activities are also a critically important part of this program. Most programs that we surveyed do not provide follow-up support for enhancing continued learning, growth and individual transformation. Through our students, we have seen the need for this support, particularly, when students return to their lives in the United States.

One important part of this support system is a postprogram debriefing session that brings students together to share their experiences after being back in the United States for a month. This session gives students an opportunity to reconnect with the new friends and classmates that they lived with in a semi-communal home for an entire month. In the traditional South African culture the study abroad group becomes a *mophatho*, a group that you belong to by going through an initiation process, a right of passage.

Upon their return to the United States, students quickly discover that not everybody at home is positive about or welcoming of the changes they have gone through while living in South Africa. Students come back to this country much more conscious of and wide-awake to issues of poverty and injustice in South Africa as well as in the United States. Some students have found that the responses they get from their family and friends are sometimes so negative they no longer feel comfortable with their families or friends. These experiences can negatively impact their relationships with significant others. These difficult encounters provide another opportunity to help students to process their experiences and promote further learning, transformation, and growth. The difficulty that students often encounter in returning to their home country and to their families and friends helped us to see the importance of supporting students through this transition process and illuminated the need to teach students how to communicate their experiences to people who have not shared it. It also prompted us to develop a list serve for the group so that communications could continue among the students and with us long after the formal components of the program were over. In recent years, Facebook has become an easy way to allow continued connection long after they complete their education and leave school.

While in South Africa, we want students to spend their time meeting and talking with people from South Africa not sitting and doing research on a computer or in a library, therefore, when students return to the states, they have to turn their attention to writing up what they learned in their inquiry projects. Students have three weeks after they return to the United States to complete their final paper for the course, which means that their learning and thinking about their experiences in South Africa continues both formally and informally as they write up their studies. With this overview of the purposes and structure of the program, we turn to how this program plays out in the experiences of the students and discuss what we have learned from them.

Transformation and Growth: The Student Experience

It is not unusual to hear students say that the program and their experiences in South Africa were "life changing." Our students at NYU are not unlike students at other universities in the United States. Many students who choose to travel with us are using a passport for the very first time. Specifically, 51% of our former students had never traveled abroad prior to going to South Africa. Of those who had traveled abroad previously, a small number of them had participated in study abroad programs previously, but most of these students had traveled for vacation purposes with family and friends only. Also, fully 86% of these students had not traveled internationally beyond Canada, Mexico or Europe. These data help us to see that study abroad programs like this do encourage students to travel to and learn about developing countries. For example, when the students were asked why they chose to participate in this particular study abroad program, they expressed a desire to go to South Africa coupled with the belief that going to South Africa through a study abroad trip would make travel there more manageable and more meaningful. One student said,

> I don't think that I would have gone to S. Africa if it weren't for the study abroad program. I have always wanted to go there, but I wasn't comfortable enough to travel there on my own or with just one other person. So when I saw that I could study in South Africa, I knew I wanted to do it. Going with the program, I just felt that a lot of the things that would be difficult on my own, logistical things, like knowing where to stay and how to get around the country would be taken care of by people who knew what they were doing.

For this student, the study abroad program provided an opportunity to go to a country that he would like to see, but would not likely visit on his own. Many students expressed this same reluctance to visit South Africa on their own. The structure provided by a study abroad program made many students more comfortable about and willing to travel to a country that they felt they could not navigate on their own.

For other students, study abroad was a better way to see South Africa than traveling on their own because they knew that they would have an opportunity to get to know the culture and the people of South Africa in far greater depth. One student said:

> I could never have experienced South Africa the way I did if I was traveling on my own. I wouldn't have had access to all of the people we talked to. People just opened their doors to us. We had opportunities to interview some very highly placed and influential people in South Africa. I wouldn't have known who to talk to, and I wouldn't have been able to get in some of the places we went. You need connections to meet the people we got to know and to get into some of the communities we visited. Also, most of the places we went aren't listed in any guidebook for tourists, like seeing the Vhavenda ceremony that initiates boys into manhood. So, I know that we had experiences that very few people get to have when they travel to another country.

Students recognized that through this program, they had access to people and places that they would not have had if they were traveling on their own. Because Professor Moja is from South Africa and is a former Aide to the Minister of Education, she has immediate access to policy makers and communities throughout the country. As a result, students have important opportunities to meet people and visit communities as if they were "insiders" rather than "outsiders" or tourists. Students value meeting with leading policymakers who are shaping the direction of South Africa. They also are deeply affected by doing homestays and experiencing life in the rural communities of Venda. In Venda, they are able to participate in life in this ethnic community as it is unfolding postapartheid rather than going to one of the artificially constructed cultural villages that has been established near the larger cities to entertain tourists and introduce them to the ethnic communities of South Africa. The cultural villages do provide tourists with access to village life without going into real villages. In many ways, they are not a bad thing, they provide needed work for many people in South Africa and they do a good job of introducing tourists to the culture, music dance and living traditions of several ethnic all located in one place. In one day, tourists can get a glimpse into the many cultures and traditions of South Africa such as the Xhosa, the Zulu, the Ndebele, the Venda the Ntwana, and the Tswana to name a few. However, these cultural villages are in many ways not unlike Disneyland where everyone is happy, clean, well dressed and well fed. For educational purposes, however, there is no substitute for the real villages that offer a richer, more complex and revealing picture of village life in South Africa today.

Opening Students Minds to Traveling to a Developing Country

Students' interests in participating in this particular program were often triggered by taking courses that introduced them to international issues in education, health, and social reform and issues of social justice in education. Many students had taken either a course titled, Education and Social Reform with Professor Moja or the Politics of Multiculturalism course with Professor Larson. One student said,

> I never really thought about global issues in education and reform until I took this course as an elective in my program. I started reading more about international issues in education, and when I heard Professor Moja talk about the study abroad program there, I thought it would be amazing to go there and study education reform.

Another student said:

> When I took the class on issues of multiculturalism with Professor Larson I became more aware of who my students are and then I became more interested in where they come from. I have children in my class who come from all over the world and I realized that I have never been out of the country! I just knew that I wanted to travel more and to be able to bring my experiences back into my classroom.

Many students expressed the importance of taking previous course work to prepare them for studying in a developing country and noted the important role that these courses played in encouraging them to travel to a developing country.

Students also reported that they made the decision to go to South Africa when former students in the program shared their experiences with them. One student said,

> I just heard so many great things about the program, and when my friend told me about his experience, like meeting people in the communities, visiting schools and helping in classrooms and seeing the work of local artists, I became very excited about going.

Another student said,

> A friend of mine told me about all of the people he had met there. He had an amazing experience. And when he showed me his photos, it just made me want to go too.

Knowing someone who had traveled to South Africa previously was an important factor in motivating students to want to go there. Students have many preconceived ideas about what traveling to South Africa would be like and many of these ideas are rooted in a fear of the unknown. However, when students return from South Africa and share their experiences of helping out in schools or in orphanages, buying children's books to establish a library in a school, or just doing daily routines like shopping in a grocery store or doing the laundry, students begin to see that life in South Africa in many ways is no different from life anywhere else—and in other ways far more interesting.

In the next section, we share the stories that our students' tell about how they experienced the learning, transformation and growth process throughout the program, and how these experiences are impacting their participation in a wider global community.

Confronting Personal Narratives and Talking Across Difference

Designing a program that encourages students to open themselves up to learning about and participating in the life world of another nation and its people requires finding an important balance between formal and informal learning opportunities. Students felt that both planned and serendipitous moments in South Africa contributed to their learning, transformation and growth while living in South Africa. Valuable learning opportunities occurred between members of the study abroad group as well as with the people that they met each day in South Africa.

When it comes to racial issues, our students do not always find what they expect to see in S. Africa. They are often taken aback by the stark racial segregation that persists in this country fifteen years after apartheid. One student said:

> I was so surprised to see how segregated S. Africa is today—fifteen years after apartheid. You never saw people of mixed races together walking down the street. And that made us really stand out. We were a very racially and ethnically mixed group and when we walked down the street together, people would just stop and stare. I don't think they are used to seeing people of all races traveling, eating, partying or laughing together as friends. We would go into bars and it was either a Black bar or a White bar. And

when our group came in, people just stopped to watch us. I think for that reason, we were good for S. Africa, too.

Another student said:

I get frustrated because the United States is so very racially segregated in many ways, but it is very normal to see people of mixed races and ethnicities together on the street or at a bar. It helped me to see the progress that we have made in the United States and I really didn't appreciate that before going to South Africa.

Most students were surprised to find that in many ways, the United States was much further along the path toward creating greater equity and opportunity for people of color than they realized and that South Africa still had a lot further to go than they had expected. However, they also realized that unlike in South Africa, issues of race in the United States are not a part of the general public discourse. One student said,

What surprised me is that race is such an open topic for discussion in South Africa. You would get into a taxi and the driver would start talking to you about race and racism or apartheid. That wouldn't happen in the United States. People don't talk about race, especially with people of other races. But people in S. Africa talk about it a lot, or at least with us they did. At first, I was pretty uncomfortable with that. The driver would say something negative about White people, and I'd look at Karen (who is White) out of the corner of my eye to see how she was taking what the driver was saying, and she was fine with it, but that helped me to see that we just don't talk about race in the United States.

Being in the S. African context, students found themselves engaged in conversations about race in racially mixed groups. To many of the students in the program, talking about race with racial others was new and not always comfortable for them, but as the program evolved and as students became more accustomed to discussing racial issues, they overcame some of their fears and began developing more confidence in their abilities to talk across racial difference. One student said,

Here in New York, I have often felt like I should say something when racial issues come up, but I don't, thinking, oh, let it go—keep the peace. We like to pretend we don't have racial problems anymore, but of course we do, we just don't talk about it. But when people in S. Africa raised the issue of race, it forced us to talk about it in our classes and especially in our Indabas. It wasn't always easy, but I think we all learned a lot from each other. So now I find that I can handle it better and I am less inclined to let it go if somebody says something racist. Being in South Africa, I realized that the only way to help people understand racial issues is to talk about them.

Early in the program, we realized, however, that not all students develop confidence in their capacities or willingness to talk across difference. For example, upon returning to the United States, one student confided, "I just learned to keep my mouth shut. To this student, talking about race was risky, and when she tried, she found that it did not always go well. As a result, an issue that could have been discussed in class sessions or during an Indaba was not shared until we returned to the United States. Therefore, we found that occasionally issues that could have been discussed and that would have enhanced students' opportunities for further learning, transformation and growth were never confronted or effectively processed. Typically, these discomforts arose from racial problems that students had with one another. For example, after returning to the United States, one student shared a problem that arose in South Africa that the group was not able to handle. She explained that a White student in the program began dating a Black S. African man who was an activist and worked for the ANC (African National Congress). Given the group's very recent examination of the atrocities of Apartheid, and amidst a context of heightened feelings of racial solidarity within the group, a few of the Black women in the program became particularly sensitive to this situation. These women were disturbed to find that after all that Blacks had gone through in S. Africa to attain equality, this South African Black man who fought to end Apartheid remained trapped in problematic images of White superiority and he privileged a White woman over Black women in the group. This man's attraction to a White woman created a serious rift between a few of the Black women and the White women in the group. One White woman expressed her disappointment:

> I was just surprised by the whole thing. I thought that the people who were choosing to take this trip would understand and be more accepting of racial diversity. We tried talking about the whole dating thing, but they (the Black women) were just adamant that Black men shouldn't date White women. That seemed rather racist to me.

This story of racial conflict elevated our concern for developing students' capacities and willingness to talk across racial (and religious, gender, ethnic, class) difference in study abroad programs if our goal is to enhance social justice, increase multiracial cooperation and understanding, and develop a wider global community. However, when students confront serious challenges to deeply held perceptions and bias, they make choices about trying to work through their beliefs and feelings or becoming more deeply entrenched in their own way of seeing.

We have relied on students journals for several years to help us surface issues that needed to be discussed within the group. We found that students easily raise racial issues that they encountered or observed in South

Africa, however, they were far more reluctant to raise racial issues that arose between members of their own study abroad group. Seeing this, we were convinced that we needed to become much more intentional about raising racial issues between students. This concern resulted in adding Indaba sessions to the evening program. The Indaba sessions were scheduled for 11/2 hours but they rarely ended in that timeframe. We found that students wanted to talk and this more relaxed setting created a needed space for difficult heart to heart conversations. An Indaba is not unlike a town hall meeting and it is based on the belief in the power of people to come together to address and resolve issues that concern them. Several students reflected on the power of the Indaba session. One student said:

> I remember when we had that evening session by the fireplace. You asked us to think about the how our early experiences with race shaped who we are and how we are experiencing South Africa. That conversation was so powerful. People just opened up and shared some very deep feelings.

Another student recalled:

> Some people had such painful memories, and when someone talked everybody listened so closely, you could hear a pin drop. When you heard people's stories, you began to understand why they seemed so angry or were so frustrated by some of things that were happening in our group. That was a very cathartic night. A lot of pressure was released. After that, people got along a lot better. They were kinder to each other, and less judgmental.

Many people believe that racial, ethnic, and religious differences are irresolvable. This fear causes many people to avoid talking about issues of race and inequity entirely. Students fear these conversations because they, typically, do not have the abilities they need to talk across difference in a way that allows their message to be heard and understood. This insight helped us to see that if we wanted students to grow in their abilities and willingness to create a more just and connected world, they needed stronger skills in communicating with others about critical and potentially volatile issues.

This insight prompted us to begin teaching students about communicating across difference. We talked about the importance of communicating what we believe in a non-threatening and non-judgmental manner. Students who want to grow in their abilities to talk across difference have opportunities to practice their skills in a variety of settings in South Africa. Through a careful analysis of the success or failure of their efforts to communicate, students soon learn the importance of owning their own feelings and expressing them without blame or judgment. Through successful and unsuccessful efforts, they also begin to understand that if their goal is to truly communicate, they need to do so in a way that allows people to consider new ideas, thoughts, beliefs, or attitudes.

One student said:

> I just had this really big ah-ha when we were talking about communication. So that's why people sometimes turn off when I am talking! I didn't mean to sound like I was self-righteous or something, but I guess that's how I came off sometimes. I realized that I don't like it when people judge me when they don't even know me, so it made me more aware of not only what I was trying to communicate, but *how* I was communicating what I wanted to say.

This insight helped us to realize that if we are to create a broader global community in which students have capacities for creating greater understanding, programs must help students develop their understanding of and capacities to talk across difference and effectively confront the difficult and divisive issues that consistently stand in the way of creating stronger cross-racial, cross-ethnic, and cross national understanding.

Becoming Active Citizens in a Wider Community

Eleanor Roosevelt once said "It is not enough to be compassionate. You must act." But what makes people move from compassion to action? What makes them decide to become active citizens in a wider global community? Over the past few years, we are noticing that our students are, increasingly, choosing to become engaged citizens in a broader global community. We have found that our students are also becoming more active in their own home communities as a result of their experiences in South Africa. Having worked in poor communities in S. Africa, the students wondered, "why aren't we doing that in the U.S. too? One student said:

In South Africa, I was working in a poor community, and helping to raise money to build a library for a poor school serving Black African children. And I began thinking,

> why wasn't I doing this in New York? We have a lot of schools that need books and money and I've never done anything like that before. It just opened my eyes to the fact that I can do more for poor children and their families in New York.

Another student took Eleanor Roosevelt's words about the importance of action to heart while she was in South Africa, saying:

> Traveling to S. Africa made me more aware. It made me question, what can I do? We had the opportunity to visit several schools. At one of the schools we visited, we stood outside with the students and talked on their lunch break. And they were asking a lot of questions about America, like what it is like to live there, but one girl stood out to me. When the other kids started to go inside to eat lunch, she just stayed outside, so I asked her if she was going to eat lunch, and she explained that she didn't have any lunch. So we started talking and she told me that her family had no money. Her mother was out on the street trying to provide for them, but she might have to quit school. She just seemed so sad, and hopeless. I could relate to her because I went through the same stuff. I grew up without money. I know what it's like to not have money for school supplies or books and I know how that affects your education. So after we left that day, I couldn't get her out of my mind.
>
> I found out that parents had to pay 100 Rand per year for their children to go to school. And a lot of parents don't have the money to do that. 100 Rand is only $10.00! I'm a poor person. I don't have money. I had to borrow money to go on this trip and I don't know where my money for my tuition this fall is coming from, but $10? I can blow 10 dollars a day at McDonald's or on small stuff. So when I realized that I could have used that 10 dollars to send someone to high school for an entire year—I felt so, I don't know, embarrassed, ashamed. So the next day, I went back to the township and I went to the girl's house and talked to her mother. I explained that I wanted to pay for her daughter's education, and she was so happy. She started to cry. It made me see the importance of taking more personal responsibility for doing what I can to help others. And that made me feel so good, because I don't have much, but I can do something.

Upon returning to the United States, this student continued her connection to this girl and her family, exchanging letters and photos, sending small gifts, and money when she could. Her relationship with this family continued to grow, and recently she fulfilled this young woman's dream by getting her a passport and bringing her to New York for a visit. Finishing high school, traveling to New York, and now having the very real possibility of going on to college all happened because one individual saw a need, and reached out to offer help.

This student connected with this child and her family because she, too, knew what it was like to be poor, to do without. It is interesting to note that students who were once truly poor are, typically, the ones who reach into their pockets or offer assistance far more quickly than their more affluent peers. However, even students who do not share the experience of childhood poverty, began to change their thinking about wealth as a result of the time they spent in rural communities and townships.

Most of the students who travel to South Africa do not see themselves as wealthy. These students often struggle to pay large tuition bills and have accrued significant debt, stemming from school loads to attend

NYU, an expensive and prestigious private university. However, after taking program-sponsored trips into poor townships and visiting schools in impoverished communities, many students turned inward, and began rethinking their attitudes about their own wealth. One student said:

> I've never thought of myself as a wealthy person before, but being in S. Africa and traveling to the townships and the rural communities made me see just how wealthy I really am. Oh, I don't have a Rolex, and I don't drive a Lexus—this is what I used to think wealthy meant—or, really, just having the money to blow on whatever you want to do. I don't have that. But I have so much that so many people there live without, things that people shouldn't have to live without. It made me really take stock and think about money in a new way. It's made me more generous. I used to ignore homeless people on the street in NY but now I dig in my pocket more often. And when people ask for donations for the homeless, I want to do what I can to help. I didn't feel that way before. I thought—I don't have enough money for myself, but now I realize I really do.

Like this student, other students in the program expressed feeling very different about money after spending time in communities where there was very little of it. This experience helped these students to see as one woman said, "what having very little really means." It also helped them to see the importance of giving, "even when you feel you have so little yourself."

Another student recalled visiting a classroom where the teacher had no wall maps, and held up a book from the front of the class to show the location of the country she was discussing. One student said,

> I couldn't believe it. There were 50 little kids, two or three of them sharing one desk and they had no books. But they sat there just entranced as this teacher pointed to a small map in a book. I'm sure the kids in the first row couldn't see it, much less the last row. But they were all so eager to learn. You could just see it.

Another student had a similar reaction:

> I teach in a school where the children are about the same age as the kids in one of the classrooms I visited at the township school, and I was amazed. If I stood in front of my 28 students holding up a book like that, they would be going crazy. They would not be listening. But these kids wanted to learn. When I went up to them to offer help, they were just so excited and eager to listen. At my school, the kids don't want you coming to them to give individual help because they are afraid you will notice that they didn't do their homework or they'll be embarrassed that they don't know the answer. So it was very different for me. And even though my school is in the inner city, and we don't have the newest books or the best library, we at least have

books. I just thought, why can't these kids have a better education? What is the government doing? We all walked away from there wanting to do something to help.

After returning from the school, the students talked about what they had experienced. At first, they thought of going shopping for the school. The students quickly saw that the school needed maps, paper, books, and pencils, but then they wondered, what else did the school need that they couldn't see? After some discussion the students decided that the teachers and principal in the school ought to decide what they needed most. So they pooled their money and made a donation to the school. Another student reflected on that decision:

I felt good about that. Everybody in our group wanted to do something, but we didn't want to make a big deal about it. So we had somebody go back and take the money to the principal.

Seeing a lack of resources and finding ways to help people in need was a strong theme that emerged in the experiences of students in the program. However, students do not give money only. Several students are volunteering to assist in schools, to teach classes, to work in an orphanage or to speak with students about life in New York. Free afternoons and days set aside for working on field projects made these volunteer opportunities possible.

Creating a Broader Community: Global Citizenship

Other students have found that South Africa continues to call them back to see people they have met there during the program, and to go to places they wanted to go to but did not do so during their program. Many of these students have goals rooted in concerns for global citizenship. Several doctoral students have returned to South Africa to complete doctoral research based in South Africa. Upon completing her doctoral dissertation, one student joined the Peace Corp and returned to South Africa for two years to work in an impoverished community, and another student returns regularly to visit a school she has adopted. For these students, study abroad has helped to make South Africa a part of their newly formed global community.

Several students have chosen to return to South Africa. One student explained: "I see myself not only a citizen of the U.S. but of South Africa too." This student has stayed in touch with people she met in South Africa who share her interest in and passion for politics and advocacy. Another student said:

I decided that my graduation gift to myself is to go back to South Africa for a month, hopefully longer. My passion and love for South Africa has never diminished since our trip together and I have been yearning to go back there. I have kept in touch with my host family over the years and they consider me their American cousin. That connection could not have been fostered if this program had not introduced me to the family.

Another student decided that she wants the opportunity to teach in South Africa, saying:

I am still quite interested in returning to South Africa, and I would love to find a teaching job. Is there any way you could help me with this, or at least point me in the right direction I should be going?

The depth of experience that these students had in South Africa was crafted through thoughtfully planned activities that brought students and the people of South Africa together in meaningful ways. The relationships many of these students forged during their time there continued to flourish long after returning home. Students now care about what is happening in South Africa because the country is no longer just a place on a map. For these students, South Africa has become personal because they know and care about people who are directly affected by what is going on there. This sense of connection and care for people in another country is vital to expanding cross-nation relationships and global citizenship.

CONCLUSION

In this chapter, we argue that one way we can better address our global failure to understand one another is through education, broadly, and through the increasing use of traveling to and studying abroad, specifically. However, if our experience is not atypical, study abroad programs that hope to enhance students' capacities to understanding and connect with people around the world will have to be specifically designed for those purposes. Universities can choose to develop programs of study that emphasize academic tourism only, which encourages students to travel to a new country, experience the culture of another nation, and make progress on their program of study; or, they can do all of that and reach for the more lofty goals of creating greater global tolerance, enhancing cultural understanding, and instilling a sense of global responsibility and citizenship through education. Like Anan, we believe that education for tolerance and global understanding is needed in this world now more than ever.

When a country or an entire continent, like Africa, is a place on a map only, people in other countries can care too little about what happens there or how the policies of its own nation affect that country and its people. However, when people have been to countries in Africa, as the students portrayed in this study have, they form relationships with the people who live there, and they pay greater attention to what is happening there because they are newly connected to that land and its people.

By encouraging cross-national relationships and global citizenship, educators have an opportunity to open students' minds and hearts to learning about the lives and perspectives of people who may not share their racial, ethnic, geographic or cultural roots. Like Annan, we believe that developing students' abilities to understand issues and problems from multiple perspectives is critical to ensuring that narrow intolerance and global indifference do not take root in America's youth.

Educating youth who are comfortable around people from a variety of cultures is also important given the ever-growing diversity in the United States. Greater diversity in the United States increases contact with people and cultures beyond our borders. Therefore, an appropriate education for today's youth includes appreciating and understanding cultures and perspectives other than their own.

Over the past decade, we have learned a good deal about how to design a study abroad program that advances issues of equity and social justice and increases students' feelings of connectedness to people who are from or living in another land. We know that students have experienced a meaningful process of learning, transformation and growth when they tell us that they are forever changed by their experiences in South Africa. We also know that our students have experienced a process of personal transformation in their understanding of equity and social justice issues when they tell us that they can no longer look at themselves, the country they visited, or their own country in quite the same way after living and studying in South Africa. And finally, when students tell us that they continue to be connected to one another, to South Africa and to the people who live there, we recognize the power and value of using personal narrative to help people understand and communicate with one another across racial, ethnic, gender, class and national borders.

Each year, our students' engagement in South Africa continues long after their return to the states. This means that they are expanding their global community and embracing people who are approximately 7, 970 miles away. These newly awake global citizens are engaged in the world in a new way. Rather, than caring about me, my family, and my community only, these students are reaching out to connect with people beyond the boundaries of home, city, state, and country. Through our students stories, we see that when students have the opportunity to travel to a developing country like South Africa and spend time examining their received views about racial, ethnic and class others, and when they meet people who enhance their cultural awareness and who connect as friends and allies, they begin to realize that it is people who make up their world, and that good people are found in all places. These newly awake global citizens are becoming ambassadors for the country they visited and for the people they met, making the shift from US citizen to global citizen. As global citizens they are committed to creating greater global tolerance, enhancing cultural understanding, and instilling a sense of global responsibility and citizenship through their relationships with others.

Our global world desperately needs these new citizens, global citizens. We must imagine a time when we are no longer locked into the perilous path of caring about our own country and ourselves only. Global souls have a different sense of obligation. They are not connected to one single, fixed community; rather, they are a part of many communities forged through many bonds and relationships made all over the world. These human bonds have no racial, ethnic, cultural, class, religious or national borders. Thomas Paine captures the heart and mind of the truly liberated global soul, best, saying:

> My country is the world, and my religion is to do good.

NOTE

1. The term used in South Africa for a barbeque.

REFERENCES

Annan, K. (2001, November 28). *Intolerance is taught and can be untaught* (Press Release, SG/SM/8046). Institute of International Education. New York

Annan, K. (2006) *Study abroad now more than ever.* United Nations Center for Global Education Report. Retrieved from www.globaled.us/now/politicalleaders.html.

Bruner, J. (1990). *Acts of meaning.* Cambridge, MA: Harvard University Press.

Burch, K. (2003). An interview with Paul Simon. *Thresholds.* (Vol. XXIX.4). DeKalb: Northern Illinois University Press.

Coles, R. (1989). *A call to stories.* Boston: Houghton Mifflin.

Denzin, N. (1983). *Interpretive interactionism.* Thousand Oaks, CA: Sage.

Kristof, N. (2009, June 5). Cum laude in evading bandits. *New York Times*, p. 23.

Kuhn, T. (1962). *The structure of scientific revolutions.* Chicago: University of Chicago Press.

Mezirow, J. (1981). A critical theory of adult learning and education. *Adult Learning, 32*(1), 3-24.
Valian, V. (1998). *Why so slow? The advancement of women.* Cambridge, MA: M.I.T. Press.
Witz, L, Rassool, C., & Minkley, G. (2001). Repackaging the past for South African tourism. In *Why South Africa matters. Daedalus.* Cambridge, MA: American Academy of Arts and Sciences.
American Association of State Colleges and Universities. (2002). *Leading the way: A showcase of best practices in global education.* Retrieved from www.aascu.org/Dec 2001
University of British Columbia. (2005). *Towards 2010* (2004-5 annual report). Retrieved from www.publicaffairs.ubc.ca/annualreports/2005/citizenship.html

SCENIC OVERLOOK

Chapters 7 and 8

Guidelines for Discussions and Reflection

For school leaders:

1. What are your experiences in traveling internationally? What are you experiences in traveling to emerging or developing countries? Share these experiences. If you have not travelled internationally, to what extent would you engage in such travel? Why or why not?
2. What are your experiences with studying abroad as a student? What are your experiences with facilitating study abroad programs in schools? Share these experiences. If you have not had these experiences, what is your response to Kofi Annan's insights?
3. What opportunities are afforded to school districts to discuss and/or offer study abroad programs for educators, students, and families? Why or why not?
4. How do you understand the difference between academic tourism and global citizenship? To what extent are you willing/able/interested in participating in academic tourism? To what extent are you willing/able/interested in participating in global citizenship programs? Support your position.

5. Discuss the students' experiences in South Africa. What impact do you think experiences such as these would play in shaping your identity as a school leader? Support your position.

For those preparing school leaders:

6. What are your experiences in traveling internationally?
7. What are your experiences with researching international issues?
8. Does your school leadership preparation program implement study abroad programs for students? Why or why not?
9. What are your experiences with facilitating study abroad programs? If you have not had these experiences, what is your response to Kofi Annan's insights?
10. What opportunities should be afforded to school districts to discuss and/or offer study abroad programs for educators, students, and families? Why or why not have these opportunities been afforded?

Colleen Larson and Teboho Moja's 9-year case study provides us with insights to consider when encouraging school leaders to deepen their understanding of our global society. The authors suggest that exposing students to international contexts is vital to enhancing global understanding and cooperation. Larson and Moja reveal their passion to transform the lives of children and families in schools by transforming the lives of aspiring school leaders through active global leadership.

In the next chapter, Bruce Barnett and Gary O'Mahony reconsider the influence transcending global leadership through international collaborative efforts. Such efforts consider the influence of larger contexts, including, economic, cultural, political and educational. Their experiences provide a blueprint for international collaboratives that center on meaningful exchanges.

CHAPTER 8

UNLOCKING THE DOOR TO INTERNATIONAL COLLABORATION

The Power of Interpersonal Relationships and Learning Communities

Bruce G. Barnett and Gary R. O'Mahony

The print and electronic media leave no doubt we are living in a global community. Newspapers, television reports, internet sites, and the popular literature provide constant information about political, economic, social, and athletic events almost as they are occurring. Recent reports, such as Thomas Friedman's (2005) *The World is Flat*, examine global political, social, and economic trends as well as future ways in which governments and societies can cope with and benefit from the realities and tensions of globalization. Although the term *globalization* is becoming a household word, there is no one agreed-upon definition; however, many define the term as the interrelationship between commerce, power, and culture (Ohmae, 2000; Rosenberg, 2000), and it also can refer to "*multiple* economies, political systems, and cultures globally as well as a *single* integrative economy, political system, and culture" (Levin, 2001, p. 8, emphasis added).

As world economies, political systems, and cultures are becoming more connected, societies and individuals are developing a greater awareness of the need to understand how globalization affects their perspectives of international trends and events. Lumby (2008) makes a distinction between two types of international perspectives—traditional and expanded. The *traditional* international perspective typically consists of visiting or vacationing in other countries, participating in exchange programs, or consulting with colleagues in other countries. Engaging in these types of practices is important to connect people from different cultures; however, Lumby (2008) contends that an *expanded* international perspective only occurs as individuals gain a broader, more inclusive appreciation of the worth of nonindigenous values and practices. When individuals experience the expanded international perspective opportunities to understand indigenous social justice issues can occur. As nonnatives immerse themselves in the everyday lives of people in different countries, they are confronted with the realities of the economic, political, and social issues that affect various levels of these societies. An excellent example of social justice consciousness is illustrated in the chapter by Larson (this volume), who describes how students who studied and lived in South Africa have taken on social causes in South Africa as well as back home in the United States. As this example illustrates, these lived experiences in international settings have the potential of influencing nonnatives to move beyond being academic tourists (i.e., traditional international perspective) to becoming active global citizens (i.e., expanded international perspective).

Not only are international trends and events influencing political, social, and economic systems, but educational research and practice also is becoming more globally connected. Despite discrepancies in how international education has been defined and practiced, Dolby and Rahman (2008) reveal these predominant approaches to conducting international research: comparative education, higher education, international schools, teaching and teacher education, K-12 education, and globalization education. Within the field of educational leadership, international research and dissemination is becoming more prevalent. Examples include cross-cultural comparative research studies as well as publications and professional conferences aimed at disseminating information to international audiences. For instance, cross-national research includes:

- The Trends in International Mathematics and Science Study (TIMSS), initiated in 1995, reports math and science achievement results for fourth and eight graders from countries around the world as well as information on educational access, resource equity, and quality of school outputs. Besides comparing achievement scores, educational researchers have mined these data to contrast teachers' working conditions and compensation packages (Akiba, 2008) and how principals are spending their time (Wiseman, 2008).

- The International Successful School Principal Project (ISSPP) is a multinational study launched in 2001 to examine the knowledge, skills, and dispositions of successful principals (Leithwood & Day, 2007). In addition to case studies of over 70 schools and surveys of school leaders in six countries, researchers are returning to the original case study sites to determine if these schools' success has been maintained (Drysdale, Goode, & Gurr, 2008).
- Studies comparing mentoring programs for school leaders in the United Kingdom and Singapore reveal similarities and differences in how the process is perceived and practiced, depending on cultural context (Coleman, Low, Bush, & Chew, 1996).

Furthermore, professional publications and conferences are connecting international researchers and program providers involved in the preparation and development of school leaders. For instance, the recently published *International Handbook on the Preparation and Development of School Leaders* (Lumby, Crow, & Pashiardis, 2008) provides in-depth information on leadership preparation in Europe, North and South America, Africa, Middle East, China, and Australia. In addition, professional journals, such as *International Studies in Educational Administration*; *Education Management, Administration and Leadership*; *Journal of Educational Administration*; and *International Journal of Leadership in Education*, encourage and promote international studies of educational leadership. Finally, international conferences on educational leadership are being sponsored by professional associations, such the Commonwealth Council for Educational Administration and Management (CCEAM); British Educational Leadership, Management and Administration Society (BELMAS); and International Congress on School Effectiveness and Improvement (ICSEI).

Despite the increased interest in educational leadership preparation and research around the globe, caution is needed to ensure that the representation of leadership concepts and practices in other contexts is authentic. Because the majority of educational research and practice has been dominated by western perspectives, there is a tendency to generalize (or globalize) these models, frameworks, and practices to other cultural contexts. The problem is that this perspective overlooks local customs and contexts, leading to "fallacious conclusions regarding the appropriateness of policy and practice" (Walker & Dimmock, 2000, p. 228). The domination of theory and practice from western countries may well marginalize the contributions of less-industrialized countries (Brown & Conrad, 2007), leading to misrepresentation at best and intellectual domination at worst. Calls to reduce this type of intellectual colonialism and to better understand the complexities of cross-national educational theories and applications are being voiced by noted scholars around the world (Astiz, Wiseman, & Baker, 2002; Chu, 2003; Hallinger & Kantamara, 2000; Heck, 1996).

In an attempt to honor different cultural conceptions of research and practice, this chapter examines the intersection of collaboration, relationships, and learning communities when developing international professional development programs and conducting cross-cultural research. The two authors (one from Australia, one from America) describe their 10-year collaborative journey, which underscores the critical nature of developing cross-national personal and professional relationships in order to learn the social norms, values, and customs in different countries as well as the economic, political, and educational contexts, all of which are essential for successful entrée into a new culture.

Our perceptions illustrate the "narrative inquiry" (Li, Mitton-Kukner, & Yeom, 2008) and "narrative dialogue" processes (Brooks & Tooms, n.d.), which frame our discussion of how collaborative international relationships result in connecting practitioners, developing professional development programs, and conducting and disseminating research. Narratives come in various forms, including storying the curriculum, storytelling, and autobiographies (Merriam, Caffarella, & Baumgartner, 2007). Writing this chapter has allowed us to create a narrative of our ten-year journey and we are indebted to the editors of this book for their encouragement and permission to recount our story. While we have verbalized or written about our professional work in scholarly publications, this is the first time we have been able to recount our entire journey and our personal and professional relationships in conducting research and program development. This opportunity has allowed us to gain greater insights about the values and beliefs driving our relationship (see the Conclusions and Implications section), an outcome others have described as being one of the major benefits of storytelling (Clandinin & Connelly, 1992; McCollum, 1992), especially as a way of authentically capturing human action (Greene, 1991).

Furthermore, our perspectives on international leadership preparation and research reflect Lumby's (2008) traditional and expanded definitions of internationalization. For instance, we describe specific collaborative international research and development projects we have engaged in over the past decade (the traditional international perspective). In addition, we examine how these experiences have allowed us to gain a broader, more global appreciation of nonindigenous values and practices (the expanded international perspective), an outcome Lumby (2008) suggests is the ultimate goal of international collaboration. We also agree with James, Dunning, Connolly, and Elliot (2007) that dispositions are shaped by our experiences, reflection, and collaboration; therefore, in reflecting on our experiences as international colleagues, we realize we have gained a more global and less narcissistic world view. The relevance of gaining an international perspective for educational leaders is central to our argument. As leaders and those who prepare them are exposed to a broader understanding of local and global cultural and political systems, they can better understand issues of social justice and equity from multiple perspectives.

The chapter is divided into several sections. We first examine the guiding principles and concepts associated with developing productive international collaboration and learning communities. We then turn our attention to how international collaboration is being conducted by researchers and program developers in America as well as our personal experiences as program developers and researchers. The chapter concludes by describing our reflections on establishing cross-cultural collaboration, gaining an international perspective on leadership development and social justice, and exploring ways of expanding these types of international connections on a larger scale.

COLLABORATIVE LEARNING COMMUNITIES

Collaboration and learning communities have become two of the latest fads to climb onto the educational bandwagon. While many people acknowledge the value of collaboration and learning communities for effective organizations, how do these concepts apply to an international global community? This section will address this question by examining what these two terms mean in a global context where individuals are working across organizational boundaries to conduct research and/or develop programs (Huxham & Vangen, 2000). After defining and examining the guiding principles of these two concepts, we describe the factors affecting the successful creation of a collaborative learning community. The section concludes with a description of two prominent models that can be adapted to understand how effective international collaborative learning communities can be established between researchers, program developers, and practitioners.

The Intersection of Collaboration and Learning Communities

Collaboration and Its Purpose

Collaborative relationships are evidenced in many ways, such as strategic alliances between universities to partnerships between school districts, foundations, and private agencies. The term appears extensively in the literature on economics, sociology, business management, and policy management, and reflects a number of theoretical constructs, such as institutional theory, social network analysis, and critical management theory (Huxham & Vangen, 2000). A host of terms are used interchangeably to capture the essence of collaboration, including alliances, associations, partnerships, networks, and learning communities. For example, collaboration and partnerships have been used synonymously since both rely on accomplishing "goals that cannot be achieved by either party acting alone" (National School Boards Association, 1991, p. 3).

Effective collaboration between individuals and organizations relies on human interaction, learning, and leadership. For instance, Peterson and Brietzke (1994) suggest that collaboration within educational organizations needs to be seen as a combination of social and professional dialogue and interaction associated with cooperation, collegiality, and commitment. Intrilligator (1992), however, argues that collaboration is far more complex than cooperation or coordination. She contends that *cooperation* is appropriate when projects are short term, rely on informal arrangements between partners, and do not require additional funds; *coordination* emerges when organizations are willing to relinquish some of their autonomy and control, projects have longer time allocations, and an interagency unit is created to complete the project. *Collaboration*, on the other hand, demands high levels of organizational interdependence, including more time, finances, and commitment of human resources. Typically, collaboration occurs when one organization has capabilities not possessed by the other organization (Swan & Morgan, 1993); projects will take long periods of time, requiring the sustained effort of multiple partners (Intrilligator, 1992; Lugg, 1994); partners are willing to share authority and responsibility (Hannay & Stevens, 1984); and they demonstrate concern for the well being of the other partner (Appley & Winder, 1977).

Learning Communities and Their Purpose

What then are learning communities and how are they related to collaboration? Kilpatrick, Jones, and Barrett (2006) assert the age of individualism where the learner was portrayed as a lone seeker of knowledge has been supplanted by the spirit of community where individual learners are surrounded and embraced within a community of learners. This manifestation underpinning learning communities, most commonly attributed to Feldman (2000), is reflected in different cultural contexts. Much of the European literature about learning communities emphasizes learning towns, learning cities, and learning regions where the definitions tend to identify geographic location as a key element in learning communities (Kilpatrick et al., 2006). This conceptualization also fits the Australian context because of the country's physical isolation from many other countries. Yarrit (2000) asserts that the popularity of learning communities grew out of the changing context of the European context and are products of the political, economic, geographical, and social tenor of the times. Similar to collaboration, learning communities have been associated with alliances, coalitions, and social networks. The connection in learning occurs when:

> A learning community addresses the learning needs of locality through partnerships. It uses the strength of social and institutional relationship to bring about cultural shifts in perceptions of the value of learning. Learning communities explicitly use learning as a way of promoting social cohesion and economic development which involves all parts of the community. (Yarrit, 2000, p. 1)

Kilpatrick et al. (2006) suggest that two major issues should be considered when defining learning communities. The first deals with the human element and the rewards that accrue from building synergies of individuals in a common location or with common aims as they work towards sharing of understandings, skills, and knowledge. The second issue deals with the curricular structure for schools as the means of developing deeper learning of curricular content. Because of the geographical distance between the two authors as they sought to form a collaborative learning community, we will emphasize the first element, namely the importance of forming strong interpersonal relationships.

A variety of concepts have been used to capture the essence of learning communities. Feldman (2000), for example, maintains that learning communities are characterized by shared values and vision, supportive leadership, collective learning, supportive learning conditions, and peers supporting one another. Within educational settings, learning communities have been promoted as a means not only to establish close collaboration by adults, but also to improve student learning as evidenced by these features:

- A collaborative culture where shared responsibility for student learning outcomes occurs through regular teacher team meetings for learning, inquiry and implementation of research-based teaching practices (Haar, 2003);

- Collective inquiry is emphasized using reflective dialogue focusing on curriculum development, formative assessments, instruction, and job embedded professional development (DuFour & Eaker, 1998; Langston, 2006; Mitchell & Sackney, 2000);
- Supportive conditions exist when there is adequate time for teachers to meet and physical proximity fosters interaction (Langston, 2006); and
- A results-oriented culture emerges as teaching is assessed on the basis of student results (DuFour, 2003), results show whether students have learned the essential curriculum (DuFour, DuFour, Eaker, & Many, 2006), and results of common formative assessments are shared among team members (Langston, 2006).

As collaborative learning communities are formed, benefits can accrue to the organization and to individual members. Schools work more effectively by reducing duplication of effort, coordinating professional development, improving accountability, expanding networks, increasing access to technology, and improving staff morale (Barnett, Hall, Berg, & Camarena, 1999; Reichstetter, 2006). Similarly, international researchers and program developers who collaborate gain by:

- Increasing their awareness and understanding of shared values underpinning their work;
- Developing training to address discrepancies and gaps in their knowledge and skills;
- Identifying ways of working closer together and sharing resources; and
- Encouraging joint action planning (Hoffman & Schlosser, 2001).

Factors Affecting Collaborative Learning Communities

Collaborative learning communities are fragile and can be influenced by numerous organizational and human factors. Because these types of relationships evolve through a series of stages (e.g., Grobe, 1990; Huxham & Vangen, 2004; Turbowitz, 1986), trust, shared vision, mutual interdependence, and strong interpersonal relationships must be maintained or the collaborative partnership will flounder. Cultural, regulatory, and personal barriers also can inhibit the development of collaborative partnerships (Barnett et al., 1999; Huxham & Vangen, 2000). Cultural barriers include different reward structures, visions, and jargon used in the organizations; regulatory roadblocks occur when their policies conflict; and personal concerns arise when individuals are hesitant to participate due to time commitments, lack of understanding of the collaboration, and inadequate knowledge and skills.

Furthermore, individuals involved in international research and program development must confront a variety of challenges (Murakami-Ramalho & Barnett, 2008). First and foremost, language differences (even in English-speaking countries) can undermine a shared meaning of international leadership terms and trends. The principals' role as an instructional leader, for instance, has become a widely accepted description used throughout the United States; however, scholars and practitioners in the United Kingdom and Australia tend to avoid this term, preferring to describe principals as educational leaders. Similarly, the tendency to present a Eurocentric perspective in the English-speaking research journals raises concerns about marginalizing other international perspectives (Flowerdew, 1999; Schiele, 1994).

Second, a host of practical problems can compromise international collaboration. The geographical distance between collaborators results in costly travel expenses and time commitments, which ultimately affect opportunities for face-to-face interaction. Although email, internet, and teleconferencing are cost efficient forms of international communication, they do not allow for the personal contact which is so critical for building relationships and experiencing local cultures firsthand. Compounding the cost problem is the lack of funding for international travel and collaboration to support educational research and development projects. Although resources for international experiences are provided by organizations such as the Fulbright Program, Fund for the Improvement of Post-secondary Education (FIPSE), and the European Union, these grants and scholarships are extremely competitive and tend to focus on student exchanges and/or scholarships to attend universities in other countries, rather than funding long-term collaborative research and program development initiatives.

Models of Collaboration and Learning Communities

Framework of Collaboration

Another way of capturing collaborative learning communities is through conceptual frameworks or models. Robertson (2008), for instance, offers an innovative way of thinking about conceptualizing collaboration. Although applied to the business environment, it offers a lens through which to consider the elements that form the essence of any international collaborative effort. Figure 8.1 summarizes the three tiers representing effective collaboration. Robertson (2008) argues that each tier builds on the one below, starting with capacity (pre-requisites for col-

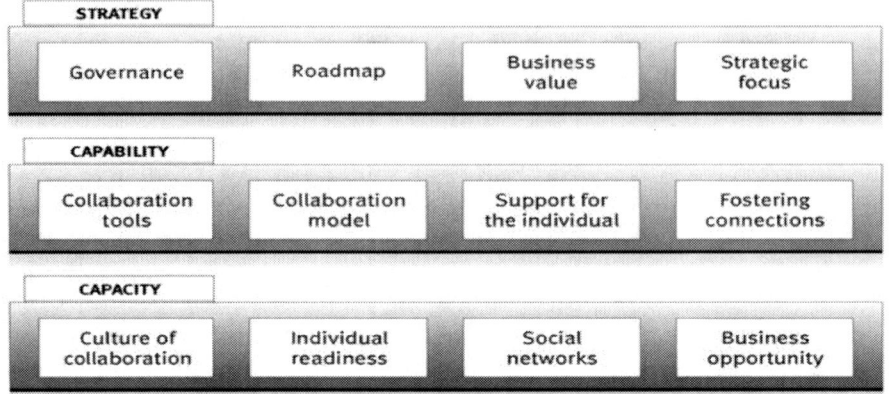

Source: Robertson (2008).

Figure 8.1. A three-tiered model of collaboration.

laboration), to capability (strength of collaborative activities and approaches), to strategy (overall focus on collaboration). Robertson's (2008) model assumes these tiers are not hierarchical, but that each one forms part of a jigsaw that forms an overall picture collaborative thinking.

Tier 1: Building Capacity for Collaboration

This level of collaboration is essential for developing the capacity for individuals and teams to collaborate. Several factors must be accounted for in establishing this capacity:

- **Culture of collaboration**—integration of collaborative practices into "the way we work" with organizations and others in the international context being sensitive to varied cultural contexts.
- **Individual readiness**—the skills, background, practices and personality of individuals to engage in collaboration brought to the international arena of learning.
- **Social networks**—strengthening and expanding the breadth and strength of existing and new social and interpersonal relationships within organization and throughout the educational community.
- **Business opportunity**—the time and opportunity for collaboration within existing work practices and overall agreed collaborative

model needs to be modeled between people and associated supporting groups and organizations.

At this foundational level, collaborative learning develops as its members learn about and become socialized to this process. As they begin to determine how to best to work together, members of the organization can address several key questions to gauge their level of commitment to and interest in developing a collaborative relationship: (1) is this venture a good match of our talents? (2) what might we gain or lose by participating? (3) what should we invest? and (4) if we decided to collaborate, how should we organize ourselves? (Barnett et al., 1999).

Openness and commitment to collaborative learning rely on two elements: (1) creating a foundation of trust and (2) developing shared meaning and understanding of how to collaborate. Trust is an essential factor in building the high-quality relationships needed to foster any type of collaboration (Hoffman, Sabo, Bliss, & Hoy, 1994). As Judge and Ryman (2001) explain: "Collaborative and collective approaches create trust in alliances; competitive and individualistic approaches create distrust. This trust is an essential glue that holds strategic alliances together, but it is very difficult to develop and maintain" (p. 75). Trust becomes a tool that aids and abets collaborators to overcome cultural differences and conflict; encourage better collaborative participation to manage the unforeseen and unintended circumstances associated with change; make more rapid adjustments to circumstances; and provide an alternative to reliance on control mechanisms.

Because trust between individuals or organizations is critical for developing a climate of openness and healthy exchange of ideas and information, researchers stress that trust relies on:

- Building relationships;
- Developing an identification with the mission of the community and with the other members;
- Creating a feeling of belonging and mutual respect;
- Openly sharing learning while building on knowledge about practice;
- Continuing to develop as a community because of meaningful engagement; and
- Developing shared norms that encourage truthfulness, openness, routine collaboration, and the ability to address difficult issues or conflict (Cullen, Johnson, & Sakano, 2000; Sobero, 2008).

In addition to establishing trust, members of collaborative learning communities must develop shared meaning and understanding about the purposes of the collaboration. Shared meaning is frequently posited as a critical component for any multiparty collaboration (Bechky, 2003; Miranda & Saunders, 2003; Standifer & Bluedorn, 2006). The development of shared meaning is not something that occurs when collaborative parties first meet, but rests on the assumption that eventually, if the collaboration is successful, that the parties will have some common interpretation. Vangren and Winchester (2007) note that other scholars have been often more circumspect about collaborative partnerships reaching mutual understanding (Donnellon, Gray, & Bougan, 1986; Weick, Sutcliffe & Obstfeld, 2005) or establishing shared aims (Huxham & Vangen, 2005), raising questions as to whether or not shared meaning is an essential component of collaborative partnerships.

Tier 2: Establishing Capability for Collaboration

The next level of collaboration provides the tools and resources necessary for these relationships to flourish. As outlined in Figure 8.1, the guiding principles of tier 2 include:

- **Collaboration tools**—designing and deploying effective collaboration tools.
- **Collaboration model**—overall model for collaboration, using individual face-to-face contacts, electronic exchanges, and group meetings or forums.
- **Support for the individual**—providing individuals with personal tools and support for and development of designated initiatives through collaboration.
- **Fostering connections**—skills and support for fostering interaction and relationships.

Without effectively managing those individuals most affected and involved in the collaboration, especially during change processes, collaborative alliances are doomed to fail. As Hutt, Stafford, Walker, and Reingen (2000) highlight, "many collaborative alliances fail to meet expectations because little attention is given to nurturing the close working relationships and interpersonal connections that unite the partnering organisation" (p. 51). To enable connections to occur between members of any collaboration, effective communication is crucial. As Davies (2001) suggests, "The merging of interests, the sharing of privileged information, and intimate collaboration and cooperation are all dependent on the ability of the partners to communicate" (p. 187). In addition, Hutt et al. (2000) argue that effective communication and information exchange result in better understanding of goals, roles and relationships, which expands boundary-spanning activities connecting different levels of the organization.

Tier 3: Devising a Strategy for Collaboration

For the building of good interpersonal relations, alliances need to be professionally planned and organized for the full potential of the cooperation to be realized. Figure 7.1 provides the ingredients necessary for a successful organizational strategy for collaboration:

- **Governance**—determining ownership, resourcing, and decision making processes for collaboration.
- **Roadmap**—overall strategy and roadmap for the adoption and growth of collaboration within the organization.
- **Business value**—demonstrated organizational values for collaboration, and their alignment with core goals of the organization.
- **Strategic focus**—recognition that collaboration is an important element of overall success and strategy of the organization.

Perhaps the most important aspect of organizations that are intent on developing a strategic alliance for collaboration is leadership (Huxham & Vangen, 2000). Leaders must attend to three important ingredients when attempting to develop a strategic collaboration: structures, processes, and network participants. Collaboration is influenced by the nature of existing distributed power and underlying politics because "structures influence process designs and what participants can do" (Huxham & Vangen, 2000, p. 1168). Given that structures can both enable and constrain collaborative initiatives, it is crucial to achieve an appropriate alliance structure for success. Astute leaders, therefore, must not only take into account the structures in their own organizations, but also the complementary or conflicting structures of the participating organizations. In a similar way, processes affect organizational collaboration because leaders control the resources allowing the partnership members to work together, communicate, and monitor their progress. Finally, participants' knowledge and skills need to be considered, especially if they are to take formal and informal leadership roles in solidifying the collaboration. According to Huxham and Vangen (2000), these three leadership issues are clearly interlinked. Structures influence processes and network members' behavior; processes influence the emergence of structures and who can set agendas; and participants influence the design of both structures and processes. Consequently, leadership in developing collaborative networks is not only enacted by the formal leadership, but also by the network members who are championing the change process.

Learning Community Framework

Kruse, Louis, and Bryk (1995) have developed a framework conceptualizing professional learning communities in school settings. Table 8.1 serves as a theoretical and practical basis for identifying and framing ideas and activities related to capacity building in relation to schools as professional communities, but their framework also is relevant for international collaborative communities. As administrators and teachers strive to develop a professional learning community focusing on student learning, they engage in reflective dialogue, share practices publically, collaborate, and develop shared values and norms. Moreover, certain structural conditions, such as time, adequate meeting locations, and communication structures, must be provided in order for professional communities to evolve. Finally, as leaders provide necessary human and social resources, members of the professional community gain positive attitudes and cognitive skills regarding change and improvement, develop trust in and respect for one another, and become socialized to how to work collaboratively with their colleagues.

Use of These Models

Taken together, these conceptualizations of collaboration and professional learning communities have important implications for engaging in international collaboration. First, both approaches highlight the importance of *human capacity building* in order to establish strong personal bonds and commitments for collaboration to flourish. Robertson (2008) refers to these as the tier 1 elements of collaborative culture, individual readiness, and social networks, all of which are essential in developing individuals' attitudes and capacities to engage in collaborative learning communities. The Kruse et al. (1995) framework reflects important human and social resources, especially positive attitudes toward change and mutual respect and trust, which must be accounted for professional learning communities to flourish. As these models suggest, when colleagues trust one another, see value in engaging in a collaborative project, and set shared norms for their involvement, meaningful collaboration stands a good chance of occurring. In essence, collaborative learning communities only work when strong interpersonal relationships are established, a point we will emphasize later in describing our international collaborative journey.

Second, these two frameworks can be used in practical ways as the basis for a self-assessment in order to identify areas of strength and weakness in collaboration strategies, learn about collaborative approaches, collect

Table 8.1. Framework for Analyzing School-Based Professional Community

Elements of Professional Community	Examples of Professional Community
Characteristics	Reflective dialogue Collective focus on student learning Deprivation of practice Collaboration Shared values and norms
Structural conditions	Time to meet and discuss Physical proximity Interdependent teaching roles Teacher empowerment/school autonomy Communication structures
Human/social resources	Openness to improvement Trust and respect Supportive leadership Socialization Cognitive/skill base

Source: Adapted from Kruse, Louis, and Bryk (1995).

information on collaborative techniques and approaches, and develop a shared model to build understanding between practitioners of collaboration (Robertson, 2008). By reflecting on these elements, any organization can determine its own development as a learning community and explore ways to become more effective. They also provide a basis for focusing on how schools can change their thinking and practices and how collaborative partnerships can be formed to help them achieve the reality of an effective school learning community. The starting point is for individuals and organizations to look within because true learning communities reflect on their own practices to determine if they are modeling what they espouse (Vescio, Ross, & Adams, 2006).

PROMOTING AND ENGAGING IN INTERNATIONAL COLLABORATION

Our personal experiences with international collaboration over the past decade are not new; partnerships between individuals and organizations interested in educational leadership have existed for quite some time. For instance, over 40 years ago, the University Council for Educational Administration established collaborative relationships with international colleagues and organizations (Culbertson, 1995). In this section, we describe in some detail the ways in which our collaborative relationships have grown over the years. Before describing our personal experiences, we provide a brief overview of the types of international projects and activities being implemented between researchers and practitioners in the United States and other countries.

University Collaboration

Recently, one of the coauthors (Bruce Barnett) became the associate director of international affairs for the University Council for Educational Administration (UCEA), an international consortium of universities that offer doctoral programs in educational leadership and administration. The organization's mission is to advance the preparation and practice of educational leaders for the benefit of all children and schools by: (a) promoting, sponsoring, and disseminating research on the essential problems of practice, (b) improving the preparation and professional development of school leaders and professors, and (c) influencing policy and practice through establishing and fostering collaborative networks. Approximately 1,200 professors in the 80 member institutions and 800 additional faculty affiliates are involved in various aspect of the UCEA program. Recent events have provided momentum for UCEA's role in advancing an international educational leadership agenda: (a) several international universities have become UCEA members (University of Lincoln, University of Southampton, Chinese University of Hong Kong), (b) the publication of *The International Handbook on the Preparation and Development of School Leaders* (Lumby, Crow, & Pashiardis, 2008), a collaborative effort between UCEA, BELMAS, and CCEAM, provides in-depth information on leadership preparation in Europe, North and South America, Africa, Middle East, China, and Australia, (c) the 2007 UCEA Convention theme examined international educational leadership issues, and (d) an associate director position dedicated to increasing the organization's international involvement was created.

In his role as the associate director, Bruce is responsible for: (1) increasing international cooperation and partnerships, (2) encouraging international memberships in UCEA, and (3) developing international research and learning opportunities. To determine the types of international projects UCEA members were engaged in, an electronic survey was distributed to member institutions in the fall of 2008 (Barnett, 2009). Survey responses from 35 UCEA members revealed the breadth of current work being conducted in international settings as well as possible future directions for international research and development initiatives. Of the 35 responses obtained, the majority of program faculty ($n = 23$ or 66%) currently are engaged in international research or program development. The trends that emerged from members' responses are briefly summarized below.

Current International Projects

UCEA faculty members are conducting research studies all around the globe, from New Zealand and Australia, to North America, Central and South America, to England, Central and Eastern Europe, to the Middle East, and Africa, and to Asia. Studies are examining diversity, organizational citizenship, superintendents, principal preparation, democratic schooling and student achievement, and professional socialization and identity. Furthermore, UCEA institutions are delivering doctoral and master's degree programs in other countries. Some institutions are engaged in collaborative projects with international organizations in Kenya, Jordan, Norway, Bulgaria, Mexico, Peru, and South Korea dealing with faculty, teacher, and graduate student exchanges and curriculum development projects, such as language and culture development, gifted education, and school improvement.

Desired International Projects

Great interest was expressed by respondents to continue or begin working with international colleagues and organizations. Engaging in research studies examining teacher leadership, social justice, diversity, secondary and tertiary alignment, and leadership preparation were popular as well as organizations they would like to collaborate with (e.g., National College for School Leadership) and/or countries or geographical regions where they would like to work (e.g., Africa, Latin America, Scandinavia, Middle East). Higher education institutions already delivering graduate degree programs abroad wanted to broaden their outreach by expanding these programs in Canada, Mexico, Belize, Thailand, and China. In addition, faculty expressed a desire to continue or begin cross-cultural projects. Examples of cross-cultural projects included working with indigenous groups in the United States and Mexico; developing exchange programs for graduate students, professors, principals, and aspiring school leaders; and establishing programs focusing on leadership development, digital learning, and school improvement.

Our Personal Experiences With International Collaboration

As these examples indicate, international relationships between colleagues in different countries are alive and well. Our collaborative journey over the past decade is quite similar. In sharing the evolution of our relationship, we rely on the "narrative inquiry" process because we believe our "practices are conceived as having been composed over time as our lives unfolded in various contexts alongside and in relation to different people" (Li, Mitton-Kukner, & Yeom, 2008). In this sense, we present a personal narrative of our experiences often found in studies using a biographical methodological approach (e.g., Shields & Edwards, 2005).

Our initial encounter was a chance meeting at the University of Northern Colorado where Bruce was a faculty member and Gary was visiting a mutual colleague, Gene Hall. We never imagined that the hour spent together learning about the work Gary was doing as a Project Director at the Australian Principals Centre (APC) in Melbourne, Australia would bear such professional and personal fruit. The APC was created through the formation of a multi-organizational alliance between the Victorian Department of Education, the University of Melbourne, and principals' organizations in Victoria and throughout Australia (as well as other Australian universities, independent and Catholic schools sectors) with the intention of establishing a model for principal accreditation and professional leadership learning. The APC leadership was interested in forming collaborations and alliances within Australia and beyond, which provided a strategic opportunity for us to launch our international partnership. Without the support and encouragement of the APC, our relationship never would have materialized.

On Gary's invitation, Bruce spent a fortnight in Melbourne during February 2008 visiting schools, meeting his APC colleagues, and presenting seminars. This 2-week experience blossomed into a sabbatical for Bruce and his family at the APC the following year. Since that time we have engage in a variety of projects and research studies, which have included: (a) study tours, (b) program development and delivery, (c) university team-teaching experience, and (d) research and dissemination. Background on these professional arrangements is described below.

Study Tours

Study tours to other countries can be a stimulating and stretching experience to sample a new cultural experience, but they can be wasteful and frustrating if they are not well planned in advance. If the host organizers are not clear about the nature of the tour and the needs of the participants, then they may create a smorgasbord of activities based on what they think participants want and desire. We have found that for Australian regional study tours coming to the United States to visit schools, universities, and professional associations the following guidelines are essential:

- Ensuring contacts in the participating organizations jointly plan the scope of the tour and develop events and activities directly related to the needs of the visiting group;
- Gathering expectations and requirements from tour participants and then checking to make sure the planned activities provide opportunities for individuals to explore these ideas in a new context, such as differentiated teaching, team teaching for improving student assessment, and cohort learning;
- Identifying common areas for the group to explore (e.g., leadership and school improvement, differentiated teaching) can ensure that participating groups can share similarities and differences in how leadership is conceived in differing cultural contexts;
- Providing prereading materials (e.g., articles, websites) related to the visitation contexts and initiatives can help stimulate discussion prior to and during the visit;
- Allowing time and opportunities for participants in both contexts to set aside time for sharing and exchanging ideas about their observations; and
- Ensuring on the return home that tour participants share their learning experiences with colleagues in networks or through material gathered through the study tours.

An Example of a Jointly-Developed Study Tour

The tours we have co-developed typically have been for about two weeks. One week is devoted to visiting the town where the American Educational Research Association (AERA) is being held to attend the conference, visit local schools, and meet with members from professional associations. The second week is spent in San Antonio, Texas, where Bruce is a faculty member at the University of Texas at San Antonio. Once again, participants attend graduate classes on campus, visit local schools, and meet with professional associations. We implemented such a tour in April 2005 and conducted another tour in April 2009 for a group of principals and regional office administrators from the Western Metropolitan Region (WMR) in Melbourne, Victoria, Australia. The following goals shaped the 2009 tour:

1. Attend the American Educational Research Association Annual Conference in San Diego (California) to learn of the current research and initiatives in school improvement, school development, and leadership;
2. Visit and study school improvement initiatives and exemplar student learning programs in San Diego (California) and San Antonio (Texas);
3. Attend seminars and professional development sessions arranged by San Diego University and the University of Texas, San Antonio and visit schools in San Diego and San Antonio; and
4. Visit with district and professional association leaders to learn about important professional learning opportunities being delivered for teachers and school administrators.

Program Development and Delivery

During the time Bruce spent his sabbatical at the APC, he and Gary delivered a variety of workshops on reflection, strategic leadership, and teambuilding. The reactions of participants to these sessions, as well as Gary's knowledge of the leadership development context in Victoria, led to creating a series of multiple- and single-day programs for principals, assistant principals, and teacher leaders. When establishing these programs, we wanted to ensure they not only addressed the needs of participants, but also modeled the best adult development principles (Merriam et al., 2007). Some of the underlying principles we consciously attempted to build into these programs included:

- Using research as a yardstick on which to build and design learning;
- Incorporating the components of adult learning (e.g., needs-based, ownership, involvement, job-related, high engagement); and
- Blending opportunities for the use of reflection as a necessary component of the learning process (Barnett, O'Mahony, & Matthews, 2004).

The sabbatical served as a catalyst for continuing our collaborative relationship. Early in our relationship, we created APC-sponsored programs (SAGE, PRISM, Coaching for Experienced Principals). After Gary retired, the programs we implemented were based on his involvement as an independent consultant (Journey into Leadership) and thematic workshops dealing with the series of books we have written (Reflective Practice, Teams, Building School Culture). Below we highlight the various professional development programs we have delivered.

SAGE Mentor Training

This program was developed by the APC for experienced principals to support beginning principals, which grew out of beginning principal research, indicating that novices need differentiated mentoring support from designated mentors in their first year in the role (O'Mahony, 2003). The SAGE acronym stands for Supporting, Accomplishing, Guiding, and Enriching and was initially piloted with principals in the Western Metropolitan Region in Melbourne, Australia with the support of the Victorian Department of Education and Training (Barnett & O'Mahony, 2005). Following the pilot, the program has prepared over 1000 school leaders across nine regions in the state of Victoria. By building a cadre of trained mentors for succession planning, SAGE was instrumental in developing induction, leading teacher accreditation, and deputy principal programs.

During the program, participants engage in the following activities:

- Completing a learning style instrument, revealing the mentor's and the protégé's preferred styles;
- Using a written inventory to examine mentors' tendencies for interacting with others, controlling situations, and developing trusting relationships;
- Creating a jointly developed memorandum of understanding, which specifies the mentor's and protégé's working agreements, timelines, and expected outcomes;
- Practicing how to ask reflective questions and provide meaningful feedback; and
- Anticipating how to accommodate the changing nature of the mentoring relationship (Barnett & O'Mahony, 2008, pp. 242-243).

PRISM

Modeled after the Peer Assisted Leadership Program developed at the Far West Laboratory (Barnett, 1987), PRISM entailed shadowing and cohort learning for regional and interstate groups of school leaders. PRISM stands for Peers/Reflecting/Inquiring/Sharing/Mastering and sought to reduce the isolation of school leaders through peer observation and feedback and to improve their problem solving expertise to meet the rigors faced in everyday school life. Participants were involved in three phases over the course of the year. Phase 1 provided training in shadowing and reflective interviewing; phase 2 involved partners shadowing and providing reflective feedback as they engaged in a school improvement project; and phase 3 allowed participants to reconvene to share their experiences (O'Mahony & Barnett, 2006b). The program was guided by the following principles:

1. Know yourself—school leaders examine their leadership styles, values, and behaviors underpinning their effectiveness. Before they can lead others, they must be able to lead themselves.
2. Know your organization—school leaders understand the elements that make their schools effective and are able to build strategies for continuous school improvement.
3. Know what you and your school are capable of achieving for children—school leaders need to know their own and their schools' capacities and limitations to be able to concentrate on the achievable, ensuring the best possible outcomes for students.
4. Know the value of reflection—school leaders and their peer partners reflect on the school improvement projects that they are implementing (O'Mahony & Barnett, 2006b, p. 7).

Coaching for Experienced Principals

As part of their Blueprint, the Victorian Department of Education and Training (2005) emphasized the importance of providing professional development programs to build school leaders' leadership capacities. The APC responded to this initiative by instituting the Coaching for Enhancing the Capabilities of Experienced Principals Program (CEP) based on an executive coaching model (Zeus & Skiffington, 2000) for supporting experienced principals. One unique aspect of CEP was its focus on experienced principals since most leadership coaching programs are aimed at novices or school administrators who are flounder and need special assistance. During the course of the school year, participants were expected to:

- Actively participate in all program activities;
- Implement an action plan for school improvement with their coach;
- Complete a confidential 360-degree Educational Leadership Feedback Instrument (ELFI) to be used with the coach as starting point for their discussions; and
- Maintain a reflective diary or electronic portfolio of their coaching interactions (O'Mahony & Barnett, 2008, pp. 19-20).

Retired and practicing principals, state department employees, and corporate consultants served as coaches. Prior to entering their coaching relationships, coaches attended a 2-day training program to examine how to develop effective coaching skills, assist experienced principals in developing their transformational leadership skills, and clarify their roles and expectations (O'Mahony & Barnett, 2006a; Barnett & O'Mahony, 2007a, 2006b). Each coach was encouraged to spend a minimum of 10 hours in the relationship; however, most coaches exceeded this expectation. Four cohorts of principals and coaches participated in the program and experienced principals engaged in a variety of transformational leadership projects. They also reported being better at delegating responsibilities, improving their self-confidence, and becoming more strategic in implementing school improvement (Barnett & O'Mahony, 2008).

Journey Into Leadership

Besides developing the capacities of practicing school leaders, the Victorian Department of Education and Training (2005) also saw the need to improve leadership succession planning by developing the knowledge and skills of aspiring school leaders. In his role as an educational consultant, Gary and his colleagues developed Journey into Leadership (JIL), a year-long program for teachers and assistant principals to develop the skills and knowledge necessary to progress towards the principalship. Aspirants engaged in four program phases: (1) determining personal awareness, (2) planning a school-based leadership project, (3) learning the leadership skills for implementing the project, and (4) reporting and reflecting on the progress of leadership projects. Besides attending regularly-scheduled professional development sessions and completing a school-based leadership project, JIL participants shadowed successful principals and worked with a mentor principal. To support the implementation of their leadership projects, aspirants attended workshops conducted by mentors, completed learning modules focusing on school improvement, and learned how school leaders support teachers and manage the curriculum (Leithwood, Seashore-Louis, Anderson, & Walstrom, 2004). They also spent time working with a mentor principal to plan and reflect on their leadership projects, shadowing a principal for five days to better understand school improvement leadership practices, and participating in mock job applications and interviews.

Thematic Workshops

As we gained experience delivering these professional development programs for Australian educators, we sensed they wanted to learn more about many of the topics we were addressing. We solicited the involvement of one of Gary's long-time colleagues, Robin Matthews, a professor at Deakin University, to determine his interest in collaborating with us to share his expertise in program development and dissemination. Robin has a strong background in change and innovation and has prepared numerous publications and workshops dealing with these topics. They also had experience publishing books (O'Mahony & Matthews, 2005) with the Australian publisher, Hawker Brownlow Education in Melbourne. Therefore, we approached Elaine Brownlow to determine their interest in developing a book series. Their editorial leadership team saw great value in producing these publications for school leaders, particularly ones that we could use in workshop settings. Most of our professional development programs rely heavily on the use of reflective practice, so we began by writing the book, *Reflective Practice: The Cornerstone for School Improvement* (Barnett, O'Mahony, & Matthews, 2004). Besides examining the guiding principles and concepts of reflective practice, the book offers practical approaches for promoting reflection for leaders, teachers, students, teams, and school-wide development. We used this book in workshops dealing with reflection for school improvement and team development (descriptions appear below). Based on the positive response to these initial reflective practice workshops, we wrote two more books on school improvement, one on school culture building (O'Mahony, Barnett, & Matthews, 2006) and the other on change management (Matthews, O'Mahony, & Barnett, 2006). We presently are completing our fourth book in the series on coaching for school improvement (O'Mahony, Matthews, & Barnett, 2009). Examples of the thematic workshops incorporating our books that we have conducted in throughout Victoria, Australia include:

- *Reflective Practice for School Improvement.* This workshop examines how strategic leaders can apply reflective questioning techniques to address their school improvement initiatives (Barnett & O'Mahony, 2002). After examining the guiding principles of reflection and strategic leadership, participants are introduced to our Model of Reflective Thinking and Practice (Barnett, O'Mahony, & Matthews, 2004). Individuals apply this information by crafting and practicing reflective questions representing the phases of the model and consider ways of assisting others in the organization to become more reflective about how their practices are supporting school improvement efforts.
- *Improving Schools Through Reflective Team Practices.* Advertized for teams of teachers and school leaders, this workshop is aimed at assisting teams to reflect on their current practices and to ascertain ways of improving their future (Barnett & O'Mahony, 2002). After learning about our Model of Reflective Thought and Action, team members review the phases of team development and the features of effective and ineffective teams (Larson & LaFasto, 1989; Lencioni, 2002). Using these elements as a guide, teams reflect on their current practices, noting ways in which they are functioning well and poorly. Based on this reflective assessment, they develop plans for how to build on their strengths and address their limitations.
- *Building a Teacher Development Culture for School Improvement.* School-level teams are encouraged to attend this workshop, which focuses

on ascertaining the healthy and unproductive aspects of their school culture. Participants are introduced to our Framework for Analyzing School Culture (O'Mahony, Barnett, & Matthews, 2006) and identify cultural practices and artifacts in their schools that exemplify elements in the framework. Using several inventories (O'Mahony, Barnett, & Matthews, 2006), teams reflect on current strengths and weakness of their school culture and then determine ways to maintain their strengths and improve their deficiencies.

We also have conducted workshops on reflective practice and mentoring for professional associations in Australia and university programs in other countries. During the height of our involvement in SAGE, we delivered an abbreviated version of this mentoring program for Lutheran educators in South Australia and Queensland. In 2005, we conducted a workshop on reflective practice for the School Leadership Centre at the University of Auckland in New Zealand and worked with assisted with mentor development for principals at the University of Victoria in British Columbia, Canada. These experiences allowed us to adapt program materials and activities for practitioners in different contexts and cultures.

University Team Teaching

During Bruce's tenure at the University of Northern Colorado, Gary came to Colorado to team teach leadership preparation courses with him during a concentrated 4-week period in the summer. We thought that combining the expertise and experiences of an academic (Bruce) and a former school principal (Gary) would be an innovative way to allow American aspiring school leaders to gain an international perspective on leadership and school effectiveness. Two courses, The Principalship and Supervision of Curriculum and Instruction, comprised the content and students were exposed to practical case studies, dilemmas, and leadership situations reflecting the Colorado licensure standards for school leaders. Besides incorporating a variety of readings, local experts, school visits, and community advisers ensured that the cohort was exposed to the reality and demands faced by school leaders. Significant elements included:

- Having the instructors present during the entire experience to offer different perspectives on course content and students' experiences;

- Using a core set of references to ensure that group discussion and debate were actively encouraged;
- Encouraging cohort learning and presentations to ensure students became a team and took ownership and responsibility for their own learning; and
- Applying course content by having students develop personal vision statements, create an entry plan, and anticipate practical ways of collecting and interpreting student performance data, being an effective ethical leader, building a school culture, and holding people accountable.

Research and Dissemination

As noted earlier, we have produced a series of books on important issues related to school improvement, which have proven to be invaluable in delivering the thematic workshops. We also have used a variety of outlets to capture our programs, examining the types of learning outcomes and ways practitioners have applied this information in their school settings. To provide a sense of our program research and dissemination, we examine the various mechanisms for sharing our work and the types of outcomes and benefits reported by program participants.

Types of Dissemination

The Hawker Brownlow book series was intended to capture what we have learned about reflection, culture, change, and coaching. Although we used these books in the thematic workshops we conducted, they also served as stand-alone products that have been marketed by the publisher throughout Australia. We also have been intentional about disseminating information regarding the programs we have produced in other professional publications and at conferences. Examples include the following:

- Our ideas about reflective practice have appeared in journals, including *Reflective Practice* (Barnett & O'Mahony, 2006a) and the *Journal of Staff Development* (Barnett & O'Mahony, 2002).
- SAGE has been reported in book chapters on international trends in leadership preparation and development (Barnett & O'Mahony, 2008); in Australian journals, such as *Teacher* (Barnett & O'Mahony, 2005) and *Prime Focus* (Barnett, O'Mahony, & Miller, 2002); and in APC publications (Barnett 2001a). The program also was featured in Weindling's (2004) description of succession planning programs

operating around the world, which was disseminated by the National College for School Leadership in England.
- The PRISM program has been promoted in several Australian publications, including *The Victorian Education Magazine* (O'Mahony & Barnett, 2006b) and APC publications (Barnett, 2001b).
- Descriptions of CEP have been disseminated in book chapters (Barnett & O'Mahony, 2008); in the journal *Leading & Managing* (O'Mahony & Barnett, 2008); and at professional conferences, including the Commonwealth Council for Educational Administration and Management (Barnett, Henry, & Vann, 2008), American Educational Research Association (Barnett & O'Mahony, 2007a; O'Mahony & Barnett, 2006a), and University Council for Educational Administration (Barnett & O'Mahony, 2006b, 2007b).
- JIL has been presented at the American Educational Research Association Conference (Barnett & O'Mahony, 2009).

Outcomes of Program Participation

Besides describing these programs' guiding principles, operating procedures, and activities, we also have sought to learn how participants' knowledge and skills have been affected by their involvement. Through informal discussions and survey instruments, program participants have acknowledged outcomes that have affected their thinking and actions as teachers and school leaders. Typically, information was collected while participants were engaged in a program or at its conclusion; however, a recent study of JIL aspirants and their mentors examined their reactions one to two years following their involvement (Barnett & O'Mahony, 2009). While many of these benefits have been reported elsewhere, we summarize below the major outcomes participants in various programs have reported.

1. **Study tours.** The expressed intent of these visitations is to investigate research and school practices on leadership and school improvement from an international perspective. Study tour participants note the following outcomes associated with the experience:

- Incorporating ideas and materials into their work in schools and the regional office;
- Serving as resource teams for school networks engaged in school improvement;
- Gaining a better appreciation for their practices and for other ways of leading and managing schools;

- Distributing samples, exemplars, videos and photos, and booklets for use by the group; and
- Forming long-term relationships for personal and professional support.

In their own words, study tour participants' comments reveal how this international learning experience stimulates personal growth and creates a learning community among members of the group: "The study tour experience engenders great pride in our own educational organizations and their achievements and builds a wonderful sense of common purpose and corporate commitment to making a difference in our schools when we return." "The study tour stimulated a great deal of reflection on my own practice, a great deal of professional discourse with colleagues enabled me to develop lasting professional and personal relationships both within Australia and overseas." "The main benefit was the development of networks of people vitally interested in leadership for school improvement. These networks both in the United States and Australia have continued to be strong and remind us all that we are a global learning community." "Personally I improved my reflective and critical thinking processes by being surrounded by rich conversations at the end of each day. Our professional learning journey continues 4 years later with our commitment to visit our own schools as a group and attend a variety of professional learning activities in small groups or altogether."

2. **SAGE.** Mentors and the new principals with whom they work have expressed a host of benefits from the experience (Barnett & O'Mahony, 2005). Mentors often feel they have gained more than the novices, reporting the benefits of examining their own leadership tendencies, developing collegial relationships, and understanding the importance of having support from the regional office. As one mentor mentioned, "If you want to improve the morale and enhance the capacity of your leadership team and yourself, then explore the potential positives of a mentoring program like this. The rewards are enormous and career changing." New principals appreciate mentors providing them with a more realistic perspective, reducing their sense of isolation, and considering new ways of handling problems as evidenced by these comments, "This program assists thinking through broadening and crystallizing of ideas. It is about improving the practice of leadership" and "[I have benefitted by] sharing and obtaining different perspectives on leadership and the mentoring role in learning to solve problems."

3. **PRISM.** During their year-long relationship with a peer partner, program participants not only value having a trusted colleague collaborate on a school improvement initiative, but also sense they are more stra-

tegic and make more-informed decisions (O'Mahony & Barnett, 2006b). Typical comments include, "[PRISM] creates an opportunity to reflect actively on my personal actions as a principal," "[I have] the ability to see the diversity in leadership styles and skills ... [and the] perceptions from my staff were very rewarding, as I think I am too critical of myself," and "[I have reaffirmation] of what leadership is [and I can] focus on an area of school improvement in a supportive environment" (O'Mahony & Barnett, 2006b, p. 7).

4. **CEP.** Data from experienced principals and coaches reveal the ways their relationships allowed principals to grow professionally (O'Mahony & Barnett, 2008). Principals acknowledge that the experience raised awareness of: (1) their own leadership styles, (2) how to utilize the skills and talents of other staff members in implementing their school improvement projects, and (3) how to be more strategic about school improvement. Coaches also noticed these same outcomes, noting the importance of establishing their credibility as a supportive, respected, and trusted colleague. The power of the coaching relationship is evident in CEP participants' comments: "[My coach's] willingness to listen to the conversation and tease out the important elements was terrific throughout the program... and I have plans to continue working with [her] in some capacity." "[My coach] acted as a trusted facilitator who continued to seek my views and responses rather than spoon feed suggestions to me." "[My coach] has been a great encourager and was determined to keep our meetings to task, a characteristic I greatly appreciated. [Her] spot on questioning techniques [were used] to get to the core of the situation."

5. **JIL.** One or 2 years following their participation, aspiring principals and their mentors were asked to reflect on the effectiveness of various program elements, the outcomes of the program, and aspirants' readiness to become school leaders. The results of this investigation revealed the value of shadowing other administrators and being mentored as well as the benefits aspirants obtained, such as knowing the job roles and requirements of principals, understanding their own leadership styles, having the capacity to become a school administrator, and being prepared to take on the role (Barnett & O'Mahony, 2009). These comments from participants reveal the power of the experience, especially in developing their perspectives and self-confidence: ""I was looking for a next step in my career and this JIL experience allowed me to see a number of leadership styles and gain a greater insight into school leadership." "Since the program I have had the confidence to apply for two positions ... and there has been a degree of personal and professional confidence that I can work with a variety of administrators in different contexts." "I found the shadowing of an experienced principal and her generosity on sharing insights into why she operated in the way she did to be invaluable to my growth in both confidence and under-

standing of leadership styles." "The program gave me time to reflect and consolidate my skills and showed me a pathway of furthering my career without compromising my educational morals."

6. **Thematic workshops.** Many participants have commented on how they have adapted and used ideas from the workshops, particularly the books we have incorporated. This feedback has been particularly useful to us when we are approached by other schools, districts, or regions. Participants indicate they have used the books and training materials in the following ways:

- Forming study groups to present selected chapters of the book at staff meetings;
- Establishing work teams to conduct action research;
- Adapting workshop activities on reflection for their school staff;
- Using inventories and frameworks to assess the current school culture;
- Developing school mentoring and coaching programs; and
- Using reflective practice to underpin their work in student learning by developing rubrics and linking teaching practice to annual performance goals.

CONCLUSIONS AND IMPLICATIONS

As global awareness and communication increase, individuals, groups, organizations, and agencies will be presented with opportunities to collaborate and establish learning communities spanning regional and national boundaries. To ensure these interactions are productive requires thoughtful consideration of the advantages and rationale for entering into these agreements as well as the structural arrangements and organizational support necessary for sustaining collaborative relationships. In anticipating how current and future collaborations between individuals and organizations are productive, this section summarizes our personal reflections on developing international collaborative relationships as well as the implications for developing international collaboration and learning communities.

Reflections on Our Collaborative Journey

Collaborating to write this chapter has been an example of how narrative inquiry and biographical methods (Li, Mitton-Kukner, & Yeom, 2008;

Shields & Edwards, 2005) can be used to capture the genesis and evolution of our relationship. Over the years, we have commented on how our personal and professional lives have been enriched by our decade-long collaborative relationship. However, writing this chapter has been an excellent way to summarize our experiences and what we have learned about international collaboration. Our international passports have allowed us to work together, share ideas and revelations, and acknowledge our strengths and shortcomings, without which our relationship would be bereft. The true test of our international collaboration is that our personal and professional relationships have survived and still thrive today. We have traveled the high and low road, confronted one another at times, experiencing the situational rapids or the hot springs of testing human relationships; we have sometimes been blown into the winds of doldrums or encountered neither rhyme nor reason in our search for better approaches to delivering and disseminating information about our programs.

In describing our journey, we have focused on our professional interactions, noting the advantages and benefits we have reaped; however, perhaps more crucial, are the personal relationships we have established with one another, our families, and mutual friends. We have taken vacations together with our spouses in Australia and China, have stayed in one another's homes, have attended sporting events in Australia and America, and have celebrated holidays and festivals together. Because our relationship goes well beyond professional interactions, we have learned to appreciate one another's personal values, beliefs, and aspirations; however, we also have learned so much more about the norms, values, and aspirations of our two countries. This deeper level of interaction has provided us with numerous opportunities to directly experience the social, economic, and political fabric of our two countries, allowing us to gain an expanded international perspective, so vital to understanding other cultures through their eyes (Lumby, 2008). And the chance to recount our story, as suggested by Clandinin and Connelly (1992), has been an excellent way to capture our personal, social, and emotional experiences, which have been the glue binding our relationship. Our professional interactions were a means for beginning our partnership and for continuing to explore ways to stay connected. However, our relationship remains vibrant because of our personal affection for one another and our families and friends, not simply because we have similar professional interests.

In reflecting on our professional journey, we rely on several sources. First, we use a framework for understanding the pillars of visionary leadership developed by Cox and Rock (1997). We then examine how our experiences reflect the three tiers of collaboration advanced by Robertson

(2008). Each framework provides a unique lens for examining our relationship.

The Visionary Leadership Lense

In their book, *The 7 Pillars of Visionary Leadership*, Cox and Rock (1997) describe seven pillars, or foundations, that serve as a moral compass for visionary leaders to manage their own learning: visioning, mapping, journeying, learning, mentoring, leading, and valuing. The ways in which these pillars capture our collaborative international journey are considered below.

- *Visioning*. Gary's familiarity with educational trends and issues in Victoria coupled with his experience as a school principal and APC staff member were instrumental as we envisioned projects and programs that would meet the needs of practicing and aspiring school leaders. We designed and developed new and innovative ways to package and present professional development around a number of needed areas, particularly mentoring for principal succession (SAGE), coaching for principals and teachers (CEP), and developing aspiring school leaders (JIL). Although there have been many mentoring programs offered in Victoria, the fact that the SAGE program was implemented for nine years and prepared over 1,000 mentors is a true testament to its relevance. In addition, our creation of the HBE book series was envisioned as a way of capturing our learning and using it for future workshops and presentations, which continue today.
- *Mapping*. We each have varied and distinct backgrounds, one a professor and researcher in a university, the other a former school principal and Principal Centre project director. Blending our knowledge and talents was extremely important for examining issues from multiple perspectives. Tapping our strengths was particularly evident when we were creating leadership development programs. Gary is extremely creative, ensuring we incorporated symbols, artifacts, and metaphors into our teaching. Bruce, being a bit more pragmatic, provided structure and organization to the planning. Our combination of talents was never more evident than when team teaching in Colorado. While Bruce knew the Colorado licensure system and the University of Northern Colorado principal preparation program, Gary exposed students to new ways of thinking about curriculum, instructional practices, and professional development.
- *Journeying*. During our decade-long relationship, we have engaged in a variety of professional experiences, which has allowed us to

explore new ideas in different contexts. Our international journey has taken us from delivering mentoring and coaching programs in Australia, team teaching on the Western Slope of Colorado, working with mentors in British Columbia, and conducting study tours in Southern California and Texas. These experiences not only have helped us to better understand different schools systems, but also have allowed us to adapt our leadership development programs for different cultures and contexts.

- *Learning*. One of our norms was to use the feedback from participants to change program materials and delivery. For example, although SAGE ran for nine years, we constantly changed and adapted the program based on participants' reactions. Furthermore, writing about and presenting our work has forced us to capture the rationale for and outcomes associated with our professional development programs. Preparing manuscripts when living so far apart has been a struggle at times; however, it also has been a labor of love because we have challenged one another, stimulated new thoughts, and honored our writing commitments and timelines, resulting in numerous books, chapters, journal articles, and presentations at conferences around the world.
- *Mentoring*. We each have mentored one another at various stages of our relationship. The serendipitous circumstances through which we met at the University of Northern Colorado provided the impetus to explore how we could collaborate together. Being hosted by the APC for an initial two-week visit was the chance for Bruce to experience firsthand the culture of the "land down under." Being a stranger in a new land was eased by Gary's knowledge of school operations, professional development approaches, and social norms. Bruce, having more experience in the world of academia, sought professional outlets for our work, including this chapter.
- *Leading*. Just as we have mentored one another, we also have taken on leadership roles when the need has arisen. For instance, Gary has been proactive in initiating programs that meet local needs and address the Victorian Department of Education's initiatives. His efforts have resulted in several long-standing programs, particularly SAGE, CEP, and JIL, and the creation of the HBE book series. We have coled activities, such as our team-taught course and study tours. Bruce has tended to take the lead in disseminating our work, particularly journal articles and conference presentations; recently, he accepted the position as the UCEA associate director of international affairs.

- *Valuing.* Throughout our relationship, we have taken time to ruminate on our work and its direction. An enormous advantage has been the large blocks of time we have spent together. Examples include Bruce's four-month sabbatical at the APC, the 4-week team teaching experience in Colorado, and the recurring trips to Melbourne over the last 10 years that have lasted from three to four weeks. The opportunity to have concentrated time together has provided opportunities for constructive and sustained dialogue about current programs and future initiatives.

The Lens of Collaborative Learning Communities

Another way of analyzing our relationship is to examine how our experiences mirror the elements comprising successful collaborations. Using the three-tired model of collaboration presented earlier (Robertson, 2008), we illustrate how each tier of the framework is exemplified by our experiences. These tiers include: (a) *collaborative capacity*, or the willingness and ability of individuals to engage in collaborative activities, (b) *collaborative capability*, which requires resources and tools to support these types of ventures, and (c) *collaborative strategy*, or the thoughtful planning and organization necessary to sustain collaborations over time.

Capacity for Collaboration

When our relationship began, we both had experiences collaborating with organizations (e.g., regional offices, departments of education, foundations, universities) in our own countries and with colleagues in other countries. Gary had been to the United States on earlier occasions, attending conferences, meeting with professional associates, and visiting schools. Bruce's international background included visiting schools and presenting workshops, primarily in England, but had never ventured below the equator. Early in our conversations we realized our sense of shared values about the power of reflective practice, the importance of building programs based on adult learning principles, and the advantages of leadership development programs that blended cross-national perspectives. As these shared values emerged, our trust and respect for one another grew, which served as the foundation for building a personal professional learning community (Kruse, Louis, & Bryk, 1995).

Capability for Collaboration

Besides our desire to collaborate, having the sanction and resources of the APC was instrumental in launching our collaboration. During Bruce's sabbatical in Melbourne, Gary arranged for the APC to provide an office, telephone and email communications, contacts with regional offices and Catholic school educators, and access to state and national professional organizations (e.g., Victorian of Secondary School Principals, Australian Council for Educational Research). Spending concentrated time together provided ample opportunities for planning and determining our roles and responsibilities, which are critical for professional learning communities (Kruse, Louis, & Bryk, 1995). The resources and entrée provided by Gary and his APC colleagues allowed Bruce to access and dialogue with key decision makers, principals, and teachers, resulting in the initial thematic workshop sessions on reflection, teambuilding, and strategic leadership offered to regional offices and conferences around the state of Victoria. Similarly, the interest in our work and the resources provided by Hawker Brownlow Education were instrumental in publishing and marketing the book series across Australia.

Besides the professional support provided by these two Australian organizations, the other crucial contribution has been our mutual investment in the relationship. To save costs, we have stayed at one another's homes during extended periods of time. Attending sporting events, visiting museums, watching movies and plays, discussing current events, and touring the local region has solidified our relationship. As a result, our families have taken vacations together in Australia and China. The blending of professional, personal, and social experiences has enriched our international relationship far beyond what would have occurred had we only engaged in professional activities.

Strategy for Collaboration

When we began our collaborative relationship, we did not create a long-term strategy for program development and delivery beyond the activities associated with Bruce's sabbatical. However, Gary began to envision ways of continuing and expanding our collaboration, the most notable being the piloting of the SAGE Mentoring Program near the end of Bruce's sabbatical. Therefore, we submitted a tender to the Victorian Department of Education to deliver SAGE training annually for nine regions across the state. The tender was accepted and beginning in 2000 Bruce began a series of annual trips to Melbourne to co-present the program with Gary and his colleagues Ian Miller and Robin Matthews. As the popularity of SAGE grew, we began to map a longer-term collaborative strategy for delivering additional leadership development programs (e.g., PRISM), marketing thematic workshops, collecting information and disseminating our work in articles and at conferences, conducting study tours to the United States, and approaching HBE about a books series. In hindsight, our strategic plan for collaboration has evolved over time, rather than being clearly laid out at the beginning of our relationship. As we gained trust and confidence in one another's knowledge and talents, our plans for future collaboration unfolded.

Clearly, our journey reflects many of the qualities of visionary leadership and successful collaboration identified in the professional literature. Key resource providers (e.g., Australian Principals Centre, Hawker Brownlow Education) legitimized and supported our interests and we devoted sustained time working together (e.g., sabbatical, yearly visits) to promote dialogue and planning. As our programs (e.g., SAGE, thematic workshops) were accepted by practitioners and disseminated in various professional outlets (e.g., HBE book series, journals, conferences), tangible benefits of our collaboration surfaced. Rather than being merely a professional odyssey, our relationship has been a personal journey as well, one that cannot only be understood using theoretical conceptualizations and principles of effective collaboration.

By starting small and making no long-term commitments, we were able to determine if our initial interactions warranted more sustained involvement. As we identified mutual interests and commitments, our relationship grew in ways we never imagined. Perhaps the greatest lesson we have learned from our international relationship is not to create ambitious, long-term goals from the outset. There is an ebb and flow to international collaboration that cannot always be predicted ahead of time. Instead, we believe it is far more productive to find common ground, complete short-term projects, and then determine what makes sense in continuing longer-term involvement. Over promising what can be delivered at the beginning of a relationship may doom it to failure. However, as trust and respect develop, partners are much better able to make informed decisions about how to implement their international collaboration

Implications for Future International Collaboration

If educational leadership is to become a globalized profession, then practitioners, researchers, and program developers need to become better informed about the trends that are shaping schools and the issues school leaders are confronting around the world. As these groups become more internationally savvy, there is a greater likelihood they will understand and accept the worth of nonindigenous values and practices, which is the ultimate outcome of internationalization espoused by Lumby (2008). As we have argued, one step toward achieving this goal is to encourage and support engagement in international collaborative relationships. Important lessons from our relationship and others' experiences with international collaboration may inform future generations from different countries seeking to collaborate to promote leadership preparation and development. We conclude this chapter by identifying the types of support required for these collaborations to thrive.

Overcoming Barriers to Collaboration

As noted earlier, regulatory, cultural, and personal barriers can inhibit the development of collaborative partnerships (Barnett et al., 1999; Huxham & Vangen, 2000). Regulatory roadblocks occur when there is conflict and misalignment between the policies and practices of the collaborating organizations. Fortunately, our professional journey has not been compromised by the rules and policies of the organizations with which we worked. In fact, these organizations (Australian Principals Center, University of Northern Colorado, and University of Texas at San Antonio) have encouraged and supported our relationship. Cultural barriers include the lack of congruity between the reward structures, visions, and jargon existing in different organizations and nations. Overcoming these barriers, especially language differences and social norms, requires "cultural insiders" to anticipate and navigate these issues for nonnatives. As insiders provide these insights, outsiders can better understand and experience the social, economic, and political fabric of another culture, which can reveal how social justice is defined, practiced, supported, and compromised. Again, having an insider to open doors is one of the best ways to obtain an expanded international perspective (Lumby, 2008). Each of us has served in this role, especially when coordinating extended visits to one another's countries to deliver professional development programs, team teach, and conduct study tours. Finally, personal barriers to international collaboration arise because of a lack of knowledge of people and programs operating in other countries, the distance between collaborators, and the financial costs associated with travel and lodging. The financial costs supporting our collaboration have been lowered based on the generous contributions of our sponsoring organizations (APC, VDE, regional offices in Victoria, and universities where Bruce has worked) and our individual commitment (e.g., lodging at one another's homes). Clearly, without the blessing and sponsorship of these organizations and our families, being able to visit one another's countries would have been greatly diminished.

As our personal journey reveals, individual initiative coupled with organizational endorsement for international collaboration are necessary for initiating these relationships and helping them to survive over time. Individuals need to determine their motivation for engaging in international research and program development by answering several questions, such as: (1) is this venture a good match of our talents? (2) what might we gain or lose by participating? (3) what should we invest? and (4) if we decided to collaborate, how should we organize ourselves? (Barnett et al., 1999). For us, what began as a traditional approach for engaging in international collaboration by spending time working on projects of mutual interest, has evolved into an expanded international perspective as we have gained respect and appreciation for other ways of leading and managing schools, developing and delivering leadership development programs, and disseminating research on programs (Lumby, 2008). Therefore, our attitudes about leadership practices, professional development, and dissemination have been positively affected by our experiences (James et al., 2007).

Besides the lessons learned by our personal experiences, other sources provide insights about how to support international collaborative relationships. In particular, the survey of UCEA institutions described earlier captured respondents' perspectives input about how UCEA can support international research and program development (Barnett, 2009). Although this survey addressed UCEA's role in supporting the globalization of knowledge and practice of educational leadership preparation and development, we believe the results are applicable to other professional organizations and agencies, such as BELMAS, CCEAM, International Congress for School Effectiveness and Improvement, European Educational Research Association, National College for School Leadership, and international research centers housed at universities. Numerous suggestions were provided, however, responses focused on two general categories: (a) disseminating information and (b) advocating for international research and development.

Information Dissemination

Respondents mentioned UCEA should serve as an information clearing house, including the most important types of information to exchange and how best to communicate this information. As a clearing house, information can be shared regarding individuals who currently are engaging in international research and program development, people who would like to participate in international projects, and examples of international projects being implemented. Because of the high financial costs required to conduct international initiatives (e.g., travel, housing, salaries), information on potential funding sources (e.g., proposals from foundations, grants from professional organizations) would be extremely useful. A variety of dissemination formats were recommended, including electronic communications (e.g., email blasts, website announcements), print media (e.g., UCEA's quarterly newsletter), and special issues of UCEA's flagship journal, *Educational Administration Quarterly*, devoted to international research.

Advocacy

As a long-standing professional organization, respondents commented that UCEA should be an advocate for international research and program development. Advocacy can be provided by collaborating with other professional organizations, dedicating funds to support international projects, and publicizing international initiatives at the annual convention. Interorganizational collaboration would occur by having UCEA cosponsor international conferences, which not only would increase understanding of cross-cultural commonalities and differences in leadership preparation and development, but also would allow participants to gain a greater appreciation for the quality of research and programs being implemented in different parts of the world. Small start-up grants and stipends could be dedicated to: (a) establishing a new journal devoted to global education and leadership, (b) financing comparative research studies, (c) providing travel expenses for faculty, student, and practitioner exchanges, and (d) offsetting expenses for trips to other countries to learn about educational leadership preparation and development. The annual UCEA Convention can serve as an important venue for identifying important international trends; therefore, international faculty and graduate students could be supported to attend the session to report comparative studies and encourage cross-national networking opportunities for convention participants.

Despite being a relatively small survey study, these results point out several encouraging trends regarding internationalizing the dialogue and connection between educational leadership researchers and program developers around the globe:

- Strong linkages already exist between colleagues and organizations around the world in conducting comparative research, delivering degree programs, and implementing curriculum projects;
- Interest in conducting international research and development is extremely high not only among faculty who already are engaged in international projects, but also for individuals who have no previous experience with international initiatives; and
- Professional organizations, like UCEA, are viewed as key players in supporting and shaping the international discourse on leadership preparation and development.

We have been privileged to become part of a global learning community and are indebted to the organizations and individuals who have supported our collaborative partnership. Our lives have been greatly enriched because of the new friends and professional associates we have made, the leadership development programs we have developed, and the opportunity to share these programs in professional publications and at conferences. Ours, however, is not a unique journey. Many other researchers and program developers have established collaborative relationships with colleagues around the world to advance the cause for internationalizing educational leadership, such as conducting large-scale, comparative studies of school leaders in different countries (e.g., Drysdale, Goode, & Gurr, 2008; Leithwood & Day, 2007), examining programs for aspiring school leaders in developing countries (e.g., Bush, Duku, Kiggundu, Kola, Msila, & Moorosi, 2008), and offering educational leadership degree programs in other countries and supporting faculty and student exchanges (Barnett, 2009). We believe that these types of international partnerships and collaborations have the potential to grow in the future, especially as "global processes become increasingly a transparent and obvious part of the everyday lives and practices of our educational communities and the research agendas of educational scholars worldwide" (Dolby & Rahman, 2008, p. 710). However, this potential will be realized only as individuals are exposed to international trends and perspectives, resources are widely-publicized to support the high cost of international collaborations, and opportunities are provided for publishing and presenting international research and program development. Our hope is that if this groundswell of interest in examining educational leadership preparation and development occurs, our profession will benefit immensely. Not only will educators gain a better sense of the realities leading schools and educating children beyond their own physical borders, but also will better understand and appreciate how social justice issues drive schools, communities, and societies.

An important caveat is that educational researchers, leaders, and policymakers run the risk of understanding social justice issues at an intellectual level when they engage in short-term cooperative efforts (Intrilligator, 1992). Brief visits or conversations between educators from different cultures are important in beginning international dialogue, as is evidenced by our story; however, understanding the realities of working and living in other cultures requires sustained collaboration, where mutual trust and commitment are established. If the educational leadership profession is to become a true global community, one where non-Western values and conceptualizations are understood and appreciated, then long-term, sustained collaboration between individuals and organizations must develop. Although there is a time and place for "academic tourism" (Larson, this volume), the attitude of "seek first to understand, rather than be understood" is essential for building trust among international colleagues. As our personal journey suggests, once this level of trust is developed, there are endless opportunities for meaningful, sustained collaboration between international colleagues and friends.

REFERENCES

Akiba, M. (2008). *Working conditions of middle school mathematics teachers: A comparison of the United States, Australia, and Japan.* Paper presented at the annual convention of the University Council for Educational Administration, Orlando, FL.

Appley, D. E., & Winder, A. E. (1977). An evolving definition of collaboration and some implications for the world of work. *The Journal of Applied Behavioral Science, 13*(3), 279-290.

Astiz, M. F., Wiseman, A. W., & Baker, D. (2002). Slouching towards decentralization: Consequences of globalization for curricular control of national education systems. *Comparative Education Review, 46*(1), 66-88.

Barnett, B. (2009). UCEA's involvement in international research and development: Current trends and future implications. *UCEA Review, 50*(1), 31-32.

Barnett, B. (2001a). Mentoring for practising and aspiring school leaders: The "SAGE" model. *Australian Principals Centre Monograph, No. 4.* Hawthorne, Victoria, Australia: APC.

Barnett, B. (2001b). Preparing to face the challenges of the principalship: The "PRISM" model. *Australian Principals Centre Monograph, No. 3.* Hawthorne, Victoria, Australia: APC.

Barnett, B. G. (1987). Peer-assisted leadership: Using peer observations and feedback as catalysts for professional growth. In J. Murphy & P. Hallinger (Eds.), *Approaches to administrative training in education.* Albany, NY: State University of New York Press.

Barnett, B. G., Hall, G. E., Berg, J. H., & Camarena, M. M. (1999). A typology of partnerships for promoting innovation. *Journal of School Leadership, 9,* 484-510.

Barnett, B., Henry, D. A., & Vann, B. (2008). *Coaching teachers and principals: Influence on resiliency, student learning, and school improvement.* Paper presented at the Commonwealth Council for Educational Administration and Management Conference, Durban, South Africa.

Barnett, B., & O'Mahony, G. (2009). *Journey into leadership: Aspirant leader development in Australia.* Paper presented at the annual meeting of the American Educational Research Association, San Diego, CA.

Barnett, B. G., & O'Mahony, G. R. (2008). Mentoring and coaching programs for the professional development of school leaders. In J. Lumby, G. Crow, & P. Pashiardis (Eds.), *International handbook on the preparation and development of school leaders* (pp. 232-262). New York, NY: Routledge.

Barnett, B. G., & O'Mahony, G. R. (2007a). *Developing productive relationships between coaches and principals: The Australian experience.* Paper presented at the annual meeting of the American Educational Research Association, Chicago, IL.

Barnett, B. G., & O'Mahony, G. R. (2007b). *Mentoring and coaching for aspiring and practicing school leaders: International trends and future implications.* Paper presented at the annual convention of the University Council for Educational Administration, Washington, DC.

Barnett, B. G., & O'Mahony, G. R. (2006a). Developing a culture of reflection: Implications for school improvement. *Reflective Practice, 7*(4), 499-523.

Barnett, B. G., & O'Mahony, G. R. (2006b). *Peer coaching for experienced principals: Building their capacity as transformational leaders.* Paper presented at the annual convention of the University Council for Educational Administration, San Antonio, TX.

Barnett, B., & O'Mahony, G. (2005). Sage mentors. *Teacher, 164*, 46-51.

Barnett, B. G., & O'Mahony, G. (2002). One for the to-do list: Slow down and think. *Journal of Staff Development, 23*(3), 54-58.

Barnett, B. G., O'Mahony, G. R., & Matthews, R. J. (2004). *Reflective practice: The cornerstone for school improvement.* Victoria, Australia: Hawker Brownlow Education.

Barnett, B., O'Mahony, G., & Miller, I. (2002). The promise of mentoring. *Prime Focus, 29*, 23-26.

Bechky, B. A. (2003). Shared meaning across occupational communities: The transformation of understanding on the production floor. *Organization Science, 14*, 312-330.

Brooks, J. S., & Tooms, A. K. (n.d.). *A dialectic of social justice: Learning to lead through reflection and dialogue.* Unpublished manuscript.

Brown, L., & Conrad, D. A. (2007). School leadership in Trinidad and Tobago: The challenge of context. *Comparative Education Review, 51*(2), 181-201.

Bush, T., Duku, N., Kiggundu, E., Kola, S., Msila, V., & Moorosi, P. (2008). *Zenex ACE school leadership research: First interim report.* Paper presented at the Commonwealth Council for Educational Administration and Management Conference, Durban, South Africa.

Chu, H. (2003). Principal professionalization: Knowledge base and support systems. *Educational Administration Review, 1*, 223-252.

Clandinin, J., & Connelly, M. (1992). Teacher as a curriculum maker. In P. Jackson (Ed.), *Handbook of research on curriculum* (pp. 363-401). New York, NY: Macmillan.

Coleman, M., Low, G. T., Bush, T., & Chew, O.A. J. (1996). *Re-thinking training for principals: The role of mentoring.* Paper presented at the annual meeting of the American Educational Research Association, New York, NY.

Cox. M., & Rock, M. E. (1997). *The 7 pillars of visionary leadership: Aligning your organization for enduring success.* Toronto: Harcourt Brace & Company.

Culbertson, J. (1995). *Building bridges: UCEA's first two decades.* University Park, PA: University Council for Educational Administration.

Cullen, J., Johnson, J., & Sakano, T. (2000). Success through commitment and trust: The soft side of strategic alliance management. *Journal of World Business, 35*(3), 223-240.

Davies, W. (2001). *Partner risk. Managing the downside of strategic alliances.* West Lafayette, IN: Purdue University Press.

Dolby, N., & Rahman, (2008). Research in international education. *Review of Educational Research, 78*(3), 676-726.

Donnellon, A., Gray, B., & Bougon, M. (1986). Communication, meaning and organized action. *Administrative Science Quarterly, 3*(2), 43-55.

Drysdale, L., Goode, H., & Gurr, D. (2008). *International comparative study of successful school leadership: Moving from success to sustainability*. Paper presented at the Commonwealth Council for Educational Administration and Management conference, Durbin, South Africa.

DuFour, R. (2003, May). Building a professional learning community. *The School Administrator*, 13-18.

DuFour, R., DuFour, R., Eaker, R., & Many, T. (2006). *Learning by doing: A handbook for professional learning communities at work*. Bloomington, IN: Solution Tree.

DuFour, R., & Eaker, R. (1998). *Professional learning communities at work: Best practices for enhancing student achievement*. Alexandria, VA: Association for Supervision and Curriculum Development.

Feldman, D. H. (2000). Foreword. In V. John-Stenier (Ed.), *Creative collaboration* (pp. ix-xiii). New York, NY: Oxford University Press.

Flowerdew, J. (1999). Attitudes of journal editors to nonnative speaker contributions. *Journal of Second Language Writing, 8*, 123-145.

Friedman, T. J. (2005). *The world is flat. A brief history of the 21st century*. New York, NY: Farrar, Straus & Giroux Publishers.

Greene, M. (1991). Foreword. In C. Witherell & N. Noddings (Eds.), *Stories lives tell: Narrative and dialogue in education*. New York, NY: Teachers College Press.

Grobe, T. (1990). *Synthesis of existing knowledge and practice in the field of educational partnerships*. Washington, DC: Office of Educational Research and Improvement.

Haar, J. M. (2003). Providing professional development and team approaches to guidance. *Rural Educator, 25*(1), 33-35.

Hallinger, P., & Kantamara, P. (2000). Educational change in Thailand: Opening a window onto leadership as a cultural process. *School Leadership & Management, 20*(2), 189-205

Hannay, L. M., & Stevens, K. W. (1984). *The principal's world: A case study of collaborative research*. Paper presented at the annual meeting of the American Educational Research Association, New Orleans, LA.

Heck, R. H. (1996). Leadership and culture: Conceptual and methodological issues in comparing models across cultural settings. *Journal of Educational Administration, 34*(5), 74-97.

Hoffman, J. D., Sabo, D., Bliss, J., & Hoy, W. (1994) Building a culture of trust. *Journal of School Leadership, 4*(5), 484-502.

Hoffman, W., & Schlosser, R. (2001). Success factors of strategic alliances in small and medium-sized enterprises—An empirical survey. *Long Range Planning, 34*, 357-381.

Hutt, M., Stafford, E., Walker, B., & Reingen, P. (2000, Winter). Case study defining the social network of a strategic alliance. *Sloan Management Review, 51-62*.

Huxham, C., & Vangen, S. (2005). *Managing to collaborate*. London: Routledge.

Huxham, C., & Vangen, S. (2004). Doing things collaboratively: Realizing the advantage or succumbing to inertia? *Organizational Dynamics, 33*(2), 190-201.

Huxham, C., & Vangen, S. (2000). Leadership in the shaping and implementation of collaboration agendas: How things happen in a (not quite) joined-up world. *Academy of Management Journal, 43*(6), 1159-1175.

Intrilligator. B. A. (1992). *Establishing interorganizational structures that facilitate successful school partnerships.* Paper presented at the annual meeting of the American Educational Research Association, San Francisco, CA.

James, C. R., Dunning, G., Connolly, M., & Elliot, T. (2007). Collaborative practice: A model of successful working in schools. *Journal of Educational Administration, 45*(5), 550-572.

Judge, W. L., & Ryman, J. (2001). The shared leadership challenge in strategic alliances: lessons from the U.S. healthcare industry. *The Academy of Management Executive, 15*(2), 71-79.

Kilpatrick, S., Jones, T., & Barrett, M. (2006). Learning through research: A regional university and its community. *International Journal of Pedagogies and Learning, 2*(2), 36-49.

Kruse, S. D., Louis, K. S., & Bryk, A. (1995). An emerging framework for analyzing school-based professional community. In K. S. Louis & S. D. Kruse (Eds.), *Professionalism and community: Perspectives in reforming urban schools* (pp. 23-42). Thousand Oaks, CA: Corwin Press.

Langston, V. (2006). *What is a professional learning community?* Unpublished manuscript.

Larson, C. E., & LaFasto, F. M. J. (1989). *Teamwork: What can go right/what can go wrong.* Newbury Park, CA: Sage Publications.

Leithwood, K., & Day, C. (2007). *Successful school leadership in times of change.* Toronto: Springer.

Leithwood, K., Seashore-Louis, K., Anderson, S., & Wahlstrom, K. (2004). *How leadership influences student learning.* New York, NY: The Wallace Foundation.

Lencioni, P. M. (2002). *The five dysfunctions of a team: A leadership fable.* San Francisco: Jossey-Bass.

Levin, J. (2001). *Globalizing the community college.* New York, NY: Palgrave.

Li, Y., Mitton-Kukner, J., & Yeom, J. (2008). Keeping hope alive: Reflection upon learning to teach in cross-cultural contexts. *Reflective Practice, 9*(3), 245-256.

Lugg, C. A. (1994). *Schools and achieving integrated services: Facilitating utilization of the knowledge base.* Paper presented at the annual convention of the University Council for Educational Administration, Philadelphia, PA.

Lumby, J. (2008). *International perspectives on developing educational leaders.* Paper presented at the Commonwealth Council for Educational Administration and Management Conference, Durbin, South Africa.

Lumby, J., Crow, G., & Pashiardis, P. (Eds.) (2008). *International handbook on the preparation and development of school leaders.* New York, NY: Routledge.

Matthews, R. J., O'Mahony, G. R., & Barnett, B. G. (2006). *Managing change: Leading school improvement.* Victoria, Australia: Hawker Brownlow Education.

McCollum, M. (1992). Organizational stories in a family-owned business. *Family Business Review, 5*(1), 3-24.

Merriam, S. B., Caffarella, R. S., & Baumgartner, L. M. (1999). *Learning in adulthood: A comprehensive guide* (3rd ed.). San Francisco, CA: Jossey-Bass.

Mitchell, C., & Sackney, L. (2000). *Profound improvement: Building capacity for a learning community.* Lisse, The Netherlands: Swets & Zeitlinger.

Miranda, S. M., & Saunders, C. S. (2003). The social construction of meaning: An international perspective on information sharing. *Information Systems Research, 14*(1), 87-106.

Murakami-Ramalho, E. & Barnett, B. (2008). Globalizing conversations in educational leadership. *UCEA Review, XLIX*(2), 1-4.

National School Boards Association (1991). *Link-up: A resource directory. Interagency collaborations to help children achieve.* Alexandria, VA: Author.

Ohmae, K. (2000). *The invisible continent: Four strategic imperatives of the new economy.* London: Nicolas Brealey.

O'Mahony, G. R. (2003). *Learning the role: Through the eyes of beginning principals.* Unpublished doctoral dissertation. Melbourne, Victoria, Australia: Deakin University.

O'Mahony, G., & Barnett, B. (2008). Coaching relationships that influence how experienced principals think and act. *Leading & Managing, 14*(1), 16-37.

O'Mahony, G. R., & Barnett, B. G. (2006a). *Advancing school improvement in Australia: The influence of peer coaching on experienced principals.* Paper presented at the annual meeting of the American Educational Research Association, San Francisco, CA.

O'Mahony, G., & Barnett, B. (2006b). Principals supporting principals: The PRISM experience. *The Victorian Education Magazine, Term 1*, 7.

O'Mahony, G. R., Barnett, B. G., & Matthews, R. J. (2006). *Building culture: A framework for school improvement.* Victoria, Australia: Hawker Brownlow Education.

O'Mahony, G. R., & Matthews, R. J. (2005). *A climate of mentoring: Building teams for school improvement.* Victoria, Australia: Hawker Brownlow Education.

O'Mahony, G. R., Matthews, R. J., & Barnett, B. G. (2009). *The power of coaching: Nurturing talent and building capacity for school improvement.* Victoria, Australia: Hawker Brownlow Education.

Peterson, K. D., & Brietzke, R. (1994). *Building collaborative cultures: Seeking ways to reshape urban schools.* Oak Brook, IL: North Central Regional Educational Laboratory.

Reichstetter, R. (2006). Defining a professional learning community: A literature review. *E & R Research Alert*, Report No. 06.05.

Robertson, J. (2008). *Three tiers of collaboration.* Retrieved from http://www.steptwo.com.au/columntwo/three-tiers-of-collaboration.

Rosenberg, J. (2000). *The follies of globalisation theory.* London: Verso.

Schiele, J. (1994). Afrocentricity: Implications for higher education. *Journal of Black Studies, 25*, 150-169.

Shields, C. M., & Edwards, M. M. (2005). *Dialogue is not just talk: A new ground for educational leadership.* New York, NY: Peter Lang.

Sobero, P. M. (2008). Essential components for successful virtual communities. *Journal of Extension, 46*(4). Retrieved from http://www.joe.org/joe/2008august/a1.shtml.

Standifer R., & Bluedorn, A. (2006). Alliance management teams and entrainment: Sharing temporal mental models. *Human Relations, 59*(7), 903-927.

Swan, W. W., & Morgan, J. L. (1993). *Collaborating for comprehensive services for young children and their families: The local interagency coordinating council.* Baltimore, MD: Paul H. Brooks

Turbowitz, S. (1986). Stages in the development of school-college collaboration. *Educational Leadership, 43*(5), 18-21.

Vangen, S., & Winchester, N. J. (2007). *Managing culture in cross-national collaborations.* Paper presented at the EURAM annual conference, Paris, France.

Vescio, V., Ross, D., & Adams, A. (2006). *A review of research on professional learning communities: What do we know?* Retrieved from http://www.nsrhatmony.org./research.vescio_ross_adam.pdf

Victorian Department of Education and Training. (2005). *Annual report 2004-05.* Retrieved from, http//www.det.vic.gov.au/edulibrary/public/govrel/reports/05DET-rpt.pdf

Walker, A., & Dimmock, C. (2000). Mapping the way ahead: Leading educational leadership into a globalised world. *School Leadership & Management, 20*(2), 227-233.

Weick, K., Sutcliffe, K., & Obstfeld, D. (2005). Organizing and the process of sensemaking. *Organization Science, 16*(4), 409-421.

Weindling, D. (2004). *Innovation in headteacher induction.* Retrieved from http://www.ncsl.org.uk/index.cfm?pageID=randd-research-publications

Wiseman, A. W. (2008). *What are we training educational leaders for? A cross-national analysis of school principals' activities by school type and context.* Paper presented at the annual convention of the University Council for Educational Administration, Orlando, FL.

Yarrit, M. (2000). *Towns, cities and regions in the learning age: A survey of learning communities.* Retrieved from http://www.ala.asn.au/learningcities/LGALearningLayout.pdf

Zeus, P., & Skiffington, S. (2000). *The complete guide to coaching at work.* Sydney, Australia: McGraw-Hill.

SCENIC OVERLOOK

Chapters 8 and 9

Guidelines for Discussions and Reflection

For school leaders:

1. How do you see issues of international collaboration impacting your students' lives?
2. What are learning communities? What steps have you taken to create learning communities as a school leader? Discuss your experiences in leading this collaboration.
3. What are the factors influencing your ability to foster collaborative learning communities?
4. Using Robertson's three-tier model of collaboration, where would you place yourself, the school, and the school district?
5. How might you use the Learning Community Framework on your campus? Predict and discuss possible outcomes.

For those preparing school leaders:

1. How do you understand international collaborations and K-12 schools?
2. What are your experiences with international collaborations with K-12 schools and/or school leadership preparation?

3. How does your preparation program foster collaborative learning communities
4. for faculty and/or graduate students?
5. To what extent do the learning communities established within your program address issues of social justice?

Bruce Barnett and Gary O'Mahony reconsider the influence of larger cultural systems that impact how we lead for social justice. The authors examined the importance of developing meaningful personal relationships with international colleagues to deepen their understanding of economic, political and educational contexts. As nonnatives, they immersed themselves in the everyday lives of people. Such experiences expanded their international perspectives and enhanced their ability to respond to the needs of their local professional communities.

In the next chapter, Steven Jacobson affords the reader to consider the implications of looking inward with the presumption that one educational system outweighs another. The author deepens our understanding of how the University Council for Educational Administration (UCEA) re-emerged as an international presence, suggesting international collaborative efforts foster a myriad of ways to address school policy and practices.

CHAPTER 9

PERSONAL REFLECTIONS ON AN ORGANIZATIONAL TRANSFORMATION

UCEA's Re-Emerging Role in a World of Interdependent Nations

Stephen Jacobson

In October 2008, I delivered the University Council for Educational Administration's (UCEA) Presidential address at the council's annual conference in Orlando, Florida. As the out-going president, I decided to use my last official function as a bully pulpit to advocate strongly for UCEA's re-emergence on the international scene. My arguments for taking this position were based on an articulation of a personal vision, personal reflections and a review of the UCEA's past, in anticipation of its transformed future. I opted to address this issue though the use of a personal narrative because I felt it was the best way to share my passion for this initiative. Moreover, my own enthusiasm for the idea of building a stronger worldwide community in educational administration was fueled by the personal narratives of others, most notably Jack Culbertson and Oliver

Gibson, both of whom I am indebted to. This chapter gives me a chance to elaborate on several points that time constraints precluded during my address in Orlando.

I begin the chapter by answering a very simple question, "Why should UCEA and educational leaders in the United States look outward?" I believe that the answers to this question provide an excellent rationale for UCEA's transformative initiative, but that these answers can ultimately be boiled down to the simple observation that national borders can no longer contain our collective commitment to education. The world's nation-states are now so interdependent that any examination of educational policy and practice, especially as it relates to school leadership, is limited without looking at educational policy and practice more globally. Next, I present a brief review of past UCEA achievements in the international arena, specifically the development of the International Intervisitation Program (IIP) in the 1960s through to its subsequent demise in the late 1990s. This review is especially important to those unfamiliar with UCEA's 50 plus-year history, because the past can often serve as prologue for future efforts. I then describe UCEA's transformative agenda as it relates to internationalizing the Council and new directions and international activities already under way, including an example of a relatively successful cross-national research project—the International Successful School Principalship Project (ISSPP), which reveals both the potential and pitfalls of doing this type of research. The chapter concludes with several recommendations for future steps that UCEA might consider as it pursues its transformative agenda, as well as a reaffirmation of the importance of this initiative.

WHY LOOK OUTWARD?

When I ran for UCEA president in November 2006 at the annual meeting in San Antonio, I told the plenum that 2 months earlier, during his September 2006 visit to the University at Buffalo (UB), the Dalai Lama had called the twentieth century the bloodiest in human history. In an address titled "Promoting Peace Across Borders Through Education," he recommended that the twenty-first century would have to be characterized by dialogue and warm-heartedness if the world was ever to be brought back into harmony. Specifically, the Dalai Lama urged educators to address, "the widening gap between the rich and the poor, both globally and nationally, because this inequality, with some having abundance while others go hungry or die of starvation, is not only morally wrong, but the source of most of the world's problems." Equally important, he argued, was the issue of freedom, "for as long as there is no freedom in many parts of the world, there can be no real peace or freedom for the rest of the world." He concluded the address by encouraging a throng of over 30,000 in attendance to think more compassionately, especially toward our children, pointing out that the responsibility for addressing these issues does not only lie with the leaders of our countries, but with each of us individually (Office of International Education [OIE], 2006).

I was very moved by the Dalai Lama's comments and felt that he had described eloquently the direction I was hoping UCEA would head. Social Justice has been a central theme of UCEA for over a decade, but the Dalai Lama's position could be seen as an explicit plea to take our efforts beyond our borders. With that goal in mind, my program cochairs, Lauri Johnson of UB and Andrea Rorrer of the University of Utah, helped me develop the theme for the 2007 UCEA conference, "Fostering Compassion And Understanding Across Borders: An International Dialogue On The Future Of Educational Leadership." I believe that the theme, and the conference program we constructed around it, resonated with our members primarily because educational organizations such as UCEA are fundamentally about compassion for children, much in the fashion suggested by the Dalai Lama. I would dare say that many, if not most, faculty members at UCEA institutions chose their career in order to improve the lives of children, and not just American children. It is that basic understanding that I believe is the fundamental rationale for an international initiative on the part of UCEA.

LANGUAGE, INTERNATIONAL DIALOGUE AND MESSAGE

Before going into the narrative of my presentation, let me explain its title and a little about how the language we use can effect the dialogue for building international relationships and the messages being conveyed about collaboration and partnership.

The original address was to be called, "UCEA's emerging role in a world of interconnected nations." But upon rereading Jack Culbertson's 1995 work, *Building Bridges: UCEA's First Two Decades* (a personal narrative chronicling Culbertson's experiences during the formative years of UCEA), particularly chapter 7 "Reach Across the Seas," it was clear that I would be talking about a "re-emerging" role, because UCEA has had an international presence going back over 40 years. I also switched to "interdependent" nations rather than "interconnected" after hearing Bill Clinton use the term during his speech in support of Barack Obama at the Democratic Convention. Dependence suggests a far tighter relationship between nations than mere connection and the use of the term was quite prescient in light of the subsequent financial crisis that has gripped the world, with national economies so inter-dependent that, for example, the collapse of the housing market in the US led to the near collapse of the banking system in Iceland.

These concerns about economic interdependence were echoed in Petros Pashiardis' 2008 Presidential address to the Commonwealth Council for Educational Administration and Management (CCEAM). Since the theme of that conference was, "Think Globally, Act Locally," Pashiardis argued that understanding globalization requires a redefinition of several key relationships, including those between individual nations and the rest of the world, between public and private institutions, and especially between economic prosperity and poverty (Note the parallels in Pashiardis' position with those of the Dalai Lama). Furthermore, globalization requires the formation of regional and international networks of nations, international and nongovernmental organizations, and even multinational companies, especially for smaller nations, if they are to avoid marginalization (Pashiardis, 2008). As a result, the educational policies of any one nation should no longer be examined without looking at educational policy worldwide. But the downside of such relationships, as Pashiardis points out, is that the educational policy decisions of these supra-national entities often have little to do with local realities. So for example, while standardized cross national testing such as TIMSS may enable a nation to learn about its aggregate performance relative to that of other countries, it may contribute little to addressing its own educational needs.

In another CCEAM keynote, Tony Townsend (2008) argued that, unlike the conference theme, thinking globally and acting locally was an inadequate strategy for future educational leaders; instead future leaders need to start thinking *and* acting *both* locally and globally. Charting the evolution of public education in terms of delivery, impact, and paradigm (see Table 9.1), Townsend contends that the impact of thinking globally and acting locally is limited when compared to the emerging universal paradigm that educates *all* children, with each child considered a unique individual. Clearly, Townsend's conception of a universal delivery of public education is a compassionate vision of educating children in a fashion that aligns with that of the Dalai Lama.

Unfortunately, this noble goal of universal education is challenged by current economic realities. Martin Prew (2008), for example, in a CCEAM presentation that included the issue of expanding access to education in the Republic of South Africa and three other African countries, found that there have been unintended consequences of having taken on this enormous task too quickly. These negative consequences include having far too few teachers, having too many teachers who are poorly trained (a problem exasperated by the HIV/AIDS pandemic that

Table 9.1. Evolution of Public Education in Terms of Delivery, Impact, and Paradigm

Period	Focus of Delivery	Those Effectively Educated	Dominant Paradigm
1000-1870 AD	Individual	Few people	Thinking and acting individually
1870-1980 AD	Local	Some people	Thinking and acting locally
1980-2000 AD	National	Many people	Thinking nationally and acting locally
2000-2010 AD	Global	Most people	Thinking globally and acting locally
2010-onward	Universal	All people individually considered	Thinking and acting both locally and globally

Source: Townsend (2008).

continues to ravage parts of Africa where they must often train three people to fill one job, in anticipation of the deaths of the trainees succumbing to the disease). These factors have led to oversized classes and very high dropout rates from primary school, as parents prefer to pull their children from school in order to work for the family. Ultimately, the result is limited student learning. Specifically, Prew reports that 70% of South Africa's youngsters drop out of primary education before Grade 7, and of those who remain, only 20-40% are functionally literate, meaning that perhaps only 10% of South Africa's students enter secondary education literate.

But lest we see this as just a problem of the developing world, a recent report entitled *Cities in Crisis* (Swanson, 2008) revealed that high school completion rates in the principal school districts serving America's 50 most populated cities was just over 50% (51.8%), and that there are four cities (Baltimore, Cleveland, Indianapolis, and Detroit) below 35%, with Detroit actually at 25% graduating high school. Let me repeat that last statistic, only one in four students in Detroit's public schools currently graduates from high school! This loss of human potential is staggering. My own city, Buffalo, has just dropped below 50% graduating high school, a factor that fuels the research my colleagues and I are doing on successful leadership in high need schools as part of the ISSPP study to be discussed later (Jacobson et al., 2007). But first, I think it would be helpful to review past UCEA international activities, in order to make clear why my advocacy is for a re-emergence of a focus that was once quite central to the Council's mission.

THE PAST AS PROLOGUE—REVISITING THE INTERNATIONAL INTERVISITATION PROGRAM (IIP)

I first became aware of UCEA when I arrived at UB in 1986. During my doctoral studies at Cornell University, the professional associations we focused on were the American Educational Research Association (AERA) and the American Education Finance Association (AEFA). But UB was one of UCEA's founding institutions and the late Ollie Gibson, professor emeritus at UB, quickly drew me into conversations about the organization and its history. In fact, this chapter is a "thank you" to this brilliant scholar who was always so generous with his time. In addition to Ollie's personal narratives, the events I'll be reporting are informed by Culbertson's 1995 book and by my own experiences. I begin with a brief history of the IIP.

In 1963, Culbertson recognized that, "path breakers around the world lacked formal opportunities to discuss their ideas with one another. More importantly, the field of educational administration had no structures for nurturing international development." (Culbertson, 1995, p. 178).[1] Culbertson wondered whether UCEA could make a contribution to the internationalization of the field, so he proposed a conference to the Kellogg Foundation, but was encouraged to rethink the idea. He then substituted instead the idea of the IIP, a three-week exchange of scholars from the U.S., England, Scotland, Canada and Australia. Being the only country with a system of pre-service administrator preparation at the time, it was felt that visits to U.S. institutions would be instructive to others. IIP 1966 attracted 78 participants from the five nations and began with a weeklong seminar, followed by two weeks of visits to UCEA institutions and concluded with three days of evaluation and follow-up. Among other things, the discussions at IIP66 revealed that common terms such as "principal," "college," "decentralization" and even "educational administration" were used in different ways in different countries. In England and Scotland, for example, they preferred the terms head teacher or master to principal or administrator. It proved to be a classic example of two, or in this case, five peoples divided by a common language. Interestingly, there still persist differences in how key descriptors of our field are used, especially the terms management, leadership and administration. So, for example, in the U.S., we call our lead organization the University Council for Educational Administration (UCEA), in the Commonwealth[2] it is the Commonwealth Council for Educational Administration and Management (CCEAM), while in Britain all three terms are used in the title of the British Educational Leadership, Management and Administration Society (BELMAS), yet each is working in what is essentially the same field.

As an aside, I run into similar differences in English language terminology in my classes at UB when we discuss differences in educational policy in the United States and Canada. In Buffalo, we can claim the same expertise about Canadian education as former Republican vice-presidential candidate Sarah Palin infamously did about foreign affairs, because just as she said she could see Russia from Alaska, we can see Fort Erie, Canada across the Niagara River from Buffalo. Yet Canadians call the chief officer of their schools systems the director while Americans call that person, superintendent, a title more commonly used in Ontario to describe second tier officials, whom New Yorkers would call directors. More importantly, American students do not understand how Ontario's Roman Catholic Separate Boards[3] are legally able to receive public funds, believing that Canada operates under the American principle of separation of church and state—which it doesn't. In other words, proximity alone does not translate into expertise, especially in societies with a propensity towards insularity and provincialism, such in the United States.

Australian scholar, William Walker summarized the key outcomes of the first IIP as helping to break down insularity and provincialism; laying the groundwork for an international conception of administration; and demonstrating somewhat unexpectedly the variety in U.S. preparation programs—a variety that still exists (Culbertson, 1995, p. 183).

The first IIP was such a success that a second was planned for 1970 in Australia. The conference themes were bureaucracy and centralization, planning and systems analysis, accountability and assessment, and teacher negotiations, with visits to several Australian state capitals. IIP70 led to the formation of the Commonwealth Council for Educational Administration (later CCEAM), a development Walker later called "the jewel in UCEA's crown."

The 1974 IIP was probably the most famous. Built around the theme, "Educational Administration: New Directions in Practice and Theory," it featured three weeks of presentations and visitations that began in Bristol and ended in London, by way of Glasgow—with most conferees traveling together by train that July. IIP74 led to the formation of both the European Forum on Educational Administration and the British Educational Administration Society (currently BELMAS).

Don Layton's report in the *UCEA Review* (1974) noted that Dan Griffiths' keynote presentation upset the conference hosts when he criticized Britain's emphasis on structures and organization, as opposed to educational goals and purposes, with Griffith going so far as to say, "No modern country offers so little education to its youth." Heated rebuttals in subsequent issues of the *Review* revealed that the felt insensitivity of Griffith's remarks by many Commonwealth participants clouded the intent of his message. The perceived arrogance of this keynote statement, whether intended or not, should serve as a forewarning as to how Americans should respectfully engage in international dialogue as we go forward.

The conference also featured T. Barr Greenfield's presentation, "Theory About Organization: A New Perspective and its Implications for Schools," which challenged the basic assumptions underlying the existing orthodoxy of systems theory, offering instead an alternative 'phenomenological' perspective (Greenfield, 1975). The result of this presentation was a conversation that echoed through the years in what became known as the Greenfield-Griffiths debate—much of which played out in the pages of the *UCEA Review* in the late 1970s. This debate has arguably had the greatest impact of any in our field and reshaped research in educational administration to this day. Eighteen papers from IIP74 can be found in *Administering education: International challenge*, edited by Meredydd Hughes (1975).

THE IIP, WAS IT A JUNKET OR PROFESSIONAL SERVICE AND DEVELOPMENT?

Subsequent IIPs were held in Canada (1978), Nigeria (1982) and Hawaii, Fiji and New Zealand (1986). IIP86, which examined Equity and Diversity: Challenges for Educational Administrators, was undoubtedly the most far-flung IIP and it received mixed reviews. For some it was the opportunity of a lifetime, a chance to experience educational equity and diversity in a most holistic fashion, especially the time spent with the Maoris in New Zealand. Yet for others, it was a more of a junket than an academic event. To this latter critique, I would like to go off on a brief tangent to consider the virtues of travel from an article I found in an issue of Delta's *Sky* Magazine, January 2008 (pp. 60-63).

I happened upon this article during a flight from Buffalo to UCEA headquarters in Austin, Texas, where I was headed to research my presidential address using their archive of *UCEA Review*. There was something incredibly fortuitous about coming across the article, "Just causes—Traveling with Martin," a conversation with Ambassador Andrew Young about his time spent with Dr. Martin Luther King, Jr. In it, Young notes that Dr. King referred to travel as a "pacifying force," because it raises people's cultural awareness and, in turn, reduces stereotypes and prejudice. Dr. King so strongly believed in travel as an approach to peace that he scheduled a pilgrimage to the Holy Land for September 1967. Five thousand people signed up for an event that was to take place in an amphitheater and on a boat in the Sea of Galilee. The crowd was to be so large that the governments of Jordan and Israel agreed to open the gates on their common border so that people could go back and forth between the two nations. Unfortunately the Arab-Israeli 6-day war broke out in June 1967 and Dr. King was assassinated the following April, so the event never took place, but the idea of travel as mere junket is markedly undercut.

PERSONAL REFLECTIONS: HOW IIP AFFECTED ME AS A SCHOLAR

I attended my first event in 1990 in Manchester, England, at the University of Manchester Institute of Technology. I attended because the conference proposal I had co-authored with Edward Hickcox of the Ontario Institute for Studies in Education (OISE) to co-host the 1994 IIP in Toronto and Buffalo had been accepted and Ed and I had to meet with the IIP Standing committee to discuss our plans.

The IIP90 conference organizers were Peter Ribbins, Ron Glatter, Tim Simkins and Len Watson under the auspices of the British Educational Management and Administration Society (BEMAS, later BELMAS). Their conference theme was "Developing Educational Managers for the Future," later called *Developing Educational Leaders* in the Ribbins et al. 1991 edited book of the event for Longman. (Note the change in terminology from educational 'managers' to 'leaders,' which reflects an ongoing tension in our field about the appropriate terminology for those who inhabit it).

What I recall most about IIP90 is first hearing about the notion of VISION during Jim Guthrie's keynote address, and even more importantly, hearing directly from English Heads as they dealt with the consequences of Margaret Thatcher's Educational Reform Act of 1988. Little did I know how much I was peeking into the future of education in the U.S. and now much of the rest of the world. IIP90 also gave me my first opportunity to present my work on performance-related pay and educational leadership to an international audience and get feedback that was informed by other educational policies and practices (Jacobson, 1991a, 1991b). For those interested, I had the pleasure of sharing my perspectives of the event, along with Richard Rossmiller and Edward Hickcox, for the Fall 1990 issue of *UCEA Review*.

IIP94, that Ed Hickcox and I organized, was held in Toronto and Buffalo and several memories are worth sharing (Hickcox & Jacobson, 1994). The first was a day of remembrance in honor of the late Thomas B. Greenfield's contributions to educational administration. Richard Bates of Deakin University gave the keynote address in Toronto, with other notable presenters including Dan Griffiths, Peter Ribbins, Colin Evers, Carol Harris and Ollie Gibson. In Buffalo, Larry Cuban of Stanford University delivered the conference keynote, "Reforming the practice of educational administration through managing dilemmas" (Cuban, 1996).

Two of the 5 days spent in western New York involved school visits and I will never forget as our international delegates waited excitedly for the little yellow school buses that would take them to several rural districts. For most of the children in those schools, it was the first interaction they had ever had with someone from another country and teachers and principals thanked me for an opportunity that proved to be the highlight of the school year.

I also remember taking a group of about 10 international educators to Emerson Vocational High School, a school that focuses on preparing students to work in the culinary arts trade in Buffalo. Students served as our guides, wait staff and cooks for what turned out to be an unforgettable meal. When the student chefs came out to meet the IIP delegates they were greeted by a sincere standing ovation. It was a wonderful day for all involved. Again, for those interested, eighteen papers presented at IIP94 can be found in *School administration: Persistent dilemmas in preparation and practice*, a 1996 book I coedited with Ed Hickcox and Robert Stevenson, my colleague at UB.

My most vivid memory of IIP98 in Barbados was of the school visits, because it was stunning the extent to which music and art were infused throughout the curriculum and day-to-day activities of students. These were not affluent schools, but it was an implicit affirmation of life that I wish I saw more of in American schools, especially as curriculums are being narrowed in light of NCLB.

Unfortunately, attendance by UCEA members declined so markedly over the years (perhaps as few as five Americans were in Barbados) that the CCEAM governing board changed IIP to a Commonwealth biennial conference. By the time the conference took place in Sweden in 2002, the IIP name was gone and many in attendance wondered when Sweden had become part of the Commonwealth. Sweden's hosting of the conference was originally to have been an IIP event, but at present, IIP is no more, instead subsequent quadrennial meetings—2006 in Cyprus and the 2010 conference to be held in Sydney, Australia—are solely CCEAM events.

I think several factors explain why UCEA members stopped participating. First, Americans have never felt any urgency to look beyond our 50 states, with the possible exception of an occasional look to our neighbors in Canada to the North, but far less so to Mexico, Central and South Americas. When one considers the diversity of policies and practices that result from educational control vested at the state level, which is then often delegated to the districts, there is already a plethora of natural laboratories for researchers and policymakers to consider. As a result, Americans have long been rather inward looking and isolationist, with the presumption that our educational system matches our predominance in other areas. That perception changed markedly after the publication of a

Nation at Risk in 1983, which pushed Americans to begin comparing the performance and practices of their schools with those of other nations, especially those international "competitors" perceived to be doing better, such as Japan in the 1980s and Finland today. In our quest to be number one, public attention is most often drawn to our students' shortcomings as they compete with nations at the top of the rankings. Far less attention is paid to those lower on the scale, as if, in a world of interdependent nations, low reading scores among students in Venezuela or Botswana are any less important than scores in Mississippi or California. I think this competitive model diminished our natural curiosity about the full range of educational policies and practices happening elsewhere. In other words, if there was no perceived competitive advantage to be gained by studying another nation, then why bother? I think we lost sight of what Culbertson understood so well, what participants at the IIPs experienced and what I learned by attending these events, i.e., there is as much, if not more, to be learned about our own system of education by studying and visiting the systems of others. For me, every IIP served as a mirror in which the reflection of American education was constantly in my mind's eye as I came to terms with how education was conducted elsewhere, and how that approach compared and contrasted with my experiences at home.

The second reason I think Americans stopped attending IIP was the introduction of UCEA's conference. Although the development of the conference has been wonderful for the growth of UCEA, it made the cost of attending an international conference prohibitive. Assuming that most UCEA attendees also go to AERA, IIP became a budget buster in that given year. Moreover, unlike AERA, which has increasingly attempted to reach out to greater international participation (this may be easier for AERA since its membership is individually based rather than UCEA's institutional membership), UCEA has not been especially inviting to the same audience.

During my visit to UCEA headquarters mentioned earlier, Katherine Mansfield, a doctoral student at University at Texas-Austin, helped me review the archive of UCEA conference programs to determine the percentage of sessions at every annual conference since its inception in 1987 that had either an international presenter or an American presenting on an international topic as compared to the totally number of sessions at that conference. We found that it was not until UCEA's 13th conference in 1999 that the percentage of international presentations exceeded 10%, with the figure hovering below 5% during the first decade of the annual meetings. From 1999 until 2005, the figure remained between 10-15%, then rising to just over 20% in 2006. When the 2007 UCEA conference theme focused explicitly on engaging an international dialogue, these presentations spiked to 45% of the entire conference, but then dropped to just under 20% the following year. This rather simple analysis suggests that if UCEA chooses to focus on cross-national issues, in order to re-emerge on the international scene, it is well positioned and its efforts should be well received.

Before moving on to the potential of UCEA's re-emerging role, let me quickly note that in his book Culbertson also talked about UCEA's efforts in the late 1970s to link North and South American scholars through the development of the InterAmerican Society for Educational Administration. This endeavor did not prove as successful as the early years of the IIP, nevertheless, Culbertson ends chapter 7 with the following note of hope and his personal sense of accomplishment:

> As we strove to unfold path-breaking programs, I felt in my more elated moments that UCEA's international accomplishments alone were sufficient rewards for the 22 years I labored in its expanding vineyards. (Culberston, 1995, p. 204)

UCEA'S TRANSFORMATIVE AGENDA

At its Leadership meeting in summer 2007 at the University of North Carolina-Chapel Hill, several of us helped then-UCEA President Fenwick English draft a transformative agenda for the future of UCEA. Among the key items listed was Transformative Agenda Initiative 3: the Internationalization of the Educational Leadership Preparation Conversation. In this section of the report, we recommended that UCEA should take a lead in fostering greater international collaboration and cooperation through:

- Expanded international membership;
- Enhanced intellectual, conceptual, and epistemological horizons for preparing educational leaders to deal with greater cultural diversity and a deeper understanding of the appropriate role of preparation for citizenship;
- Developing comparative research projects that can inform educational leadership and educational policy making across the globe.

At the 2007 UCEA plenum, I met with a group of 11 plenary session representatives (PSR) to discuss these recommendations and they unanimously supported making internationalization a UCEA priority. The PSRs urged that we survey UCEA member institutions about what they already do and what they want in terms of internationalization. It was felt that UCEA should facilitate exchanges to develop a better understanding of what leadership looks like international, perhaps through conference sessions or by helping scholars fund international projects; using media and technology to make international linkages more accessible—even during the annual conference; and by creating a Request For Proposal (RFP) for a new UCEA international program center. This group of PSRs also suggested that UCEA should go after more international members and partners, and hold its conference outside the U.S., perhaps in the Canadian cities of Toronto, Montreal or Vancouver to start.

But, in addition to these recommendations, there were also several cautions and concerns. For example, the group felt that UCEA should be careful not to impose its Western viewpoints; that instead we must consider the culture and values of other countries and potential partners. This same sentiment was expressed by Benno Sander in 1979, when he argued that if the InterAmerican Society for Educational Administration was to be successful, interactions had to be transactional, not interventionist, "otherwise, the builders of schools and educational systems run the risk of destroying national cultural values" (Sander, 1980, p. 4, in Culbertson, 1995, p. 199).

The other concern expressed was that a re-emerging international initiative would take resources and attention away from problems in American schools. This is not an inconsequential issue, but I would argue that this position holds only if one looks at it from a zero-sum perspective. My own experiences suggest otherwise in that almost all of my international experiences have informed my domestic research in a variable-sum way. Over the past 20 years, I have had the opportunity to visit schools in such far-flung places as Australia, Barbados, Canada, China, Cyprus, England, Ethiopia, Germany, Israel, Mali, Malta, Mexico, Netherlands Norway, South Africa and Sweden, and each of these experiences has given me new insights into American education and offered me alternative ways to think about how to improve the life chances of children, especially those in western New York. For example, in March 2007, I visited a high poverty, primary school in Monterrey, Mexico where a class of sixth graders quickly switched from science instruction in Spanish to English in order to accommodate their monolingual American guest. It seemed obvious to me that such facility with two languages could only improve the life chances of children in American schools, and that other language instruction should begin in the early grades.

ACTIVITIES CURRENTLY UNDERWAY

In January 2008, UCEA created the role of associate director of international affairs (ADIA), and appointed Bruce Barnett of the University of Texas-San Antonio to the position. The ADIA's first tasks include many of the suggestions made by the PSRs, such as surveying our members to determine existing partnerships and how they are resourced, as well as interests and needs regarding partnership development. This survey will produce a database of international partnerships that UCEA can then disseminate to its member institutions. The ADIA will also seek funding to support international activities such as visitations, study tours and joint research. The initial challenge will be to raise membership awareness of and interest in research and learning opportunities and then to help identify potential funding sources to make these initiatives a reality.

Bruce and I discussed the idea of developing reciprocal agreements between international institutions that could facilitate faculty and student exchanges, which might range from a week to a semester or year, depending on the resources of the host universities and the availability of the scholars. For example, these exchanges could involve scholars in teaching special topics classes to graduate students, conducting seminars for faculty and students, and conducting cross-national research with graduate students interested in international leadership and development.

In order to get the ball rolling, Bruce and I met with CCEAM's governing board in September 2008 in Durban, South Africa to share UCEA's transformative agenda and get a sense of CCEAM's interests. We found that the goals of these two organizations converge around two key points: (1) both want to increase partnerships with one another and with other international associations, and (2) both are encouraging of cross-national research and program development. We agreed that these common interests could be facilitated through sessions at one another's conventions; publicity of one another's publications; exchanges and study tours; a data bank of training programs; the creation of funding opportunities; and by encouraging and disseminating comparative research studies. Before considering an example of the type of cross-national research UCEA and CCEAM might support, I want to first highlight a significant outcome of such an organizational partnership, specifically the recent publication of the *International Handbook on the Preparation and Development of School Leaders* (2008), coedited by Gary Crow, Jacky Lumby, and Petros Pashiardis, which attempts to take a global perspective on the conceptual underpinnings of school leadership and then describes the diverse approaches taken to prepare school leaders worldwide.

AN EXAMPLE OF INTERNATIONAL RESEARCH: THE ISSPP

An example of the type of comparative research that could be supported by the transformative agenda is the International Successful School Principalship Project (ISSPP). ISSPP began in 2001 as an eight-nation study of the practices of principals who had successfully improved the academic performance of students in their schools. More details about the ISSPP, its history and descriptions of participating research teams from Australia, Canada, China, Denmark England, Norway, Sweden and the U.S. can be found at www.oise.utoronto.ca/research/schoolleadership/ssl.html or www.ils.uio.no/english/research/project/ssl/index.html

The ISSPP attempts to connect a concern for outcomes found in the school effectiveness research to issues of process found in the school improvement literature. The project focuses specifically on the practices of a school's formal leader and then expands this inquiry trans-nationally by addressing the following questions:

1. What practices do successful principals use?
2. Do these practices vary across contexts?
3. Under what conditions are the effects of such practices heightened or diminished?
4. What variables link principal's leadership to student achievement?

In 2005, the *Journal of Educational Administration* (JEA) devoted a special issue (volume 43, number 6), to ISSPP and published seven country reports that included a total of 65 case studies of successful school principals (Jacobson, Day, & Leithwood, 2005), making it one of the largest international studies ever undertaken in this field.

In his analysis of these reports, Leithwood (2005) concluded that the ISSPP has produced "progress on a broken front." For example, while findings from these qualitative, primarily descriptive and informative cases are limited in how much transference can be made to other contexts; the scope and quantitative breadth of the ISSPP go some way in overcoming this limitation. Furthermore, the ISSPP cases support the existence of a set of core leadership practices: setting directions, developing people, and redesigning the organization, necessary for improved student achievement in almost any context (Leithwood & Riehl, 2005). But it was found that principals adapted these practices to their specific contexts in order to achieve the desired effects. In the U.S., for example, principals' direction setting was rather short-term, driven by required NCLB annual achievement gains (Jacobson et al. 2005), especially when compared to successful Australian principals who tended to focus on learning over a lifetime (Gurr et al., 2005). In contrast to this type of academic achievement oriented direction setting, principals in Norway (Moller et al., 2005), Denmark (Moos et al., 2005) and Sweden (Hoog et al., 2005) focused far more on the development of democratic values. In other words, direction setting was found in every case, but the actual directions set were context-specific and sensitive to policies and/or values prominent in each nation.

When it came to developing people, successful principals in every national context were highly visible and readily accessible to staff, students and parents, often modeling the type of professional practice and behaviors they expected of others. Although specific expectations of good practice were often contextually sensitive, the more general practice of helping others to reach that goal was common to all.

Finally, successful principals in these seven countries redesigned their organizations by fostering cultures of collaboration through teamwork, especially in England (Day, 2005); distributed leadership, particularly in the Scandinavian cases; broad based governance structures in Australia; and, deprivatizing teaching practice in the United States. In the northern European cases, leadership as participation did not need to be developed, as it already exists as a traditional value. This was particularly the case in Norway, where the term "team on top" was used to explain the preeminence of collective over individual leadership. But in Shanghai, China, there was a much different meaning of leadership distribution—one in which people demonstrate considerable respect for hierarchy, position, age, and formal authority and, as a consequence, Chinese principals involved their staff in decisions about "how" things should be done, but far less so in deciding "what" should be done.

Not only have the findings from the ISSPP added to the literature on successful school leadership across diverse contexts—by helping to identify both the isomorphic and idiosyncratic characteristics of leadership, but the presentations themselves, at UCEA, CCEAM and AERA, have generated so much interest in cross-national research that participation in the project has grown from the original eight nations to 14 over the past few years. Research teams from Cyprus, Israel, Kenya, Mexico, Slovenia, South Africa and Turkey have recently joined the project, as well as four additional research teams from the United States—with teams from the University of Texas-San Antonio, Vanderbilt University, Indiana University and the University of Arizona joining UB.

I believe this expansion was, in part, the result of some very honest conversations at these presentations among team members about both the challenges, as well as the potential, of doing this type of research. The challenges were probably best exemplified during the development of a survey instrument for multinational research that was eventually produced in five different languages. We were never entirely sure whether these translations were understood the same way from country to country. Also, certain demographic proxies, such as free and reduced lunch commonly used to represent community wealth in the United States, do not exist across all national sites. Moreover, conceptions of what defines a "challenging" school varied across contexts. In the United States, a challenging school referenced socioeconomic status and we were looking explicitly at high need, high poverty schools. Similar schools could be found in Australia and England, but in Denmark, Norway and Sweden, the notion of what defined a challenging school had more to do with the number of different languages spoken in a school, since disparities in community wealth and school funding were far less than in Australia, England and the United States.

Funding was also a major obstacle for this cross-national research project. While some country teams had national funding and/or governmental support made available, others had to scramble for sufficient resources. Needless to say, members of the ISSPP teams would be desirous of UCEA's or joint UCEA/CCEAM involvement in helping to access fiscal support for this type of multinational research. But, obviously, concerns about these pitfalls were outweighed by the potential gains of such cross-national analyses, given the level of interest the work has generated among new teams of researchers. Let me offer another example, this time drawing from the research on high need schools that a subset of ISSPP researchers have been working on (Ylimaki, Jacobson, & Drysdale, 2007).

Using the original 65 cases from the ISSPP, we identified 13 schools in Australia, England and the United States that could be classified as high need and found several commonalities among their principals. For example, the successful leaders in these schools brought a passion for the socially just and equitable education of the children and the communities they served. Their enthusiasm was accompanied by persistence and optimism, and in the high accountability contexts of England, Australia and U.S., these principals used external demands as a tool for overcoming resistance to change on the part of those teachers who questioned the innate academic abilities of their students (Ylimaki, Jacobson, & Drysdale, 2007).

In many cases, the principals we studied had knowingly assumed the leadership of a school in a poverty stricken area with high needs and few resources. While they recognized the barriers to learning that poverty can produce, none would allow those conditions to be used as an excuse for low expectations or poor performance. Instead, they believed in the ability of their students; focused on improving the learning environment; applied pressure early in the process to encourage adherence and then used whatever resources they could generate to engage teachers in professional dialogue and development. They also worked hard to involve parents and other community members in school activities and decision-making because they believed that reconnecting the school to its community was absolutely central to their school improvement efforts (Ylimaki, Jacobson, & Drysdale, 2007).

The benefit of comparative research like that found in the ISSPP is that it speaks to what I believe is the fundamental rationale for an international initiative on the part of UCEA, for example, it addresses the need to take the Council's concerns about Social Justice beyond our borders in order to improve the life chances of all children, irrespective of where they live. Having teams from UT-San Antonio, Vanderbilt, Indiana and Arizona eager to join the efforts of UB suggests that this international research initiative has landed on very fertile ground and UCEA ought to be using its organizational clout to help support and encourage such work.

CONCLUSIONS AND RECOMMENDED FUTURE DIRECTIONS

I hope that by articulating a personal vision, reviewing past UCEA efforts and offering my own reflections on some of those UCEA events, I've made some headway in engaging the reader's support for UCEA's Transformative Initiative to Internationalization the Educational Leadership Preparation Conversation. In fact, I hope that I've developed a persuasive argument for a more comparative perspective within the field of educational administration, management and/or leadership (whatever your preference), whether or not the reader is involved with a UCEA member institution.

Among the recommendations to internationalize UCEA suggested by the PSRs, the one I think will have the most immediate return is to encourage more non-U.S. institutions to join the organization. Currently UCEA has only three non-American members, the Universities of Lincoln and Southampton, both in England, and the Chinese University of Hong Kong. I would love to see a return of former member institutions from Canada, as well as new members from Central and South America and elsewhere around the world. UCEA should also continue in its collaborative efforts with CCEAM, BELMAS and a growing number of other organizations serving educational leadership around the world.

Another recommendation that could help UCEA re-emerge as a leader on the world stage would be to hold our annual conference outside the United States, perhaps every 4 or 5 years. As noted earlier, this would probably have to begin in a North American city to see how well the idea was accepted by the membership. The idea of taking the conference abroad could be coupled with the revival of the IIP. Such an event would combine presentations and school visits in the host nations and should be cosponsored by several international associations to defray costs and guarantee it being held in different parts of the world. Finally, we should make this international event and our existing conferences far more technologically innovative so that there are interactive sessions involving virtual global participation.

No matter which paths we pursue, Jack Culbertson's case for engaging on the world scene rings as true today as it did decades ago:

1. We gain a deeper understanding of school administration in our own culture by examining it in other cultures;
2. Leaders and policymakers have more options and insights when they access ideas from other countries;
3. The limits and uses of educational ideas can be better identified in cross-nation analyses as compared to single national contexts;
4. Working cooperatively across nations, it is possible to achieve research and development objectives that may not be possible if pursued alone.

With the wealth of nations so interdependent, we can no longer ethically or practically allow any child to be left behind, whether that child lives in San Francisco or Sao Paolo, Baltimore or Beirut, Canarsie or Kabul. We must take Townsend's argument to heart and make thinking and acting both locally and globally our habit of practice.

I believe that UCEA should once again be leading the way in helping educational researchers and policy-makers worldwide find new and innovative ways to partner and collaborate. In much the same way that UCEA was at the forefront in helping to promote national and cross-national associations during the 1960s and 70s, UCEA should be at the forefront of researching and helping educators correct social inequities worldwide in 2009 and beyond. As noted earlier, I think most educational researchers and school leaders enter the profession because of their compassion for children. I think that UCEA's re-emergence on the world scene would show our collective commitment to the world's children at this critical time.

NOTES

1. Note that at that time, there were only the very beginnings of academic publication networks in educational administration with the first issues of the *Journal of Educational Administration* appearing in 1963 and then UCEA's own *Educational Administration Quarterly* in 1964.
2. The Commonwealth is an intergovernmental organization of 53 independent member states, most of which were formerly part of the British Empire.

3. The Roman Catholic Separate Boards in Ontario are publicly funded school districts that include religious education in their curriculum.

REFERENCES

Crow, G., Lumby, J., & Pashiardis, P. (2008). *International handbook on the preparation and development of school leaders*. Thousand Oaks, CA: Sage.

Cuban, L. (1996). Reforming the practice of educational administration through managing dilemmas. In S. Jacobson, E. Hickcox, & R. Stevenson (Eds.), *School administration: Persistent dilemmas in preparation and practice* (pp. 3-17). Westport, CT.: Greenwood Press.

Culbertson, J. (1995). *Building bridges: UCEA's first two decades*. University Park, PA: UCEA.

Day, C. (2005) Sustaining success in challenging contexts: Leadership in English schools. *Journal of Educational Administration, 43*(6), 573-583.

Day, C., & Leithwood. K. (2007). *Successful principal leadership in times of change: An international perspective*. Dordrecht, The Netherlands: Springer.

Giles, C., Jacobson, S., Johnson, L., & Ylimaki, R. (2007). Against the odds: Successful principals in challenging U.S. schools. In C. Day & K. Leithwood (Eds.), *Successful principal leadership in times of change: An international perspective* (pp. 155-168). Dordrecht, The Netherlands: Springer.

Greenfield, T. (1975). Theory about organization: A new perspective and its implications for schools. In M. Hughes (Ed.), *Administering education: International challenge* (pp. 71-99). London: Athlone Press of the University of London.

Gurr, D., Drysdale, L., & Mulford, B. (2005) Successful principal leadership: Australian case studies. *Journal of Educational Administration, 43*(6), 539-551.

Hackler, J. (2008, January). Just causes: Traveling with Martin. *Delta Sky,* 60-63.

Hickcox, E., & Jacobson, S. (1994). IIP94: 8th International Intervisitation Program. *UCEA Review, 11*(3), 7-8.

Hughes, M. (1975). *Administering education: International challenge*. University of London: Athlone Press.

Jacobson, S. (1991a). Performance related pay for teachers: The American experience. In H. Tomlinson (Ed.), *Performance related pay in education* (pp. 34-54). London: Routledge.

Jacobson, S. (1991b). Future U.S. educational leaders. In P. Ribbens, R. Glatter, T. Simkins, & L. Watson (Eds.), *Developing educational leaders* (pp. 198-213). London: Longman.

Jacobson, S., Brooks, S., Giles, C., Johnson, L., & Ylimaki, R. (2007). Successful leadership in three high poverty urban elementary schools. *Leadership and Policy in Schools, 6*(4), 1-27.

Jacobson, S., & Day, C. (2007). The International Successful School Principalship Project (ISSPP): An overview of the project, the case studies and their contexts, *International Studies in Educational Administration, 35*(3), 3-10.

Jacobson, S., Day, C., & Leithwood, K. (Guest Eds.). (2005). The international successful school principalship project. *Journal of Educational Administration, 43*(6).

Jacobson, S., Hickcox, E., & Stevenson, R. (1996). *School administration: Persistent dilemmas in preparation and practice*, Westport, CT: Greenwood Press.

Jacobson, S., Johnson, L., Giles, C., & Ylimaki, R. (2005) Successful leadership in U.S. schools: Enabling principles, enabling schools. *Journal of Educational Administration, 43*(6), 607-618.

Johnson, L., Møller, J., Jacobson, S., & Wong, K.C. (2008). Cross-national comparisons in the International Successful School Principalship Project: The United States, Norway, and China. *Scandinavian Journal of Educational Research, 52*(4), 407-422

Layton, D. (1974). The third International Intervisitation Programme: An eye-witness account. *UCEA Review, 14*(2), 8-11.

Leithwood, K. (2005) Understanding successful principal leadership: Progress on a broken front. *Journal of Educational Administration, 43*(6), 619-629.

Leithwood, K., & Riehl, C. (2005). What do we already know about educational leadership? In W. Firestone & C. Riehl (Ed.), *A new agenda for research in educational leadership* (pp. 12-27). New York, NY: Teachers College Press.

Moller, J., Eggen, A., Fuglestad, O., Langfeldt, G., Presthus, A., Skrovset, S., Stjernstrom, E., & Vedoy, G. (2005). Successful school leadership: The Norwegian case. *Journal of Educational Administration, 43*(6), 584-594.

Moos, L., Kresjsler, J., Koford, K., & Jensen, B. (2005). Successful school principalship in Danish schools. *Journal of Educational Administration, 43*(6), 563-572.

Office of International Education. (2006). Reflections on the Dalai Lama's visit. *UB International, 15*(2), 1-10.

Pashiardis, P. (2008, September). *The dark side of the moon: Being locally responsive to global issues.* Keynote presentation at the CCEAM conference, Durban, South Africa.

Prew, M. (2008). School and district accountability: A dream too far? Paper presented at the CCEAM conference, Durban, South Africa, September 2008.

Ribbens, P., Glatter, R., Simkins, T., & Watson, L. (1991). *Developing educational leaders.* London: Longman.

Rossmiller, R., Jacobson, S., & Hickcox, E. (1990). IIP 1990 in the United Kingdom. *UCEA Review, 11*(3), 9, 14.

Swanson, C. (2008). *Cities in crisis.* Bethesda, MD: Editorial Projects in Education.

Townsend, T. (2008). *Third millennium leaders: Thinking and acting both locally and globally.* Paper presented at the CCEAM conference, Durban, South Africa, September 2008.

Ylimaki, R., Jacobson, S. & Drysdale, L. (2007) Making a Difference in Challenging, High-Poverty Schools: Successful Principals in the US, England and Australia. *School Effectiveness and School Improvement, 18*(4), 361-381.

SECTION III

THE REFLECTING POOL

CHAPTER 10

LOOKING BACK ON THE ROAD NOT TAKE

Autumn K. Tooms and Christa Boske

When Autumn was a senior in high school, she was a mediocre student and not exactly an icon of popularity. In an effort to make Autumn feel special, one of her teachers invited her to participate in the process of designing the graduation invitations for her senior class. Autumn learned that her job would be to select a phrase that would stand the test of time for the students in her graduating class. So began the very first literature review of Autumn's life. The result of this treasure hunt was the oft used poem referenced below by Robert Frost:

> "Two roads diverged in a wood, and I—
> I took the one less traveled by,
> And that has made all the difference."
>
> From *The Road Not Taken* by Robert Frost (1920)

These lines are so very true that some may argue they have become trite. However, that does not take away from their potency or relevance. And it helps to clearly illustrates the influence one person can have in choosing a path other than the predictable and ordinary. Such is the story of how Autumn and Christa became involved with this book. In congruence with the narratives in other chapters, we begin this discussion with a brief history of how we came to work, think, and learn with each other as well as our fellow authors. This is followed by a discussion of the previous chapters along with their implications for practitioners and those who train them. We look at where we have fallen short as a field and what we should do about our shortcomings. Finally, we end with suggestions and a rationale for how you, the reader can write your own narrative.

THE ROAD NOT TAKEN WINDS THROUGH KENT

Autumn had been a principal for several years in Phoenix, Arizona. Like Christa, she had a taste for urban schools and enjoyed the gritty work of reform. Upon entering academia, Autumn described herself (as she does now) as a scholar who is focused on the micropolitics of schools because that is how she was trained as a doctoral student. Christa, upon applying for the position at Kent State University in 2007, described herself as a tempered radical in her cover letter. Autumn would tell you that "social justice" is a somewhat uncomfortable phrase for her because she wrestles with an unfair bias that being known as a social justice scholar somehow means that one is less of an academic, less of a thinker. Reading any of the previous chapters quickly rectifies this unfair assumption on Autumn's part, but it is there none-the-less, lurking in the back of her mind. By contrast, Christa, who boasts a background as both social worker and principal, finds great ease in identifying as a social justice scholar. This in part is due to Christa's training to critically examine and respond to institutionalized discrimination or ways in which power acts as a barrier of exclusion. In naming and actively addressing social justice issues, both Autumn and Christa do not simply recognize injustices, they challenge the notions of equity, emphasizing solidarity across differences as a necessity to bring about justice.

We have immensely enjoyed working together to bring this book to fruition. Christa has teased Autumn for describing herself as an onion because she is guarded and reticent to speak from her heart (who wouldn't be if their line of inquiry was politics and discourse?). Autumn, who enjoys a more acerbic world lens, teased Christa for using phrases that are "mushy." In between the mush and the acid, we found a common place that sees leadership from a stance of humanity, hope, and service. Occasionally, we found ourselves mesmerized by the sheer grit of our co-authors. For example, upon being introduced to Dr. Catherine Marshall for the first time, Christa said with awe, "I have your book by my bed." And, while Autumn enjoys a mischievous repartee with Bruce Barnett, she finds his compassion and commitment to service an incandescent inspiration. Like all the authors, Dr. Catherine Marshall and Dr. Bruce Barnett's everyday work enables community building, the recognition of basic human rights, and promotes the value of an equitable society. Ultimately, this book is important because it is rooted in a shared commitment to how we understand, correspond, and respond to the elimination of oppressive practices in institutions of learning.

Lessons of the Chapters

This experience has reinforced to us that social justice is an entire framework of responsibility that *undergirds* leadership; but because of the power structures in societies, it is understood by many in our field as a supplementary effort; worthy only of the occasional chapter in mainstream leadership texts. This is no longer acceptable. If anything, the insights offered by the authors confirmed that social justice work is integral to ordinary, everyday, leadership efforts. Advocates of social justice work do not speak of one vision of the ideal society or leadership practice. They argue that such a stance would just be another form of elitism with one group identifying the "right" way to lead schools. What social justice leadership *does* is offer possibilities. In the testimonies found in the preceding pages, such work shifts our focus from exerting power and promise to leveraging struggle and action.

Because leaders face a myriad of distractions, the urge/courage to improve the lives of others can be lost easily to the siren songs of standardized test scores, policy mandates, and the desparate search for new ways to finance the business of school. Such pressures and demands tend not to serve the interests of all groups of people. Pursuing politically guided leadership practices that address the nature of oppression, lived social realities, and a vision of social justice for all coincides with what Freire (1985) refers to as conscientization:

> A political illiterate regardless of whether she or he knows how to read and write—is one who has an ingenuous perception of humanity in its relationships with the world. This person has a naïve outlook on social reality, which for this one is a given, that is, social reality is a fait accompli rather than something that's still in the making. (p.103)

Through such a process, Freire believes people learn to critically think about the world in which they live, understanding there exists different versions of truth. By advocating for social justice work, school leaders deepen their understanding of the impact of unfairness and humanity, and work toward practices that empower communities, define their purpose, and a more human society. The assumption here is that changing the lives of people will significantly change peoples' lived experiences, including their attitudes, beliefs, and practices. We believe that while the work begins with introspection, it is the collective that brings about social changes larger than what individuals can do alone.

We see from the chapters that reflection is critical to social justice work. And we could not applaud more the efforts to promote a global dialog across cultures. Here too, we find the importance of reflection as a singular and shared activity. Not only must our field understand how vital social justice work is to leadership, it must also acknowledge the myriad of ways that it is carried out in the everyday moments in schools around the world. Kumashiro (2002) suggests many of us who say we want to see injustices eliminated tend to resist acting, because we are uncomfortable with what he defines as "commonsensical" (p. 57). Our tendency to resist antioppressive practices challenges us to reconsider how we feel about those who are different than us and how we think and feel about ourselves. For example, some of us might be uncomfortable to engage in Queer theory because it calls attention to the role each of us play in perpetuating hegemonic practices or critical race theory because it calls attention to the influence of White privilege. In order to deepen your understandings of social justice and leadership, we invite you to analyze the circumstances of your own life. We invite you to consider the questions offered below as a springboard to constructing your own narrative that we hope begins with looking inward and transitions into looking outward.

We ask you to consider what social justice means to you. We hope you are able to identify real world instances within your work and social community that involve resistance, If you are unable to, it would interesting to think about why that is. Determine for yourself the level of involvement you and your colleagues can claim in terms of recognizing and addressing forms of oppression within your work. Examples of real world resistance might include, but are not limited to:

- Examining the impact of immigration legislation in your community;
- Becoming a historian and analyze how problems shape the lives of children, families, and community members;
- Examining school community food services and who benefits from the types of services rendered;
- Considering the influence of tax incentives within a school community; analyzing of community housing patterns;
- Examining how leadership practices can affect structures that reinforce oppressive environements (For example, are all the Spanish-speaking children segregated from the English speaking children

Looking Back on the Road Not Take 285

in a school? What is the policy on bullying? Is the word "fag" considered a slur in the same way that the word "nigger" is?

- Examining to what extent pedagogical practices create processes in which teachers and students are partners in creating democratic spaces;
- Questioning the impact of poverty on the lives of children and families within a school community;
- Questioning what is valued in terms of social justice discourse by the leadership preparation program that you work in or are served by.

As Margaret Grogan noted in the foreward, the words *social justice* are used more often, yet we still find it difficult to find common ground in school leadership. *We* have created a space below for you to get involved in this discussion by reflecting and addressing questions related to topics covered in this book. As you consider the meaning of social justice, which frameworks reflect your own discursive style? You may find yourself "mushy" like Christa or a member of the onion family like Autumn. Either way is just as potent. The point is to understand stylistically how you define social justice for yourself and how you share that definition with others.

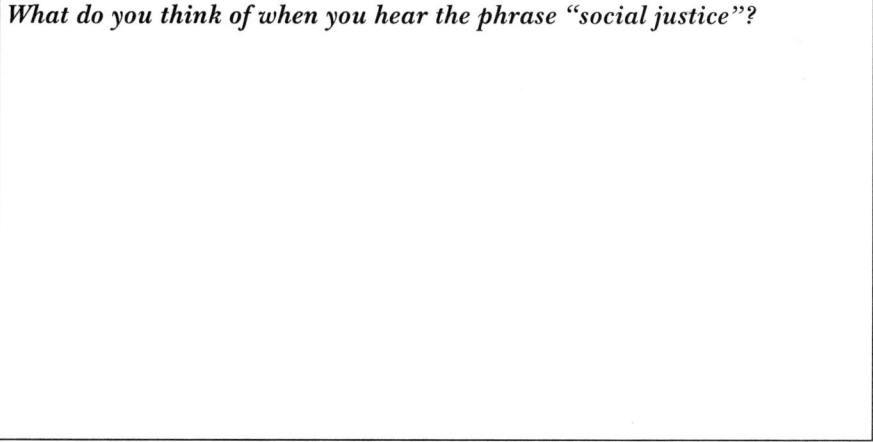

What do you think of when you hear the phrase "social justice"?

Developing social action skills, which intend to bring political, social, and economic changes (Bennett, 2002), bring political issues, such as race, class, and gender inequalities to the forefront. We would like you to consider times in which you made a conscious effort to challenge dominant ideologies.

> *Describe instances in which you have disrupted/changed/affected the culture. What happened?*

Advocates of social justice work recommend we consider real world resistance experienced by students, families, and community members within our school communities (Beane, 1995). We would like you to examine the real world resistance in your school community, examining the limitation placed on the lives of those you serve.

> *What topics of equity create resistance in your school community?*

Next, we want you to consider how people on your campus (be that a university or a K-12 school) participate in the democratic life of schools by addressing oppressive practices. Advocates for social justice work recommend people not only recognize oppressive practices within schools, but they play an active role in eliminating them. The authors would like for you to consider what guides the decisions you make regarding social justice work.

> *Is oppression a word used in your school's culture? Who at your campus or university engages in pointing out inequities or oppressiuve frameworks? How do they do this? What impact has such work had on the democratic life of your learning institution?*

Understanding how our life circumstances influence our beliefs, attitudes, and actions provides a means of tracking our progress as leaders for social justice. As continue to seek to understand diverse points of view, consider your own willingness to probe deeper. How can you renew and strengthen connections with those you serve through empathy and respect in real every 7-day ways?

> *To what extent have you been involved with addressing organized forms of resistance? What enables or prevents you from doing so? If so, what happened?*

Finally, we urge you to consider that leadership demands a critique and challenge of the assumptions of rightness and forces of dominance. Looking within and understanding the complexities associated with human oppression is the first step. Changing ourselves, our practices, and committing to the work of improving the lives of others is pertinent to the ongoing process of leadership development. The reflective process offered here is intended to support, extend, and compliment the work of the researchers in this book as well as other scholars in the field of school leadership. We have a choice to grow as individuals as well as a profession. And in an effort to consider social justice and ordinariness we ask you to consider talking about this with your students (if you prepare school leaders) or your team members and teachers (if you are a school leader).

Did This Book Meet Our Expectations?

What we liked about this book is the collective voice of authors who both embrace and struggle with how they see their work in relation to social justice. Our responsiveness and capacity to connect with the lives of those we serve *is critical to leadership*—not "leading for social justice." Deepening our engagement with students, families, colleagues, and community members contributes to our ability to develop a more authentic self, aware of both purpose and commitment as leaders. Honoring the lived experiences of others in an effort to foster democratic spaces in both large and everyday ways *is* being responsive to the communities we serve. There is no work more important than this.

The conversations about what we shared and what we did not eventually became the outline for this book because we realized our challenge to think about what leadership and social justice *means* internationally and locally are no different than that of our colleagues. And thus, was born the idea of collecting the histories of those who made seminal contributions to leadership and social justice linen of inquiry. We wanted this book to be easily digestible and have a rawness to it in the same way that war stories and philosophical arguments do around a table of beers at one in the morning. We wanted our book to be a collection of voices from those, who like Christa, easily conceive of social justice as an epistemological stance and those who like Autumn, believe in humanitarian leadership and struggle understand and use the words social justice with comfort and ease. We hope this book provides spaces for considering the impact of working together in committed communities. We realize this might be the first time you have been asked to consider such transformative possibilities. Do not be intimidated, because schools and institutions of higher learning can be places of oppression or liberation. We understand that people tend to plant themselves along a continuum of resistance and activism for different issues. This is due in part to a level of comfort and the cost benefit analysis of risk taking. We encourage you, the reader, to identify the dangers, enormous tasks, and possibilities for social healing as a way to connect deeper with your commitment to leadership.

Where Do We Fall Short as a Field? (And What Can We Do About That?)

Student success is central to our imperative as school leaders. We strive to work with students, parents, and community members in ways that honor, respect, and value their lived experiences. However, as a group of nations it can be argued that the meaning of success is up for debate. Guenier and Torres (2003) best encapsulates this argument when she explained a study of three classes of Harvard law school's graduates. The purpose was to determine what correlates with success as Harvard defined it. Harvard defined success as financial satisfaction, professional, satisfaction, and contribution to the community. Two things were found to correlate with the Harvard definition of success: Low SAT scores, and a blue collar background. And thus it is demonstrated that test scores, the de rigeur choice of the new millennium, are essentially feckless. But this is a fantastic example of how testing does not predict success of students and how we must continue the push to focus on a very everyday word " success", and how it constrains our understandings of school leadership and the purpose of school. Oppressive practices and forces of domination must be actively resisted.

Such forces must be defied not only in our professional lives, but in our personal lives as well. School leaders, like other leaders concerned for the welfare of others, utilize the people around them as resources to address inequities in the education process. Advocacy, therefore, is at the heart of what we do as school leaders. As school leaders continue to understand the influence of collective action, the field of school leadership has the potential to be perceived as a tremendous political force. Part of our work as school leaders is to make our communities aware of dominant forces, the commitment to eliminate human oppression and urgency to uphold democratic schools. This is the unfinished work which haunts our profession.

The Road(s) Less Traveled

How do we know when we see social justice work transforming the lives of those we serve? When Christa was working in an inner-city school as an assistant principal, one of the roads not taken was to address years of discriminatory disciplinary practices within both the high school and middle school. She documented disciplinary practices as well as aligning such practices with school outcomes. What Christa discovered not only changed the disciplinary practices of school leaders and teachers, but the lived experiences of children and families. A disproportionate number of Black/Latino/a children who received free/reduced meals missed thousands of hours of school each year due to office referrals. As means of challenging the belief that "these students can't learn," children who frequented the office were provided opportunities to participate in democratic decision making, building on their strengths and lived experiences. Such experiences included, but were not limited to, examining oppressive pedagogical practices, analyzing culturally responsive school resources, building school-community relations, promoting positive race relations, as well as exploring issues facing Black/Latino/a students working with predominantly White teachers.

The result of this change was a significant decrease in the number of student referrals/suspensions, improvement in student attendance, and for the children who most often frequented the office, seeing their names for the first time in their academic careers on the honor roll, contributing a student-written book on their "truth" to the DuSable Musuem and Black Holocaust Museum, as well as receiving a standing ovation from the Illinois State Senate in Springfield, Illinois. Some might ask, "How is this a road less traveled?" Christa would argue that this parable has hallmarks of a road less taken. For example, the number of teachers who submitted written complaints to the union regarding the consideration of more humane approaches to schooling children, the threats made to her personal safety, and increasing racial tensions all were bumps in her road less traveled. Christa witnessed and encouraged a collective effort to challenge the forces of dominance within the school, and after four years of committing to social justice issues, the children and families were respected, honored, and valued. She describes her efforts with her colleagues as "relentless in a passion to serve" furthermore, stakeholders in the school, especially the children, were understood as stewards of democracy.

Autumn has a different take on a familiar "less traveled road." At the time of this writing ten years had passed since she lead a team to implement a dual language program at the K-8 elementary school she served as principal. This program essentially desegregated the school. The work was fraught with the wrath of unions, weak district leadership, and racist parents and governing board members. Like all politicians, she knew when it was time to leave. She rarely looks back on a chapter in her life that was defining, as she endured painful lessons in success and defeat as a leader. Ironically, in the midst of writing this chapter (two days before

Looking Back on the Road Not Take 291

the typing of this very sentence), she was contacted by one of the teachers at her former school that had just retired. This colleague was the school's literacy coach, had built partnerships with Shearson Leeman Brothers, and had taken several students on field trips to the Simon Wiesenthal Museum in Los Angeles. She did this work thanklessly, of her own accord, and she understood what it meant to promote an equitable learning environment. The teacher called to catch up on the adventures of Autumn's life in academe and to share what the 10 years after Autumn's departure had been like.

Admittedly, Autumn was curious as to what happened to the school that boasted an inclusive dual language program, 1300 students, and a staff with a split commitment to educating diverse students. To no great shock, Autumn was informed that the principal who replaced her dismantled the dual language program, then was eventually fired. Her former superintendent had left under questionable circumstances, the student membership had dropped from 1300 to 200. The school was on its way to being closed and the district had now been taken over by the government as it was recognized as one of the worst performing districts in the state.

Unlike Christa's story, Autumn's does not necessarily have a happy ending. Except perhaps for this: Every night when Autumn goes to sleep, and is alone with her own mind and her own heart she asks herself "Did I do everything I could have as a leader to serve in the places I have been?" And every night she sleeps very well because she can honestly say "yes." We offer that a happy ending is not mandatory on the road not taken. Leadership on the road not taken calls for tenacity, for sense of self, and a willingness to reflect on decisions and learn from them. The road not taken calls for the strength to do the hard work over and over in every context imaginable because that is what modern considerations of leadership demand.

Like Christa, Autumn chose to serve others on a long and bumpy road as both principal and academic. What she found was that over time you learn things about the path you are on. You learn that many of the challenges you face become familiar kinds of obstacles and thus, not so formidable. You learn to rise above the toxic actions of colleagues who are insecure. You begin to understand that anger is actually based on fear and therefore something not to be bothered with for too long. You learn that the road less traveled can be painfully lonely both personally and professionally.

However, you also learn these obstacles are temporary because the more tenacious you are the more like you are to find others on your path equally committed to improving the lives of learners and teachers. You find extraordinary comfort and courage in everyday small interactions. Your best friend may call with a silly joke to keep your footing steady and your spirits up. Or you find strength in the example of others, like the authors of this book.

If you are lucky, the road not taken eventually brings you to vistas that are direct reflections of your contributions. They are the sum of all the everyday, ordinary actions: The farther you walk, the stronger your confidence becomes because you realize leadership on the road not taken makes a difference in the lives of others. Therefore, hope is always looming around the corner. *And that makes all the difference.*

REFERENCES

Apple, M. W., & Beane, J. A.(1995). *Democratic schools*. Alexandria, VA: Association for Supervision and Curriculum Development.

Bennett, C. I. (2002). *Comprehensive multicultural education* (5th ed.). Boston: Allyn and Bacon.

Freire, P. (1985).*The politics of education: Culture, power, and liberation* (D. Macedo, Trans.) South Hadley, MA: Bergin & Garvey.

Frost, R. (1920) *Mountain interval*. New York, NY: Henry Holt.

Guenier, L., & Torres, G. (2003). *The miner's canary: Enlisting race, resisting power, transforming democracy*. Boston: Harvard University Press.

Kumashiro, K. (2002). *Troubling education: Queer activism and anti-oppressive pedagogy*. New York, NY: RoutledgeFalmer.

CHAPTER 11

EPILOGUE

Ira Bogotch and Dilys Schoorman

For us, this collection of essays succeeds on many levels: it presents, perhaps for the first time, multiple histories of social justice within the field of educational leadership; secondly, it challenges us to consider the specific methodology of personal reflective narratives as a valid medium for researching social justice struggles across diverse contexts; and, thirdly, it breaks new ground toward building bridges across two cultural/professional divides, that is, (a) the divide between U.S.-centric views of social justice and collaborative international work inside educational leadership; and, (b) the divide between educational leadership researchers and our brother and sister researchers in teacher and special education.

The book's successes, however, reveal how far we must still travel inside the ordinary to undo the many faces of institutionalized social injustices. We agree with Tooms and Boske that it is inside the ordinary that educational leaders must work to find new ways to build leadership capacities for all educators, regardless of their positional roles. For, it is on the level of practice that social justice struggles will continue to be fought and hopefully won. That said, we cannot ignore how the ordinary, the taken for granted structures, cultures, policies, and practices of our educational institutions—K-12 and universities—have conspired to work against implementing socially just reforms. These all too familiar barriers have been documented long before the term "social justice" was ever appended to educational research studies (see Foster, 1986).

Our purpose in this epilogue is to take the ideas already presented and implied, and to project forward new social justice discourses and practices in our educational institutions. We came to our themes, *troubling history* and *troubling epistemologies*, by engaging in a critical dialogue with one another that has been our mode of research, teaching, and service for the past few years. That is, we use our points of disagreement to ask questions, provide arguments, and stay engaged with one another in order to work through our differing perspectives. We have remained critical friends as well as collaborators in research, teaching, and service.

From beginning to end, the personal reflective narratives, many of which were written in an "I was there" genre provide readers with up-close, first person accounts of the many historical and contemporary struggles for social justice within the tight disciplinary borders of the field of educational leadership. Most of the book's essays describe why and how the sum of a person's professional life of teaching, research, and service can rise above the norms established by job descriptions, professional associations, doctoral degree granting universities, and other socio-cultural determinants, including misinformed expectations. It is in the ordinary that the book's authors trouble the water.

Thus, while we applaud the book's successes—outlining history, offering new research designs and methods, and bridging cultural divides professionally and geographically—we are still confronted with the challenges of injustices at home and around the world. To these purposes, we suggest that it is important to make trouble intellectually by troubling history and troubling epistemology.

TROUBLING HISTORY

What this book has done well is to reveal how personal-professional lives have reshaped our largely forgotten histories. As history, readers may already be familiar with the work of Catherine Marshall. Here, we can read her ideas in a first-person reflective narrative, not only detailing her earliest struggles for professional recognition, but also in the larger contexts of transforming the dominant discourses of educational leaders away from a bastion of white male privileges, and away from a total reliance on survey research and quantitative methodologies. There is an almost steady progression wherein the construct of social justice evolved as a valid next stage in a lifetime of feminist struggles for educational leadership. That progression emerges in the authorship of women and men who today are able to conduct their research in new ways and with authentic voices because of the doors opened by pioneering individuals like Catherine Marshall. It is not for us to retell anyone's story, but it is obvious how many authors in this text (and we assume readers, too) have directly benefitted by her life's work.

These stories "belong" in the discourse on social justice only to the extent that the injustice of institutional practice is fore-grounded. Our response, then, is not just to applaud these writers as "role models" for the marginalized, but to interrogate how and why their institutions' practices continue to be seen as the intractable "models" (Sarason, 1990) for our own places of work. Collective agency is central to this quest for social justice because it maintains our focus on institutional settings and the need for challenging hierarchical, isolationist and competitive structures. Too often, the focus on individual theorists, teachers, and/or scholars, rather than collectives, frame social justice as an individual struggle, a conceptualization that works in favor of maintaining a status quo. Each of the essays of this book addresses a challenge to or transformation of the status quo, either in terms of the repositioning/reframing of the "marginal" or a reevaluation of "standard" practice. In so doing, however, they move from individual struggles to institutional struggles.

As professors in teacher education and educational leadership, we have found common interests in social justice as a way to bridge the institutional divides that have isolated our respective fields. As U.S.-centric educators, we share a history grounded in Horace Mann's vision of the common school movement, John Dewey's progressive ideas on experience, art, and democracy, George Counts and Harold Rugg's beliefs in social action, and access issues raised by DuBois, Washington, and Brown v. Board of Education (see Boyles, Carusi, & Attick, 2009). Beyond these seminal authors and events, our parallel narratives of history take flight along different trajectories separating teaching from administration. Cuban's (1988) call for educators to unite has been drowned out by Callahan's (1962) thesis of vulnerability and Tyack's (1974) one best system. Unfortunately, these canonized historical narratives have not been contested or led to reinterpretations and critiques that would honor the memories of those educators who struggled then and now to change the status of educators and education (Bogotch, 2005).

By the middle of the 1970s, our educational imaginations whether in teacher education or educational leadership seem to have given way to educational strategies promoting cultural assimilation, student achievement (aka test scores) and the distribution of resources—as proxies for social justice. That is, instead of educational purposes driving new theories, new visions, and new actions, we witness an intellectual shift away from education to ideas emanating from business, organizational theory, social theory, politics, and even philosophy. While voices of educators can still be heard, as minority voices, they are now subsumed under the hierarchies of disciplines, political power, unfunded mandates, and policies. Whereas educators alone have deep knowledge of curriculum, pedagogies and children's learning, the managerial shifts to centralization, standardization, measureable outcomes, accountability, and distributing resources are combined into the dominant leadership paradigm, which is to say that mandates, management, strategies, and quantitative measures all matter most: today, more than ever.

In contrast, in the delimited context of "multicultural education" courses, we draw on Freire and advocates of Critical Pedagogy such as McLaren, Giroux, Kincheloe, Sleeter, and Nieto, or collectives such as Rethinking Schools or Teaching Tolerance and multiple centers for social justice in universities and communities. As a multicultural educator, the history of education in this country is front and center to what Dilys does; it is - by and large - a history of injustice. Although this history might not serve as the backdrop to Teacher Education in general, the complicity of education in social injustice was well known, even before the advent of Freire's notion of the pedagogy of the oppressed, liberatory education or social justice pedagogy in educational discourse. That schools functioned as sites for the "miseducation of the Negro" (Woodson, 1933/1998), deculturalization through "killing the Indian and saving the child" (see Grande, 2004, p. 14; Spring, 2010) through segregation and boarding schools, for colonization and imperialism through the Americanization of Puerto Rican and Mexican students, where girls at first did not belong or when they did were tracked into subservience, where the presence of and service to students with disabilities had to come about through administrative/legal mandate rather than by the human capacity to do what is right, and where students continue to encounter violence (or the daily threat of it) because of their sexual orientation, must necessarily be "front and center" to our everyday efforts in the classroom (see Williamson, Rhodes, & Dunson, 2007.) Not only because it is a stark reminder of what was or can be, but because we are deeply embroiled, everyday, in the struggle to either remake (i.e. break out of historical structures) or rewrite (i.e., present from diverse/alternative viewpoints) this history; sometimes doing both simultaneously.

There is certainly a shared history of social injustices inside educational leadership; but our understandings of history and our field's collective responses have not been equal to the challenges raised by leaders for social justice in this book or elsewhere. Not only have we not continuously troubled the histories of Tyack, Callahan, and Culbertson, we have not made historical understandings a prerequisite for building educational leadership standards and measures of accountability (English, 2008) or for building educational leadership conceptual frameworks (Blount,

2008, e.g., reviews of literature and theories; see section troubling epistemologies below). The historical canon offers us pathways for disrupting business models and definitions imposed upon education (Callahan, 1962, p. viii) and Tooms and Boske's book takes reflective narrative histories beyond "personal anecdotes" (Culbertson, 1995). In other words, Tyack and other historians know about the "kaleidoscopic surface and hidden dynamics of everyday life (1974, p. 4), and so should we as educational researchers.

As educational leaders, we have to use history to rediscover our uniquely powerful voices. The authors in this book show us how. Lugg goes back to primary and secondary sources weaving in her autobiographical methods: "my understandings of sexuality and identity were largely formed by the Baptist church, public TV, and broadcast news." Each of her sources is so carefully documented that when she synthesizes the personal with the historical, we trust the validity of her conclusions. Marshall, of course, was a participant observer who understood the events happening around her and struggled to change them professionally. Jacobson was both a participant as well as an "eyewitness" to the internationalization of educational leadership. Larson and Moja use two reflective focus questions "who are you" and "who am I" to help educational leaders learn how to bridge their personal selves with a deeper understanding global issues. Jean-Marie describes how remaining connected to her Haitian heritage even today helps her, and by extension us as well, to related to representations of being "other," "different," and "foreign." Each of the book's authors shares who she/he is and why their histories and ours matter.

But as we said in opening the epilogue, such successes document the "necessary," but not the "sufficient" aspects of being leaders/researchers for social justice. Following, English (2008):

> There is nothing in the [leadership] standards which would propel leaders prepared by such standards to question larger socio-economic practices nor even the pervasive Jim Crow laws by which racial segregation was practiced legally in public schools for many years (p. 115).... My line of argument ... is that if educational leadership preparation programs are to instruct their graduates to engage in the kind of change which Carolyn Shields (2004) has called *transformative*, social justice has to be conceptualized as more than "being against" or protesting or complaining about assumptions and practices which are unjust, unfair, and/or discriminate on criteria which serve to marginalize and erase the viewpoints of persons who are poor, of color or of a non-heterosexual orientation. (p. 116)

There are too many concepts in educational leadership that do not serve us well in making transformative changes. For example, change theories across social science and science disciplines are not as relevant to educators unless we begin with the *educational* meanings of change (Fullan, 1982). Similarly, for social justice, until we figure out how to recenter education in these debates, social justice will remain outside the ordinary experiences of classroom teachers and school-based administrators (Bogotch, 2008). Recentering social justice as an educational construct means that we must subject the theories of philosophers and social theorists to close educational scrutiny. Intellectually speaking, we cannot allow the second-hand theories of John Rawls or Iris Young to define for us the *educational* meanings of social justice. That is our responsibility as educational researchers. But even as we continue to do so, whether through historical analyses, reviews of literature, or systematic analyses of data, we need to believe that history is not just about the past. It is relevant to our present and futures.

The final historical lesson to have emerged from the Tooms and Boske book is also troubling, but for a very different reason. It was a lesson learned by Ira as he was conducting research for this epilogue. He literally stumbled across a short article written in 1988, four years prior to the seminal essays published by the *Journal of School Leadership* edited by Margaret Grogan. The forgotten author, Laverne Smith, had been a professor at York University. Her 1988 article was titled "Social Justice and School Administration: An Agenda for Our Future" and it appeared in the *Journal of Educational Thought*. Smith challenged school leaders to "seize opportunities to promote positive societal trends with the microcosm of school" (p. 228). She argued that debates grounded in speculative futures distract leaders from "current predicaments" (p. 229). For Smith, attention should be focused on developing pedagogies which are responsive to diverse learners, on curricula linked to students' backgrounds and needs, on naturalistic methods of evaluation based on pluralistic conceptions of intelligence, on restaffing schools with an eye on both diversity and community, and, lastly, on inclusive styles of leadership.

Her connection of schooling, leadership, and social justice targeted

> ensuring opportunities for each individual, regardless of social class, gender, religion, ethnicity, race, or alleged disability, to attain her or his full potential. And, of course, the notion of social justice goes beyond equality of opportunity to include the affirmation of such basic human rights as participation in making decisions which affect one's life, freedom of speech without fear of reprisal, and assurance of respect for human dignity. (Smith, 1988, p. 229)

Imagine if Smith's definition had been "discovered" and cited earlier during the initial stages of developing the agendas of leaders for social justice? Would the intersections of educational leadership and social justice today be the same? Would its inclusion have given NCATE accreditors the courage to maintain social justice in their criteria or made ISLLC standards more relevant to managing the learning environment? Clearly, Smith's intent was to insert social justice into the educational agenda—leadership and teacher education. But who actually read the original article? Was it read and dismissed as "before its time"? As with any historical interpretation, we may never know the line of events had this or that interrupted history, but surely Smith insertion as an historical footnote even today allows us to belatedly reinterpret social justice in 2009.

History demands that it be troubled with new interpretations as new facts become apparent and made relevant to researchers. In so doing, we connect history to epistemology—another troubling aspect of our research.

TROUBLING EPISTEMOLOGIES

We begin with what seems to be everyone's central question: what is the definition of social justice? On the one hand, we hold that is it the responsibility of the researcher to define terms as concretely as possible. But when it comes to validity, whose voices should we privilege, the researcher or the practitioner? To the extent that the researcher is also a participant—in history—we should take seriously the researcher's voice. But for the most part, is it not the educators themselves to decide whether or not their institutions are fulfilling the role of social justice to all stakeholders in society? Is not social justice more a consequence of years of hard work by educators to redress grievances and to build more equitable relationships beyond schooling than an a priori definition? Given the difference between causes and effects, might not the researcher be the last, rather than the first, to see this societal dynamic? All of which makes any definition of social justice an ongoing struggle. It is at this intersection where the epistemological/methodological issues of construct validation meet the more constructive radical notions of catalytic validation and merge into new conceptions for research questions, designs, and methods.

Our own work has progressed through these struggles with a priori definitions and labels as we conceptualized doing traditional research in the 'cause' of social justice. Without a valid definition, we invariably struggled with how to connect our research with social justice or with any one of the many "proxy" variables used in the literature to describe social justice—be it literacy, achievement gap data, SES, access issues, drop out graduation rates, and so on. While these proxies underscored the complex nature of discussing educational, economic, and social injustices, their indiscriminate uses contribute to concerns that "social justice" itself was being seen as a "fad" among well-intended scholars, and this perceived "bandwagonism" is something we now consciously seek to avoid. In fact, MacDonald and Zeichner (2009) and Montano, Lopez-Torres and DeLissovoy (2002) foreground the notion of activism as they contrast it with the role of a critical educator who teaches (or writes) *about* injustices; they criticize those who adopt social justice "in thought only" and call for a definition of social justice as a "call to action" (p. 267).

Doing SJ Research

The authors in this book drew on the tradition of reflective narrative as they presented their scholarly analysis of the field of educational leadership and the conceptualization of social justice that emerged from their work. Commenting on the liberating potentiality of narrative as a process and a product, Tyler (2003) noted, "Our stories are our theories and our methods" (p. 9). Yet, for too many of us, this approach to research is still marginalized within our institutions where positivism, an outgrowth of the white male cannon of research, has been fossilized into the institutionalization of "what counts" as research, thereby perpetuating hegemonic research norms and practices guised as "objective" and "neutral" which de-legitimize the voices of narrative research and activist scholarship. "Mainstream research practices are generally, although most often unwittingly, implicated in the reproduction of systems of class, race, and gender oppression" (Kincheloe & McLaren, 2005, p. 304). Conducting social justice research within the context of hegemonic academic research cultures places us within epistemological "borderlands" where we undertake research as counter-hegemonic praxis. We regard our work as "the first step towards forms of political action that can redress the injustices found in the field site or constructed in the very act of research itself" (p. 305), perpetually searching for evocative and compelling ways to detect and understand power and oppression and to "irritate dominant forms of power" (p. 306) and/or develop hybridized approaches to research through bricolage, dedicated to a form of rigor that is conversant with numerous modes of meaning making and knowledge production (p.318).

To this end, Hostetler (2005) challenged us to redefine how we view "good" research: moving away from solely methodological criteria to explore the purposes for which the research was undertaken, to ensure that, "Good education research is a matter not only of sound procedures but also of beneficial aims and results; our ultimate aim as researchers and educators is to serve people's well-being" (p. 16). However, he also warns us that a higher education culture that that values quantity of publications might not be especially hospitable to such research. While we acknowledge the courage required by the individual researcher to break free of the research norms within mainstream research culture, and we recognize that there is no one way to do social justice research, echoing Audra Lorde's (1984) famous question on whether the master's tools can bring down the master's house, we must ask to what extent our participation within the "traditional" culture of research allows us to address the injustices perpetuated by the very practices in which we engage. Such criticality must be engaged as we navigate through institutional review boards that on the one hand question whether you are doing "real" research and on the other forbid publication without requisite paperwork, 1-year academic evaluation cycles that require predesigned research plans and "results" at the end of the academic year to validate scholarship, perspectives that assert that legitimate research cannot entail advocacy and/ or activism that further shape and limit the borderlands within which social justice researchers function.

Yet our quest is not to decouple methodological rigor (however it is defined) from social justice purposes; on the contrary, methodology matters. What we must address is how we, as we engage in this work, redefine, if necessary the meanings of rigor, relevance, and validity.

Redefining the Role of the Professor Within a Social Justice Framework

Our own engagement with the principles of social justice has prompted us to rethink our roles as professors. We recognize that in order for social justice to become 'normal' in our daily professional lives, it is important that the principles of social justice pervade all aspects of our professional assignment: teaching, research and service.

For most of us, teaching *about* social justice (i.e. having students read about social justice principles and activists, discussing social justice theory, and conducting research on issues central to social justice concerns) is central to our lives as professors. While this alone has proven to be risky for many of us, we must be honest about acts of courage and acts of complacency in our teaching. For example, when Dilys first became a faculty member she asked if sexual orientation was a topic that she should place on her undergraduate syllabus and was advised by 'insider' colleagues that she should talk about the topic in class, but perhaps not place it on the syllabus. She put it on the syllabus anyway. And while it was true that the department was extremely insular and unsupportive of diversity generally, it turned out that this was not an issue on her evaluations toward tenure and promotion. Thus, today, putting this topic of discussion on the syllabus is no longer an act of courage, and to act as if it were would be an indicator of laziness or complacency. "Teaching *about*" social justice also requires that we do so effectively. Having learned that teachers associate "social justice" with the jargon of the university classroom and unconnected to the "real world" of teachers and students (see Schoorman & Bogotch, 2007) our challenge now is to find ways to engage in teaching *for* social justice, where lessons are grounded in the everyday injustices of education/ schooling, injustices in which the lives of students, teachers and administrators are interwoven (see, for example, Center X at UCLA).

By grounding our teaching and research in our own community work, as we strive to be "engaged public intellectuals," we have begun to make our struggles for social justice "front and center" in our teaching and research. As we noted in the critical reflection on four of our current research projects (Schoorman & Bogotch, 2008), most of our current research emerges from our service work, which was initially undertaken as purely community engagement. This 'research as service' emphasizes several key characteristics: it is undertaken primarily as a service to members of the community, where the research is a collaboration between "researched" and the "researcher," where the research product serves as a pedagogical tool in the classroom and in community contexts and where the traditional demarcations of teaching, research and service are undeniably blurred.

Extending social justice principles to our daily service undertakings within the university has been especially insightful. In traditional institutional perspectives "service" is seen as the dreaded but necessary committee work in which one typically has to engage, in order to be favorably evaluated each year. At best, it is seen as being a "good citizen" within the department, college, university or professional organization and doing one's share of the chores required to keep the institution going. Yet these activities seldom question or transform the existing administrative structures, and in so doing also run the risk of perpetuating structures that could well be inherently unjust.

Redefining the Role of Colleges and Universities Within a Social Justice Framework

Yet, despite the tremendous efforts we all make at the individual level, we must recognize that social justice comes to fruition once we have had an impact on the standard operating procedures of our institutions. This is the message of many of the narratives of this book: the ability of individuals to make institutional change, making inroads from the margins to the mainstream. Yet educational institutions are themselves an enigma with both liberatory and oppressive potentialities. As we reflect on our own struggles within our institutional contexts we recognize that our actions would be even more far-reaching if we worked in professional contexts that valued social justice; or better yet, that actively pursued such goals. Yet, many of the scholars who write about social justice identify schools as the site of social injustices, not our own colleges and universities. Indeed, we must recognize that transformation must "begin at home" so to speak, especially if we are to move social justice beyond the 'borderlands' of academia.

What Bush and Saltarelli (2000) said about the two faces of schools, could well apply to our colleges and universities, even as those of us in academia seek to transform schools at the local and global level.

> Education is often used as a panacea for a broad spectrum of social ills, from racism to misogyny. While the impact of such initiatives has been mixed, their starting premise is the same: that formal education can shape the understandings, attitudes, and ultimately, the behavior of individuals. If it is true that education can have a socially constructive impact on intergroup relations, then it is equally evident that it can have a socially destructive impact. (p. 9)

Both extremes are always possibilities for and against social justice. At their best, schools, colleges and universities can be places where we develop new theories which expand our educational imaginations (Britzman, 2007) across contexts "which stretch from the intimacy and immediacy of local circumstances to reach and intersect with broader social frames, nationally and internationally, communally and globally." (Kemmis, 1996, p. 213). At their worst, historically in Nazi Germany, "[schools] tend to dull native curiosity" while still successfully imparting ready-made information (Dewey, 1939, p. 149). Here, schools may be peace-destroying and conflict-maintaining (Bush & Saltarelli, 2000), perpetuating violence against those who are different, uneven distributions of education in order to preserve privileges, manipulating history, promoting cultural repression, diminishing self-worth, encouraging hate, and, as stated above, impoverishing the imaginations of all of us to address the everyday, ordinary conflicts. All these possibilities, both good and evil, happen inside the ordinary, the commonsense of education.

For us, who work closely with public school students, teachers and principals, the need to reconceptualize our workplaces as sites for social justice struggle is rooted in the marginal role that schools and universities (especially colleges of education) have been accorded within the neoliberal, standardization cult of recent educational policymaking. As we watch the role of educators in educational decision making completely vanish, only to be replaced by compliant, robotic, technocrats beaten into a hegemonic acceptance of instructional drills that belie all theory, research, professional and intuitive judgment, the "fire in the belly" (Jean Marie, this volume) must necessarily burn within all of us.

In this regard, we see both positive steps and some potential pitfalls. We both belong to departments that have a high interest in global education and research. The need to contextualize our practice within this international framework is readily acknowledged and steadily practiced in coursework, research partnerships, service endeavors, student admissions and in faculty expertise and background. Internationalization has moved from being a buzzword to being reflected in multifaceted institutional practice. The potential pitfall in these activities is a complacency that might set in, where the diversity or difference of such experiences becomes proxy for social justice. In her dissertation on internationalization efforts in higher education, Schoorman (1997) warned about hegemonic and counter-hegemonic efforts. Simply engaging in international activity, though it might expand one's previous knowledge base on the one hand, might perpetuate a hegemonic practice at a different level. Over sixty years after the world said, "Never again" to the atrocities committed by educated oppressors, as we engage in social justice pedagogy within the shadow of the Frankfurt School that underscored the role of educators in the midst of injustice, a quick scan of the world today will indicate that—as educators—we have not lived up to our historic resolve, which we have forgotten, and have allowed those around us to forget. Until the material lives of the world's citizens are improved, such work does not rise to the level of social justice regardless of the titles affixed to groups, programs, courses, journal articles or books.

And so, we should not only trouble the histories of social justice, but also the status of personal narratives as research methods for advancing educational research. The reason this is most important in education is that the processes of teaching, learning, and leading are ongoing and not consigned to the category of historical research *per se*, but rather to contributing to the understanding of contemporary practices. To quote Pulitzer prize-winning historian, Joseph Ellis (2007),

> My approach ... was to assume that narrative is the highest form of historical analysis, that by inhabiting certain propitious moments and telling their stories, I stood the greatest chance of encountering and hunting down my quarry. (p. x)

For all of us who come to this work with a sense of urgency beyond institutionalized schooling and traditional research methods, we can take valuable lessons from the authors of this book: to question (Brooks), reflect (Jean-Marie), participate (Jacobson), collaborate (Barnett and O'Mahoney), connect (Lugg), transform (Shields, Larson, & Moja), fight back (Boske), and rebuild (Marshall, Shields). Whether these meanings translate into one methodology, that is, reflective narratives, or one construct, that is, social justice, the quarry we all must hunt down is social injustice.

REFERENCES

Blount, J. (2008). History as a way of understanding and motivating. In I. Bogotch, F. Beachum, J. Blount, J. Brooks, & F. English (Ed.), *Radicalizing educational leadership: Dimensions of social justice* (pp. 17-38). Taipei, Taiwan: Sense.
Bogotch, I. (2008). Social justice as an educational construct. In I. Bogotch, F Beachum, J. Blount, J. Brooks, F. English, *Radicalizing educational leadership: Dimensions of social justice* (pp. 179-112). Taipei, Taiwan: Sense.
Bogotch, I. (2005). A history of public school leadership: The first century, 1837-1942. In F. English (Ed.), *The Sage handbook of educational leadership* (pp. 7-33). Thousand Oaks, CA: Sage.
Boyles, D., Carusi, T., & Attick, D. (2009). Historical and critical interpretations of social justice. In W. Ayers, T. Quinn, & D. Stovall, (Ed.). *Handbook of social justice in education* (pp. 30-42). New York, NY: Routledge
Britzman, D. (2007). Teacher education as uneven development: Toward a psychology of uncertainty. *International Journal of Leadership in Education, 10*(1), 1-12
Bush, K. D., & Saltarelli, D. (2000). *The two faces of education in ethnic conflict: Towards a peacebuilding education for children.* Florence, Italy: Innocenti Research Center, UNESCO
Callahan, R. (1962). *Education and the cult of efficiency.* Chicago: University of Chicago Press.
Cuban, L. (1988). Managerial imperative and the practice of leadership in schools. Albany: State University of New York Press.
Culbertson, J., & Culbertson, J. (1995). *Building bridges: UCEA's first two decades.* University Park, PA: UCEA
Ellis, J. (2007). *American creation: Triumphs and tragedies at the Founding of the Republic.* New York, NY: Knopf.
English, F. (2008). Towards a theory of social justice/injustice. In I. Bogotch, F. Beachum, J. Blount, J. Brooks, & F. English, *Radicalizing educational leadership: Dimensions of social justice* (pp.113-146), Taipei, Taiwan: Sense.
Foster, W. (1986). *Paradigms and Promises: New approaches to educational administration.* Amherst, NY: Prometheus Books
Fullan, M. (1982). *The meaning of educational change.* New York, NY: Teachers College Press.
Grande, S. (2004). *Red pedagogy: Native American social and political thought.* Lanham, MD: Rowman & Littlefield.
Hostetler, K. (2005) What is "good" educational research? *Educational Researcher, 34*(6), 16- 21.

Kemmis, S. (1996). Emancipatory aspirations in a postmodern world. In O. Zuber-Skerritt (Ed.), *New directions in action research* (pp. 199-242). London: The Falmer Press.

Kincheloe, J., & McLaren, P. (2005). Rethinking critical theory and qualitative research. In N. K. Denzin & Y. S. Lincoln (Eds.), *Handbook of qualitative research* (3rd ed., pp. 303-342). Thousand Oaks, CA: Sage.

Lorde, A. (1984). *Sister outsider: Essays and speeches.* Berkeley, CA: Crossing Press.

MacDonald, M., & Zeichner, K (2009). Social justice teacher education. In W. Ayers, T. Quinn, & D. Stovall (Ed.), *Handbook of social justice in education* (pp. 595-610). New York, NY: Routledge

Montano, T., Lopez-Torres, L., & DeLissovoy, N. (2002). Teachers as activists: Teacher development and alternate sites of learning. *Equity & Excellence in Education, 35*(3), 265-275.

Sarason, S. (1990). *The predictable failure of educational reform—Can we change course before it's too late?* San Francisco, CA: Jossey Bass.

Schoorman, D. (1997). *Internationalization and its pedagogical implications: Understanding and implementing global perspectives in higher education.* (Unpublished doctoral dissertation, Purdue University, 1990). ProQuest document ID:736843301. Retrieved from http://80proquest.umi.com.ezproxy.fau.edu/pqdweb?did=736843301&sid=5&Fmt=2&clientId=3326&RQT=309&VName=PQD

Schoorman, D., & Bogotch I. (2008, March). *What is a critical multicultural researcher? A self-reflective study of the role of the researcher.* Paper presented at the annual conference of the American Educational Research Association, New York.

Schoorman, D., & Bogotch, I. (April, 2007). *Implementing critical multicultural education in a high-performing, "Blue Ribbon" university lab school: Implications for university-school articulation.* Paper presented at the annual conference of the American Educational Research Association, Chicago.

Spring, J. (2010). *Deculturalization and the struggle for equality: A brief history of dominated cultures in the United States* (6th ed.). Boston: McGraw-Hill.

Tyack, D.(1974). *One best system: A history of American urban education.* Cambridge, MA: Harvard University Press.

Tyson, C. (2003). Research, Race and an epistemology of emancipation. In G. R. Lopez & L. Parker (Eds.), *Interrogating racism in qualitative research methodology* (pp. 19-28). New York, NY: Peter Lang.

Williamson, J. A., Rhodes, L., & Dunson, M. (2007, March). A selected history of social justice in education. *Review of Research in Education, 31*, 195-224.

Woodson, C. G. (1933/1998). *The mis-education of the Negro.* Trenton, NJ: Africa World Press.

ABOUT THE AUTHORS

Bruce Barnett is a professor in the Educational Leadership and Policy Studies Department at the University of Texas at San Antonio, having entered the professorate in 1987. Besides developing and delivering master's, certification, and doctoral programs, his research interests include leadership preparation programs, particularly cohort-based learning; mentoring and coaching; reflective practice; leadership for school improvement; school-university partnerships; and the realities of beginning principals. Recently, he has become involved in international research and program development, authoring books on school improvement; researching mentoring and coaching programs operating around the world; and presenting workshops in Australia, New Zealand, England, Ireland, and Canada. In January 2008, Bruce was appointed as the associate director of international affairs for the University Council for Educational Administration. This role is intended to: (1) increase international cooperation and partnerships, (2) encourage international memberships in UCEA, and (3) develop international research and learning opportunities.

Ira Bogotch is a professor of educational leadership at Florida Atlantic University. His research interests include leadership pedagogies, social justice, the principalship, school reform, and critical research methods. He currently serves as the associate editor for the *International Journal of Leadership in Education* and is on the editorial boards of *Urban Education* and the *Professional Educator*. Ira is also a regional editor on US Perspectives for a new *International Handbook on Leadership for Learning*. His latest books include a coedited (with Tony Townsend) volume titled *The Elusive*

What and the Problematic How: The Essential Leadership Questions for School Leaders and Educational Researchers and a multiauthored book titled *Radicalizing Educational Leadership: Dimensions of Social Justice*.

Christa Boske is an assistant professor in preK-12 educational administration at Kent State University. Christa works to encourage school leaders to promote humanity in schools, especially for historically disenfranchised children and families within America's educational system. Her scholarship is informed by her work in residential treatment and inner-city schools as a school leader and social worker. Her research appeared in the *International Journal of Educational Management*, the *Multicultural and Education Technology Journal*, the *Ohio Literacy Resource Center*, *Academic Exchange Quarterly*, the *Journal of Educational Considerations*, the *National Council of Professors in Education Administration Yearbook*, and *Connections*. Christa serves as Kent State University's plenum representative for The University Council of Educational Administration.

Jeffrey S. Brooks is an associate professor in the Department of Educational Leadership and Policy Analysis at the University of Missouri and a J. William Fulbright Senior Scholar alumnus. His research interests include high school leadership and reform, teacher leadership, ethics, and sociocultural dynamics of leadership practice and preparation. Dr. Brooks' work has been published in *Educational Administration Quarterly*, the *Journal of Educational Administration*, *Educational Policy*, the *Journal of Cases in Educational Leadership*, the *Journal of LGBT Youth*, the *International Electronic Journal of Leadership for Learning*, *Science Education* and the *Journal of Values and Ethics in Educational Administration*, among other scholarly journals. Dr. Brooks is editor of the *Journal of School Leadership*, chair of the AERA Leadership for Social Justice SIG, and series editor of the Information Age Publishing Educational Leadership for Social Justice Book Series.

Margaret Grogan is currently a professor of educational leadership and policy, and dean of the School of Educational Studies at Claremont Graduate University. Originally from Australia, she received a bachelor of arts degree in ancient history and Japanese language from the University of Queensland. After graduating from Washington State University with a PhD in educational administration, she taught in principal and superintendent preparation programs at the University of Virginia and at the University of Missouri-Columbia. She has served in many leadership roles at her institutions and in her professional organizations including a term as president of the University Council for Educational Administration in 2003-2004. Together with coauthor Charol Shakeshaft, she is working on a forthcoming book to be published by Jossey Bass tentatively entitled *Women Leading Collectively in Education.*

Stephen Jacobson is a professor and associate dean for the Graduate School of Education at the University at Buffalo (UB). His research, which has examined teacher compensation, the reform of school leadership preparation and practice, and effective principal leadership in challenging schools, has appeared in *Educational Administration Quarterly, Journal of Educational Administration, Journal of Human Resources, Educational Evaluation and Policy Analysis* and *Urban Education.* He has presented often throughout the United States, as well as in Australia, Austria, Barbados, Canada, China, Cyprus, England, Germany, Israel, Mali, Malta, Mexico, the Netherlands, Norway, South Africa and Sweden. He was president of the University Council for Educational Administration and the American Education Finance Association. He is codirector (with Kenneth Leithwood) of the UCEA Center for the Study of School-Site Leadership and coeditor (with Leithwood) of *Leadership and Policy in Schools.* In 1994, he received the UCEA Jack Culbertson Award for outstanding contributions to the field of educational administration by a junior professor.

Gaetane Jean-Marie, PhD, is an associate professor in educational administration, curriculum, and supervision in the Department of Educational Leadership and Policy Studies at the University of Oklahoma. Her prior work experiences include North Carolina's Teaching Fellows and precollege programs in urban school districts in New Jersey. Her research focuses on urban school reform, educational equity, leadership for social justice, women and educational leadership, and cross-boundary leadership. Her recent works include a forthcoming coedited book, *Educational leadership Preparation: Innovation and Interdisciplinary Approaches to the Ed.D. and Graduate Education* (2010, Palgrave), a chapter in *Gender and Women's leadership* (2010, Sage) and a chapter in *New Perspectives in Educational Leadership: Exploring Social, Political, and Community Context and Meaning* (2010, Peter Lang). Her work has been published in the *Journal of School Leadership, Journal of Educational Administration, Leadership and Organizational Development Journal, Journal of Women in Educational Leadership,* and other refereed academic journals.

Colleen Larson is a professor and director of programs in leadership, politics and advocacy in the Steinhardt School of Culture, Education and Human Development at New York University. Illustrative publications include: *Sinking like quicksand: Expanding Educational Opportunity for Young Men of Color* with N.S. Anderson, *in Educational Administration Quarterly,* 45(1), 2009; *The Color of Bureaucracy* (Wadsworth Press; 2001), with C. J.

Ovando; and *Re-Presenting the Subject: Problems of Collaboration in Autobiography and Personal Narrative Inquiry*, in the *International Journal of Qualitative Studies in Education*, *10*(4), 1997. Her research interests are rooted in sociopolitical and economic theories of equity underpinning social and institutional reform in industrialized and developing nations. Her teaching unites her interests in issues of equity and inquiry methodology, offering courses in the politics of multiculturalism and case study and ethnographic research. With Professor Teboho Moja, Professor Larson also serves as research faculty for the NYU study abroad program in South Africa, focusing on issues of institutional equity and access in post-Apartheid S. Africa.

Catherine Lugg is an associate professor of education in the Department of Theory, Policy, and Administration, Graduate School of Education, at Rutgers, the State University of New Jersey. Her research interests include educational politics and history, and the influences of social movements and political ideology have on educational politics and policy. She has focused much of her research on queer issues and people, and the politics of U.S. public schooling. Her research has appeared in *Educational Policy*, *Educational Administration Quarterly*, the *Journal of School Leadership*, the *Journal of Curriculum and Practice*, the *American Journal of Semiotics*, *Pennsylvania History*, and *Education and Urban Society*. She is also the author of two books, *For God & Country: Conservatism and American School Policy* (Peter Lang), and *Kitsch: From Education to Public Policy* (Falmer).

Catherine Marshall is a professor of educational leadership and policy at the University of North Carolina, Chapel Hill. In 2009, the Politics of Education Association awarded her the Stephen Bailey Award for "Shaping the Intellectual and Research Agendas of the Field." In 2008, the University Council for Educational Administration awarded her the Campbell Lifetime Achievement Award for contributions that changed the leadership field. Her education career began as a teacher, when Title IX had just passed, and a woman thinking of school administration was an anomaly. Since then her scholarly agendas have often combined gender issues and politics. Her nine books include *Reframing Educational Politics for Social Justice* (Allyn & Bacon), *Feminist Critical Policy Analysis* (Falmer), *The Assistant Principal* (Corwin), *Designing Qualitative Research* (Sage), and *Activist Educator* (Routledge). Catherine was vice president of Division L, Politics and Policy, in AERA, and was the 2003 recipient of AERA's award for activism and research on women and girls in education and also of a Ford Foundation grant to support leadership for social justice (LSJ), thus supporting many of the projects that maintained LSJ momentum.

About the Authors

Teboho Moja is a clinical professor of higher education at New York University. She has a PhD from the University of Wisconsin-Madison and has taught in South Africa, the United States, and guest professor in Norway. She teaches courses that include study abroad courses to South Africa, Israel and India in addition to higher education courses she teaches at NYU. She has been a policy analyst with a focus on the South African higher education system and an adviser to two ministers of education in South Africa since the first democratic elections in 1994. She also served as the executive director for the National Commission on Higher Education in South Africa. She researches education in South Africa particularly higher education as well as the implications of globalization on higher education. She served on UNESCO committees and has also served as an advisor and consultant for international development agencies including the World Bank.

Gary O'Mahony is formerly a project director at the Australian Principals Centre where he was instrumental in implementing a range of professional career development programs for novice and experienced principals. He also has been a primary school principal, a state government senior project manager for principal professional development, and a consultant with a range of professional education consultancy groups. Gary is the director of his own consultancy company, O'Mahony & Associates Consulting, which provides state-based and regional programs in leadership for aspirant leaders, principals, and school teams. Currently, he is involved in international research and program development, co-authoring books on school improvement; researching mentoring and coaching programs operating around the world; and presenting workshops in Australia, United States, New Zealand, and Canada.

Dilys Schoorman is an associate professor in the Department of Curriculum, Culture and Educational Inquiry at Florida Atlantic University where she teaches courses in multicultural/global education, curriculum and instruction, and critical theory. Her research and service interests include critical multiculturalism in teacher education, internationalization of curriculum, immigrant education and family literacy. Her scholarship is informed by her work with preliterate Maya immigrants and their struggles for equitable education for their children in school systems where teachers' creative potential for working with difference is hampered by testing regimes and standardization mandates; and her collaboration with teachers, in the United States and in Sri Lanka, committed to serving the needs of diverse populations despite the institutional challenges they face.

Dr. Carolyn Shields, is a professor of leadership in the Department of Educational Organization and Leadership at the University of Illinois at Urbana Champaign, is past president of the Canadian Association for Studies in Educational Administration and former Canadian representative to the Board of the Commonwealth Council for Educational Administration and Management. Her teaching is in the area of transformative leadership and ethics, deep democracy, equitable policy, social justice, and research methodology. Her research focuses on how educational leaders can create learning environments that are deeply democratic, socially just, inclusive of all students' lived experiences, and that prepare students for excellence and citizenship in our global society. These interests are reflected in her presentations and publications—over 100 articles and seven books—the most recent of which is *Courageous Leadership for Transforming Schools: Democratizing Practice*. She has received recognition for both her teaching and her career contributions to the field of educational leadership.

Autumn K. Tooms is an associate professor of educational leadership at Kent State University. Her experiences as a biology teacher and school principal contoured a research focus dedicated to unpacking the politics related to the principalship along with dynamics related to those who aspire to positions of school leadership. As an academic she has done a great deal of work with the nation of The Bahamas to increase leadership capacity in Bahamian schools through a partnership between The College of The Bahamas and Kent State University. She serves as the program director for this partnership. Her research has appeared in *Educational Administration Quarterly, The Journal of School Leadership, The Journal of Cases in School Leadership, The International Journal of Leadership, Kappan, Educational Leadership, The School Administrator,* and *Principal*. She is the author of *The Rookies Playbook: Insights and Dirt for New Principals* and *The Principal's Guide to Literacy in the Elementary School* (with Nancy Padak, and Tim Rasinski). Currently she serves as the associate editor of *The Journal of School Leadership*. More importantly, she is the humbled student of Dr. Robert Stout, the finest teacher she ever met. Her work continues to be a respectful nod to his profound legacy as a scholar and mentor.

LaVergne, TN USA
05 May 2010
181578LV00001B/21/P